PLAYING THROUGH
THE PAIN

PLAYING THROUGH

THE PAIN

—

KEN CAMINITI
AND THE
STEROIDS CONFESSION
THAT CHANGED
BASEBALL FOREVER

—

DAN GOOD

ABRAMS PRESS, NEW YORK

Library of Congress Control Number: 2021949393

ISBN: 978-1-4197-5363-3
eISBN: 978-1-64700-256-5

Printed and bound in the United States
10 9 8 7 6 5 4 3 2 1

Abrams books are available at special discounts when purchased in quantity
for premiums and promotions as well as fundraising or educational use.
Special editions can also be created to specification. For details, contact
specialsales@abramsbooks.com or the address below.

Abrams Press® is a registered trademark of Harry N. Abrams, Inc.

ABRAMS The Art of Books
195 Broadway, New York, NY 10007
abramsbooks.com

CONTENTS

INTRODUCTION

Ken Caminiti's world was falling apart, again, but he was in New York City trying to make things right.

The veteran third baseman spent his career waiting for this moment—he'd endured so many lost years on bad teams in worse uniforms. He was finally playing for a winner, the 1998 National League champion San Diego Padres. Going into the World Series. Four wins away from baseball glory.

But there was a problem. Those four wins would have to come against baseball's most successful franchise—the New York Yankees—in its most successful year. The Yankees steamrolled the American League in 1998, winning 121 games during the regular season and playoffs. No team had ever won that many games in a season.

But minutes before the start of Game 1, Ken's mind wasn't on the Yankees, or the lost seasons, or that night's pitcher, or his hitting approach. He was dealing with other problems. Ken was back to using drugs and surrounding himself with the wrong people, leaving his marriage frayed and fueling an endless cycle of disappointment and frustration and shame.

* * *

Ken shouldn't have been playing.

His legs were failing him . . . but that never stopped him before, and this was the World Series, dammit. Bruce Bochy—the legendary skipper managing in his first World Series, who adored Ken like a son—wrote his name on the lineup card, as usual. What other options did he have? A hobbled Ken Caminiti meant more to the Padres at third base in reputation alone than a healthy George Arias or Andy Sheets (no offense meant to either, but they weren't badass former MVPs whose scowls intimidated fellow players). There was always the hope that Ken would rise to the occasion, just like he had in Monterrey, Mexico, two years earlier when he got food poisoning and took IV fluid and ate a Snickers bar and, barely able to stand upright, still smacked two home runs. He wobbled as he rounded the bases that day, his accomplishments burnished into legend. Or weeks before the World Series, in the playoffs against the Atlanta Braves, when he slugged a tenth-inning home run to put the Padres one step closer to the Fall Classic.

History was not on San Diego's side. The Padres had reached the World Series once before but lost. The Yankees, meanwhile, had won twenty-three world championships on the strength of players like Ruth and Gehrig and DiMaggio and Mantle and Berra. One more title would tie the Yankees for the most championships in North American professional sports.

On paper, Yankees versus Padres in 1998 made David versus Goliath look like an even matchup. As if the challenge wasn't difficult enough for San Diego, the World Series was opening in Yankee Stadium, a concrete-and-steel cathedral that had experienced more winning than a two-headed coin.

The night of Game 1, October 17, 1998, was crisp and clear, 56 degrees—fans brought long-sleeve shirts and 60-grit-sandpaper personalities. The 4 and D subway lines shuttled the sardines decked in navy and white to 161st Street. The unfortunate souls who chose to wear San Diego gear could expect to face death threats and *Fuck-the-Pad-res* chants. It wasn't personal. It was the Yankees.

Red, white, and blue bunting covered the stadium's edges, a patriotic touch for the extra-special occasions such as the 1998 World Series—the capstone to one of major league baseball's magical seasons, when a home run chase between sluggers Mark McGwire and Sammy Sosa enthralled the nation. The two men went on a summer-long testosterone tour, smacking dingers at a prodigious rate. Few questioned the home run display, and those who did were brushed aside. We were blinded by power. We were back in love with baseball.

* * *

The drive from Yankee Stadium to the Bronx's Hunts Point section takes less than fifteen minutes if traffic is thin.

The direct route takes you east on 161st Street, underneath the elevated subway platforms, swerving around pesky double-parkers. The route twists and turns, and you follow it. Along the way, the rust and graffiti and decay become more prevalent. Duck under a highway overpass, and then you reach the 1200 block of Seneca Avenue.

If heroes are made at Yankee Stadium, people are overlooked on Seneca Avenue. A man sits on a stoop, scanning the passing cars. Children play in the shadows of surveillance cameras, throwing matchbox cars at birds. An apartment building is wedged in the middle of the block, identified by a stucco sign on the front: the ruth ap't.

On a different October day not far removed from his World Series appearance playing in "the House That Ruth Built," Ken Caminiti spent his final moments here.

He could have been anywhere else.

CHAPTER 1

BATMAN

Kenny was always trying to fly.

That's what he was doing on the stairs at two and a half years old—he thought he was Batman, the caped crime-fighting crusader played on TV by Adam West. Instead of flying, Kenny tumbled down the stairs, 30 pounds of energy and dreams and rug burns. Come to think of it, Batman never actually could fly. . . .

Given Kenny's aerial and athletic pursuits, Cordoy Lane was just about the perfect place for him to grow up. The street—part of the Cambrian Park neighborhood in southern San Jose, California—was developed in phases, starting with Kenny's section in the 1960s, then growing to include a perpendicular addition so it resembled a curved L shape. The curve at the intersection of those two ends made an ideal spot for pickup games.

The neighborhood was surrounded by plum orchards and open fields and rock quarries, and given the proximity of schools—more than a dozen within two miles—you could usually find a baseball, football, or basketball game in progress by hopping on your bike and riding around for a few minutes. With so many young families, kids' voices served as a neighborhood soundtrack. The neighborhood and houses and street and schools and sports fields were all new, a reflection of San Jose's growth. It was a nice middle-class upbringing, in contrast to the city's overlooked minority and lower-income neighborhoods and the ritzy town of Los Gatos a few blocks south.

Kenny's family lived at 5129 Cordoy Lane, a split-level home with a garage and four bedrooms. Their house had a swimming pool in the backyard. Families living nearby would become the Caminitis' friends. The Rosses. The Weedens. The Costantinis and Noriegas. Steve Rienhart lived across the street from the Caminitis and was Kenny's age. "It was a dead-end street for a lot of years, so out in front of the houses, out in the orchard next to us or the field a few blocks away or the quarry, there was plenty of open dirt to go play in," Rienhart said.

Peggy Weeden recalled Kenny being a sweet, innocent, inquisitive boy. When he was five or six years old, before the neighborhood was fully developed, the Weedens had the last house, and beyond their house was a large field that filled up with water whenever it rained. "There were frogs there. Kenny was fascinated with the frogs, and kept pointing out, 'Look, there's a double-decker . . . and another, and another . . . ,' not realizing they were mating," Peggy Weeden said.

Chris Camilli's family lived one street over on Elrose Avenue. "If I went outside my front door and I threw a tennis ball over two houses and bounced it on the street, I could probably one-hop it to his house," Camilli said.

Chris and Ken normally got grouped together because of their names—strong, powerful Italian surnames starting with "Cami-." The curly-haired, soft-spoken Chris came from a sports family. His grandfather Dolph played twelve seasons of major league baseball during the 1930s and '40s, hitting 239 career home runs and winning a Most Valuable Player award, while his uncle Doug caught one of Sandy Koufax's no-hitters for the Los Angeles Dodgers.

Chris and Ken would spend hours playing traditional sports and inventing their own games, like seeing who could hit a rock with a bat the farthest. *Ping! Ping!* They'd play until someone hit a house—*Ping!*—or they got into trouble, and that would be the end of it, until they came up with something else to do. Kenny wasn't one to stay indoors. "He was a restless kid," Camilli said. "He didn't like to play board games and watch TV."

Kenny and the other kids were expected to be outside all day, and parents generally weren't keeping track of what their children were doing. You'd ride your bikes to the rock quarry, and bike on a trail or do some jumps, and when it got too hot you'd go to someone's house and hose yourself down, then sit in the shade and cool off, then maybe go to 7-Eleven and get a Slurpee, then go out and ride your bikes some more, and you came home for dinner, and stayed out until dark, and everything seemed so innocent, even if it wasn't.

* * *

Glenn Caminiti was tough, the kind of kid who would truck you in a flag football game *just because.* But he was also nurturing and protective of his brother, who was two years younger—a trait he shared with their sister, Carrie, who was four years older than Kenny. Glenn could have dumped Kenny and left him behind, embarrassed and ashamed to hang out with his kid brother. Instead, he included Kenny in games with the older kids.

Kenny consistently tagged along and played sports against Glenn's friends, the smallest kid on the field. Kenny was talented, but he was also pint-sized. No matter how hard Kenny hit, no matter how hard he tried to prove himself, he was known as Glenn's little brother.

Glenn was the three-sport star who towered over everyone—a physical beast and a badass in football, basketball, and baseball. Glenn's little brother happened to play the same sports. Given the Caminitis' competitive household—even something as casual as Ping-Pong could turn into all-out warfare—Kenny inevitably found himself locked in a sibling rivalry, losing the arms and legs race against his older, bigger brother. Glenn and Ken couldn't help but get grouped together: two brothers, two years apart, with the same interests and passions, jockeying for attention and approval and respect. Their names even rhymed. *Glenn and Ken.* It was his oldest, truest rivalry, one born from love and lineage.

"Glenn was always riding him. And that's what kind of made Ken the person he is," Kenny's childhood friend Peter Morin said. "He always tried to be as good as his brother."

But Kenny wasn't Glenn—Kenny was more sensitive than his older brother, a reflection of his closeness to his mother, Yvonne. His father, Lee, meanwhile, encouraged his athletic pursuits. "He was his mom's boy," Peggy Weeden said, adding, "He worshipped his dad, and he always tried to work hard to make his dad proud."

Nick Duerksen and Kenny used to ride their bikes to Little League practice together, two boys with their baseball mitts over their handlebars and wads of Bazooka in their cheeks. They played together in 1973 and 1974 in Union

Little League. For Duerksen, one quality made Kenny stand out above everyone else—his cannon arm. Kenny could rifle throws from the hole in shortstop. With Kenny's arm strength, no runner was safe on a ground ball. He'd rear back and fire, and the ball became a blur of white heat. An arm like Kenny's could dominate Little League, with him pitching every few games and shifting between the mound and shortstop. After all, his daddy was a pretty good pitcher. . . .

But that was the problem—Lee Caminiti, a former prep pitching and catching star himself, didn't want his son pitching or catching in Little League. Kenny's arm and body were too valuable. Too much wear and tear and Kenny's gift would be gone, another boy who could've been something. So Lee Caminiti forbade Kenny's Little League managers from allowing his son to pitch or catch. Kenny was an infielder. As a result, the best arm in Union Little League was largely hidden away. There would be time for Kenny to show off his arm strength.

* * *

Dave Moretti was six years old when he first met Kenny. Their brothers played on the same Little League team, and eight-year-old Kenny was the batboy, and Dave wanted to be a batboy, too. So for the next game, Dave dressed the part—he wore his San Francisco Giants pajamas. The pj's looked enough like an actual baseball uniform to suffice, so Dave and Kenny started serving together as batboys.

"Ken wasn't real thrilled," Moretti said. "He didn't want to share duties."

Kenny's mother, Yvonne, encouraged him to be nice, and halfway through the game he came up to Dave, and they started talking, and that's how their friendship began. In a way, Dave represented the younger brother Kenny never had. They were both loyal and competitive and fiery, and they loved each other, and they butted heads, and then they wouldn't talk for a while, and then they'd reconnect and pick up like nothing had happened.

Moretti remembers going over to the Caminitis' house with his older brother Mark when he was in fourth or fifth grade. Someone showed up with a six-pack. "The older guys were having a beer, and Glenn was bribing Ken not to tell his mom, with Popsicles," Moretti said.

Glenn didn't want to explain to his parents why the Popsicles were gone . . . but the alternative would be worse. "Little Moretti's not gonna say anything to his parents, and I gotta bribe you with Popsicles," Glenn told his brother.

Kenny got his Popsicles, and Little Moretti and Kenny both kept their secret. They were good at keeping secrets.

* * *

Lone Hill Elementary School was north of Kenny's neighborhood, and the middle school was to the west, and the high school was south.

The setup allowed the same children to go to school together from kindergarten to high school, a tight-knit bond that they'd carry throughout their lives. These are the people you grew up with. San Jose lifers identify themselves by their elementary school, and these were Lone Hill kids. The school was located next to a creek, and there was a culvert underneath a chain-link fence.

Kenny showed off his mischievous side at Lone Hill, pulling pranks he learned from older kids, and he'd giggle and give you that playful glance, letting you in on the joke with a glimmer of childishness in his eyes.

"Kenny always had two sides to him," Camilli said. "He had a side that he would be the kid that every parent would just love. And then he had the mischievous side where, when he was away from adults or around people he was comfortable with, he liked to push things a little bit. He'd like to make people laugh."

For Kenny and Chris Camilli and a group of their classmates, recess was all about sports—they would draft teams and play five-game series of football or basketball over the course of a week, then the next week they would draft new teams and play a new series. Stats were kept from the games. This was serious business.

By fifth grade, when the boys began playing basketball, "some guys didn't want to play on the same team as Kenny because he always shot," Camilli remembers. A couple of them decided to keep track of Kenny's stats and calculate his shooting percentage.

"I think they did it over two days and then they shared that with everyone, and I remember Kenny was really hurt by that," Camilli said. "People were laughing and stuff like that, and he just took it really, really bad."

Kids can be mean. But Sharon Rossell never saw that from Kenny.

Rossell lived at the corner of Elrose Avenue and Michon Drive in the summer of 1974, so Kenny, then eleven years old, walked past her house with his bat and glove whenever he went to the park or elementary school.

"He was like the Pied Piper, because he had all the neighborhood kids with him and they would follow him," she said. "And if they were going to the park, fifteen or twenty kids would be following Kenny to the park."

Sharon would be outside with her son Greg, then a toddler, when Kenny returned from the park, and she would give Kenny cookies and lemonade.

"Mrs. Rossell, I'm gonna teach Greg how to play baseball," Kenny promised.

"As soon as he's walking, Kenny," Sharon said. "He isn't walking yet."

Soon enough, Greg started walking, so Kenny would go over to the Rossells' and gently throw the ball underhand to Greg, and Greg would pick up the ball and throw it back.

"He was so sweet," Sharon said. "There were some bratty kids in the neighborhood, but he was never one of them."

* * *

The glass bottle spun on the cold concrete, warping and twisting the view of the pretty faces as it landed on its target.

Kim Eicholtz-Novielli was in the Caminitis' garage, along with Glenn and Ken and another neighborhood girl, playing "spin the bottle"—whoever spins the bottle has to kiss the person sitting where the bottleneck points. Kim's family lived in the house that shared a backyard fence with the Caminitis. She was three years older than Ken. Her brother and Glenn were good friends.

"Ken was so young. I was in high school, and I was the first girl he ever kissed," she said. Kim remembers Kenny being "very shy," with a smile perpetually on his face when he was young.

Many of Kenny's female classmates wish they could have traded places with Kim. The girls all loved Kenny. He was shy and unassuming and so damn cute, with his effortless laugh and those eyes that would burrow into your soul. "He was such a beautiful person," said Claudia Henderson Druhan, a classmate from kindergarten through high school.

Debbie Eason, who started attending Lone Hill School as a quiet ten-year-old, thought Kenny was "crush-worthy"—so much so, she was happy to learn that her dog Peki had run away to Kenny's house so she'd have a reason to visit.

* * *

Chris Camilli's mother, Karen, loved cooking big breakfasts full of pancakes or waffles or French toast, bacon and eggs—heapings of food. By the time sixth grade rolled around, and for years after that, Kenny would come over every morning to eat breakfast with his friend's family.

"It got to the point where he didn't even knock on the door, he would just come in and eat breakfast," Chris Camilli said. "He kind of became part of the family."

After three or four years of breakfasts with the Camillis, Chris was talking to Kenny's parents and realized that they weren't aware that Kenny had been eating with his friend's family.

"He was eating two breakfasts," Chris said. "I think he was eating cereal at his house and then he'd come over to our house and have breakfast, and then we'd go to school. That went on for years and years, and his parents had no idea."

That's how things were back then in the neighborhood. Secrets—little ones and big ones—remained buried away, and parents remained largely in the dark on what their children were doing. "We knew nothing. I thought we were very observant and talked about [things] with each other and the kids. And we just, we didn't know a thing about what was going on," said Margit Sparks, a friend of Yvonne's whose son became friendly with Ken and Glenn.

Some of the secrets were innocuous. Peggy Weeden's house had a large plate glass window in the front. One day, the window was broken by a baseball. Her two boys, Darryl and Brian, tried to explain what happened.

"Darryl can't throw," Brian said.

"Brian can't catch," Darryl said.

It was only years later that Peggy learned the truth, that Kenny's errant throw had broken the window.

"There's a lot of stuff that I learned way long after the fact about keeping secrets, and there'd be things that would happen in the neighborhood," Peggy Weeden said. "There was that secrecy thing." That secrecy extended to the use of drugs and alcohol, which were everywhere in San Jose during the 1970s—readily available for kids who had lots of freedom and little supervision. Older siblings passed things down to their younger brothers and sisters.

Kenny began drinking beer by middle school. It was easy to obtain. If Kenny and his friends wanted alcohol, they could ride their bikes to 7-Eleven and wait for the right person to "shoulder-tap," standing outside the store and asking an older customer to pick something up for them. No one thought much of it. Beer made Kenny feel less self-conscious. Beer helped him turn his mind off and stop judging himself. Beer helped him escape. "Alcohol, to me, I guess growing up it was something that changed my mood," Ken told ESPN's Tom Friend in 1998. "I mean, I got invincible. I had this suit of armor on."

CHAPTER 2

THE VALLEY OF HEART'S DELIGHT

Leroy Caminiti could have played pro baseball.

Caminiti was a standout pitcher and catcher, and also played football and basketball, at Murray F. Tuley High School on Chicago's West Side in the years following World War II.

Leroy, also known as Lee, showed lots of talent while playing for Tuley. On May 1, 1950, he pitched a no-hitter against Kelvyn Park, despite walking three batters and giving up two runs. Lee had those intangible qualities scouts are always looking for. He was analytical and bright, smart enough to finish a *New York Times* crossword, and with the body of a dancer—a thin waist, firm shoulders, and a muscular build. He was good at figuring things out and getting things done.

Leroy's parents were both second-generation Americans. His paternal grandparents were born in Italy, while the relatives of his mother, Mary, hailed from Lithuania. Leroy, born in 1932, and his brother, Donald, a year and a half older, grew up in the height of the Great Depression. Their father, Samuel, worked as an auto mechanic.

Some of Lee's high school teammates entered the pro baseball ranks after graduation, playing for minor league teams like the Janesville Cubs and Keokuk Kernels. But Lee was meant for a life beyond baseball, and that's what he found after graduating from Tuley in June 1950.

* * *

Yvonne Bye was a go-getter.

The blond-haired stunner—of Norwegian and French heritage—participated in numerous clubs and committees during her time at Tuley High, from secretary of the Marionette Club to a Hall Guard captain and member of the Class Night Dance Committee.

Her busy high school career exemplified the school's academic focus. Alums include Saul Bellow, the Pulitzer- and Nobel-winning writer. Famed football coach Knute Rockne attended Tuley but didn't graduate.

"Tuley was never a jock school; it produced lovers and authors," said Dan Maxime, who attended the school at the same time as Lee and Yvonne and later became a Tuley historian.

Yvonne, born in 1931 in Cicero, a suburb of Chicago, was Loren and Thelma Bye's second child, coming three years behind her brother, Eugene. Her father spent decades working at Belden Electrical Company in Chicago.

* * *

Yvonne and Leroy were high school sweethearts. They made a stunning couple, his olive skin and his hair as sharp as a well-manicured golf green, her pale skin and clear complexion and warm smile. She was drawn to his eyes, those lovely eyes.

* * *

The war between North and South Korea began the month Lee graduated from Tuley High, and Lee was one of the 1.7 million brave Americans who participated in the conflict. The war—which took millions of lives between 1950 and 1953—pitted the Communist-backed North against the United Nations–supported South. Both sides staked a claim as Korea's one true government. North Korea invaded South Korea on June 25, 1950. Within days, President Harry S. Truman ordered U.S. troops to the Korean Peninsula. Years of bloodshed ensued.

Although an armistice was signed in 1953, a settlement of the war was never reached.

Lee was still stationed in Korea in 1954. His former Tuley classmate Dan Maxime bumped into him at a Seoul air base, a chance meeting 6,500 miles away from home. The classmates snapped a photo together. Lee's belt is cinched tight around his narrow waist. His badge-covered shoulder sleeves hint at the muscle underneath.

The badges identify his rank and company as a sergeant with the 7th Infantry Division, a unit that was involved in some of the war's key battles, including the battles of Pork Chop Hill and Old Baldy. Lee never talked much about his wartime service. He didn't talk about a lot of things.

* * *

After Lee returned to the States, he settled some unfinished business. He and Yvonne married on April 28, 1956, in Illinois. He also had a fling with that other love he left behind, playing some semi-pro baseball.

The young couple bounced around the country. They moved to Florida in 1957, and Lee got a job at the Martin Company, which made bombers and rockets. The Caminitis moved to California by the end of the decade. Their family expanded. A daughter, Carrie Lee, was born in 1959. A son, Glenn Scott, followed two years later. They were living in Lemoore, near Hanford in south-central California, when their third child, another son, was born—Kenneth Gene Caminiti came into the world on April 21, 1963, at Hanford's Sacred Heart Hospital. When their baby boy was a few months old, the family moved north to San Jose so Lee could take a job at Lockheed, the aerospace and defense company.

* * *

San Jose wasn't known as a tech hub or the sprawling nexus of Silicon Valley when the Caminitis moved there. Instead, it was famous for its orchards, "the Valley of Heart's Delight." The city—located in northern California's Santa Clara Valley, south of San Francisco Bay—housed miles of plum and apple and cherry trees, making the air sweet enough to taste. San Jose's temperate climate and arid soil made it a prime growing location. The city is buttressed by mountains, and the Santa Cruz Mountains separate it from the Pacific Ocean.

The Caminitis moved along Southwood Drive in West San Jose in 1963. The Caminitis, young and friendly and fun, quickly bonded with their neighbors.

"Mr. Caminiti was like my idol," said Rob Hart, whose family lived next door to the Caminitis during the mid-1960s. "He was the ideal dad. He played Wiffle ball with us."

After a few years on Southwood Drive, the Caminitis settled into the house on Cordoy Lane, the street that eventually shaped into a curved L, and that's where Lee and Yvonne would stay for four decades, through the successes and struggles and jubilation and tears.

As the years passed, Lee's duties at Lockheed remained a guarded secret. Ken's friends would needle him about his father's mysterious profession, jokingly calling him "I Spy," referencing the 1960s TV series. Even Ken didn't know what his father did for a living, only that it was at Lockheed. His friends didn't need to waste their time.

"He won't tell you; don't ask about it," Ken would say.

No one generally bothered asking Lee because they were too afraid. Lee wouldn't tell them anyway, about his work tracking Russian subs using water displacement (at least that's the rumor) or whatever else he was doing for Uncle Sam. Eventually Yvonne started working there too, as an executive secretary. They remained a stunning couple. She continued to be drawn to his eyes, those lovely eyes.

CHAPTER 3

(NOT SO) BIG MAN ON CAMPUS

Kenny tried to hold back the tears. He didn't want to let anyone know his pain.

Especially not his freshman football coach, Hal Kolstad. Kenny's arm was a four-alarm fire whenever he moved it, so he held the arm firm as he ran off the field, pleading with Kolstad to let him stay in the game.

"He never cried in public about anything . . . but he cried when he couldn't go back in," said Kolstad, who also coached Ken in baseball at San Jose's Leigh High School. The next day, Kenny showed up at school in a cast.

Despite the bumps and bruises and the occasional broken bone, Kenny gravitated to football, where he could hit as hard as he wanted, a locomotive with a departure time every thirty seconds or so—the Little Engine That Could. "At a buck 25, Ken could put a wallop on you like no one's business," said Mark Buesing, a classmate who played high school football with Kenny. "He would just dive into you, you know, helmets and shoulder pads, that he's ringing your bell, even at a buck 25."

Playing with Glenn and other local kids helped make Kenny fearless. He was always matching up against bigger kids. And holding his own. "Saturday mornings, I'd go to the high school after I graduated and just play pickup games. And Kenny was always there, and he was a small kid back then," remembers Michael Volzke, who graduated in 1977.

Glenn was Big Man on Campus at Leigh High School, a renegade football player, the tallest player on the team, with perfectly feathered hair to match. He also played baseball and basketball. Kenny, just scratching five feet tall, was a pint-sized boy stuck in his brother's shadow. "Glenn was a grown man. Ken was just a kid. Glenn was protective of him, that's for sure," said Hardy Watkins, who played football and baseball at Leigh with both of the brothers.

The brothers' contrasts went beyond their size and maturity. Glenn was cocksure and extroverted; Kenny was sensitive and quiet. Glenn was more of a troublemaker. Kenny was kind. There was a sibling rivalry brewing between Glenn and Kenny—it's bound to happen with two brothers so close together pursuing the same interests, baby birds seeking the same worm—but underneath the rivalry was love, an older boy who would do anything for his younger brother.

With an older brother leading the way and involved, caring parents, Kenny had a strong support network. Someone else would enter his life, too, someone who would bring love and stability and would stand by Kenny through so many of his ups and downs.

* * *

Kenny's early relationships would emerge and recede gradually, waves brushing the sand, background noise to his truest, oldest love of sports. Tammy Ivancovich Cabri was his girlfriend in ninth grade, and they spent about half the school year dating. "I always kind of had a crush on him in middle school. . . . It wasn't until our freshman year that things kind of sparked, and then we started dating," Tammy said. "He was a great athlete, a great person, he was attractive. There was a lot that drew me toward liking him.

"He was always a nice guy. It just didn't work for us."

High school friend Jackie Vitale said she and Kenny would set each other up with their classmates—she would play matchmaker for him, and he would make connections for her. "I don't think he was very confident as a guy as much as he was in sports," she said.

After one of Kenny's relationships ended, he wanted to start dating Nancy Smith, a shy cheerleader at Leigh with kind eyes. Nancy lived in Morgan Hill, a well-to-do city on the opposite side of Leigh High. Friends worried that the studious, reserved Nancy and quiet Kenny would have little to say. Nancy's friends wondered what she was doing with Kenny, who had a reputation for not taking much in life seriously (having Glenn as a brother helped build that reputation). But Kenny wasn't like the other boys, and Kenny and Nancy officially started dating, becoming their class's "it" couple. Nancy was a rock. She was responsible. She was trustworthy. She was *so sweet*, the kind of girl you'd want to start a family with someday.

"She kind of kept him settled down and gave him stability and confidence and kind of kept him, I think, from getting into even more mischief," said Kenny's close friend Chris Camilli.

Sometimes when Kenny was going to Nancy's house, he'd urge his friends to come over in an hour to bail him out. "Come over to the house, tell me you've got uneven teams and you need me to come and play," he'd tell friends like Dave Moretti. So Moretti would go over to Nancy's house and knock on the door, and he would recite his rehearsed lines. "Nance, they need a guy," Kenny would tell Nancy, and Nancy would see through the caper and roll her eyes, but he was off to play anyway. "He loved Nancy, but he loved playing basketball," Moretti said.

* * *

By sophomore year, Kenny was still pretty small, but his athletic talent couldn't be ignored. He wound up making the varsity football team in tenth grade, one of only a handful of sophomores to do so—which allowed him to play alongside Glenn. He'd also make varsity as a sophomore in basketball and baseball, an uncommon feat at a school with nearly two thousand students. At Leigh, sophomores typically played for the frosh-soph or JV teams before playing varsity for eleventh grade. But Kenny wasn't a typical athlete.

"You went from one sport to the next. We'd butt heads and knock each other silly on the football field, get up and shake hands, and see each other six weeks later on the basketball court and do the same, and then meet each other from the pitcher's mound and the batting box eight weeks later," said Jeff Melrose of Campbell High, one of the West Valley Athletic League's top all-around athletes at the same time Kenny played.

While Kenny spent his sophomore year of high school squarely in his brother's shadow—it was Glenn's senior year, after all—Kenny started to establish himself, especially during baseball season, when Glenn quit the team (there was no one particular reason) and Kenny ended up starring as Leigh's starting shortstop.

"His first game on varsity, he went five-for-five. . . . Yeah, he was in the right place," Leigh baseball teammate Jim Evans said.

Teammates, while impressed by Kenny's talents, soon learned to avoid warming up with him. "I remember warming up with him before games or practice. If you were the one unlucky enough to be warming up with him, you knew you'd have a sore hand afterward," Evans said.

Hal Kolstad, Kenny's high school baseball coach, had one of those major league careers that might have been completely forgotten if not for the Topps bubblegum cards. The flame-haired Wisconsin native pitched for the Boston Red Sox in 1962 and 1963, compiling an 0–4 win-loss record and an ERA somewhere past Saturn. After his playing days had exhausted themselves, Kolstad turned to teaching and coaching. He's remembered fondly by his former players for wearing those teeny-tiny Pony-style shorts that were oddly popular with coaches in the 1970s, as well as the tobacco that was invariably wadded in his mouth. Sometimes, if Kolstad was perturbed during practice, he might call a player over and spit his chew into their glove, or take the wad of Red Man from his lip and put it in the player's hand.

"I can remember being in his PE class and he used to send me to 7-Eleven to buy him some Red Man. I think he gave me a dollar, and I went and got him two packs of Red Man every once in a while," said former Leigh baseball player Mike Thorpe. "But Coach Kolstad was great. He had a good personality. He could be hard when he needed to, and he liked to have fun with us, and he was fun to play for."

In Kenny, Kolstad found a polite, well-mannered kid—and a natural talent. "He came in playing very well. He just did everything naturally, and there wasn't really a lot of coaching that I had to do except work on his footwork as an infielder," Kolstad said. "He had the coordination and the sense about what was going on around him all the time. Even though other players would never pick that up, he knew his presence early on."

Kenny was out of Glenn's shadow for the first time, and it was comfortable for him. Baseball was breezy and carefree for Kenny—for the final time in his life. There were no expectations, just fun, the thrill of competition, something to do before football season started again.

And boy, did Kenny love to compete. He batted .423 in sixteen league games his sophomore year—22 hits in 52 at bats, 11 runs, 1 triple, and 1 home run. He also compiled 30 putouts and 21 assists as the team's starting shortstop (along with 9 errors). The Longhorns went 10–6, and Kenny earned a selection to the all-league first team. Branham pitcher Roger Samuels, a lanky lefty, won MVP honors with an 8–0 record and 1.40 ERA, while Leigh outfielder Kevin Kevorkian and pitcher Dave Resh, with a 4–1 record, were also named to the all-league team.

* * *

Drugs and alcohol flowed freely in San Jose, and the Cambrian Park neighborhood, and Leigh High. It was ingrained in the region's DNA.

Kenny had been drinking since his middle school days—despite California's legal drinking age being twenty-one since the 1930s, it wasn't strongly enforced—and by high school, he'd occasionally smoked weed, too. Cocaine and anabolic steroids were floating among his circle of friends. Kenny wasn't partaking in those things himself back then—that would come later—but for Kenny and his friends, there wasn't a big stigma around drugs. People close to him used. It was all no big deal.

At most schools, athletes wouldn't touch drugs. At Leigh, some athletes would get high before games. "The culture of drugs in California was different. In the Midwest, you could tell the people who did drugs in high school and who didn't. Athletes never did drugs," said Dino Sontag, who transferred to Leigh High and was three years behind Kenny. "Moving to California, you play high school football, those guys would get high before games. I couldn't understand that. And no one made a big deal about that."

Beyond street drugs, Leigh football players were known to use DMSO, or dimethyl sulfoxide, a solvent that was normally meant for horses—but when applied to the skin, it can speed up recovery time and serve as a pain reliever. It also left a garlic aftertaste in your mouth.

A series of factors contributed to Leigh's drug culture. The teens generally had latitude from their parents to do as they wished, and for many of them, what they wished to do was to drink and smoke dope. At the time Kenny was in high school, San Francisco ranked fourth in the country—behind Miami, Los Angeles, and New York—in the cocaine trade, a port of entry for drugs. Some of those drugs stayed local. And the middle- to upper-middle-class student body had money to spend.

They'd do things they weren't supposed to be doing, but what the hell, it was fun while they were doing it.

Beyond substances, the campus culture could be cliquey, a series of over-lapping circles—jocks and nerds, bookworms and burnouts, skiers and surfers, and drinkers and dreamers. While it was easy for Kenny to insulate himself among the athletes, he floated among numerous groups, someone who was warm to classmates regardless of their popularity or the company they kept.

"The football players and the cheerleaders, they had these little circles, these little cliques, but he would talk to everybody," classmate Harriet Armstead said of Kenny, who was quick with a smile and a wave. "We were African American, and in that school, there were six of us. There were a lot of kids that didn't speak to you."

Kenny could have skated by on his athletic talent, or his looks, with his inviting blue eyes or his smile that made you feel warm inside, but he had a depth to him, a preternatural talent at making people feel more comfortable about themselves. He looked out for those who were liable to get picked on, like unpopular kids and those with disabilities. He'd stand up for someone, walk them between classes or to and from school, and you knew not to pick on them because Kenny had their back.

"He was the cool dude on campus. He was the kind of guy who everyone gravitated toward. He was always the guy I wished that I could be like," said Tim Halverson, who played sports with Kenny. "He was like a magnet for the girls, and the other guys just wanted to hang out and be around him and talk to him and be a part of his life. He was such a good athlete and had that coolness factor. Plus, he was a good-looking guy. Everyone wanted to be around him."

* * *

Mike Druhan was the life of the party, someone who was always ready to respond with a witty reply—or a punch. He and Kenny became fast friends through football and weight lifting and parties. Druhan was nicknamed "Egghead"—"he had kind of an egg-shaped head," said his brother Vic. In Druhan, Kenny found someone who could match his zest for life, his recklessness. Druhan was more vocal and animated. Kenny was more subdued, at least until he got a few beers in him and he loosened up.

"My brother was known for being a big partier around town. So Ken's parents hated my brother; they thought he was bringing Kenny down. But the fact of the matter was, my brother and Kenny were like Siamese party twins," Vic Druhan said.

In time, Mike Druhan began selling coke, and drug use became more and more common for Kenny's circle of friends.

"Anyone who was friends with Mike, for the most part, snorted coke," said their classmate and friend Dan Lillis, who ended up rooming with Druhan for about a year in the early 1980s.

* * *

The thrill-seeking didn't all revolve around drugs and alcohol. Kenny became a meticulous diver in his family's backyard pool, jumping off the diving board again and again before graduating to the roof of their two-story split-level. Pretty soon he was diving off a rock overlooking a nearby reservoir that he and fellow teens knew simply as "the rock." It was forty feet up, high enough to give most kids—but not this one—pause.

"All of a sudden I see this guy just walk right to the edge and do a gainer, a backward flip, and I said, 'Holy shit, who was that?'" longtime friend Will Vince recalled of the moment he met Kenny.

Diving aided Kenny's body control and helped teach him how to maneuver his body through space. He was graceful and precise in his dives—a counterbalance to the battering ram effort on the football field that left him with numerous injuries, including a jammed neck his senior year.

Ken tried to keep quiet about the bumps and bruises, doing whatever he could to stay on the field. He'd grit it out or use a splint and tape. Glenn would help him conceal his injuries, too.

"His shoulder problems started from playing football," high school teammate and friend Vito Cangemi said of the injury that would linger during Caminiti's professional baseball career. "It was a football injury that he had his junior and senior year."

The injuries carried from football to basketball, where coach Ron Deetz could tell Kenny wasn't able to play at 100 percent. "His senior year wasn't quite as good because he had damaged a thumb or maybe both thumbs in football, which of course he wouldn't tell you about or say anything about," Deetz said.

* * *

If Kenny's first true love was sports and his second was Nancy, cars were his third love, a passion passed down from his father.

When Kenny started driving, he ended up with a 1973 Chevy Stepside pickup, driving fast and wild, laughing all the way. Other times he'd be driving a little more carefully, when Nancy was with him.

And then he'd drop Nancy off at the end of the date, but instead of going straight home he'd meet up with his friends, catching up with whatever he'd missed.

In spite of, or maybe because of, Kenny's incorrigible side, Nancy became more involved in curating his circle of friends, pushing out those she didn't like or trust, from his female friends to people she thought were bringing out his wild side. Kenny didn't always listen, but he often did. He wanted to keep Nancy happy.

* * *

Kenny was Leigh's best baseball player, and by his senior year, everyone knew it. Opposing pitchers focused on him, either trying to bring their best stuff or pitching around him—they knew better than to groove one down the middle of the strike zone, and since Kenny wasn't selective, it meant he was swinging at tougher stuff as he developed from a contact hitter to a power hitter. While his batting average dropped season to season, from .423 to .370 to .344, he was learning to drive the ball. In 1980, his junior year, he collected three doubles and six triples. His senior year, in 1981, he had three doubles, three triples, and two home runs. Kenny ended up being named all-league first team in each of his three varsity seasons, but each time he missed out on the league MVP award, his senior year to Dave Collishaw of league champ Los Gatos, who went 5–3 with a 1.16 ERA as a pitcher and also batted above .450. "Since I pitched, it was a dual merit. So they honored me with MVP over Ken, which is surprising, 'cause he was a hell of an athlete, as we all know," Collishaw said.

With each hit and each great play in the field, Kenny felt a deeper obligation to his teammates, his coaches, and his father most of all, a well-intentioned man who was seldom satisfied. Lee was quick to point out the mistakes and missed opportunities. Still, he looked out for his boy. And Kenny would do anything to make his father proud.

"His dad was really intense. One of those parents who pushed the kids, and pushed him pretty hard to be as good as he could be," Tim Halverson said.

The tough love was encouraged by Yvonne, who noticed qualities in Kenny that she previously recognized in her brother, Eugene, who struggled with alcoholism. She urged Lee to be hard on Kenny. Maybe it would keep him on the right path.

Given Kenny's football injuries, playing his favorite sport in college wasn't in the cards. There was always baseball. But where would he continue his career? The issue wasn't talent. He didn't have the grades for four-year schools like Stanford University or Santa Clara University or Cal Poly or the University of Hawaii or San Jose State, solid universities with established baseball programs that would have been interested if his grades were better.

"I liked his hands. I thought he was a good player, and I liked the way he swung the bat, his approach and stuff, but academically, he was not one of the top students in the area," said Jerry McClain, then the baseball coach at Santa Clara University.

That left junior college. California's two-year junior colleges were divided into geographic districts, and Ken's district covered West Valley College and Mission College. Sam Piraro, then the head coach at Mission College, wanted Kenny to play for him. "I was on Ken pretty heavy," Piraro said. "I can remember him sitting in my office, talking to him. He was pretty quiet, reserved, didn't say much.

"At that point in time, he was kind of a skinny kid. He had not filled out at all, but the one thing that I remember about Ken, when I went out to see him play, was his arm strength. He had the arm strength at an early age, and it was a nice throwing action. It was a powerful release out of his hand. And so you could tell he had a chance, he probably was going to be pretty good."

Junior college coaches were forbidden from directly contacting student-athletes located outside their district, but nothing was stopping players from reaching out to coaches themselves. And the juco coaches could try to connect with players through their high school coaches. So Hal Kolstad slipped his star shortstop a piece of paper with a phone number on it and told Kenny to call. Kenny dialed the number, and a man named John Oldham answered, and Kenny's future started coming into focus.

CHAPTER 4

COLLEGE TRY

Despite his talent, Ken still had a lot to learn about baseball.

Lucky for him, John Oldham, the head coach at San Jose City College, was a stickler for fundamentals. A lifetime earlier, Oldham was a player himself, a pretty damn good pitcher, good enough to get called up in 1956 by what was then called the Cincinnati Redlegs. He entered one game for Cincinnati as a pinch runner and never made another major league appearance. Decades after his day in the sun, Oldham ran a baseball factory at City College. Practices were split into blocks and scheduled minute by minute. A practice might consist of fifteen or sixteen workstations, with each station devoted to an aspect of hitting or fielding or baserunning.

"John Oldham was such a fundamentalist. He made us better ballplayers, there's no doubt about it. He threw our gloves away for a day and made us take infield bare-handed, and played with paddles, and you know, shit, we've never done that before," said Max (Greg) Sosebee, who played against Ken in high school and, as a college teammate, quickly befriended him.

In order to play the right way, Oldham thought, you needed to practice the right way. His program was an academy, and some of his former pupils included big leaguers like Dave Righetti and Dave Stieb. Ken's course load included learning a new position. No more shortstop for Ken—Oldham shifted him to third base, where he'd have to face screaming line drives and bunts down the line and pop-ups into foul territory and slow choppers.

"I didn't think he had enough lateral movement to be a shortstop," Oldham said. "So I moved him to third base, and he was probably the best third baseman that I ever had. His first step was so quick; he had really good hands and a strong arm. He was just a prototypical third baseman."

The angles at third base were different. Shortstops had to cover lots of ground, and Ken, while a smart base runner, wasn't especially fleet of foot. At third, the ball was on top of you. Ken had good impulses and first steps. He was fearless. At third, he could unleash the weapon that was his arm. Call it a rifle. Laser. Cannon. Rocket. Bazooka. No matter what, it was deadly to base runners trying to reach first base, with an optimum distance of about 130 feet.

For the first time, Ken's life revolved around baseball. He worked out in the morning, practiced, went to classes, played games, and partied with his teammates. There was no shift to another sport. No more football, his actual favorite sport to play, but one that his body couldn't withstand. No more basketball, his winter reprieve. At City College, baseball came with a year-round commitment. He devoted himself to weight lifting, too, something that helped to build his strength. He went from gangly and thin to muscle-bound and stockier.

Oldham's program helped to reinforce Ken's work ethic. It showed him the effort required to be great.

But despite so many adjustments for Ken, Oldham wasn't ready to allow one more change—for Ken to switch-hit in games, something he'd been toying with and something that his father wanted. While many players who switch-hit learn the skill as a youngster, when muscle memory is still being forged, Ken was picking up switch-hitting in college. Lee Caminiti thought his son would be a fast study hitting lefty. Switch-hitting could help Ken get extra attention from major league scouts, Lee believed. Of course, in Ken's case, switch-hitting meant even more commitment, more batting practice, more frustration, more struggle. It was a specialized skill—only a few dozen major league players switch-hit at any given time, mainly because of how difficult it is. It's tough enough becoming proficient at hitting from your natural side of the plate. Now switch sides, hold the bat differently, use new muscles, the opposite side of your brain. . . . A swing is like a fingerprint, unique for each hitter, and switch-hitters effectively develop a second fingerprint.

Despite Lee's intentions, and Ken's practicing hitting left-handed out of season, Oldham said no to Ken switch-hitting in games. Which put Ken in a difficult spot, since his dad—the person he most wanted to impress—had problems with his coach, the person he most needed to impress.

"I think it was a tough time for Kenny because he believed in John and he needed discipline. . . . He really felt like he was learning," said Joe Cucchiara, a college teammate of Ken's. "If he didn't do something right at practice, his dad would come to most practices and most games, and his dad would literally stand right behind the backstop watching everything. And I think that put a lot of pressure on Ken."

That rift—the competing aims of his coach and his father—fueled Ken's internal pressure. He was a rubber play toy being pulled in two different directions. Every at bat was a do-or-die moment for him, liable to disappoint one or both of these forces, and if he didn't perform, he'd carry that into the field with him, making him more likely to boot a ball at his new position.

The expectations and frustrations wore on Ken. He wanted to quit.

To walk away.

To leave baseball behind.

His love of baseball was gone. The feeling had been brewing in him since the end of his high school days, and during his freshman year of college, Ken had it with baseball. It wasn't even his favorite sport, but now his entire life revolved around baseball. And he was *good*, really good, at baseball. Ken knew how gifted he was. He struggled with his burden. He worked as hard as anyone, but his talent surprised even him sometimes. Even with his heart not fully in it, he was still better than other guys.

Lee knew how talented his son was, too. Which is why he wouldn't let Ken quit.

"I think you should give it one more year," Lee told Ken.

Ken didn't want to let his father down. And he didn't want to throw his gift away. The shame would have been overwhelming. Shame wasn't something he needed more of, especially the shame of potentially walking away from his destiny. And if he quit . . . he could look at Glenn's life to see a potential view into his baseball-less future. Glenn was working as a carpenter and had hurt his back in a motorcycle wreck. It wasn't a glamorous path.

Ken would keep playing, not out of love of the game, but out of a sense of obligation. Through baseball, people saw value in him, even if he didn't always see it in himself. Being a part of the team gave him a connection—he did always love the team aspect of sports. His teammates loved his dedication, his commitment to his craft. They loved his commitment to everything.

And baseball was a venue for him to compete and to challenge himself.

"Life's all about competition. We compete for girls. We compete for jobs. We compete for a spot on the team, whatever. Everything's competition," Ken told his friend and teammate Mark Triplett during their year together playing for the City College Jaguars.

"He loved competition. He got it. He got it young. He was only nineteen. I was twenty-one, thinking, 'Wow, that's kind of deep.' It stuck with me," Triplett said. "He competed. And there's no end to his competing. He had that fire inside."

Triplett was a high-octane center fielder who might have been the only player with a dirtier uniform than Ken's, thus the nickname "Pigpen," like the character from the *Peanuts* comic strip who was surrounded by a cloud of dust. From the outfield, Triplett watched Ken make play after play at third, and he felt a connection—this guy was playing the game the way he played it, too. "He was like a Labrador retriever going for a ball. The way he charged bunts was nuts. And that's where he developed diving behind third base, popping up, sticking his chest out, waiting for a second . . . and then just letting it go. He had a laser. He's the one guy who fired me up more than anybody else I played with," Triplett said.

But being the older guy, Triplett used to ride Ken, too. It was mostly playful, tongue in cheek, but every now and again, he'd push Ken's buttons a little bit.

"He's playing third, the batter hits a bullet, and the ball takes a bad hop, hits him in the cheek, rolls into foul ground. He stands up, kind of rubs his cheek, and walks over and picks up the ball," Triplett said.

After the inning was over, Triplett confronted Ken in the dugout.

"What the fuck was that?" Triplett asked.

"What are you talking about?" Ken said.

"George Brett picks up the ball, throws him out, then decides if he's got a face or not."

Triplett quickly laughed off the conversation and forgot about it. Not Ken.

"I swear to God, two or three weeks later, the same thing happens. Roller takes a bad hop, he takes it off his face, picks up the ball, throws him out, and I'm like, *holy shit!* When I got into the dugout, he comes up and goes, 'Hey, how'd George Brett like that?'" Triplett said.

Older players like Mark Webb and Joe Cucchiara would look out for Ken, serving as mentors and helping him to harness his talents. The best player on the team—more polished and refined than Ken—was pitcher Randy Kramer. The Aptos High product was the best juco pitcher in the region and maybe the state that year. In 1982, San Jose City College was going to go as far as Kramer would take them.

"He was the most complete pitcher I've ever seen at that level. He had all the pitches, he had all the pickoff moves, he could field his position like a cat. He had it all," Triplett said of Kramer. "He was lights out. He was throwing ninety with stuff, and he was composed. At that level, he was amazing. Smooth. The only thing we'd make fun of is he was perfectly dressed. He was well groomed, pearl drops, a stellar smile."

Ken settled in at third base, providing steady defense and pop at the plate as City College jumped out in front of the Golden Gate Conference standings.

Despite Ken's emergence, his partying became a concern for Oldham. He started hearing whispers, *that Ken likes to drink....* Sometimes there were hints about drugs. Ken wasn't even twenty, and lots of kids his age were doing the same things. Whenever they had an overnight road trip, the players would wait until after curfew and sneak out. One time, Oldham overheard some of the players talking about their plans, so he asked Triplett to have a team meeting to send a message. "No partying tonight," Triplett warned his teammates. As the meeting ended and the players prepared to disperse, the conversation changed with coaches out of earshot: "So, where are we going?"

As the Jaguars jelled, players noticed something odd: Wallets and money disappeared from their lockers during practice. They dubbed the unknown thief the "Dugout Bandit." The situation fueled distrust and resentment. Who was doing this? Why? Players got creative to avoid getting their pockets picked. "Guys on the team were on the field with their wallet in their uniform pocket. Instead of a can of Skoal, they had their wallet," said infielder Billy Smith.

The situation got pushed aside as the wins piled up. Behind Kramer's pitching and a solid lineup, the Jaguars spent most of the season ahead of rival Laney College out of Oakland, the conference champs from the previous season.

City College wrapped up the regular season with a 20–7 record. Laney finished second, one game back. The second- through fifth-place teams entered a playoff—whichever team won the playoff would face San Jose City for the chance to advance to the state playoffs, which attracted lots of major league scouts.

A chance for Ken to showcase his talents.

But City College needed to qualify first—against Laney, which advanced out of the bracket with a dramatic extra-inning comeback win.

All San Jose needed to do was win one game of its doubleheader against Laney to advance. And the team had the league's hottest pitcher.

But days before the doubleheader, the "Dugout Bandit" struck again. The coaches did some investigative work and finally, after a season of everyone's items disappearing from the locker room, the coach's suspicion fell on a surprising figure: Randy Kramer.

Oldham, believing the "Dugout Bandit" to be Kramer, made the tough decision to boot the ace with all the pitches and all the pickoff moves and the perfect outfits and stellar smile, three players on the team said.

Kramer would go on to pitch in the majors and live an upstanding life. But he wouldn't be pitching in the playoffs for City College, which was welcome news to Laney.

"It was real crazy. We didn't find out until we got there," Laney pitcher Joe Odom said of Kramer's dismissal. "The moms made cupcakes with everybody's number on it. They ended up giving us all the cupcakes. They just knew they were gonna win one out of two."

City College could have used Kramer against Laney. Odom's arm was rubber—he went deep in the first game, a Laney win, and after San Jose went up in the second game, Odom came back out and threw some more, and Laney came back to win.

Laney advanced to states. City College was eliminated. No state playoffs. No scouts.

* * *

It would have been neat for Ken to play for his hometown team, the San Francisco Giants. In the early 1980s, the team hosted open tryouts at Candlestick Park—players were recommended by coaches or learned about the tryout through word of mouth. Ken attended the tryout with Max (Greg) Sosebee, his friend and City College teammate. Ken made the final fifty players, but that's as far as he got. *Thanks, no thanks.* Ken would play at Candlestick again. Someday.

* * *

Chad Roseboom packed up his life and moved from Illinois to California to take a graduate assistant position at San Jose State University, but since grad assistants don't make much money, he lined up a delivery job at a Budweiser distributorship, and one of his supervisors needed someone to coach a summer ball team, and Roseboom said why not, and that's how he was introduced to Ken Caminiti.

"He had the most unbelievable arm you've ever seen for a kid that age," Roseboom said. Ken also had a pretty swing from both sides of the plate. And he was tough as hell. Even after badly spraining his ankle and barely able to walk, Ken continued showing up to play.

The grad assistant called his new boss, Gene Menges, a barnacle of a man who washed up at San Jose State as a quarterback in 1948 and spent the next four decades there coaching football or baseball. One of the players he coached on the gridiron was Dick Vermeil, the Super Bowl Champion NFL head coach.

"Hey, you gotta come look at this guy," Roseboom told Menges. They weren't necessarily planning to steal away Ken from City College. But Menges (pronounced Meng-Guess) came out and watched this Caminiti guy, and talked to him, and assured him that they didn't have any problems with him switch-hitting (hell, they'd let him take double the batting practice), and pretty soon Ken was transferring to San Jose State.

Which was news to Oldham, who expected to work with Ken another year and help him develop into a pro prospect. While Ken's aggravations at City College—aided by his father's switch-hit demands, along with a spat over sliding headfirst due to his bad shoulders—were well-known to his friends, Oldham didn't recognize the fractures and frustrations that had been brewing inside Ken. "I had heard that he was leaving, and I spent the summer trying to chase him down to find out what was going on," Oldham said. "I finally caught up with him one day, and he said he was leaving."

Ken's parents, concerned by his increased partying, hoped a change of scenery would be good for him. The transfer meant that Ken would have to wait until his junior year before turning pro—the eligibility for four-year colleges and universities was different from that for junior and community colleges, from which you can be drafted at any time. If Ken had stayed at City College, he could have entered the 1983 draft. Transferring to San Jose State meant he'd wait until 1984.

Nabbing Ken was a nice coup for State baseball, which went 14–39 the season before Ken arrived, a forgotten program behind the money-generating forces of football and men's basketball. Donations to the Spartan Foundation by the father of a player, Marko Trapani, and other fans and parents freed up scholarship money that helped San Jose State recruit Ken.

The campus was located in downtown San Jose, which by the 1980s was run down, with a row of dilapidated buildings lining its western edge.

"There was nothing," former San Jose State field hockey coach Carolyn Lewis said of the area surrounding the campus. "It was pretty much a total commuter community." One coach at the time had a process for bringing recruits for campus visits: "I pick them up in the dead of night, bring them to campus, have them here for the full campus visit, and then take them back at night to the airport," so they couldn't see downtown San Jose.

Some of those run-down buildings housed fraternities, and without pledging a frat, there wasn't much to do at the school. Ken ended up rushing Sigma Alpha Epsilon, a frat full of jocks—Baseball, football, and basketball players. One frat brother, Bob Berland, became an Olympic medalist in judo. Another, Dan Clark, played "Nitro" on the sports competition TV show *American Gladiators*.

One time, the SAE brothers had rushes—timid recruits who wished to join the frat—line up blindfolded at midnight at a softball park for an initiation event. The brothers had ordered a pile of ice shavings from a local ice company and dumped them on the ground. Ken and the other brothers started making balls out of snow and ice, and throwing them at the recruits.

Woooosh!

"Ken had fire in his eyes, and with his arm . . . oh boy. He was chucking them at some of the guys. Whoa, watch out, guys, this is gonna be something else. . . . I stayed clear. I knew this guy's got an arm, and it's gonna hurt. It's not fun and games anymore," said Kevin Sullivan, a baseball teammate and friend of Ken's.

* * *

Rick Schroeder spent years cultivating a relationship with Ken and his family.

Schroeder drifted from coaching to scouting after an unspectacular playing career. His area was northern California, and Rick adored Ken's game—his instincts, his arm strength, his gap power. Ken had *it*. The Texas Rangers scout was first tipped off about Ken by a scout and coach named "Red" Walsh, an old Milwaukee Braves farmhand (you may have heard of his granddaughter Kerri Walsh Jennings, the beach volleyball legend).

The Rangers had a team in the Peninsula Winter League, known affectionately as "scouts league"—scouts assembled teams of top Bay Area college players and low-level minor leaguers. The league gave players a chance to mature, and scouts a snow globe view of prospective draft picks playing against talented competition.

"He'd come by my place, and most of the time he'd come with me to the games," Schroeder said of Ken. "Kenny surfaced in that league, and that's where he became a player."

Schroeder became close with Ken and his family—what wasn't there to like? Ken was great, and so was his family. This was a deep bond between Schroeder and the Caminitis, something that went beyond a scout simply trying to steer a prospect in his direction. For years, Schroeder would eat Thanksgiving dinner with the Caminitis. Rick Schroeder was family. And he had the inside track on getting Ken drafted.

* * *

It took Dana Corey watching Ken for one play—in one practice—before he knew he'd have to find a new position. Corey was the big dog on San Jose State's team, a senior, entering the 1983 season. He started at third base the season before.

During the first practice of Corey's senior year, the infielders were taking ground balls, and Corey fielded the ball and threw to first. Right on the money. His backup Jeff Crace was next. And then this "skinny transfer kid" was up. The coach hit a ball down the line. "And he made a backhanded play on the chalk and threw an absolute howitzer across the diamond," Corey said.

"I went up to the coach after practice and told them I could play second base, too."

Ken announced his presence to the rest of his new teammates and competitors during a doubleheader on February 14, 1983, at Stanford, a College

World Series finalist the year before. The games were initially scheduled for that Saturday, but rain turned Sunken Diamond to soup, necessitating a two-day delay. In the first game, a 9–2 Stanford win, Ken hit a homer from the left side against pitcher Brian Myers, then turned around in the second game, a 15–11 defeat, and slugged another from the right. After the second home run, Corey went up to Ken in the dugout.

"What'd you get?" Corey asked Ken.

"Whatya mean?"

"What was the pitch?"

"I dunno."

Corey was trying to scrape and grind for any advantage he could get, and here was Ken, making it all seem so simple. See the ball, hit the ball.

Despite the simplistic approach to hitting, Ken became more of a student of the game during his time at San Jose State. If there was a rainout and no practice, "Ken would go to the batting cages for four hours and hit from both sides of the plate, just working on little things," teammate Rudy Escalante said. "It was amazing." He also practiced switch-hitting on his own, having his friend Will Vince throw him BP so he could get more comfortable hitting lefty.

As a switch-hitter, Ken was forced to see the ball differently. From the dugout when his team was at bat, Ken began focusing on the ball coming out of the pitcher's hand, studying release points and trying to give himself an edge when he was in the batter's box.

* * *

Teammates noticed Ken separating from the pack during his sophomore season. His intensity and defensive prowess became otherworldly.

Mark Webb, who played with Ken at City College and San Jose State, recalled a play Ken made against UC Berkeley on a liner on the backside of the line. Ken dove and snared the ball in his glove. "He gets up and he's still kind of falling away and he throws a rocket across the diamond that I swear to God just barely cleared the top of the mound, that was rising as it got to the first baseman. And that's the first time that I was kind of in awe of something he did, and not only the agility, but the power of his arm. That's when I just said, *Holy shit*," Webb said.

"That's the first time I saw that boy become a man. We're kind of in a sunken level in the diamond, so you can see the throw. I don't think it ever got twenty-four inches off the ground, but it was right by the time it got to first base. You know, that's a long throw. He was off-balance, and he just threw a lace across the diamond to make a play. And it was one of those things where everybody starts laughing. You can't believe he did it, right?"

In a game against Fresno State, John McLarnan was on the mound and the catcher called for an outside pitch, and the ball was lined to third base about three feet in front of Ken.

"The ball bounced up, hit off his forehead, and went right by me on the pitcher's mound," McLarnan said.

"Ken walked up, you could see this knot growing off his forehead, with the emblem of the ball and the threads, and his eyes rotating. The coach, everybody, ran out to see what was going on, and he refused to come out of the game.

"His toughness was never, never questioned."

* * *

San Jose State opened its league schedule on March 25 and 26 with doubleheaders, and they swept all four games—this from a team that had won eight league games the prior season. But the Spartans quickly settled back to earth, losing five straight against Fresno State, including a string of nineteen innings without a run.

San Jose State hung in behind steady pitching by McLarnan and Ed Bass, the speedy play of shortstop Ed Krause, and timely hitting from Ken, Corey, and Dwayne Graybill. After a three-game sweep at San Francisco, San Jose State entered an April 20 doubleheader only two and a half games behind St. Mary's College of California in the NCBA standings. The Spartans saw the postseason within reach. . . . But the Gaels won the opener 8–0, then squeaked past in the nightcap, 8–7, sending San Jose State to 8–8 in league play and all but ending the team's hopes of making the playoffs.

Ken found a way to contribute wherever he was playing. In a 5–3 win against Santa Clara on May 11, he made a key play in left field to stop a rally. With a runner on third, Jeff Nollette hit a sinking liner to left field. "Left fielder Ken Caminiti sprinted in and slid to one knee to snare the ball just above the turf, saving a run and ending the inning," the *Spartan Daily* reported. Ken also led off the fifth inning with a single and scored on a double by Dana Corey, then hit a sacrifice fly an inning later to drive in another run.

Against Santa Clara on May 15, Ken went 5-for-7—slugging a key home run in the first game of the doubleheader, then adding two doubles in Game 2. He finished his sophomore season with a .299 batting average, 7 home runs, and a team-leading 36 RBIs. He was on his way.

* * *

Being so close to home meant the party continued with Ken's high school friends.

One time when they were nineteen or twenty years old, Ken spent the night drinking with John Belmont and Mike Druhan—Belmont had a fake ID, so they went to get beer at a 7-Eleven across from Los Gatos High School, no "shoulder-tapping" necessary. Dozens of people were congregating outside.

"Kenny, stay in the truck," Belmont told him. "Don't hurt nobody."

Kenny didn't usually look for fights—sometimes they found him. Belmont and Druhan went to buy beer. "We came out, and Kenny was beating the heck out of this guy," Belmont said. "Kenny had him in a headlock and ran him through a redwood fence, a backyard fence, headfirst."

The friends sped away, but the police pulled them over and put them into the back of the cop car. The police ended up letting them off with a warning: *Stay out of Los Gatos!* Ken wasn't always apt to follow directions, however, and he was back in Los Gatos the next week. And he was speeding. Got pulled over. He rolled down the window, and there was the same cop who had told him not to come back. The cop looked at Ken.

"Hey, I want to personally thank you and all your buddies for putting a whupping on these kids," the officer told Ken.

Another time, Kenny and Belmont and a few other friends got pulled over by the cops after they'd left a party. They'd been drinking. But being that this was the early 1980s, drinking and driving didn't often result in handcuffs. Instead, the officer made them run—"one at a time, one beer at a time, hundred-yard sprints to a garbage can. Open the beer, pour it out, throw the can in the garbage can, then sprint back. We had to do that until all the beer was gone," Belmont said. "What he was doing was sobering us up. He was helping us, but teaching us a lesson as well."

The sprints made Kenny sick.

"John, I'm gonna throw up," Kenny said, doubling over.

"Go ahead, Kenny, I'm right there with you," Belmont responded.

Belmont, years later, was more circumspect.

"This cop was putting the hurt on us, but it was deserved," he said.

* * *

San Jose State was optimistic heading into 1984. And then, in the second game of the season, all of that got thrown into doubt. On February 4, the team was trailing 4–3 in the eighth inning against UC Berkeley. Ken was on second base, the potential tying run. Paul Mason singled to right field, and being this was Evans Diamond, with its short fence in right field, outfielder Lance Blankenship might as well have been standing at the edge of the infield. Ken rounded third, and Blankenship fielded the ball and came up firing, throwing home to Cal catcher Bob Liebzeit, a human doorstop.

The ball nestled in Liebzeit's glove as Ken was still up the line, bearing down on home plate. The catcher braced for contact. Ken momentarily considered sliding. No . . . this was a chance to lower a shoulder and bowl over the catcher, just as he'd done in his football days.

But Liebzeit wasn't moving.

"It was a bang-bang play. He was out by three, four, five feet, so I had a big advantage on him, having the ball," Liebzeit said. "I was in position to take a hit, and it's just a freak play."

Ken collided with an immovable object, and Liebzeit held on to the ball. Out. But there was something else—Ken's shoulder. The hit worsened the lingering injury from his high school football days. X-rays taken after the collision at Cal's on-campus hospital facilities were negative, but the amount of swelling meant the extent of the injury wasn't initially clear. "He could be out for the year, and he could be out for only several weeks," Menges said in the days following the collision.

It turned out to be a separation. Ken missed five games. He hated missing any games at all.

"I wish I were out there," he said, fidgeting as he watched his teammates from the stands.

Ken was back in the lineup after ten days—rushing back too soon, he later admitted. His batting average hovered around .230 for a while before he started heating up.

"(The injury) definitely affected my hitting," he said. "I came back too early. Every time I swung, it hurt."

But the bat came around. On February 21, he hit his first home run of the season, against UC Davis.

One week later, against Cal State Hayward, he smashed a ball down the right field line—a triple. But then the umpires converged, and talked, and decided to call the ball foul. No triple. And no win, either. The Spartans lost that one 4–3.

"Fricking snake-bitten," Menges told the *Spartan Daily* following the loss. "We're just fricking snake-bitten."

Being snake-bitten and traveling to face one of the top teams in the country wasn't an enviable task, but here was San Jose State on a southern swing, traveling to the University of Southern California to face head coach Rod Dedeaux's pro baseball factory. In the first game of the doubleheader, San Jose State's Ron Rooker got into trouble in the first inning, letting two runners reach base with USC first baseman Mark McGwire coming to the plate. This McGwire fellow could mash. . . . He ended up taking Rooker deep to make the game 3–0, and with future major league pitcher Brad Brink on the mound for USC, it was pretty much over from there.

San Jose State took a lead in the nightcap. Ken smashed a solo home run in the seventh inning, and the Spartans were up 5–3 . . . a lead that grew to 6–3 in the eighth. But then Kevin Sullivan walked the bases loaded before a sacrifice fly, and then a pinch-hit single by Jack Del Rio, a bear of a man who also happened to be pretty good at football, cut the lead to 6–5. McGwire scored the tying run in the ninth, and USC pulled out the win in the eleventh inning. Ken's team lost, but those games made people—namely, scouts watching McGwire and other USC players, as well as Dedeaux—notice Ken's talent. He made play after play at third base and showed off his switch-hit power.

That road trip was memorable for another reason. Mark Triplett—Ken's friend who'd bounced back from a catastrophic knee injury the previous season—was walking on eggshells because, behind his back, his mom's husband had sued the school for the way it handled his knee injury. Triplett wanted to send a message only to the training staff, and the lawsuit ended up including the baseball coach, the baseball team, the doctor . . .

Triplett tried staying on his best behavior. Which didn't last very long. "I got my school book, and I got in the van with the guys that I knew were going to study," he said. "And Cammy actually physically grabbed me, lifted me up, and carried me to the party van, and it went all downhill."

Triplett said Ken had him drinking "green lizards" with 151-proof rum and Chartreuse. After a night of drinking, Triplett was standing in the parking lot outside the team's hotel. It was four in the morning, well past curfew, but he said he was with a grad assistant and a few other people—he figured he was safe.

But there was Menges opening the door of his room—it was one of those hotels that opened onto the parking lot, and the manager was in his nightgown and nightcap, and he yelled out at Triplett . . . at that point Triplett really started to worry. Menges ended up kicking Triplett off the team. Three other players—Rudy Escalante, Mark Webb, and Steve Olson—were suspended for similar infractions. Ken very well could have been suspended, too. He was doing the same things as the other guys. But Gene wouldn't punish Ken. Ken was special. Ken was different.

"If I could run, I'll tell you, they wouldn't have kicked me off. That's how it is, you know what I mean? You get some hits, and they'll say you're quirky and funny, but as soon as you can't do any of that, they'll think it's over the top," Triplett said. "But I also did sue the team."

After the road trip, Menges made another change, moving Ken to left field so he could get Jeff Crace's bat in the lineup. Ken's arm was awesome at third base, and it was awesome in left field, too. Runners trying for second, beware. If Menges intended the punishments and changes to motivate his team, they did—San Jose State went on an eleven-game winning streak and opened league play with a 5–0 record.

The winning streak set the stage for a nonleague bout on March 27 against UCLA and star outfielder Shane Mack, expected to be a top pick in the June Major League Baseball amateur draft. San Jose State fell behind but had a rally going when Ken came to bat with two men on. Here was his chance to carry the team . . . but UCLA pitcher Bill Wenrick had other plans, striking out Ken. Disgusted, Ken threw his helmet and bat to the ground. He had a chance to help his team, and he blew it. The pressure was starting to affect his play. People were expecting him to come through, and they talked about him for the draft, or for the Olympics, and it was a lot for Ken to handle. He just wanted to disappear.

That's what he did on a road trip to Reno, Nevada, in April 1984—he apparently spent the night at the casinos, gambling and drinking. "It's in the 20s, snow flurries, just bitter cold. I roomed with him, but he was never in the room," said Dan Bajtos, who played infield and served as designated hitter at San Jose State. "He was gone the whole time. And I remember, as we were pulling out, Ken was not on the bus, and all of a sudden the bus is starting to take off, and there's Ken running down the road, putting his shirt on, chasing the bus.

"He could've been up all night long, but he was rock-solid. He never showed signs of it on the field at all. I never saw any hint that he was tired or had been up all night or anything like that. He kept it all to himself."

After Crace suffered an arm injury while warming up in frigid, thin-aired Reno, Ken shifted back to third base, where he'd stay. With Ken back at third on April 8, San Jose State swept Santa Clara to give the Spartans a half-game lead in the NorCal standings over powerhouse Fresno State.

A sweep against University of the Pacific set the stage for a three-game set against Fresno State, the reigning league champs. Fresno State was led by John Hoover, the country's best college pitcher that year. Hoover was a workhorse for the Bulldogs, pitching an NCAA record nineteen complete games in 1984—the righty took the ball and went until the game was over. He'd finish the season with an 18–3 record and 2.09 ERA.

In Game 1, San Jose State took a 5–0 lead against pitcher Vince Barger, but Fresno State tied it back up on outfielder Scott Buss's three-run home run off Ron Rooker, who battled through heat exhaustion. Rooker pitched into the tenth inning, when Fresno State's Garret Crough hit a home run to secure a 6–5 Bulldogs win.

Hoover pitched the second game, going the distance in a 10–1 Fresno State victory.

The third game, like the first, ended in an extra-innings loss for San Jose State. With the sweep, the magic ran out on San Jose State's season—the Spartans ended up losing seven in a row and eleven of thirteen.

Despite the team's downturn, Ken's bat stayed hot. On May 5 against Pacific, Ken accounted for five of the team's eight runs, including a towering blast to center field, in an 8–4 win. Next on the schedule: Fresno State, again, and megastar pitcher Hoover. Ken came to bat in the first inning and blasted a pitch off the country's best pitcher that he thought was going to clear the right field wall 394 feet away. "I went into my home run trot. I was rounding first base when the ball hit the fence. I thought, 'Oh shit.' I had to run to make it into second," he said.

Oh well. The scouts, there to watch Hoover spin another complete-game win, had something else to distract them. Ken also picked up a ball bare-handed down the line and threw, off-balance, to get the runner at first.

San Jose State's season ended unceremoniously in Honolulu with a four-game set against the University of Hawaii, the eighth-ranked team in the country—sacrificial lambs sent to the slaughter. Ken's teammates, especially the senior players, found themselves burned out from a long season.

"All the seniors were done. We were just done," Dan Bajtos said. "We get there and we all rent mopeds, and Ken is doing wheelies and he's falling. He's got blood coming down his face, his legs, and he doesn't even feel it. He was like Iron Man. And then we play our games at the University of Hawaii, and there's like twenty thousand people there. Nobody ever knew. Coaches, I don't think they knew. The guy was a Man of Steel. He could tolerate partying and being out late better than anybody I've ever known."

Back at the hotel, with the beer flowing and his team at least five stories up, Kenny was stunning and scaring his teammates by standing outside the balcony railing, climbing from one ledge to another ledge. He had so much to look forward to, but one slip and he could lose everything.

CHAPTER 5

RED, WHITE, AND BLUE

The best prep team ever assembled was exhausted.

Too many groggy 5:00 a.m. wake-up calls. Too many handshakes and smiles and autograph signings. Too many one-game road trips on behalf of Uncle Sam and a consumer electronics giant. So the team turned out the lights, lay on the floor in the Shea Stadium locker room, and for forty-five minutes grabbed some elusive shut-eye. All they needed were sleeping bags—really, really big sleeping bags—and the players might have resembled a first-grade class at nap time.

Wherever Team USA traveled during that fascinating, travel-weary summer of 1984, to New York and Norfolk and Battle Creek and Boston, fans showered the heroes with chants of *U-S-A! U-S-A!* and waved flags and cried, overcome with patriotic pride.

Los Angeles was hosting the 1984 Olympics, and baseball was back in the games for the first time in twenty years as a demonstration sport, with eight teams set to compete for a gold medal (not an official medal, but close enough). Ahead of the games, Team USA invited thirty-one of the country's top collegiate players to Louisville, Kentucky, to participate in training before hitting the road on a grueling national tour.

The ultimate goal was to make baseball a full-fledged Olympic sport for the 1988 games. Team USA's players would serve as ambassadors for their game and country, as well as brand ambassadors for their sponsor, the Louisville-based General Electric Major Appliance Business Group, because nothing says America like a GE Spacemaker microwave oven. Some of the games were played before major league games, exhibition contests that were liable to end after five or seven innings to make way for the marquee event. Other games were held in cities near key GE appliance accounts. Team USA played against local teams, minor league clubs, and some of the other countries participating in the Olympics.

"No one in their right mind would put on thirty games in thirty-three days and move seventy-five people daily," including coaches and support staff, said Wanda Rutledge, administrative director for the United States Baseball Federation, which oversaw the tour.

More than three thousand players had tried out for Team USA at one of sixty-three nationwide tryout camps the preceding fall. Ken was not one of those players. The talent pool was trimmed from one hundred to seventy-six to forty-three. During the spring 1984 college season, Ken and fifteen other players were added to the team due to their strong seasons. Ken was invited after catching the eye of Rod Dedeaux, the legendary baseball coach at USC, whose teams had won a record eleven college baseball championships. Dedeaux also happened to be managing Team USA.

The roster was trimmed to thirty-one players ahead of the tour. Players who were still standing had to endure two more rounds of culling before Team USA settled on its twenty-man Olympic roster.

* * *

About a week before Ken arrived in Louisville, his future plans came into focus with the Major League Baseball draft.

Major League Baseball reached an agreement with the U.S. Baseball Federation whereby players drafted that June could sign their contracts but continue to play with Team USA until after the Olympics—to defer the start of their pro careers. MLB teams outwardly supported the venture while privately grousing about their players' involvement on Team USA. Owners wanted to protect their prized commodities. They wanted the prospects playing for them—for green instead of red, white and blue.

Despite his strong junior season, Ken still wasn't a known national commodity, at least compared to fellow Team USA players like USC's Mark McGwire or UCLA's Shane Mack. Which gave Rangers scout Rick Schroeder hope. Schroeder had spent years cultivating a relationship with Ken and his family, watching him from his season at San Jose City College in 1982. He'd been patient and loyal, fishing the same spot each day, waiting for the day to hook his trophy catch.

After the first two rounds of the draft came and went without Ken's name being called—the third round was held the following day—Schroeder was instructed to call Ken and tell him that the Rangers would take him if he was available. Texas picked twelfth in the round.

And none of the teams that drafted before Texas picked Ken. *The Rangers were up!* The moment Schroeder had spent years working toward, all the time spent running the scout league team and watching Ken's college games and putting miles on the car—it was all building to this.

With the sixty-sixth pick in the 1984 Major League Baseball draft, the Texas Rangers decided to select . . . Sid Akins, the right-handed pitcher from USC who teamed with Ken on Team USA. Sid Akins?! "I was so mad. We had him all set to go," Schroeder said. The scout pushed back and pleaded when he learned of their plans to pick Akins. But Rangers brass thought Ken might be available in the fourth round. They hadn't considered the possibility that Bill Hallauer and Paul Weaver were interested in Ken, too.

Hallauer, who had played shortstop at UC Berkeley during the Great Depression, moonlighted as a scout in the Sacramento area. In the early 1980s, he was scouting for the Astros. "He knew immediately this kid had some intangibles others didn't," Hallauer's son-in-law, David Coffing, said of the scout's interest in Ken. "And Ken really, really stood out. He followed Ken a number of places where San Jose State played, because he really thought this kid was going to be good." Weaver, meanwhile, was establishing himself as one of the Astros' top scouts and would travel the globe in search of talent during his decades-long career.

Dan O'Brien, then Houston's assistant director of scouting, remembers making a trip to San Jose to watch Ken play in 1984. "He was a player who clearly stood out, not only for his physical abilities, but also the way that he competed and went about his business on the field. It was always 100 percent and always well focused," O'Brien said. "And quite frankly, we did not anticipate that he would fall to us in the third round. But we were delighted when he did."

With the seventy-first pick, five spots after the Rangers took Sid Akins instead of Ken Caminiti, Houston had its third baseman of the future.

Longtime Bay Area scout Gary Hughes—who'd also scouted Ken—believed such a talented player slipping so far in the draft was a reflection of San Jose State's status, "a nice program, but it's never been a powerhouse," as well as the draft's crapshoot nature. That year, Hughes was especially impressed by Mack. Looking back years later at the careers of the 1984 draft picks, Hughes believed Ken deserved to be a first-round pick.

"Ken probably could be in the top five, if not the top three," Hughes said. "After fifty years in the game, I still say it's not an exact science."

* * *

On his flight from Los Angeles to Louisville, Ken ended up sitting next to another California player competing for a spot on the team: Don August, a pitcher out of Division II Chapman College who'd been drafted in the first round by the Astros. The pair struck up a connection and ended up rooming together during part of their time with Team USA. The pattern continued for Ken, again and again—you met Ken Caminiti one time and got to know him, and he was your friend for life.

The new friends arrived in Louisville for their baseball boot camp, and it was *hot*—sunbaked, 90-degree stagnant heat. But for August, the piles of baseball shoes and gloves and uniforms at Cardinal Stadium, home park of the Louisville Redbirds and the team's training site, felt "like Christmas Day."

Life's all about competition, and here was Ken competing against the best players in the country, trying to make a name for himself.

The biggest name was McGwire, the USC super slugger whose freckles were louder than his voice—but put a bat in his hands, and the ball was liable to go a long, long way. The converted pitcher had first base all but locked up, given that his college coach was helming Team USA. The situation frustrated Will Clark, the team's other first baseman, to no end. Clark, a sweet-swinging Mississippi State product with a Southern twang and snakeskin exterior, ended up being the DH and playing the outfield when McGwire was at first base.

"I thought Will and Mark were going to kill each other before the end of the games. They fought constantly, because Will thought he should be the starting first baseman," Rutledge said. "Will was pretty much the number one asshole on the tour, especially when he didn't get to start. He'd just be a jerk to everybody."

Oddibe McDowell, the Arizona State outfielder, won the Golden Spikes Award in 1984 as the country's best amateur player, hitting .405 with 23 home runs.

Barry Larkin was on the team, too, serving as a backup shortstop one year before beginning his Hall of Fame career with the Cincinnati Reds.

Another of the team's stars was Cory Snyder, an infielder who was named to the All-American team three times during a transcendent college career at Brigham Young University before getting selected by the Cleveland Indians with the fourth pick in the 1984 draft. Snyder, playing third base, made things difficult for Ken.

Ken and Cory, and a lot of the other players, were about as chummy at the time as a pair of hamsters thrown into a tight space. You take a bunch of stars who've excelled at every level of the game, make them jockey against one another for playing time, force them to delay the start of their pro careers for *America*, and all against the backdrop that one-third of them would be sent home before the actual Olympics, and of course the players are going to worry about M-E over T-E-A-M.

"That team was the greatest collection of individuals I'd ever seen, but they didn't like each other that much," Rutledge said. "They were all superstars. And it's really hard to get a collection of superstars to play together when everybody wants to be a leadoff hitter, or bat cleanup. They fought over how much playing time they got, they fought over what bus seat they were gonna be in, you name it."

Ah, the bus rides. After wins, and there were many, Dedeaux was liable to burst into song, belting out "MacNamara's Band": "Oh, me name is MacNamara, I'm the leader of the band / Although we're few in numbers, we're the finest in the land," mixing in his own words, making it more akin to Dedeaux's Band. He mixed in his own words a lot of the time. A big win called for a "bucket of suds." He'd tell players to "never make the same mistake once." He used the same nickname for just about everyone: "Tiger." Caminiti was Tiger, and Snyder was Tiger, and Clark was Tiger, and Larkin was Tiger. . . .

"He called everyone Tiger. We thought he called everybody Tiger affectionately, but I don't believe he could remember everybody's names, all the people he's come across and who he knew," Don August said.

Wanda Rutledge wasn't called "Tiger"—she found it grating to be called "Wander." Or that Dedeaux nicknamed the bus driver "Bussy-Bus."

"Bussy-Bus" was busy that summer.

After workouts in Louisville, the tour officially kicked off June 16 in St. Louis against a group of local all-stars. The following night, Team USA was back in Louisville to play the Redbirds, the Cardinals' Triple-A affiliate.

The stands were packed, and the PA announcer played a recording of "Olympic Fanfare," majestic and patriotic, and people in the stands cried, and three Hall of Famers (Robin Roberts, who served as a GE and team spokesman that summer, along with Pee Wee Reese and Bob Feller) were there for the pregame festivities. Mark McGwire smashed two home runs, and DH Will Clark added three hits, and Team USA won 7–4 against a Triple-A team featuring former major league pitchers Jim Bibby and Dyar Miller, along with soon-to-be major league stars Vince Coleman and Terry Pendleton.

Larkin was a pinch runner. Ken didn't play. Of course Snyder was the team's starting third baseman—he was the proven, popular pick, the superstar in the making. Ken just wanted a chance to play. But as the days passed, as he'd fill in as a defensive sub or DH, Ken grew bitter and resentful. Ken wasn't a *rah-rah* type. He wanted to play, not watch. He didn't feel like he could contribute from the bench. Some players were happy just to be included. For Ken, watching Snyder play and riding the pine and getting called "Tiger" was like flossing with sandpaper.

Dedeaux tried to balance playing time among his superstar squad. But he had his favorites, his own way. He didn't give some of the underclassmen as much playing time, so that meant Larkin didn't see the field as often as he should have. The other coaches—also hailing from the college ranks—pleaded with Dedeaux to make roster adjustments and give players like Larkin more time, but Dedeaux wasn't having it. This was Dedeaux's team, and Dedeaux's way.

* * *

Even though Ken was overshadowed by other players, he left an impression on his teammates.

Bobby Witt, a hard-throwing righty, remembers coming across Ken at their hotel's pool after one of their practices in Louisville, doing jumps that he'd learned in San Jose. "Cammy was doing full gainers off the diving board. He was so athletic. It was scary. I was like, man, this guy is unbelievable," Witt said.

And then there was that arm of his. . . . It still stood out, even among the best of the best of the best. So did his intensity.

"I could see and feel what type of energy he had and how badly he wanted to contribute. He just had an intensity that was almost unmatched," McDowell said.

* * *

Anywhere was a potential bedroom for the road-wearied players. The dugout, the airport, the locker room at Shea Stadium. . . .

"We were just exhausted. We were tired all the time. If we could just get a nap for five minutes, we would take it," August said. "I remember we were playing at Shea Stadium. We were gonna play before the Mets game. And of course, with scheduling, we always had to get there super early. We get to Shea Stadium and we thought we were there too soon, so we had to wait. We were just exhausted. So we just said, 'Let's just turn off the lights in the locker room.' We went to sleep on the floor."

Funny, quirky things happened on the tour, too, circumstances the players continued to laugh about decades later. "We were somewhere in Mississippi, and Rod Dedeaux put the bus through the McDonald's drive-through," said Chris Gwynn, an outfielder on the team.

Over time, the players grew tired of the constant signing, handshakes, meet and greets, events with General Electric folks. . . . one time, Rutledge suggested the players could sign balls while sitting on the airplane instead of at an event after landing, in order to save time and energy. She passed the balls around, and the players signed them, and they handed them back. Two boxes of baseballs. "I opened the boxes, and the balls are signed 'Mickey Mouse' and 'Ronald Reagan,' everything but their names," Rutledge said. "It was just their little protest for 'We've got another freakin' city to go to? Are you serious?'"

* * *

Ken regularly made an impact when he played. But the problem was, he didn't regularly play.

At Pittsburgh's Three Rivers Stadium on June 19, Ken smashed a home run against a local all-star team, ahead of a Cubs-Pirates game.

Team USA also lost 6–5, its first defeat to an American team, fittingly on July 4, against the Michigan Stan Musial All-Stars in front of 7,300 fans at Battle Creek's Bailey Stadium. Snyder, playing third base, smashed a homer to tie the game in the fourth, and two innings later, Caminiti, the team's DH, hit a double to tie the game again, but then Team USA lost the lead late, and a ninth-inning rally fell short.

Dedeaux made a point to start a lot of players when the tour rolled to their cities, and Ken hoped to start when Team USA played in San Francisco's Candlestick Park ahead of the All-Star festivities on July 9. But when Ken started the game on the bench, his hometown fans—specifically his brother, Glenn—showered Dedeaux with insults from the stands. "You suck, Dedeaux!" Glenn yelled, loud and close enough to the dugout for Ken's manager to hear. "Put in Caminiti!"

Dedeaux acquiesced midway through the game, and Ken played a few innings in the field and made some nice plays at third base. After seven and a half innings, the game was halted—it was time for the Miller Lite celebrity softball contest, in which the "Tastes Great" team would face the "Less Filling" squad (Tastes Great won, 7–5, to the relief of fans everywhere).

Ken was unfulfilled—final cuts were looming, and he was in danger of getting cut, and there wasn't anything he could do about it with Snyder getting the bulk of the playing time.

"It's been real tough, especially mentally," he said. "At first, being part of this meant a lot to me, but now it's become a matter of survival. It's a job." Beyond getting to see the country, he did find a positive to the experience: "The one thing this experience has taught me is learning how to be a team ballplayer."

On July 14, the tour reached Houston—the Astrodome, the home of the team that drafted Ken, the Astros. Team USA was facing a team of Japanese collegiate all-stars and jumped ahead 10–0. Ken came up in the eighth inning with B. J. Surhoff on base and singled, driving home Team USA's final run.

The announcement would follow that Ken had feared—he wasn't making the final twenty-man roster. Of course Ken's run with Team USA had to end after his first game in Houston, the place where he hoped to have a long career. . . . Ken ended up getting cut along with a trio of pitchers who'd reach the big leagues—Norm Charlton, Greg Swindell, and Drew Hall—and Georgia Southern outfielder Ben Abner.

While they were in Houston, Ken's friend August signed his contract, a chance to celebrate something, to get his mind off the disappointment. Ken signed his contract that summer, too. The grudging baseball player, the guy who wanted to play football instead, was a member of the Houston Astros.

Of course, Ken could have started his pro career during the summer of 1984 and been playing in the minors if not for Team USA. Instead, he'd miss the rest of the 1984 season and report to instructional league in Arizona in the fall.

While playing for Team USA slowed down Ken's pro career in some ways, it also readied him and other players for what lay ahead. The tour gave them glimpses of every level of pro ball, from Single-A ball to the major league All-Star Game.

"As soon as I got into pro ball, I was so prepared," Witt said.

Ken stewed as his Team USA teammates went on to compete in Los Angeles at the Olympics without him. To top it all off, "the best prep team ever assembled" didn't even win gold! Team USA wound up with a silver medal. All the travel and impromptu napping, and bus trips, and handshakes, and appearances, and the team didn't even win. Which shouldn't have been surprising, given that some of the teams, like gold medal winner Japan, had played together for years ahead of the Olympics.

For players like Oddibe McDowell, the Team USA experience became more meaningful with the passage of time. The teammates who were apt to clash over playing time or seats on the bus could connect over their shared success instead of viewing one another as threats.

"It was an assembly of unbelievable ballplayers. And we were all young, and just to reflect back on it, it was really a privilege to be a part of such a group of guys playing back in that time, representing the country," McDowell said. "We were traveling, getting ready to take on our professional careers, yet winding up the amateur years."

Cory Snyder felt the same way: "We had the ability to say we did something really, really good together. So that connection was always there."

Ken would feel that way, too, in time—it became special to cross paths with his fellow Team USA players as their careers each took off. But for a long time, whenever someone would mention Dedeaux or Team USA, Ken would growl or stare through them. Still, Ken hung with the best of the best of the best—virtually the last men standing from a pool of three thousand. Some of these guys were really good. But Ken wasn't overmatched. And now he had added motivation as his professional career began.

CHAPTER 6

BUS RIDES AND EMPTY BALLPARKS

Ken's pro baseball career officially began on a rain-slicked Florida field on a night when the errors nearly outnumbered the fans.

It was an inauspicious debut for Ken and the Florida State League's Osceola Astros, Houston's brand-new Single-A affiliate. Team officials had hoped to sell 2,500 tickets for the home opener, on April 12, 1985. A pregame show featured "clowns in a baseball slapstick." But then the skies opened and the rains poured down, and the game itself resembled a clown act—with a sixty-three-minute rain delay and steady drizzle making way for a sloppy game.

Osceola took the lead in the seventh, scratching across three runs as a result of two singles, three walks, two errors, and a wild pitch. In the top of the eighth, the Daytona Beach Islanders loaded the bases against Osceola's Chuck Mathews. Reliever Doug Shaab entered the game.

Ty Nichols was batting for Daytona Beach, with the game's outcome in the balance. He hit a ground ball to third. Ken wasn't going to let a little rain stop him from making the play. He fielded the ball cleanly and fired home, getting the runner at the plate. Daytona ended up scoring two runs in the inning, but it wasn't enough, and Osceola scraped by, 9–8. Ken, batting seventh, went 2-for-3 with two runs, one double, and one run batted in.

The announced attendance for Ken Caminiti's first minor league game: 393. In actuality, a couple of dozen people stuck through the rain to watch the game. You could count the individual umbrellas.

Even if no one was watching—and there were quite a few games with low attendance—something special was taking root that season in Kissimmee, in the shadows of nearby Disney World. Osceola County had used resort tax money collected from hotel rooms to fund a new $5.5 million spring training complex, and the Astros, nonplussed by the dilapidated facilities in Cocoa Beach, decided to center its Florida operations in Kissimmee. That meant moving the Single-A team from Daytona Beach. Don Miers was the general manager with Daytona Beach, and he and his business partner didn't want to move the team to Kissimmee.

"Daytona Beach was a pretty good town to have a team and make some money, but Kissimmee is a lot smaller. So we suggest to the Astros, you want the FSL team, you buy it. So they bought our franchise—and lucky for me, they chose me to come with it, to be the first Houston Astros employee in Osceola County," Miers said. But what to call the team? Since no one could pronounce "Kissimmee" properly (it's ka-SIM-mee, not KISS-a-mee), it would have been embarrassing, Miers said, for the team to become known as the KISS-a-mee Astros, so Osceola Astros it was.

There, in ka-SIM-mee, Ken would forge the foundation for his pro career while connecting with people who would become his longtime friends and teammates. Gerald Young, a Honduras-born former Mets prospect who was an add-on in Houston's 1984 trade of Ray Knight, was pure speed—he stole 43 bases the season before and 31 more swipes in 1985, a petty thief who stole bases at will. They were the team's two most talented position players. Gerald got on base, and Ken would drive him home. Their symbiotic relationship would take them very far.

"That was Frick and Frack for a long time," pitcher Anthony Kelley, who got promoted to Double-A after starting the 1985 season with a 5-1 record at Osceola, said of Ken and Gerald. "They were close. The team itself was close, but I would say that Gerald and Ken had a really close relationship."

Sandy-haired pitcher Rob Mallicoat was another star in the making. Mallicoat was cerebral and meticulous—after his playing days were over, the Oregon native entered the computer industry and worked for Microsoft—and in 1985, he was the Florida State League's best pitcher, going 16-6 with a 1.36 ERA. At one point, the lefty was looking gaunt, so coach Charley Taylor suggested he eat out more to keep his weight up, and Mallicoat ended up ordering Domino's

Pizza and having it delivered to the clubhouse. (After his pizza delivery stunt wasn't warmly received, he began frequenting an Italian restaurant.) Mallicoat loved playing with Ken.

"He was the kind of guy that, if you were on his side, you were feeling pretty grateful. You could see when he played, he gave every ounce that he had, whether it was cuts on his arm or strawberries on his leg, a hurt shoulder, hurt knees. . . . He gave every bit he had. He burned the candle not on one or both ends, but both ends and in the middle."

Many of the players rented condos at a golf course complex, and that year Ken roomed with Clarke Lange and Bobby Parker. Lange, a University of Miami product, was a third baseman like Ken who also got drafted by the Astros in 1984. "At that point they kind of made it sound like Clarke would be the one," said Melodee Lange Christensen, Clarke's wife until his death in 2006. "And then obviously, there's Ken." Parker, a second baseman, played college ball at the University of Mississippi and was drafted in the twenty-first round in 1984. He and Ken became fast friends. Scott Houp—who'd roomed with Clarke the previous year at Asheville—served as an unofficial fourth roommate, often trying to nudge his teammates to call it a night.

Manager Dave Cripe made sure to schedule morning workouts, a way to keep the players in line and a workaround for the rain showers that commonly washed out pregame batting practice. Cripe was strict and stern, a solid presence for a bunch of twentysomethings getting adjusted to pro ball. A college football player under Lou Holtz, Cripe chose to pursue a baseball career instead of the gridiron, but as a third baseman in the Royals system during the late 1970s, with Hall of Famer George Brett blocking his path, he was about as treasured as the lukewarm sips of coffee he got in Kansas City at the end of the 1978 season. Cripe's playing days made way for his coaching days, because what else are you going to do, and in 1985 he found himself managing a player, like Brett, who was poised to become one of the game's premier third basemen.

"I think he was the only arm I ever graded out," Cripe said. "It was the best arm I'd ever seen."

Ken's arm was a weapon. Sometimes his throws would rise as they crossed the diamond, which posed a challenge for whoever was on the receiving end. "He threw a ball at third base, and it literally hit the first baseman, Jim O'Dell, in the middle of his chest because it came at him and rose, and we laughed so hard because after the game, there's this big indentation on his chest and you could see the Rawlings mark on it," Houp said.

Ken's competitive streak emerged hours before game time. Sometimes he'd saunter to the outfield, where Houp was playing, and challenge the outfielder to a throwing contest. The teammates would see who could make the best throw, and Ken would usually win, chucking it from the warning track to first base. Houp also noticed Ken's random acts of kindness, an innate sense to pick up a teammate who was struggling: "Hey, how are you doing today?" Stars are often wrapped up in their own little bubbles, but Ken's teammates found the opposite: a humble guy who carried himself like the twenty-fourth player on the team.

Ken was living on his own for the first time and learning how to take care of himself. His parents were concerned about his lifestyle—Lee, thousands of miles away, couldn't keep an eye on his boy. His parents wanted to make sure he was OK. Ken didn't want to be bothered. "I rebelled hard to where my minor league career started and they were calling me, wondering why I wasn't doing a little better here, if I was getting my sleep, and I finally said, 'Y'know, just quit it. I'm a grown-up. Don't tell me how to live,' that kind of attitude. Finally, I broke it off for a while, just not even talking to them," he said in a 1997 interview with journalist Jane Mitchell.

While Ken was emotionally and physically distanced from his parents, and scraping by on $650 a month (his teammates' monthly salaries ranged from $500 to $1,000), he found support in Florida. "He was broke. I used to take him to Denny's after the games in Kissimmee," team trainer Larry Lasky said. When Ken and his teammates couldn't afford to go out at night—which was often—they'd head to the home of Roger and Betty Ann Jones.

The couple's sons Kirk and Kevin served as batboys on that 1985 team, and the family had season tickets behind the dugout.

"These guys got done at ten, eleven o'clock at night," Roger Jones said. "They didn't have any money and they had nothing to do until noon the next day, so we kind of became a stopping point for a bunch of them. They would come over, we might play cards, Betty and I would go to bed. She had a whole bunch of taped movies on VHS. We just left them out there, and they watched movies. It was too expensive to go barhopping, and it was a place to go. Eventually they would just lock up and go home."

Players saw Roger and Betty Ann as their surrogate parents—they'd stay in touch for decades, calling the couple "Mom" and "Dad" whenever they spoke. "We were like their sons almost. . . . It was like their life revolved around our team," catcher Mark Reynolds said.

While the Joneses were a consistent presence at home games, sitting behind Osceola's dugout, the rest of the crowd didn't always fill in behind them. Attendance was an ongoing problem for the team—Kissimmee's population in 1985 was fewer than twenty-five thousand, roughly half that of Daytona Beach. The area was best known for dairy farms and transient vacationers. Locals had a tough time getting excited watching a bunch of guys they'd never heard of. "I always joke if they had dressed us up like cows and said, 'Rodeo tonight,' they would have filled the stands," Lasky said.

Don't think the idea didn't cross the mind of team leadership, which tried every promotion possible to draw crowds. Players tossed eggs and milked cows. Hall of Famer Bob Feller made an appearance, as did Max Patkin, the second "Clown Prince of Baseball." They launched fireworks and hosted donkey baseball—which, as the name suggests, involves base runners and fielders riding donkeys. On Grocery Scramble Night, six fans got to run the bases with the chance of gathering groceries, a pseudo *Supermarket Sweep* around the infield. They handed out razors on Gillette Razor Night, and Marco the Magician made a visit. Santa Claus stopped by on Christmas in June Night.

When those events failed to draw crowds—the team was bringing in fewer than 500 fans a game on average—they resorted to giving away cold, hard cash. A $10,000 giveaway on August 18 would pay out a dollar per fan and the full prize to one winner if 5,000 people showed up for the game . . . but attendance turned out to be 2,498, meaning the winner took home $2,498.

The fans who showed up got to see a solid team. A week into the season, Cripe moved Ken up to third in the batting order, and he pretty much stayed there for the rest of the season. Ken had a knack for getting timely hits and clutch RBIs, like on May 3 against Tampa when his two-RBI single won the game in the ninth.

Things were rolling—Osceola was in first place, and Ken was batting about .280—until a May 20 game at Fort Myers, when Ken fielded a ground ball and threw across his body, and *oww*. "It felt funny after I threw it, and the next day it was sore," he said. It was a strain of his throwing shoulder, a reflection of his urge to make every throw as hard as he could. Ken remained in the lineup as a designated hitter while he rested his shoulder. But he wanted to play the field. He struggled to keep his head in the game when all he had to do was walk to home plate three or four times and swing a bat. He didn't feel like he was helping his team.

But he was. He hit his first pro home run on June 2, off Cardinals prospect Greg Mathews, a Cal State Fullerton product who would pitch in the majors. Ken was still developing his power stroke and learning how to drive the ball. It didn't help that the Florida State League parks were major league size. He only ended up hitting four home runs that season, and the first three came in early June. But he was driving in tons of runs—he spent the season near the top of the league lead—and he was one of seven Osceola reps named to the league's East All-Star team, along with Mallicoat and closer Mark Baker, catcher Troy Afenir, Young, Cripe, and Lasky. Other FSL All-Stars included Yankees outfield prospect Jay Buhner, along with Mathews, Tampa catcher Joe Oliver, Fort Myers infielder Kevin Seitzer, Lakeland's Jody Reed, and St. Petersburg outfielder Lance Johnson.

The All-Star selection posed a logistical issue. Ken's high school sweetheart Nancy was coming to town and planned to spend the off days with Ken. He wasn't expecting to make the team, or maybe he didn't think that far in advance. The plan was for the players to go down in the van, play the game, and come back—the FSL sites were all within a few hours' drive of one another—and the team didn't have a problem with Nancy making the trip in the van, but when they arrived, it was pouring . . . an ongoing theme for the season, rain and lots of it.

The van pulled up at the hotel where Don Miers, the team's GM, was staying with his family. Bam! Bam! Bam! Ken knocked on the door and asked if he and Nancy could stay in Don's room while they waited for the rain to let up. Sure, Miers said. So Nancy and Ken sat on one of the beds, and Miers's then-sixty-year-old mother was in the room, too, watching TV, and the next thing she noticed was Ken and Nancy getting frisky—nothing R-rated, she just wasn't expecting to see Ken licking Nancy's fingers with his eyes closed, the two lovesick lovebirds stealing a moment and reconnecting after a long time apart.

"Cammy, my family's here, can you wait?" Don asked.

"No, we don't have much time together," Ken responded. For years afterward, whenever Miers's mother saw Ken on her TV, she responded, *there's finger sucker.*

The All-Star Game ended up getting postponed until the following day. In the first inning, Buhner hit a towering two-run homer, and Ken added a single to drive in Pete Camelo, leading the East to a 5–2 win. Mallicoat surrendered two hits in three innings pitched, and Baker got the save.

With his shoulder sufficiently healed, or at least in playable shape, Ken was back to playing the field again. But the Astros lost four of five to open the second half of the season, and they went into July 21 tied for first place with the Winter Haven Red Sox, Boston's affiliate.

The tie atop the standings lasted for only one day—Osceola swept the two-game series to take back sole possession atop the Central Division—but Winter Haven kept nipping at the Astros' heels that summer, until an August 19 game, when Ken dealt the Red Sox a knockout blow. With two outs in the eleventh inning and the game knotted at 4, Bobby Parker and Gerald Young reached base and Ken came through, driving home the winning run with a double in what was Cripe's three hundredth career win as a manager. The victory gave the Astros a five-game lead with eleven games left. Osceola clinched the division five days later, after sweeping a doubleheader, fittingly, against Daytona Beach, the city the team had vacated the previous season before moving to ka-SIM-mee.

After the regular season concluded with a home doubleheader, the playoffs loomed: Osceola would face Fort Lauderdale, the Yankees' affiliate managed by Bucky Dent, he of the famous 1978 playoff home run against the Red Sox.

Cripe had a decision to make—he could let the Astros rest and play Game 1 of its series against the Fort Lauderdale Yankees at home before playing Game 2 and, if necessary, Game 3 on the road, or he could force his team to make the two-hundred-mile trip to play Game 1, then turn around and come back home to close out the series. He chose to host Game 1, to give the team a travel break, even if it meant sacrificing home field advantage.

The series opened on August 30. Osceola started Mike Friederich, who'd been 8–9 in the regular season, instead of Rob Mallicoat—he'd take the bump in Game 2. But Yankees pitcher Bill Fulton kept the Astros at bay, pitching into the eighth inning. Fort Lauderdale staked a 4–0 lead before Osceola scraped across its first run, and despite a three-run rally that included an RBI double by Ken, it wasn't enough, as Osceola fell 4–3.

Cripe's plan backfired, and now Osceola had to win two in a row at Fort Lauderdale.

Game 2 saw Mallicoat battling with Steve George, one of the league's top pitchers. Osceola jumped to a 2–0 lead in the sixth inning before the Baby Yanks answered with three runs to spell Mallicoat. Baker gave up a run in the eighth to make it 4–2. Last chance for Osceola. Two outs. Ninth inning. One runner on base. Up came Karl Allaire with his .211 batting average and zero home runs in 289 at bats on the season. George was trying to close the door. But it's impossible to know when the baseball gods will shine down on someone, when Bucky Dent will become Bucky Fucking Dent to Red Sox fans, and so it was for Karl Allaire, who hit his first home run of the season to stun the Baby Yanks and send the game into extra innings.

The game went on, and on, and on. . . . Young threw out a runner at home to keep the tie intact, and the teams played for another full nine innings and one more to top it off, when Jim O'Dell hit a two-run double in the nineteenth to clinch the win—a game that had taken five hours and fifty-five minutes.

"That will go down as a career for me," said Allaire, who went 6-for-7. "Actually, they were all pissed at me 'cause they all wanted to go home. That would have been the end of the season. Everybody was pissed at me."

The end of the season came one game later, when Fort Lauderdale won 7–2. It was tough saying goodbye. After the loss, the players returned to Kissimmee. That night, Ken, Scott Houp, Clarke Lange, and Bobby Parker went out together and drank to the good times. For Ken, the future was blinding—he was a legitimate prospect with major league talent. How far he could go . . . that would be up to him, at least for a while. For Clarke and Scott, it was quickly the end of the line, their pro baseball dreams making way for careers and families and memories about the summer they shared in ka-SIM-mee playing baseball with their friend Ken Caminiti.

* * *

For the first half of the 1986 season, Ken might as well have been playing in hell.

Columbus, Georgia—home of the Astros' Double-A affiliate during the 1980s—felt a lot like hell anyway, with its high humidity and stagnant, dead heat. The town is located near the Alabama-Georgia border along the banks of the Chattahoochee, and yes, as the song suggests, it gets hotter there than a hoochie coochie. Instead of saying it was hotter than H-E-L-L, "we used to say, 'It's hotter than Columbus,'" said Rocky Coyle, who played for the Southern League's Huntsville Stars.

"It was burning, just burning," said Jeff Bettendorf, a pitcher on that 1986 team.

But the heat was only one reason 1986 initially felt like hell for Ken and his Columbus Astros teammates, many of whom had matriculated together from Single-A Osceola along with manager Dave Cripe, who Ken enjoyed playing for in his first minor league season. Despite reaching the playoffs the season before, and having a deep roster that included former major league players Larry Ray and Mike Fuentes, everything seemed to go wrong—injuries and bad bounces and personal conflict all fueled a nosedive that left the team mired in the cellar early into the season.

Ken couldn't stop throwing the ball away at third base. The errors piled up. The playing conditions didn't help. Where the Florida State League featured spring training facilities fit for major league players, the Double-A Southern League facilities were shabby and worn, especially where Golden Park was concerned. The infield dirt was full of rocks. The outfield ground was uneven. The ball bounced differently in hell.

Ken's minor league teammate Tim (Earl) Cash remembers closing out a game when Ken was playing third base at Columbus. A routine but hard-hit ball to third. Ken was in position to field the ball, when "the ball hits like a clump of grass or something," Cash said. "The ball takes some funky hop and kind of shoots right up toward his right ear.

"He reaches up with his bare hand and grabs it out of the air, just his fast twitch reflexes, and then throws a seed across to first base. And I'm like, you have got to be kidding me."

Back in the 1980s, minor league teams normally had a manager who also served as a hitting instructor, along with a pitching coach, and that was that—meaning that during practice, pitchers often ended up hitting fungoes to infielders. Ken would position himself playing in, as close to the hitter as possible, and urge his teammates: Hit 'em as hard as you possibly can.

"I could hit it harder than anybody else. So I'd show up to the ballpark early to do my run, and there'd be a fungo bat with three or four baseballs, and he's standing there like a puppy dog waiting to chase a tennis ball," said Jeff

Livin, a teammate of Ken's at Columbus. "And we'd go out to the field, and it's rocky ground. And if you didn't hit it as hard as you could, he would throw it as hard as he could back at you. And if you managed to duck that one, it'd come off the wall and get you on the rebound. He didn't want a routine ground ball. He wanted something to challenge him. That's the way that guy was wired."

Nelson Rood, an infielder in the Astros system during the 1980s, remembers fielding ground balls with Ken. "Occasionally when the pitchers were hitting fungoes, we would take our gloves off and catch them barehanded to let the pitcher know he wasn't hitting them hard enough. That would get under their skin, and then they'd start rocketing them," Rood said. "It was one of these days where, I don't know who initiated it, but one of us slipped off our glove and caught it with a bare hand. The pitcher started hitting some pretty good shots down the line there. And so he said, why don't we play a game catching them behind our back in between our legs—these ground balls, you have to catch 'em, you have to put the glove behind your legs, and catch the ground ball. And the pitcher's hitting them so hard."

* * *

The ballpark in Columbus was located near Fort Benning, a U.S. Army base, which meant a few games a week, the recruits would get in for free or get discounted tickets, and the team would cash in on the concessions. "There would be like three thousand guys there just drinking beer, hootin' and hollerin', and it's pretty crazy. They were out there working hard in the heat all day and doing their military stuff and that, that was their escape," Larry Ray said.

Despite the heat, Columbus wasn't seen as the worst place to play in the league.

"Charlotte was the worst. There was one faucet that worked in the shower. It was horrible," said Doug Scherer, a San Jose native who pitched for Huntsville in 1986 and 1987.

"They had trailers out there, and you had to dress in shifts, pitchers and catchers, then infielders and outfielders," Huntsville catcher Jimmy Jones said of the facilities at Charlotte.

Playing in the Southern League meant long trips. The ten teams were spread across six states—Tennessee, Alabama, North Carolina, South Carolina,

Florida, and Georgia. The teams were located as far west as Memphis, as far east as Charlotte, as far north as Knoxville, and as far south as Orlando. Given that all the locations were so spread out, the players would spend hour after hour on long bus rides—the average bus ride that year lasted more than four hours and covered nearly three hundred miles. The longest trips, more than eight hours and covering about six hundred miles, took the team south to Orlando. You can only spend so long playing cards and dominoes.

Columbus entered the 1986 season with optimism. But then the free fall began.

In a May 19 game against the Orlando Twins, Ken fielded a ball with two outs and the bases loaded, but he threw the ball away, causing three runs to score and keying a 4–1 loss for Columbus.

He made another error on May 30, causing the floodgates to open for another big inning and another Astros loss.

Ken was pressing. He was trying to be perfect. With every mistake, he could feel his manager's judgment, the need to be perfect. It was the same way his father's criticism made him feel during his high school and college days. He'd carry errors with him into the batter's box and bad at bats into the field, lingering on mistakes instead of letting them go and focusing on the play in front of him. He wasn't the only player who was pressing. Dave Cripe's management style, which had worked so well the season before, had worn thin.

"Caminiti would dive and make an unbelievable catch, and then he had to put the second piece together. He had to get up and throw to first, and he couldn't do it 'cause he was scared. He was afraid if he made an error that he would get yelled at. And that's the way Criper approached these guys. And the young guys, they didn't respond," said Ray, one of the team's veteran players, who'd spent a month in the bigs in 1982.

The players were tired. Tired of the extra practices, tired of losing, tired of Cripe's businesslike approach to practices and games.

Things came to a head, Ray said, after some of the players broke curfew during a road trip. After they arrived back in Columbus following a long bus ride, Cripe decided to schedule a practice for the following morning. Practice started—they were working on rundowns—and Ray didn't slide, and Cripe started to yell, and "we got into it right in front of all the young guys," Ray said.

The players felt a disconnect with Cripe's management style.

"We had fun all the time. We cracked jokes. We were singing, and when the game starts, that's when we put on our game face. But before that, nah. Dave wasn't like that. So he never got the best out of the players that he had [in 1986], because he didn't know how to manage us," Anthony Kelley said.

Cripe would agree with that assessment. By the time 1986 rolled around, he wasn't enjoying baseball the same way he had in previous years. He was always introverted, someone who didn't seek out friendships with his players or enjoy the public needs of being a manager, but what else was there? "I did some good years managing, but it really wasn't for me," Cripe said. "I needed to stay in baseball at that point because I didn't know what I had left to fall back on."

As Columbus sank like a rock in the standings, the losses became more and more difficult for Cripe to stomach. "We did terrible, flat out," he said. "And when I evaluated myself, I thought I did terrible. Nothing I did seemed to come off correctly. I'd never experienced that kind of failure personally."

Some of the losses were just bad luck. Baker, the Osceola closer the season before, injured his arm but tried to pitch through the injury, losing five games out of the bullpen before being shut down. A similar fate befell Mallicoat, Osceola's ace in 1985. Mallicoat hurt his ankle in spring training, tried to pitch through the injury at Triple-A, got sent down to Columbus, and went 0–6 with a 4.81 ERA before being shelved.

Ken was battling an injury, too—his right knee bothered him and would require off-season surgery. "Don't let them know that the knee's hurting," Ken told trainer Ed Duke, downplaying his injuries to stay in the lineup.

With Columbus 23–38 and stuck in last place, Houston decided to make a change. Cripe was out as manager. He flew to Columbus from Memphis, where the team was wrapping up a road trip, to clean out his locker. And then he was off to his native California, where he'd get his degree and become a teacher.

"I drove home in like two days. I didn't stop. I pulled over a couple of times, slept by the side of the road," Cripe said. "It was kind of a relief."

* * *

Gary Tuck spent so much time in the sunlight behind a baseball cap and shades, the skin around his eyes and forehead seemed to perpetually be two or three shades lighter than his cheeks. Tuck played college football and was a catcher in the Montreal Expos system for a few years before shifting to coaching and becoming a baseball nomad—bouncing from Arizona State to Tucson to Osceola, traveling wherever the game would take him.

Tuck had been coaching in Osceola in 1986 when Fred Stanley, the Astros' director of baseball operations, asked him to head to Columbus. The club was in last place, and they needed someone to fill in as manager, and what the hell, why not give "Tucker" a shot to lead a ball club.

For the Columbus Astros, things changed the moment Gary Tuck arrived at Golden Park. Larry Ray recalled the day he saw Tuck's pickup truck in the parking lot. Ray, one of the clubhouse leaders, gave Tuck timely advice.

"You got a lot of talent here," Ray said he told Tuck. "You gotta praise these guys."

"That's it?"

"No, put three cases of beer on the bus on road trips."

"Consider it done."

Gone were Dave Cripe's rules. Gone was the stress. Tuck motivated the players by encouraging them and building them up.

"I let the players be themselves. I told them they were the best players in that league. I told them individually they were the best players," Tuck recalled decades later while sitting in the Yankee Stadium dugout as a bullpen coach on his final pro baseball assignment. Along the way, he contributed to five World Series champions.

Tuck endeared himself to the rules-weary team. "How many of you are from Columbus, Georgia?" he asked the group.

"Nobody," they said.

"Neither am I," he told them. So for the rest of the year, they would wear their road uniforms.

"We never wore home uniforms. And nobody shaved. So there was no shaving, and sometimes the laundry wasn't done," Tuck said. "They wore road uniforms, they swung 3-and-0, everybody had the green light to steal, and that's how we played it."

Ken grew a "scruffy old bootleg beard," Tuck said. "He could shave and grow a beard in half an hour." Facial hair wasn't allowed by many pro baseball teams during the 1980s—Columbus's parent club in Houston disallowed anything beyond a tightly trimmed mustache. The teams that did allow it, such as

Charlie Finley's Oakland Athletics teams of the 1970s, were known for being rugged rebels in a stodgy old game. Facial hair gave Ken a presence, a swagger. He felt more secure. He looked good playing with facial hair, whether it was a bootleg beard or a goatee.

Tuck's passion for the game started from the ground up. He'd take the stereo out of his office and bring it down to the field, and he'd have the players work their positions—not with their gloves, but with rakes and shovels. The field was in rough shape, and the players were going to fix it. So Caminiti raked his plot at third base, and Gerald Young lent his groundskeeping talents to center field, and Jeff Datz worked home plate. "It was a work detail before we worked on baseball for a half hour a day," Tuck said. "You don't like the field, make it how you want it. And they did."

Once Ken was done with his groundskeeping duties, it was time to get dirty. To start, Tuck worked on Ken's positioning. "I put him at Graig Nettles depth, fifteen feet back, fifteen feet over," Tuck said. "He could actually play shallow left field because of his arm." He also focused on Ken's footwork, his preparation for each pitch. Ken had the raw physical tools—he just needed to harness and develop them further. "I actually put a chest protector on him and had him dive, practice diving in that hard dirt. And he loved it. He learned how to dive," Tuck said.

One of the biggest difference makers was Datz, a sure-handed catcher adept at handling the Columbus pitching staff. Another was first baseman Pete Mueller, who was batting all of .221 in Single-A ball when he got promoted. Mueller, a twenty-fifth-round draft pick in 1983, happened to be six feet, four inches tall, meaning Ken's wild arm was no longer a problem—it was suddenly a lot harder to overthrow the first baseman. And with Ken making so many plays at third base, Columbus's pitchers could pitch hitters inside and trust they would get the out. Ken was committed to his craft. After a game, he was known to stay behind or come back after the crowd had gone so he could put in extra work with his manager.

Tuck saw something special in his young third baseman. You spend enough time around the game, in the sunlight, and you just know when someone is destined for big things. "That year with Kenny, we went to Charlotte, where the Orioles were. And Brooks Robinson was there. I had met him a long time ago. Of course he didn't remember me, who the heck am I? But I took Kenny from our clubhouse over to the field and said, 'Brooks, I'm Gary Tuck, the manager of the Columbus Astros. This is the next Brooks Robinson, Ken Caminiti.'" A decade later, Robinson would be crossing paths with Ken again, and presenting him with a Gold Glove award.

* * *

Double-A ball in the Southern League meant long road trips, idle hours on the bus, but also stayovers for two or three nights at a time. And twentysomethings with energy and time to kill are bound to drink.

Tuck fraternized with the players in a way that Cripe didn't, and the beer flowed. Oh-for-four, have a beer to forget about it and get back to it tomorrow. Three-for-four with a homer, have a beer and celebrate. Drinking was nothing new to Ken—he'd been drinking since his middle school days, and he was known to party in high school and college, and his early professional days—but for Ken, beer became more closely intertwined with baseball in that summer of bus trips and groundwork, a way to bond with his teammates. After games, you'd go out to eat and have a pitcher or two, or three, or four, or some bottles of Miller Genuine Draft, and talk baseball. Or chase skirts (not quite so much for Ken, since things were getting serious with Nancy). And then there was beer on the bus.

Sure, Ken could drink—he had one of those trapdoor gullets that allowed him to chug. You ask Ken's minor league teammates, and yes, he drank a lot, but many of them drank a lot, too, minus some of the married or religious guys. He was twenty-three. He'd settle down eventually.

Ken played all-out on the field, and he drank all-out off of it, a competitive guy with everything in front of him. Some teammates thought Ken's drinking was within reason during his minor league days, especially since he didn't drink every night. But when he did drink . . . for Anthony Kelley, signs of trouble were starting to show.

"We knew he had a problem, and we would talk about it. We'd talk about it a lot. But it was always controlled. Never come to the ballpark drunk, high, or under the influence. Never play games under the influence," Kelley said. Ken liked drinking his beer, and he was good at it, and he didn't think he had a problem, and if his employer was supplying it for him, he didn't have a lot of motivation to change his ways.

As Ken entered his pro baseball career, friction lingered between him and his parents over his late-night habits. They wanted to help steer him in the right direction, but they were stern, and Ken didn't feel like he needed to listen. He was making money playing baseball, and consequences were an afterthought. If he wanted to drink, he was going to drink. This was all part of the baseball lifestyle. And what did they know?

Drinking wasn't impacting his play in 1986—if anything, his strong second half reflected everything starting to click. He was proving to be a strong second-half player, a pattern that would repeat during the height of his major league career. He batted .261 through Columbus's first seventy-six games, with three home runs in 279 at bats—and over the final 234 at bats, under Tuck's guidance, he batted .346 with nine home runs, tripling his home run total from the first part of the season. He played loose. He adjusted to Double-A pitching. He stopped carrying his mistakes around with him. And he played the best baseball of his life up to that point.

It didn't hurt having a familiar face around that season: Roger Samuels, a San Jose native who had played American Legion ball with Ken the summer after Ken was in tenth grade. Samuels won ten games with Columbus as a starter the year before, but in 1986 he moved to the bullpen. It would be his last year in the Astros system before catching on with San Francisco.

"Mid-season we moved in with Ken because I think his roommate left, just to make it cheaper. Nancy was coming out. So we spent the summer together," Samuels said. "He watched *Perry Mason* and cartoons; I watched *All My Children*, the soap opera."

As Ken broke out, and Kelley established himself as the league's best pitcher, in line with a Greenville Braves lefty named Tom Glavine, so did the Astros. Columbus opened the second half 19–17 before rattling off eight straight wins. Under Tuck, Columbus was enjoying baseball again, and winning.

"We wound up absolutely destroying people after that. It wasn't even close. We made a couple moves here and there, and here we go," Kelley said. "[Tuck] had the team more relaxed; he just let us go out there and play. You dropped the ball, OK, make sure to get that next time. This is what we need to do. OK. And here we go. Go out there and get your running in. OK. That's all Tuck did. "It was like we knew we couldn't be beat."

Columbus wasn't even fazed by the country's best pure athlete, Bo Jackson, the Heisman winner who was also drafted by the Kansas City Royals and made his professional baseball debut for the Memphis Chicks against Columbus on June 30. When Bo took batting practice, the Astros gathered to watch—Tuck encouraged it. Why act like this was any other minor league game? The entire country was watching. Bo batted seventh in his debut, and in his first at bat, he hit a three-hopper up the middle for an RBI single. Everything was all about Bo that day, but the Astros still won 9–5.

After finishing in last place in the first half, Columbus was poised to make a worst-to-first turnaround. But the Orlando Twins were hanging tough, sweeping Columbus in a four-game series and closing within half a game of the division lead with a week remaining in the regular season. Under Tuck, the team didn't fret. They turned things around at Jacksonville, taking three of four and keeping pace with hard-charging Orlando. After Orlando was swept in a doubleheader on August 29, Columbus had a two-game lead with three games remaining. The Astros won out, finishing the second half 42–29. Orlando ended the season three games back.

Ken and his teammates—the league's worst team in the first half—were back in the playoffs. The semifinals opened September 3 at home against Jacksonville, the Expos affiliate. And just like the year before, with Osceola, the playoffs opened with a one-run loss.

But there was no panic, and no nineteen-inning games, either. They'd already been cast aside, no one even expected them to be here, so what was one game? Columbus didn't lose again versus Jacksonville, sweeping the final three games, 10–7, 4–3, and 4–2.

The Huntsville Stars—Oakland's Double-A affiliate and the class of the league—was all that stood between Columbus and the title. Huntsville finished the regular season 78–63, the top mark in the Southern League. But by the time September rolled around, the Athletics were already raiding their minor league reserves. The team's first baseman at the start of the season, Ken's Team USA cohort and collegiate adversary Mark McGwire, had been promoted to Triple-A and then the majors, while Huntsville catcher Terry Steinbach was going to get called up to Oakland at the end of the Southern League season.

Meanwhile, Oakland shortstop prospect Walt Weiss had recently joined Huntsville. The Athletics' system of the mid-1980s was full of more talent than maybe any other system in the game.

"We had a different team headed into the playoffs," said Stars slugger Rocky Coyle.

The teams split in Columbus (Ken hit a two-run homer in the first game, a 6–1 Columbus win), and when the series went to Huntsville, the Astros couldn't be stopped. The players were staying at the same hotel as Huntsville players—they didn't want to be on the hook for another month of apartment rent—and Coyle encountered Ken and his teammates partying the night before one of their playoff games. "And I remember thinking to myself, 'Why are you guys partying this late on a night like this?'" Coyle said. But the Columbus Astros were not going to slow down. The team's mentality during its series against Huntsville: "We're coming in here, we're getting ready to take your women and kick your butts, and eat out of your refrigerator, and we'll be out of here," Kelley said.

And so it went, with Columbus winning 5–0 and 8–4 to close out the series, powered to the championship by two-run homers by Mike Fuentes and Joe Mikulik. The worst-to-first turnaround was complete.

For Ken, the second half of the season showed what he could do under optimum conditions, with a coach who lifted his spirits, a winning team around him, relative health (even with a bum knee that would require off-season surgery), and positive self-esteem.

Ken Caminiti had a ring. But when would he get the call?

* * *

Astros manager Hal Lanier stuck with two veterans entrenched at the hot corner, Denny Walling and Phil Garner, in 1987. That left Chuck Jackson—who was drafted the same year as Ken—stuck in Triple-A. And Ken, despite his torrid second half and a Southern League title in 1986, remained in hell. The two minor leaguers were on a parallel track and jockeying for the same opportunity.

"I always felt they played us off each other instead of saying, 'Hey, look, we are all going to be part of this thing together.' I just felt we had to truly compete against each other. In hindsight, there was room for everybody," Jackson said.

The Astros of the 1980s mishandled numerous prospects. Guys would have a career year, only to grow another year older and see their path to the majors change or close—case in point, Anthony Kelley, the Southern League's top pitcher in 1986, who compiled a 67–38 record (good for a .638 winning percentage) across six minor league seasons without getting the call. Eventually he injured his arm, and that was that.

Turmoil and turnover in the Astros front office didn't help. Al Rosen, a former MVP third baseman for the Cleveland Indians, was canned as Astros GM in 1985 and replaced by Dick Wagner, known for his erratic nature and for overseeing the breakup of Cincinnati's Big Red Machine. Major League Baseball's collusion scandal contributed to the logjam, too—owners made a secret agreement to avoid signing one another's free agent players, forcing the players to re-sign with their clubs at devalued salaries instead of testing the free agent market. Garner was one of the players impacted by collusion, and in 1994 he was awarded $128,063 in damages.

Ken wasn't invited to major league spring training in 1987, a common courtesy to top prospects. He was the can't-miss prospect the Astros somehow kept missing. To start the 1987 season, *Baseball America* listed Ken as the top prospect in the Southern League, directly ahead of Larry Walker and Randy Johnson—two future Hall of Famers.

Ken was frustrated. Players he compared himself to, like his Team USA teammates Cory Snyder, Mark McGwire, and Will Clark, were already in the majors, and while Astros prospects like Gerald Young and Anthony Kelley were moving up to Triple-A, he was still playing ball along the Chattahoochee.

When in hell, keep going. . . . Ken channeled his frustration into the way he approached the game. He'd work harder. And harder. And harder still. He'd work harder than anyone. He'd make it impossible for them to keep him down.

"For batting practice, you had four groups that hit, so you got an hour for batting practice. The other forty-five minutes, this guy pretty much took ground balls full speed, and our manager at that time, because it was hot in Columbus, Georgia, he would make Ken go sit in the corner down in the out-field by himself. He would threaten to fine him to make him rest," said Ken's Columbus teammate Richard Johnson.

Ken was always hurting, as evidenced by the ice packs that would cover his shoulders and knees after games, his body parts treated like soda cans in a tightly packed cooler. Nevertheless, even in the heat, there were lots of things that made Ken feel comfortable in Columbus starting in 1987. He had a familiarity with the league and stadiums. A lot of his friends, like Karl Allaire and Bobby Parker and Jeff Livin, were here. Larry Lasky, the trainer in his pro season in Osceola, was in Columbus, too. So was John Fishel—he and Ken became immediate friends, a shared connection over their all-out style on the field.

Ken's hot hitting from 1986 carried over to 1987. Through his team's first forty-five games, Ken was batting .359—even better than his .346 for the second half of the previous season—leaving him only a few points behind league leader Jim Eisenreich, a former Twins player who was back playing again after walking away from his major league career as he struggled with Tourette's syndrome, a neurological disorder that caused him to involuntarily twitch and jerk.

Columbus batboy Mark Teel remembers Caminiti and Eisenreich spending time before games standing behind the screen during batting practice, deep in conversation.

Teel, then fourteen, called Ken "Cammo" because of the camouflage grips he used on his bats. The teen struck up a friendly connection with the player. One day, Teel showed up wearing Reebok sneakers, and it had been raining the night before. Ken was worried the shoes would get ruined, so he gave Teel a pair of his cleats.

In return, Teel did something for Ken. Tobacco reps would visit the field and hand out cans of dipping tobacco. Ken's brand of choice was Copenhagen. They'd give out one or two cans for each player, and since a lot of players didn't dip, Ken would have Teel ask the tobacco rep for a few cans for so-and-so. Then Teel would stick the cans in the back of Ken's locker.

Their connection deepened one day during BP. Teel was collecting balls and putting them in a drum when Ken smashed a ball that ricocheted off the drum and hit the batboy in the face. "I was knocked out. They put an ice pack on me, and I'm on the bench and everything," Teel said. There was no major damage, just a bit of a shiner around his eye, but Teel ended up getting fined $5 in the players' Kangaroo Court. "They didn't make us pay," he said. But the next home stand, the batboys were required to wear batting helmets, which were stifling in the heat, and they smelled like something awful after a few games from all the sweat.

* * *

Chuck Jackson got the call from Triple A in May—he was headed to Houston. The third baseman and outfielder had been blocking Ken's path to a promotion.

But even after Jackson moved up, Ken stayed put as other players, mainly Dale Berra, manned the hot corner for Triple-A Tucson.

May concluded without a promotion, and all of June, and Ken's batting average started to come back to earth. Was he going to spend the rest of his days toiling away in Columbus? Did the Astros notice how good he was? Did the Astros even want him?

One time when Jeff Livin was hitting fungoes to Ken, the manager called over the pitcher. He ended up bringing him to an office at Columbus's home park. Livin thought he might be getting the call. *I've got to call my mom,* he thought. He sat down and found Astros personnel waiting.

"Jeff, it's about Ken," they said. He thought, *What about me going to the Astrodome?!*

"We know you're going to keep this to yourself," they told him, "but the front office is looking at Kenny and maybe moving him up in a couple of weeks. We'd like for you to take it a little easy on the fungoes; we don't want him hurting himself before his time comes."

Livin remembers feeling numb. He had thought he was getting the call. "And here they called me in to talk about Kenny." He returned to the field, excited for his friend but crestfallen that his own ticket to Houston wasn't getting punched.

"What'd they tell you?" Ken asked.

"Nothing, dude. Just go back out there and get some ground balls."

Ken finished the first half of the season on Sunday, July 12, near the top of the Southern League in every major offensive category: .325 batting average, 122 hits in 407 at bats, 25 doubles, 15 home runs, 69 RBIs. The great first half earned him a spot on the league's All-Star team. The All-Star Game was scheduled for the next day.

Ken thought he might soon be on the move but didn't know the team's full plans. The parent club needed a jolt and help at third base. Chuck Jackson was struggling, while Phil Garner had been traded to Los Angeles and Denny Walling was being moved around the field to plug gaps in the lineup. Houston's assistant GM, Bill Wood, called Columbus Astros GM Dayton Preston with a message: Don't let Ken out of your sight.

"We're going to bring him up to the show, but we don't know when and we don't know if it's going to be temporary," Preston said Wood told him.

Preston ended up driving Ken to the All-Star Game, in Greenville, South Carolina. On the trip, he took Ken shopping in preparation for his getting the call. "The kid didn't even have a sport coat," Preston recalled, telling Ken, "'You've got to have a coat and a white shirt and a tie and a decent pair of pants.' So we went out to what is commonly known as Jacques Penne and equipped him with a JCPenney wardrobe."

As part of the festivities, Ken attended a luncheon with the major league's home run king, Hank Aaron, and received a gold commemorative watch (though fellow All-Stars say the watches were prone to stop working within a few days).

Aaron's message to the players: Stay away from drugs. "We don't need another Len Bias," he said, referencing the Boston Celtics draft pick who'd died of a cocaine overdose the year before.

"I can tell you right now that drugs will never help you hit a home run. Drugs will never help you get into the big leagues. In fact, the only thing drugs can do is to keep you from reaching your goals.

"You have an obligation not only to yourself, but to your families, the ones that put up with you, also to your wives . . . to take care of your bodies, to take care of yourself, to reach your full potential."

That year, the league All-Stars played against the Atlanta Braves' Triple-A affiliate, the Richmond Braves. Richmond took an early 3–0 lead, but Caminiti ended the shutout in the fourth inning. Facing Glavine—who'd started making a name for himself due to his arsenal of pitches and pinpoint control—Ken hit a soaring solo blast. The Southern League All-Stars scored two more runs, and the game ended in ten innings with a 3–3 tie.

They returned to Columbus without any updates, but within the next day word came from Houston to Preston, who passed the news to Ken: He was getting promoted. *Finally!* Ken was excited. Tucson was located a few hours away from San Jose by plane. And Triple-A Tucson was only one step away from the majors. He was so close. . . .

"No, you're going to Houston," Preston corrected him.

Ken made it to the show, bypassing Triple-A. With his JCPenney wardrobe and his big-league dreams fulfilled, Ken boarded a flight for Houston. There'd be no more long bus rides. Ken was out of hell. Ken was a major leaguer.

CHAPTER 7

HOUSTON, WE HAVE LIFTOFF

You never forget your first—and Ken's major league debut was special from beginning to end.

It was July 16, 1987, and Ken was playing in the Astrodome, the "Eighth Wonder of the World," with 19,614 fans watching on, wondering who the hell this new third baseman was, *Ken Cama-who?*

The first batter of Ken's first major league game, the Philadelphia Phillies' Juan Samuel, slapped a one-hopper down the line, which Ken backhanded cleanly and threw to first for the first out—the same play he had made thousands of times before. The highlights continued later in the first inning when first baseman Von Hayes hit a slow roller. Ken charged, planted with his foot in line with the ball, picked it up, and fired off-balance in one fluid motion. Ken made two more diving stops in the second inning to keep the game scoreless.

"By the time the rookie took his first major-league at bat in the bottom of the second, he had become a crowd favorite," the *Houston Chronicle* wrote. "It mattered little that Caminiti bounced out routinely, the fans were on his side. Their reward would come later."

After his groundout to second base in the second inning, Ken came up again leading off the fifth against the Phillies' Kevin Gross—they'd later become friends, two gamers who enjoyed competing and hunting. Gross was pitching with a herniated disc. Ken, hitting from the left side, started his hands high before settling them closer to his body as the pitch came in, a fastball up. He slashed the bat head through the strike zone. *Crack!* The ball flew into right field, climbing, climbing, before landing at the warning track near the 378 sign on the wall. Right fielder Glenn Wilson tripped over himself, and the ball kicked back into right field. Center fielder Milt Thompson grabbed the ball and threw it to the infield, but by that point Ken was on third base.

"His first big league hit is going to be a stand-up triple. Holy Toledo!" Astros broadcaster Milo Hamilton said.

When Ken came up two innings later, with the Phillies up 1–0, Gross pitched him in pretty much the same spot, and Ken pounced, smooth and strong and steady, driving the ball to right field. As the ball left Caminiti's bat, manager Hal Lanier screamed from the dugout, "Get up! Get up! Get up!" The ball obliged, and it was over the fence—a home run! Ken glided around the bases, and the fans didn't stop cheering until the rookie took a curtain call, something he'd never done before.

In the bottom of the ninth inning, with the game tied 1–1, Ken came up again, this time against reliever Michael Jackson. He worked the count to 3-and-1 and fouled off three fastballs. The next fastball "just missed," Jackson said later. Ken was on base again, with a walk. He moved to third on a single by shortstop Craig Reynolds, and Jackson intentionally walked sure-hitting outfielder José Cruz, who was pinch-hitting, to load the bases.

Up came Gerald Young, Ken's minor league teammate, the two best position players for Osceola and Columbus, now playing with the parent club after being called up a week apart. Young hit the ball to where Wilson would have been playing in right field—but Wilson was positioned behind second base, a fifth infielder to guard against balls up the middle. Ken scampered home, scoring the game-winning run to cap a stellar debut. He was buzzing. All the hard work . . . all the frustration . . . all the extra BP and infield practice . . . all the time in hell . . . three years, nearly to the day, after playing in this stadium for the first time and then getting dumped from Team USA, Ken Caminiti had finally arrived.

"His first game left all the guys in the dugout just kind of looking at each other going, 'Wow, we got a player,'" said catcher Alan Ashby. "He put on quite a show."

After the game, Astros batboy Rocky Mitchell sat next to the team's newest star in the clubhouse. "I'm flying high," Ken told him. He was, for lots of reasons. The plays in the field. The home run. The triple. The game-winning run. Victory. The highest level of competition. And the pill he was given before the game, a little pick-me-up that was popular in major league clubhouses. Ken's first day in the majors, he claimed years later, was the first time he tried a "greenie," the amphetamine pills used throughout the game during the 1980s. He was familiar with recreational drugs from his San Jose days, but speed was different, a performance-enhancing drug that the older players swore by . . . not to abuse them, not an everyday thing, but a boost after a night game, a way to stay sharp when you were dragging.

$$* * *$$

It's fitting that Ken's ascent occurred for the Astros, a team that was forged with an eye to the stars. The franchise was originally named the Houston Colt .45s, but ownership decided space was a more marketable theme than guns, so ahead of the 1965 season the Colts became the Astros to reflect the team's lofty ambitions and the region's role in space exploration. An astronaut training base, the Manned Spacecraft Center, later renamed the Johnson Space Center, was located about thirty miles away.

The name change coincided with the opening of the team's new domed stadium. The Astrodome roof resembled a kaleidoscope, with 4,596 Lucite skylights radiating out along twelve lamella roof wedges. When the stadium opened in 1965, the glare from the skylights was too bright, so workers coated the skylights with off-white paint—which reduced the glare but killed the stadium's grass.

Enter Monsanto, the agrochemical company, which had created an artificial grass surface called ChemGrass. But given the building where it would be used, ChemGrass took on another name: AstroTurf. The surface changed the way sports were played. The Astrodome, with its AstroTurf, represented the future. But twenty-five years after the franchise was founded, the Astros still hadn't won a playoff series, coming painfully close in 1986 against the Mets, taking the eventual World Series champs almost to the brink in a six-game dogfight.

Lanier's approach as manager—which included platoon play and aggressive baserunning—matched the 1986 Astros nicely. Position players like Kevin Bass and Billy Doran had career years, and Houston righty Mike Scott had ace scuff, er, stuff, with a 2.22 ERA, 18–10 record, and 306 strikeouts to win the National League Cy Young Award. At the end of the season, Lanier, an old-school baseball lifer whose father had pitched for the St. Louis Browns and who had played ten years in the majors himself, was named the National League's Manager of the Year. With the same team in place and a division title under its belt, Houston players hoped the team would take the next step in 1987.

"In 1987, after we won our first six games, we thought that we were going for a ride," Ashby said. "That was my impression. And it didn't happen." The Astros fell back to earth after the hot start. Houston's offensive stats were consistent between the seasons—125 and 122 home runs, 654 and 648 runs scored, .255 and .253 batting averages—but that was the problem, since home runs across the game were being hit at a record rate in 1987, the sudden, surprising power attributed to a supposedly juiced baseball or more muscle-bound players, or . . . who knows? The flat offense made a hard-luck loser out of ageless Astros hurler Nolan Ryan, who led the league in ERA (2.76) and strikeouts (270) but went an uncharacteristic 8–16. Scott, the Cy Young winner in 1986, was 16–13.

Billy Doran, the team's second baseman, said, "It's hard to put your finger on it, but we got banged up a little bit, and things didn't work out the way we had hoped." Houston entered the All-Star break in the National League West doldrums at 44–43. The things that had worked so well the season before were less effective this time around. So Houston looked to its minor leagues for a spark.

* * *

Ken's magical week continued against the Phillies. He went 2-for-4 in his second game, a 2–1 loss (Houston mustered only eight hits). During the first inning, with runners on first and third, Phillies catcher Lance Parrish hit a slow roller down the third base line. If it was fair, Philadelphia's first run would score. A foul ball would keep the runner at third. Ken stood watch over the ball like it was a wounded bird. *Get up, fly away . . . go over to foul territory . . . c'mon, you can do it . . .* but the ball rolled and rolled, until it came to a stop near the base in fair territory to give the Phils the lead.

One day later, Ken was flexing his muscles, hitting a double and a single in a 4–2 loss. And to close out the four-game Philadelphia set, Ken slugged his second major league home run, this one off Bruce Ruffin—the only run as Houston fell 4–1. For the series, Ken batted .500 (7-for-14) and factored into five of Houston's six runs. But three of the games ended in losses, and the three-game losing streak sent the Astros under .500. "I hope I didn't bring them bad luck," Ken said.

Even with the new spark plug, this Astro van wouldn't start. But the baseball world was taking notice of his exploits. After four games, in a week that began with him playing Double-A ball and included him rubbing shoulders with Hank Aaron and hitting a homer against Tom Glavine, Ken was named the National League's Player of the Week. For Ken, the honor was a chance to reach out to some of the people who'd helped him along the way, including his manager with Columbus, Gary Tuck.

"Tuckster, I won National League Player of the Week, I just wanted to thank you for helping me get to the big leagues," Ken told him, adding, "It's really easy up here."

"Is it?" Tuck responded. "You're seeing all fastballs right now, son. See if you get Player of the Week next week when you're getting all break-ing balls."

As Tuck predicted, pitchers started throwing breaking balls at Ken, and he soon crashed back to earth after his meteoric start. His .500 average dipped to .389 . . . then to .333 . . . then to .273. . . . The hot streak wasn't sustainable. Major league pitchers exploited Ken's impatience, his frustration, and the Swiss cheese holes in his swing. Off-speed pitches kept him off-balance.

While Ken fell into a slump at the plate, his defense and arm remained otherworldly. Astros veteran Terry Puhl marveled at Ken's throws to first, with the ball rising six to ten inches as it crossed the diamond—the same tendency his college and minor league teammates recognized. One time, Puhl was throwing long toss with teammate Craig Reynolds at the Astrodome. Reynolds was at the warning track in the outfield; Puhl was near home plate. Ken approached Puhl. "Can I throw with you?" he asked.

Of course, Puhl said. So Ken took a ball, without warming up, and gunned it on a line to Reynolds.

"Didn't that hurt?" Puhl asked.

"No," Ken said.

"I bet you can't throw the ball out of the ballpark," Puhl said, testing the younger player.

Challenge accepted. Ken didn't take a crowhop or make a warm-up toss. He simply turned his shoulders and threw it—all the way into the right field stands.

"You're crazy," Puhl said, walking off.

* * *

The local boy did good, and Ken's family and friends jammed into Section 4 at Candlestick on August 10 to celebrate his homecoming. Years after attending an open tryout with the Giants, and after a stopover with Team USA, Ken was back at Candlestick as a major leaguer.

Ken stepped to the plate in the fourth inning against Dave Dravecky to raucous cheers, with his uniform in its usual state, covered in dirt. He settled in and worked the count. Dravecky tossed the ball over the heart of the plate. *Crack!* The ball flew over the fence in left field in front of the bleachers, and fans spilled over, trying to get the ball. After Ken crossed home plate and jogged back to the dugout, he glanced to the stands, looked to his cheering section, and tipped his helmet. Fans in the stands outside Section 4 booed. Local boy or not, this guy was almost single-handedly killing the hometown team.

"I heard the boos, but I heard the cheering from Section 4, too," he told the *San Francisco Examiner*'s Joan Ryan.

He got the chance to show off his defensive skills, too. In the sixth inning, Giants catcher Bob Brenly hit a grounder down the third base line that bounced near the bag. Ken sprinted toward the line, dove with his body angled to the outfield, and came up with the ball as his body thudded across the baseline chalk. He braced himself on both hands and stood in one continuous motion, then fired a laser to first, beating the runner by a step.

"This guy dives and he makes it pay off, too," quipped iconic second baseman Joe Morgan, broadcasting for GiantsVision. "That was a nice play, because Bob runs well. And he got up very quickly and he has a strong arm. This is a nice play."

"This is the play of the game, so far," Morgan's broadcast partner Duane Kuiper responded.

The game ended up being remembered for what happened in the ninth inning. Houston, up 5–4, had brought on reliever Dave Meads to close out the game. But San Francisco had other plans. After leadoff hitter Candy Maldonado hit a solo homer to tie the game, Ken's Team USA teammate Will Clark, now an emerging star for the Giants, golfed a ball into the upper deck stands in right field, walking off the game, literally—he took five or six paces, admiring his handiwork before jogging around the bases. Giants 6, Astros 5.

Despite his team's difficulties, that trip to the Bay Area was special for Ken, the perfect occasion for a welcome home party featuring a mix of Ken's San Jose friends and pro baseball buddies. Clark was there, throwing his empty beer cans into the pool, introducing himself to the ladies. Some Astros players had a playful dare, a reward for anyone who would push Clark into the pool, but Clark left before anyone followed through on it.

* * *

Ken's reputation quickly followed him to the majors. He played hard, and he partied just as hard. Twenty-four with money in your wallet is a fun time to explore the bottom of a bottle or glass, caught between grown-up responsibilities and youthful indiscretions. The veteran players with a few more rotations around the sun knew when to call it a night—pitcher Nolan Ryan would cut himself off after two beers—but Ken didn't always stop after two, or three, or four, and for a while, it was all a lot of fun.

The drinking wasn't always about getting drunk. A lot of players look back fondly on time spent sipping a beer, sitting on their stools in the clubhouse after a game, talking inside baseball with their teammates. Hitting off different pitchers, situations, the teammates you've had, playing in different cities.

The teammates had a playful streak, too. The ringleader was often relief pitching prankster Larry Andersen, who was adept at pulling off a "hotfoot," using matches and ingenuity to catch unsuspecting teammates off guard and stamping mad. Someone hung a *Playboy* centerfold in the locker of Glenn Davis, the team's devoutly religious first baseman, "and you talk about a guy blowing a gasket," remembers batboy Rocky Mitchell. A dead snake was left in pitcher Joaquín Andújar's locker in 1988—he was deathly afraid of them—and the next day, someone added a fake snake. Mitchell said, "He was gonna fight."

Beyond booze and pranks, many of the Astros players also bonded over religion. The team had a strong constituency of Christian players, and Ken wanted to make them proud, so he began attending baseball chapel, a team-based prayer service, which provided an outlet for his spiritual side. He wasn't fully invested in religion. Not yet.

"We had a prankster in Larry Andersen, and then we had the serious side," said second baseman Billy Doran. "We had a blend, everybody blended together. It was really unique."

Astros players took in Ken and liked him pretty much immediately. They adored his effort and his commitment to the team. They loved having him on their side.

"We nicknamed him Vinnie Barbarino (John Travolta's character in the 1970s TV show *Welcome Back, Kotter*), because of how Cammy would answer stuff. *'What? Huh?'*" said outfielder Kevin Bass.

For Doran, "Kenny was one of those guys that if you didn't like Kenny, there was something wrong with you."

"You knew when he played a game, at the end of nine innings, you got everything you could get out of him," said pitcher Charley Kerfeld. "And I think that's probably the best compliment you can give another player."

Ken learned lessons from his new teammates that he would apply in the years ahead. Kerfeld, one of the few other unmarried guys on the team, invited Ken to stay at his town house. "Just pay your phone bill, and that's all you need to do. I'll take care of the rest," Kerfeld told him. Being a good teammate meant opening your home to your fellow players, and Ken would later operate a pro-verbial baseball B&B over the years, giving stars and scrubs, competitors and colleagues, a place to stay, just as Kerfeld had done for him.

* * *

As Ken's rookie summer wore on, his effectiveness as a switch-hitter came into question. From the right side, Ken batted a healthy .310. From the left side, an anemic .184.

Houston considered platooning Ken and having him sit against righties, but hitting coach Denis Menke thought it would help Ken to switch-hit and play every day. "I know for a while Hal thought about platooning him, and I said, 'Don't do that. I just think that this kid's got a chance to turn it all around and be the type of player we think he is,'" Menke said.

Houston had a baseball icon on its coaching staff in the mid-1980s, someone who was quick to dispense nuggets of wisdom to the players: former

Yankees catcher and manager Yogi Berra. Berra was recruited by owner John McMullen, and Lanier knew him since he was a boy—in some ways, Berra took pressure off Lanier, especially where the media was concerned, because everyone wanted to talk to Yogi.

"No brain, no headache," Berra would tell Ken.

Another Yogi-ism that embodied Ken's approach: "You can't think and hit at the same time." Ken did his best hitting when his mind was blank, playing in the moment, not thinking too hard about things.

The fact that he was switch-hitting in the majors was a testament to his work ethic and physical ability—he'd only picked up switch-hitting in games five years earlier, after his freshman year of college, when he'd already turned nineteen. Most switch-hitters begin it when they're much younger. Ken's right-side swing was more natural, more fluid, the swing he'd been practicing all his life. From the left, Ken was more powerful but more unsteady. After his debut game, over his final one hundred at bats of the season hitting lefty, Ken had one extra-base hit, a double against Chicago's Les Lancaster on August 22.

As Ken stumbled, the Astros followed suit, losing seven straight and going 9–18 in September, deflating down the stretch like an untied balloon.

Hal Lanier's criticisms became louder as the team stumbled—he would yell at underperforming players and throw tantrums and flip over Gatorade jugs, and sometimes he'd take things away like music in the clubhouse, petty punishments that did little to motivate the players. He also warred with GM Dick Wagner, furious that the Astros didn't make any moves at the trade deadline. (Wagner fired back by criticizing Lanier's in-game decisions, naturally.)

As Astros manager, Lanier was like a bottle of turpentine—extremely useful but mildly toxic with increased exposure, apt to cause headaches and dizziness. Young players had an especially tough time dealing with his caustic nature.

"I think the pressure of trying to repeat that '86 magic might've worn a little heavily on him," Bill Wood said of Lanier.

Ken wasn't motivated by the yelling. It kept him from playing loose. "Kenny wasn't the kid you had to yell at. Kenny took it pretty hard when you yelled at him," said longtime Astros coach Matt Galante. "You got Kenny doing the things you want him to do with honey, not by yelling and screaming at him. I think the guys that were there, yellers and screamers, kind of turned him off a little bit."

Ken, reflecting on his career in a 1997 interview with TV journalist Jane Mitchell, admitted that Lanier's abrasive style was overwhelming for him. "My first year in the big leagues, I was a scared little boy, seemed like, manager throwing things, and I couldn't deal with that," he said. "Instead of saying, 'Y'know what, I'm gonna do the best I can, no matter what.' I wish I would have had my attitude now back then. I think I would've been a better player."

Despite the yelling and screaming, Ken finished his rookie season with a .246 batting average, three home runs, and stellar play at third base. He had made it. He was a major leaguer. That off-season, he took another step forward in his life, marrying his high school sweetheart Nancy. But even with domestic life, he still wasn't ready to slow down.

CHAPTER 8

DOWN

Dammit . . . dammit . . .

Ken raced his Chevy down the highway, trying to set a new Florida land speed record.

Maybe he could slip through the door and get dressed, and no one would notice that he'd been missing this time. . . . The last time Ken was late, on February 29, Astros manager Hal Lanier had to sit him down and explain that the third base job was his to lose, and how everyone needed to be ready on team picture day, whether your name was Ken Caminiti or Nolan Ryan. Ken came up with an excuse about leaving a wake-up call at the hotel front desk—who knows if that was true—and Hal suggested that from now on, maybe Ken should invest in an alarm clock or get a friend to knock on his door.

You show up late one time, and people can brush it aside. But on Sunday, March 20, the first day of spring, a day of new beginnings, Ken was late again. And then a Florida Highway Patrol trooper pulled up behind Ken's Chevy, and the lights reflected off his rearview mirror.

Dammit . . .

Ken pulled over and went through the usual steps. License, registration, emotional outpouring to Johnny Law. He was clocked going 70 in a 45 . . . probably a generous odometer reading, given his driving tendencies, but that's what the ticket shows, and it came with a $102 fine.

Strike two. And possibly out.

Be. On. Time. It was a simple mandate. Ken had been getting away with things dating back to his San Jose days because he was really talented or really likable, but he finally reached a point where those things weren't going to protect him anymore.

After Ken showed up late for the second time that spring, Lanier called him into his office. Ken slapped the ticket onto his manager's desk, *see, I tried to be here on time*, but Lanier wanted accountability, not excuses. He yelled and fined Ken $500 and sent him home for the day. Now Ken was officially in Lanier's doghouse. And that was not a fun place to be.

His teammates were disappointed, too, especially veteran players like second baseman Billy Doran, who'd taken Caminiti under his wing. It didn't make sense. Here was someone at the precipice of a boyhood dream, of making the team and establishing himself as a big leaguer, and Ken seemed inclined to flush it all away.

"You are a young kid trying to get there. You might oversleep once. You are not going to do it again. There is no way you are going to do it again," said Chuck Jackson, who was competing with Ken for a spot on the roster. "I can remember the second time it happened, and Bill Doran was just pissed. He was just like, 'You've got to be kidding me.' It was a warning signal that I don't think everybody saw early."

Denis Menke, Houston's hitting coach in 1987 and third base coach in 1988, took the young player out to eat and talked to him about baseball and responsibility. "Kenny, you want to play in the big leagues or don't you?" Menke asked him. "You have to pay a price to play in the big leagues."

* * *

The Astros were looking to Ken to take a big step forward in 1988. He participated in the Astros caravan tour stops during the off-season with Lanier, his teammate Gerald Young, new GM Bill Wood (who replaced the volatile, unpopular Dick Wagner during that off-season), and other Astros personnel. He was seen as a face of the franchise. Everyone had big expectations for Ken. But there were those *expectations* again, the same expectations that nearly drove him to quit baseball during his college days. The expectations ate at him.

For Ken, his play during spring training was inconsistent. Too many throwing errors, not enough hits. Teams are a lot more likely to look the other way when you're playing well, but start to struggle on the field, and all those quirks and imperfections suddenly matter a lot more. It was a lesson his college teammate Mark Triplett had to learn the hard way.

Ken was often a slow starter. He'd warn his managers about it in the future, urging them to be patient as he got his timing down at the plate. But this was also his first major league spring training (he was recovering from knee surgery in 1987), and he wasn't giving Lanier a confident feeling after the manager had penciled in Ken as his starting third baseman. Of course, pencils come with erasers for this very reason. On some level, Ken's struggles that spring training felt like a self-fulfilling prophecy. Ken was so worried about screwing up that he screwed up more. He should have followed Yogi's advice: "No brain, no headache." But instead, he drank and did whatever else he could in search of equilibrium, and that only threw him off further.

After winding up in Lanier's doghouse, Ken dedicated himself over the final week of spring training, trying to secure his spot. On March 29, in a game against the Phillies, he showed the Astros a sign of things to come, hitting home runs from the left and right sides of the plate in the same game. Ken ended up batting .283, but he had eight errors, a team high, that spring. After a few days of the team kicking around its options, it was decided to send Ken to Triple-A Tucson. Ken was back in the minors.

Ken's shoo-in job as the Houston Astros' third baseman ended up going to a platoon of Chuck Jackson, Ken's longtime rival for third base opportunities, and veteran Denny Walling. In the days that followed his demotion, Ken blamed the team for his struggles and tried to deflect.

"I think if they wanted me to play [at third base], they would have let me have more at bats and worked with me more," he told Houston radio station KIKK following his demotion. In a separate interview days later with the *Arizona Daily Star*, he claimed, "More people than me were late, but they looked the other way." Either way, he had to learn that being a major league player came with responsibilities and expectations. Being late wasn't acceptable.

So instead of starting the season with Houston, Ken was a thousand miles west, bonding with the most influential teammate he'd ever have.

* * *

Whenever Craig Biggio took his position behind home plate, he resembled a kid brother trying on his older brother's equipment. It all just looked so *big* on him. The Smithtown, New York, native was generously listed at five feet, eleven inches tall and 180 pounds, and his arm was the opposite of Caminiti's, and thus not catcher-like, meaning runners tried to steal on any occasion.

Biggio's value came through his heart, and his smarts, and his hitting—a scrappy player whose helmet was caked in so much pine tar, the gunk players use to help them keep a good grip on bats, it resembled a Van Gogh canvas. The 1987 first-round draft pick was being fast-tracked through the minor leagues after hitting .375 at Single-A Asheville. Biggio and Caminiti first connected at instructional league after the 1987 season—they roomed together with Karl Allaire, Ken's teammate in Osceola and Columbus—and here they were teaming again at Triple-A Tucson of the Pacific Coast League. They'd wind up playing nine seasons together and becoming the closest of friends.

They each recognized in the other a shared on-field intensity, a desire to win. The Astros recognized the amount of talent the two players represented and looked to older Tucson Toros players like Nelson Rood to serve as mentors. "It was kind of like the *Bull Durham* thing. I had to room with Craig on the road, sometimes Ken, just because they wanted me to kind of be the designated driver slash keep an eye on how many they have at night, you know?" Rood said of his time teaming with the future superstars.

While Ken wasn't thrilled to be playing in the minors again, the demotion gave him the chance to matriculate more naturally and surround himself with players he was familiar with, many of whom, like Allaire, were drafted at the same time he was. Or Anthony Kelley, the pitcher who kept on winning but, for some reason, never got the call. Or John Fishel, Ken's friend from Columbus in 1987. These were the guys he had played minor league and instructional league ball with. There was less of a bull's-eye on Ken's back now that he wasn't the new kid in town. He wasn't viewed anymore as the hotshot prospect who was going to save the Astros' season. He was just Ken.

In Triple-A, Ken rededicated himself to hitting. The jump from Double-A to the majors had deprived Ken of opportunities to mature as a hitter. Major league pitchers could exploit the holes in his swing, and the struggles sapped his confidence. In Triple-A, he could get more comfortable facing big league–caliber pitching without dealing with big league attention. Ken's detour to

Tucson meant he was also closer to his new wife, Nancy, who was wrapping up a nursing degree in San Jose.

But Ken's style of play was leaving him battered and broken, as usual. A home plate collision with longtime Chicago White Sox catcher Ron Karkovice bruised the backstop's spleen—"I held on to the ball, though," Karkovice said—while Ken wound up with a splint on his right thumb to heal a partial ligament tear. Despite the injury, and a slow start, Ken tried to stay positive as he waited to be recalled.

"It really doesn't bother me," he said as he toiled away in Triple-A. "I just want to play baseball."

After coming back from his thumb injury, Ken saw his batting average drop nearly 30 points, to .243 . . . and then things finally clicked again. Over the last week of May, he went twelve for thirty-three with two doubles and three triples, and his batting average returned to .269. It kept climbing, to .270 and .280 and .292, and he kept picking up game-winning RBIs, and making great plays in the field, and he was the Ken Caminiti of old, the talented and humble and responsible Ken who was feasting on minor league pitching.

And just like the Ken Caminiti of old, he was waiting again to get the call.

But now he had to watch his buddies like Biggio and Fishel getting promoted. Meanwhile, his rival for Houston's affection, Chuck Jackson, had struggled in his latest test and was back in Tucson playing outfield . . . and still, Ken was stuck in the minors as thirtysomething third sackers Denny Walling and Buddy Bell—acquired in a trade with the Reds—held the position for the parent club. It was difficult for Ken to figure out where he factored into Houston's plans. A few months earlier, he was supposed to be the starting third baseman. Then he showed up late a few times, and now he was an afterthought?

By the end of July, with Walling injured, and first baseman Glenn Davis also on the shelf, the Astros didn't really have any other good options, so Bell moved to first base and Ken was back with Houston. He made his presence felt in his second game back, on July 30, hitting a home run off Dodgers outfielder–first baseman Danny Heep, pitching in mop-up duty, as Houston moved to three and a half games behind the division lead. But Ken didn't fully feel like he belonged. The spot wasn't *his*; he was just keeping it warm for someone else, either Bell or Walling. And now he had to deal with more of manager Hal Lanier's tirades . . . the constant feeling that he had to be perfect to avoid getting a verbal lashing.

Still, with Ken at third base, the Astros were winning. Houston won six of seven to pull within a half game of first place on August 9. The next game, Ken tweaked his shoulder diving for a ball down the line. His shoulder again. . . . Ken kept gritting it out—he was back on the field the following night—but as Walling returned to action and Bell came off the disabled list, Ken got less playing time, and a week later he was sent back to Triple-A.

The yo-yoing bothered Ken. If the Astros wanted him, if they saw him as the future, they had a weird way of showing that. And between his balky shoulder and insecurity, Ken's bat went cold. He played eleven games at Tucson before getting recalled again to Houston, and he batted a robust .139 during that stretch. *What's the point?*

Upon getting recalled, he didn't play much. He went ten games in between at bats at one point. Houston played a three-game set at Candlestick against the Giants, and he was a defensive replacement in one of the games, and it felt a hell of a lot like Team USA all over again, when Cory Snyder was blocking his path and Rod Dedeaux kept him out of the starting lineup in front of his friends back home.

By mid-September, Houston was staging a repeat of 1987, in the midst of its annual freefall. Lanier flipped his lid after a 10–3 loss against the Giants at the Astrodome on September 18 (Ken pinch-hit for Bell in the ninth inning and grounded out), ordering the Astros back on the field after the game for additional batting practice. Lanier at the time stressed the need for his players to "have pride."

Years later, Lanier said the extra BP was actually one of his coaches' ideas, and that he was simply going along with it. Either way, he embraced the batting practice, and it forced Lanier's remaining supporters to tune him out. With Astros players still in uniform, the Giants were walking toward the team bus, which required them to walk back past left field in order to exit.

"The Giants were watching us take BP as they're leaving and just cracking up," said outfielder Kevin Bass. "I don't think any of us as a team, and as members of the Astros, took this seriously. We thought it was a joke. We knew then—stick a fork in Lanier. We knew he was done. He was toast. He was just off his rocker. His style of managing at that point in time took its course with us as a team."

GM Bill Wood felt the same way. "Hal was fiery. And I thought that sometimes that fiery approach will wear out. It has a certain shelf life, so to speak. And I got the impression during that season that the ball club had sort of tuned him out. There are only so many tables that can be overturned and yelling speeches. . . . I just felt like a change was in order," Wood said.

Lanier defended the way he managed the Astros, citing his record of twenty-two games over .500 with the team. "I think I expected a lot out of my players, and sometimes I handled it good, sometimes I probably handled it bad. No one likes losing. And again, I think I got along good with most of my players. Not every ballplayer's gonna like the manager. . . . They respect you, but they may not like you, but that doesn't mean that you're intimidating to them or you're going to make them feel scared to play the brand of ball we thought that they should be playing. I thought I got along good with all the ballplayers—99 percent of them, that's for sure."

Lanier's yelling lost its impact, and after the 1988 season, Lanier lost his job. The Astros were going in another direction. In lots of ways. That off-season, Houston made a lowball offer to pitcher Nolan Ryan, the team's local legend, only to see him leave for the cross-state Rangers and become an institution, the Ryan Express. Owner John McMullen didn't want to open the checkbooks. He wanted to make the team younger and cheaper. And maybe, if the price was right, he would sell.

For Ken, the 1988 season was a lost one—optimism washed away, in part because of his own immaturity. All he had to do was show up on time, and the job was his. . . .

Dammit.

But Ken wasn't done showing the Astros the kind of player he believed he was, a Gold Glove–caliber third baseman with power from both sides of the plate. If he couldn't prove that point during the regular season, he was going to devote his off-season to sending that message.

Ken was going to Puerto Rico.

CHAPTER 9

WINTER BALL

The sunlight shone down on Ken. He was hitting in the middle of the lineup again, and the pressure was off him, and the fans were passionate.

The winter after the 1988 season was a fun escape for Ken—he spent it taking a vacation of sorts, playing for the Indios de Mayagüez, or Mayaguez Indians, of the Puerto Rican Winter League. The team's name and color scheme—burgundy, red, and gold—were inspired by a popular brewery that had sponsored the team.

The league was a rite of passage for players like Ken who hadn't quite caught on in the big leagues. The talent level by the late 1980s was "a bit above AAA, but obviously not the big leagues," said journalist Thomas Van Hyning, who's spent decades covering the league. "It was a confidence builder. It gave a person a chance to maybe put another sixty games on their résumé."

Mayaguez, one of the oldest teams in the Puerto Rican Winter League, was owned by insurance industry executive Luis Gómez, someone who cared about the players and didn't mind paying them decent salaries. Manager Tom Gamboa—then the Detroit Tigers' minor league field director—became intrigued by Ken after seeing him play in Triple-A and was excited to have Ken on his team, which was stocked full of American "imports."

Mayaguez had so many imports that season, the league later changed its rules to limit the number of American players allocated on each team. There was Ken at third; three solid catchers in Tom Pagnozzi, Kirt Manwaring, and Chris Hoiles; Twins second baseman Al Newman; Phillies slugger Ricky Jordan at first; Pittsburgh's John Cangelosi in the outfield; a bullpen that featured Jeff Brantley, Jeff Fassero, and Roberto Hernández; Puerto Rican legends like pitcher Luis "Mambo" de Leon, who played with Ken in Tucson in 1988; and a fleet-footed outfielder in the Orioles system who would go on to play more major league games beside Ken than any other teammate: Steve Finley.

Finley wasn't the only future major league teammate of Ken's associated with Mayaguez that year. Draft pick Melvin Nieves was still a high school student—too young to play—but he regularly hung out with the team, and one time for an exhibition game, he was sitting at the back of the team bus when Ken sat next to him.

"He just started talking to me. . . . We established a friendship right there on the bus," Nieves said. "I was just like, oh my God, this is our starting third baseman. And he's actually talking to me. And we had a blast."

* * *

Ken loved the food and culture that came with playing on the island. Players had days off on Mondays, and they would regularly go to the beach together.

"It was a beach and fishing village, and I think that's what really made it neat for us," Pagnozzi said. "You go over and get fresh fish and lobster in the village over there. For me, being an Arizona boy, not seeing lots of water, it was neat."

The atmosphere at games was new and different for Ken, more festive like a World Cup soccer match than a baseball game. Music blared from the stands, and the rum flowed, and people would bet on individual pitches. The fans, he told journalist Thomas Van Hyning, were "baseball smart"—they were devoted to the game and appreciated a nice defensive play or sacrifice bunt. And Mayaguez fans had lots to cheer about. The team lost its first game, then went on a furious winning streak, a league-record fifteen straight games—an especially arduous task, Gamboa said, because of the way the six-team league was set up, where a team might play at home two nights in a row, then carpool across the island for away games.

In one game during the streak, against the Ponce Lions, Mayaguez was clinging to a one-run lead in the ninth inning. Ponce had runners on second and third with two outs. The batter hit "a sure double, a rocket down the third base line," Gamboa said. "Ken dove and backhanded it as he skidded across the chalk, then back to his feet. And of course he had a cannon for an arm, and he just threw a laser across the diamond to Ricky Jordan and got the guy.

"If the ball is past him, it's a sure loss."

The following game, Gamboa said, was being broadcast on TV, and Ken showed up at the park "sick as a dog," throwing up in the clubhouse. But Ken wanted to play. Winning streak or no winning streak, the manager said no and sent him home. It wasn't worth it. Mayaguez fell behind early but started to make a comeback. By the seventh inning, Ken, following the game's progress and feeling a little better, returned to the clubhouse and got dressed.

"If you need him, he's going to be ready," a trainer told Gamboa, passing word from Ken. If the guy wanted to play a winter league game so badly . . . *sure, why not.* So with the game tied in the eighth, Ken pinch-hit. "He sees one pitch and drives it four hundred feet to the track, a sacrifice fly to put us in the lead, then he goes in defensively and starts a 5-4-3 double play to end the game," Gamboa said. Ken's heroics that day provided a glimpse into the play-through-anything style that would fuel his most memorable performance years later.

* * *

Gamboa forged a deep connection with the third baseman. Ken and Nancy lived outside Mayaguez in nearby Cabo Rojo, in the same condo complex on the beach as Gamboa. The manager, who was single, didn't want to impose on the young married couple, but they insisted—Nancy would cook dinner, and they'd all eat together, and since they didn't have cable, they'd rent movies from Blockbuster and watch them at night to wind down after games. Ken's favorite was the Steven Seagal action flick *Above the Law*, in which Seagal plays Nico Toscani, an ex-CIA agent who takes justice into his own hands.

"We rented it like three times in the first week," Gamboa said.

Gamboa thought Ken had the perfect makeup for baseball. He'd carry himself the same way whether he went 4-for-4 or 0-for-4. "He was like a robot," Gamboa said. "His demeanor was the same all the time." But to Gamboa, Ken's balanced demeanor could be seen as both a positive and negative thing.

"It made me wonder if, internally, he wasn't looking for something that could make him feel the way other people feel," Gamboa said. "There was never any sign of internal happiness, and in a way I felt bad for him in that context."

And then there was Ken's drinking. . . .

"It was almost like he was always looking for a higher high," Gamboa said. "The Puerto Rican beer, Medalla, was really good. It came in ten-ounce cans. Over the course of dinner and a couple of movies, he would drink a dozen of them like I might have a couple glasses of lemonade."

Gamboa tried to warn his third baseman to take it easy.

"There's hardly any alcohol in it," Ken said.

* * *

Mayaguez finished second in the regular season with a 33–26 record. San Juan, led by Atlanta Braves player Lonnie Smith, the league's MVP, went 35–25. Ken, batting in the middle of the lineup, wound up fifth in the Puerto Rican Winter League in RBIs (27) and fifth in runs scored (31) and slugged seven homers.

The top four teams (San Juan, Mayaguez, Caguas, and Arecibo) faced off in a round robin, and Mayaguez and San Juan had the best records so they met in a best-of-seven series to decide which team would advance to the Caribbean Series.

Ken's team jumped to a 3–1 lead in the series, but in the fifth game, in front of a sellout crowd in Mayaguez, San Juan took a late lead. The outcome looked bleak for Mayaguez. The team was down to its final out.

Keith Hughes—who'd play parts of five seasons in the majors—came up with the bases loaded and hit a grand slam to send Mayaguez to the Caribbean Series, and the fans erupted in celebration.

The Caribbean Series was held in Mazatlán, Mexico, and included the top teams in Venezuela (Zulia), Mexico (Mexicali), and the Dominican Republic (Escogido). Mayaguez was playing solid baseball and was poised to potentially win the series, until a crucial error by Ken—in which he overthrew a ball to first base—allowed Venezuela to stay in the game. Phil Stephenson hit a homer in the thirteenth inning to sink Mayaguez's chances.

But Ken was a big reason the team went as far as it did, and his 7 RBIs tied the Caribbean Series lead. His winter in Puerto Rico was a big success. He got his confidence back, and he was poised to have a big season when he returned stateside.

CHAPTER 10

JOB SECURITY

Despite Ken's successful winter league season in Puerto Rico, the Astros still didn't know what to do with him. Houston spent the 1988 off-season flirting with the possibility of trading for Red Sox hitting machine Wade Boggs—the All-Star third baseman was persona non grata in Beantown after his mistress filed a lawsuit against him and spoke to *Penthouse* magazine about their affair. The Astros suggested a trade package that included Ken and pitcher Bob Knepper, along with outfielder Kevin Bass, but Boston GM Lou Gorman wasn't interested. "I don't like Caminiti," he said. Boggs ended up staying with the Red Sox.

Ken's name was also floated in trade rumors involving Atlanta's Dale Murphy—Braves GM Bobby Cox was interested in obtaining the third baseman after scouting Ken during his time at Double-A Columbus years earlier—but that deal also didn't materialize.

The Astros entered 1989 looking for *any* other option at third base, even if that included moving outfielder Billy Hatcher to the infield, or giving Chuck Jackson another shot. The team's impatience failed to take a number of factors into consideration. One, Ken's time playing winter ball in Puerto Rico gave him the confidence he needed to believe in his abilities, to believe that he belonged. And two, the Astros had a new manager entering 1989: Art Howe.

Howe, who wowed the Pirates at an open tryout to get his first pro contract at age twenty-four, then put together a scrappy career that saw him play third base for the Astros, was a more nurturing manager than his predecessor, Hal Lanier, who made porcupines and thumbtacks look soft. Howe built his players up, and if he had a problem, he talked to guys behind closed doors. And yeah, he'd get on your ass if he needed to, but he did it without having to bark or take the music out of the clubhouse or throw Gatorade coolers all over the carpeting to prove his point.

Howe pulled aside his unproven third baseman at the start of their first spring training together and told him, "You're my guy," and he meant it. That allowed Ken to take his mind off all of the noise and rumors and speculation. He didn't need to worry about being perfect. Someone wanted him whether he went 0-for-4 or made an error on defense. In return for that trust, Ken was going to run through a brick wall for Art Howe if that's what his skipper wanted.

"You could see he was still trying to figure it all out, but the one thing you never questioned was his effort, because effort was there every single day. He wanted to do so much and to help the team win. That's when he probably put added pressure—or maybe too much pressure—on himself at times. He had to be the guy to help win the game, whatever it took," Howe said. "But that went a long way with his teammates, because they knew how much it meant to him to win and how much he was giving forth to try to get that win."

* * *

Ken grew more secure, in part, due to measures the Astros took in his first full seasons with the team. Houston was one of the first teams to employ a sports psychologist, Fran Pirozzolo, then the chief of the Neuropsychology Service at the Baylor College of Medicine. Pirozzolo was a standout prep and college athlete himself, so he brought an inner knowledge of sports to his role with the club, helping the players unlock their full potential. He started working with the Astros in 1988, and by 1990 he was in uniform, out on the field with the players during practices and warm-ups.

Rather than push Pirozzolo away, Ken embraced him. "Great, he can help us," Ken said. Pirozzolo ended up with his locker next to Ken's. The sports psychologist helped Ken to understand that his insecurities were more common than he realized—other players just had different ways of showing their insecurities and working through them.

Ken's insecurities revealed themselves through his use of amphetamines, the "greenies" that gave guys a jolt during the long season. He started using them after getting called up in 1987. Older players had warned Ken not to overdo it, to take them only when he was dragging, like before a day game that followed a night game. But Ken felt sharp when he took them—he felt like the pill was making him play better—so he started taking them more often, like if he had a bad batting practice, and especially if he'd been drinking the night before. He feared playing "naked," without any substances in his system, as if he was disrobed at third base, stripped down to his jock strap and stirrup socks.

"He was one of those guys who believed that the drugs were the key," Pirozzolo said. "I came into the game when 90 percent of players used stimulants, and even the most straitlaced players . . . would be bouncing off the dugout walls," Pirozzolo said.

Pirozzolo spent a lot of time working with Ken on his throwing, his greatest athletic gift and the quality that set him apart, but a skill he was still learning to harness. He was liable to airmail his throws, like the key error he made in the Caribbean Series, when Gamboa recalled that Ken *almost had too much time to think.* When Ken started thinking about things too much . . . that's when he got into trouble.

Pirozzolo's advice to Ken: Throw it as hard as you can.

"That's how I got him to fix his throwing problems," Pirozzolo said. "It straightened everything out."

During spring training in 1989, the Astros also invited media figure Andrea Kirby to consult a group of players, including Ken, on dealing with reporters. "He looked like he was so thrilled to be there," Kirby said. "Ken had this real childlike persona about him. . . . He was one of my favorites because he was just so engaged." Kirby had the players complete a "personal scouting report," where they would write down seven positive things about themselves, and some would struggle to come up with seven. Then they'd each go up to the front of the room, and their teammates would help fill out the scouting report until it featured twenty-five or thirty items. For a player like Ken, who sometimes struggled to find positive traits in himself, it was powerful to hear his teammates—his peers—saying such nice things about him, and meaning it.

* * *

Playing third base is sort of like being a hockey goalie without the pads, or crossing the street against traffic. It's like wrestling a steer at the rodeo—you have to time your dive perfectly and corral the bastard around the horns. You wind up flat in the dirt, but instead of a 600-pound bovine, you're trying to subdue a white pill, a 115 mph blur, and when you get it under control you have to collect yourself and throw the ball 130 or so feet across the diamond to nab the batter in the 4.3 seconds it takes to run from the batter's box to first base.

The "hot corner," as it's nicknamed, relies more heavily on instincts than other defensive positions because the player is usually positioned closer to home plate, and since there are more right-handed than left-handed hitters, batters are more likely to hit the ball to the left side of the diamond.

Playing third base requires a specific set of skills. And few had those skills or played the position better than Ken Caminiti. Watching Ken play third base was like listening to Hendrix wail on a guitar. It was a revelation. He was a master craftsman, an artist fully submerged in his craft. He did things you didn't expect. Knock a ball down that other players would miss, gun the ball to first harder than anyone, give a glare that could melt titanium. You watched him and knew you were witnessing something special.

Third base was a reflection of Ken's influences and experiences. He played the position like he had played football, bruising and relentless. He relied on the stuntman's precision from all the jumps off his family's roof into the back-yard pool and high dives off a rock at a nearby reservoir in his youth. And then there were the endless ground balls he took, the effort he poured into playing the position. Ken had physical talent, but without putting in the hard work, expertise would have eluded him.

And expertise was what he exhibited in 1989, his first full season with the Astros. Ken played 160 games at third base that year, the most by an Astros third baseman during the Astrodome era. Diving in the Astrodome was akin to sliding on blacktop—which meant a lot of wear and tear on his "forty-six-year-old, twenty-six-year-old body," as he described it at the time.

Ken took special pride in snaring balls hit down the line, the kind of effort that would get Astros broadcaster Milo Hamilton to gleefully say his catchphrase, "Holy Toledo, what a play!" Playing third base required Ken's constant attention. He'd watch the pitcher out of the corner of his eye as he focused on the hitter's back foot—the back foot would tell him if the player was squaring up for a bunt. As the ball was released, Ken was looking directly in front of the plate, watching for the bat head, analyzing the angle at which the bat would contact the ball, and getting into position, breaking toward the line in anticipation of contact.

He started to build his highlight reel that year. In a May 9 game against Montreal, Expos outfielder Dave Martínez—a lefty—smashed an unexpected liner at Ken, who knocked down the ball, grabbed it off the carpet, and bounced the throw in just the right place for first baseman Glenn Davis to pick it for the out.

In an August 17 game against the Pirates, with the Astros up 4–2, Caminiti turned in the best play of his young career. R. J. Reynolds hit a ball down the line, and Ken was in position, diving to make the play, when at the last second, the ball took an awkward bounce. Ken, on pure instinct, "just put up my left hand and there it was," he said later. On one knee, he launched a laser across the diamond. Astros pitcher Jim Deshaies went the distance that day, scattering seven hits in a 5–3 win. But instead of taking the game ball for himself, he gave it to Caminiti due to his standout defense and signed it: "To Ken Caminiti, who made Brooks Robinson look mediocre."

No one has played third base with the finesse and precision of Brooks Robinson, the Orioles legend nicknamed "the Human Vacuum Cleaner." Where Brooks was smooth and graceful, Ken made it all look hard.

He was constantly hurting—diving on creaky knees and loose shoulders.

Playing third base like Ken Caminiti hurt. It needed to hurt for him to play the right way.

* * *

It's impossible to truly quantify Ken's talent at third base. Box scores show errors but not the would-be doubles turned into outs. Game stories touch on some of his best plays but reflect reporters' blind spots and tight news holes.

Advanced defensive statistics, while imperfect, hint at his greatness at the hot corner in 1989. Baseball-Reference credits him with 2.9 defensive wins above replacement (dWAR) that year, meaning his play in the field was worth roughly three additional wins over an average third baseman's. From 1989 to 1998, the bulk of Ken's playing career, no other National League third baseman got within 0.5 dWAR of that total for a single season. When factoring in defensive statistics, Ken was Houston's most valuable player in 1989, even though he hit twenty-four fewer home runs than slugger Glenn Davis.

That season, Ken's Total Zone Total Fielding Runs Above Average, or Rtot, was a league-leading 23—Terry Pendleton was second with 19, and Matt Williams was third with 12. By advanced metrics, Ken in 1989 turned in the best defensive season by a third baseman over the course of ten years of National League play.

But metrics and stats, many of which weren't available in the 1980s, don't capture the emotional side of seeing Ken play third—the feeling that you were bearing witness to something you'd never seen before.

Watching Ken at third base made you feel alive.

That's what happened for a boy in the Dominican Republic. The Astros were appearing on ESPN in 1991, one of the team's rare appearances on a major broadcast, and the boy was transfixed by Ken Caminiti's play—his dives, his arm, his makeup, his fearlessness, his presence. The boy adored tennis and basketball growing up, but when he saw Ken at the hot corner, he knew he had found his calling, his passion. Adrián Beltré wanted to play third base like Ken Caminiti.

"I saw how hard he played. I saw the plays he made. And I got serious about baseball," Beltré said of his idol in 1999 as he embarked on a career during which he would win five Gold Glove awards.

Ken's play at third motivated and inspired his teammates and competitors. It made them dig deeper and ask more of themselves. He was a player's player and a third baseman's third baseman. "For a lot of years there, in the National League anyway, he was the standard," said Williams, who won four Gold Glove awards.

"He was a Gold Glove third baseman before they gave him the Gold Glove," said Astros coach Matt Galante. "I'm not taking anything away from Mike Schmidt, because Mike Schmidt was great, but every year it was Mike Schmidt, Mike Schmidt, Mike Schmidt, every year until he retired. And sometimes those awards, they continue to give them to some guy, year after year—but Kenny was as good as anybody I've ever seen. I've seen him take a high bouncer, jump up in the air, catch the ball bare-handed, and throw the ball to first before he landed on the ground, with as much velocity as anybody could have."

But even though fellow players recognized Ken's talent, he wasn't getting the national attention he deserved. The 1989 Astros' diminished presence didn't help. Houston was shedding popular players like they were dead skin cells, meaning weakened fan recognition and reduced national coverage. And this was before a time of wall-to-wall video availability, before streaming services and mobile phones could broadcast a game anywhere in the world. There was no ESPN *Baseball Tonight* in 1989 (it debuted the following year), with its popular "Web Gems" feature celebrating the game's best defensive plays.

In the absence of widespread video or statistical availability, Gold Glove voting grew to resemble a popularity contest, a reward for players who'd already gotten an All-Star Game selection or MVP votes. Players were often honored for previous accomplishments.

So after Ken's magical 1989 season, the Gold Glove went to Pendleton of the Cardinals, who'd won the award two years earlier and was a more widely known player. Pendleton was deserving of a Gold Glove—he ended up winning three during his career—but in one of those years, defensive metrics and the eye test suggest Ken had a better defensive season.

It would be an ongoing problem in the years to come: Ken's mastery at third didn't translate to Gold Glove awards. Ken wasn't big on awards, but a Gold Glove would be nice. It was voted on by managers and recognized the aspect of his game that he valued most.

"To have the respect of your peers is important," Williams said. "The more offensive numbers you have, the more you're in their mind. So does that have something to do with it? Maybe. Ken had fantastic defensive years, and there are times that you think you have a better year than you had the year you won it."

* * *

A youth movement usually comes with losses—hard, painful losses—and the Astros started the 1989 season matching expectations, playing sub-.500 ball for the first month and a half of the season.

But the Astros started to jell after a fight on May 10. Larry Andersen threw a pitch up and in at Spike Owen, and Spike and his Montreal brethren weren't happy, and they were still bitter at Houston's Danny Darwin for a beanball from two years earlier, so they decided to interrupt the baseball game with a brawl. Ken raced in from third base, holding back a rushing Expos player, helping to keep the peace. Coach Ed Ott was the only Houston player or coach ejected—that's bound to happen when you put Montreal pitcher Andy McGaffigan in a headlock and wrestle him to the ground—and besides some cuts and scrapes and a 10–1 loss, the Astros emerged with a collective spirit.

The Astros rattled off a five-game winning streak after the fight—that team won and lost in bunches—and on May 26, they started getting red-hot. Win. Win. Win. Win. Win. Win. Win. Win.

Now this team was going somewhere. . . . On June 3, Houston hosted the division rival Dodgers. Los Angeles jumped to a 4–1 lead, but the Astros scraped back in the sixth inning after Houston walked three times to load the bases. And up came Ken, singling to center field to score Billy Doran and Glenn Davis. One batter later, after a single by shortstop Rafael Ramírez, the game was tied, and it would stay that way for a long, long time.

Not that there weren't a few chances to score. But no one could scratch across a run. In the bottom of the eleventh, Astros infielder Craig Reynolds was thrown out at home trying to score after center fielder John Shelby delivered a strike. In the bottom of the fifteenth inning—at 12:56 a.m.—Dodgers left fielder Chris Gwynn, Ken's Team USA teammate, settled under a fly ball and threw home in time for LA catcher Mike Scioscia to apply the tag and preserve the tie game. By that point, Dodgers ace Orel Hershiser was on in relief, and he would pitch seven innings of shutout ball. Houston countered with a series of relievers—Juan Agosto, Dave Smith, and Jim Clancy.

But Hershiser couldn't pitch forever, and Los Angeles was running out of players. So on came third baseman Jeff Hamilton to pitch at 2:32 a.m., and pitcher Fernando Valenzuela moved to first base so Eddie Murray could shift to third. Hamilton did his best, throwing into the 90s, and held Houston at bay for his first inning. The Dodgers went 1–2–3 in the twenty-second inning, and it was Houston's turn.

After Bill Doran singled to center and moved to second on a groundout by Davis, Terry Puhl was intentionally walked to increase the chances of a double play. On came Caminiti, hitting against a position player. Ken was hungry for a hit, and he smelled red meat. But he was overanxious and off-balance, mentally fatigued and swinging through Hamilton's pitches. Hamilton threw a pitch high, and Caminiti wrapped around himself trying to hit it, whiffed by *Jeff Fucking Hamilton*. You strike out to the third baseman at nearly 3:00 a.m., and the frustration is bound to boil over. He turned back toward the dugout, lifted his bat above his head, and brought it down over his knee, snapping the wood in half and dumping the fragments like discarded peanut shells. One hitter later, Ramírez lined a ball that skimmed off Valenzuela's glove, leaving just enough time for Doran to make it home in time and ending the game—FINALLY!—after seven hours and fourteen minutes, at 2:50 a.m.

The following game against the Dodgers, which started at 1:35 p.m. on June 4, less than eleven hours after the previous game ended, was the Dodgers' to lose. They jumped ahead by six runs early, but in the fifth inning, with the bases drunk, Astros outfielder Louie Meadows smashed the biggest hit of his career.

Grand slam. A one-run game.

The score stayed 6–5 until the bottom of the ninth inning, with two outs and Craig Biggio at the plate. The Astros' nine-game winning streak was bound to end, and that was OK; the players were *tired*. But Biggio had other plans, hitting a home run to left and tying the game (again). Extras. . . . This one wrapped up in *only* thirteen innings, when pitcher Mike Scott hit a ball just far enough away in center field for Ramírez to score.

The winning streak ended at ten the following night, but Ken started the Astros' next streak (six wins) in a June 6 game against the Padres. Bases loaded, bottom of the ninth, two outs, Ken on third, Alex Trevino at the plate. Trevino was down to his final strike. Pitcher Mark Davis threw the ball into the dirt, and Trevino struck out, waving at the ball feebly as though he was sweeping a broom over home plate. Catcher Benito Santiago blocked the ball so it sat there like a dead quail, but he couldn't find it. He scanned behind him—*where is it?* He looked down and it was at his feet, so he scooped up the ball—and there was Caminiti, charging hard down the line, getting ready to do his best Dick Butkus impression. Ken bruised through Santiago, and the ball popped loose, and Ken stepped on home plate to tie the game. *Pow.* If Santiago had simply stepped on the plate himself, the game would have been over. Instead, the Astros won in the following inning.

The next night, after a 3–2 win over San Diego, the Astros moved into a first-place tie, and Ken and his buddy Biggio felt like they were on top of the world, two young stars at the start of it all, when everything was new and fresh and fun. After Biggio officially became the team's starting catcher in mid-May, the Astros rattled off a 19–6 record with three shutouts, and Biggio was knocking the tar out of the ball, hitting .319 with ten extra-base hits during that stretch.

Ken and Craig were making this look easy. They were going to take this team to the top. Turn the Astros into something special, make them known for winning instead of orange uniforms and sub-.500 finishes. Bring a championship or two to H-town. This was only the beginning, and everyone loved them, and they got all the free drinks they wanted, and they saw only green lights ahead of them, and everything was speeding up, a blur of energy and excitement—until Biggio's 1988 Saab 900 swerved and nearly struck a curb, and a cop car pulled up behind them and flashed the lights and siren.

They'd been drinking at the Ocean Club and Cooter's that night, and Biggio recalled having four drinks. Ken, sitting shotgun, didn't think his friend was too drunk to drive. . . . Hell, he'd driven when drunker a bunch of times. But when the cop came up to the window, he said Biggio introduced himself with the same line he'd probably used to get those free drinks earlier in the night: "I'm Craig Biggio and I play for the Astros"—but those words didn't work as well this time. The cop asked for Biggio's license (he evidently didn't have a baseball card handy, Name: Craig Alan Biggio, Born: December 14, 1965, Ht: 5'11" Wgt: 180 . . .) and claimed Biggio handed him two $100 bills along with his license, a claim Biggio denied months later at trial.

Biggio's blood alcohol level was 0.13, above the legal limit of 0.1. The Astros put out a statement on Biggio's behalf that was written by PR director Rob Matwick, in which Biggio apologized to the fans and the city of Houston.

"I have a responsibility to the community, and I did not live up to that last night," the statement read. "I've learned an important lesson and want to put it behind me as quickly as possible," the statement continued. "I'm just sorry if I hurt anybody, especially the youngsters out there. I apologize for my actions. I was wrong."

If only Ken would have learned from that experience. . . .

About two months later, the Astros were playing in San Francisco when Ken was popped for a DUI while driving in Los Gatos, a few miles south of Leigh High School and his childhood home.

It was 1:40 a.m., and the officer saw him make a turn without signaling. Ken was also speeding—of course he was speeding—and the officer noticed booze on his breath. Ken failed a series of field sobriety tests, and the officer asked him to take a chemical test, but on the advice of his attorney, Ken declined.

"I know I really screwed up on the tests out there," he told the officer, according to a police report. "It's my fault. I should have known better than to get myself in these messes."

He'd driven drunk on these roads numerous times before. It was the 1980s. A lot of people were driving drunk back then, which is what led to the creation of Mothers Against Drunk Driving. The organization was founded after the hit-and-run death of a Sacramento-area thirteen-year-old, Cari Lightner. During Ken's college years, the cops could be more forgiving, like the time he and his buddies were forced to run off their buzz and pour out their beers. But now Ken was a pro baseball player, and his driving drunk was a news story, and not just a blurb in the fine print under the *San Jose Mercury News*'s arrests section, but an actual story with a bold headline that could embarrass him and his family.

Beyond dealing with the shame, and a court hearing that was held days after Houston wrapped up its surprising season in third place at 86–76, Ken had to answer to the Astros' leadership and meet with his manager, Art Howe, and assistant GM Bob Watson. Ken's irresponsible behavior was already on the team's radar the previous season when he failed to show up on time for spring training workouts and got demoted. He wasn't going to get shipped to Tucson for driving drunk. He was on stable ground in that way. But team employees recognized a problem, a pattern, and wanted to address it. A player could go either way on these things, to learn the lessons and make better choices, or continue heading down a difficult road.

"We just tried to tell him that he had to get himself straightened out," Howe said. "He couldn't be doing this." The conversation centered on drinking. Drinking was certainly a problem for him, but it wasn't his only problem.

CHAPTER 11

FEEL THE HEAT

As the Astros featured fewer and fewer players who fans could identify, the team in 1990 turned to their fresh faces—Ken, Craig Biggio, and Gerald Young—to draw interest.

The trio participated in one of the most sexually suggestive photo sessions in the history of the game, posing for two images in the locker room: one in their game uniforms, and one with them partially stripped down and glistening with a post-workout sheen.

Young is on the left, shirtless, the light bouncing off his ebony skin, with a bat over his shoulders. Ken is in the center, wearing a loose V-neck with his arms crossed and his fists under his biceps, which photographer Michael Hart said was Ken's idea. "I gotta pump it up," Caminiti said during the photo shoot before making a joke to Gerald about his thin, lithe arms. "Don't touch my guns, dude," Young told him. Biggio, to the right, is grasping a long, slender bat in his hands. Balls rest at the players' feet, and smoke billows in the background, and beads of sweat drip off them, and you wish for a second you were one of those droplets in this locker room fantasy. The title of the poster appears at the bottom: "Feel the Heat."

"Nobody in Houston had ever done that," Hart said. "It was a little revolutionary at the time. It was, I guess, somewhat risqué in this oil field down here."

Ken had always been popular with ladies, and his friends weren't scared to admit how attractive he was. But now he was becoming a sex symbol, a poster on women's walls, and that wasn't a natural thing for him or Nancy. How would you feel knowing women were fantasizing about your husband? That women didn't care that you were in the picture, because the third baseman was a catch? Some women—they're known as groupies or Baseball Annies—collected conquests with baseball players like stamps on a passport, *this All-Star* and *that rookie* and occasionally a journeyman catcher who spent the greatest twenty-one days of his life in the show.

Ken appreciated attention from adoring fans, but it also put stress on his young marriage. At one of Tom Koppa's card and autograph shows, Ken and Koppa were walking up the stairs—Ken was wearing faded blue jeans and a plaid shirt—and a fan snuck up behind him and took a picture of his backside.

"They just loved his butt," Koppa said.

The next show, the female fan who took the photo had an 8 × 10 of Ken's backside going up the stairs. Ken signed it across his ass. Koppa was able to get the negative, and with Ken's permission, he got two hundred copies of the Ken Caminiti butt photo printed and sold them at his booth for $5 each.

"It was really popular," Koppa said. "He was a good sport about that."

* * *

While the 1990 Astros might have been easy on the eyes, the baseball they were playing wasn't. After a lockout knocked out most of spring training and delayed the start of the regular season (fueled by owners trying to suppress player salaries and institute a salary cap), the team lost eighty-seven games, but Houston probably could have been worse, batting .242 as a team with league lows in hits, extra-base hits, and runs. But above-average pitching led by Jim Deshaies, Mike Scott, Mark Portugal, Bill Gullickson, and Danny Darwin, along with closer Dave Smith and his twenty-three saves, kept scoring down and the Astros close.

Ken was expected to take a step forward after his breakout 1989 season, especially as veteran players were sent packing, one after another, a means for owner John McMullen to save money.

Kevin Bass and Bob Knepper went to the Giants.

Craig Reynolds retired. Alan Ashby was released. Terry Puhl became a free agent and washed up with the Mets and Royals. Billy Doran was traded to the Reds, the eventual World Series champions. And reliever Larry Andersen was sent to the Red Sox, in a trade that would have a major impact in the years ahead. But for the short term, the personnel changes left a leadership void with the team.

"Cammy needed guidance. He needed to be around older players," Bass said. "When they dismantled that team, when they got rid of those older players, he was lost. I'm not saying those other kids were bad influences or whatever, but he had nobody to really look up to and to take orders from. The mentorship from some of the older guys, that was gone."

Ken showed a few glimpses of his talent in 1990, like on July 19 against the Expos, when he snared an eleventh-inning line drive by Larry Walker that was destined to bring home the go-ahead run, then singled home the winning run in the bottom half. But instead of stepping forward and filling the team's leadership void, Ken mostly disappeared that season, with only four home runs and a .242 batting average. Ken battled through injuries that season—that was a recurring problem, given the way he played. His right shoulder bothered him, and a knee injury caused him to struggle rounding the bases—his knee was jelly, so instead of planting and jogging back to first, he would slide, feet first, midway between the bases and pop back up to jog back to the bag, since it was less stressful on his leg. He suffered from "turf toe," too, a joint sprain involving the big toe that would take all off-season to heal and then would recur early in the new season. Of course, he didn't always tell the trainers the truth. . . . Even though Ken was hurting, and playing for a fourth-place team, he wasn't going to ask out of the lineup. He played in 153 games during the 1990 season. But his problems that season went much deeper than shoulder sprains and knee problems and turf toe.

* * *

You could see everything in Ken's eyes. During the good times, they were deep and piercing, Pacific Ocean blue, glistening in the sunshine. In the stormy times, they grew dark and imposing.

Some of Ken's early seasons in the major leagues were perfect beach days. But then he'd disappear for a while and return ornery like a Category 3 hurricane.

"If you were to look Cammy in the eyes some days, there was somebody else there. And you just didn't know who that was," said longtime Astros trainer Rex Jones.

The storm clouds started to gather more frequently during the early 1990s, due to his increased cocaine use. Ken had been exposed to cocaine since his high school and college days. People in his circle used it, and one of his close friends, Mike Druhan, was a dealer. At first, Ken did coke casually (as much as he could do anything casually), a sometime thing that eventually became more frequent. He'd drink, then do coke to stay awake to keep drinking, the blow a means to prolong his buzz.

Cocaine—derived from the leaves of the South American coca plant—comes in numerous forms. The most common is powder, snorted through the nose or rubbed into the gums, or dissolved and injected. Cocaine can also be mixed with heroin for a "speedball"—which can be especially dangerous. Then there's freebasing, a process that makes cocaine smokable, and more potent. The crystal rocks from freebasing can be heated, creating a crackling sound—thus the name *crack*—before being inhaled.

"There's a big difference between snorting a small white line of coke and smoking; whether it's freebase or crack, it's qualitatively a different experience, particularly in terms of its inherent compulsion," said Sheigla Murphy, one of the country's leading drug experts, who's been studying cocaine use, specifically in the Bay Area, for more than thirty years. "If you do a line of cocaine, you have somewhat of a bell curve. The top of it is a little bit longer. When you smoke crack, it looks more like a mountaintop where you go way up, but the down is the part that's really nasty. And that's what you're chasing away, is that down.

"Eventually, cocaine, if you use lots of it over a long period of time, will turn on you so that you don't get the euphoria anymore, you get discord."

Ken began dabbling with freebasing during the 1980s. Max (Greg) Sosebee, a college teammate and friend of Ken's, remembers Ken showing up at his doorstep in 1987. "That was the last time I ever touched cocaine, because we based it and I've never based before," Sosebee said. "And he had a lunch bag full. And I smoked it. It had me—it fucking had me. I couldn't wait for the next trip. I smoked one right on my doorstep as I was going back into my house. It scared the shit out of me, because it had me."

By 1990, crack cocaine became a major vice for Ken, a chance for an immediate high, even if the crash would be so, so hard and make him feel worse than before.

"Smoking crack was what got him. It was that elusive high for him," said longtime friend Dave Moretti.

Drugs helped Ken feel better about himself, this rush of euphoria, the feeling that he was good enough. They gave him confidence in his successes, which made him feel like he was in charge, and in control, that he could keep doing more.

His snorting powder cocaine was intensifying, too. One time during the early 1990s, high school classmate Peter Morin—who struggled with addiction before getting clean, and later helping others in recovery—recalled getting high with Ken and Mike Druhan. The group went to Druhan's house, and he emerged with a plastic bag full of coke, "and Ken expected me to keep up with him. . . . No way," Morin said. "My heart was going 100 miles an hour. Of course, Ken was full throttle. And that's when I realized, boy, this guy's crazy. He's crazier than I am.

"That was the highest I've ever been on cocaine. And we talked about it. I said, 'Dude, you're a nut.' He goes, 'That's me,' and then we didn't talk about it that much. . . . He didn't want to give off a negative thing that he was an addict. You've got to hide that."

As Ken battled a cocaine problem, so did his Astros teammate Gerald Young, once seen as the most promising player on the team. Young stole 65 bases in 1988, and another 34 the following season, fast as raindrops down a ravine—and then his stats fell off a cliff. By 1990, he was back and forth between the Astros and Triple-A Tucson. Young would stay with Houston for parts of two more seasons, but things were never the same as the two friends continued on self-destructive paths.

Likewise with Ken. While the hits of cocaine kept coming, the hits weren't coming as frequently on the field, especially when the Astros were on the road. In 1989, Ken batted .256 at home and .253 on the road. In 1990, while Ken batted .288 at home, his road average dipped to .191—nearly 100 points lower.

Road trips offered Ken an open suitcase of possibilities, new clubs and parties and people every three or four days. He was learning the biorhythms of major league baseball life. Each road trip had a unique feel. Sometimes wives and girlfriends were allowed, while other times, trips were only for the guys.

But Ken didn't always follow those road rules, and they were liable to get him in trouble on the home front. He was seen out with another woman in Atlanta on the last road trip of the 1991 season—a family road trip—and one of the Astros players told his girlfriend about it because they didn't share any secrets, and the girlfriend told Ken's wife, Nancy, and Nancy was understandably pissed. Ken needed to take it out on whoever ratted him out, and the rumor bouncing around was that the tattler was pitcher Rob Mallicoat, his longtime teammate and friend dating back to 1985. It wasn't, but Rob found himself slammed against a wall, with Ken's hands wrapped around his neck, wondering if his buddy was going to choke the life out of him.

"He had me with both of his hands around my throat, held me three inches off the ground, by the neck, against a wall. Looking at me with that stern face of his, saying, 'What the fuck did you tell her?' I go, 'I didn't say a word.' The interrogation continued for a while, until Ken became satisfied that Mallicoat was telling the truth.

"OK, cool," Ken told him before taking his hands off Mallicoat's neck and walking away. "He didn't say, 'Sorry,' didn't say, 'Oh, my bad,' just literally, that's how on and off he was," Mallicoat said.

CHAPTER 12

FRESH FACES

Ping!

The sweat dripped down Ken's face: another day spent baking in the Florida sun.

The other players stood behind him, waiting for their chance, gunning for his position. Their footsteps got louder, and louder, clack, clack, CLACK, and Ken had no one to blame but himself.

Two years ago, he had the third base job locked up—Art Howe went out of his way to convince him of that. No one was convincing him of that now, especially not after his lost 1990 season. He went from one of the best third basemen in the league one year to one of the worst the next. The trade rumors were swirling like starving sharks in a pool of chum. To make matters worse, Astros prospect Andújar Cedeño, a shortstop, played third base in winter ball, and a handful of players with third base experience were in camp.

If Ken didn't perform RIGHT NOW, he'd be sent packing. All those years playing summer ball, college ball, Team USA, the minors, instructional ball, Puerto Rico, the extra BP, the infield practice . . . he'd put in so much time honing his craft. If they only knew everything he'd been through, the pain and sacrifices. If they wanted his job, they were going to have to earn it. They were going to have to outwork and outsweat Ken Caminiti.

Ping!

Ken ran to his right, snared the ball off the coach's fungo bat, gunned it to first, and jogged to the back of the line, and then one of the young guns angling for the third base job—a non-roster invitee acquired in a trade with Boston, Jeff Bagwell—stepped forward.

Bagwell was toothpick thin, but he had pop in his bat. He grew up in Killingworth, Connecticut, adoring the Red Sox and got drafted by his home-town team in 1989. But Boston still had Wade Boggs, the onetime Astros trade target, at third base, meaning Bagwell was blocked. Houston spent years fol-lowing Bagwell. The Red Sox needed relief help during its 1990 playoff run, so it gave up Bagwell for Larry Andersen, only to bounce out of the postseason in the first round. Boston sacrificed Jeff Bagwell's future for twenty-two regular season innings from Andersen and a compensatory draft pick (J. J. Johnson) who never reached the majors.

The Red Sox had a knack for breaking every fan's heart at some point, and it broke Jeff's in 1986, coming within one strike of the world championship, one strike away from excising the ghost of the Babe, but then the ball rolled through Buckner's legs, and when Bagwell found out he was traded away from his boyhood team—to the *Astros? In Texas?*—it felt a hell of a lot like that ball was rolling past Buckner down the first base line again.

Now it was Bagwell's turn to prove himself to his new team. Bagwell was pissed he wasn't called up at the end of the 1990 season. But 1991 was his chance. He felt like he belonged in Houston. And he was going to give this Caminiti guy a run for the job.

Ping!

Bagwell fielded the ball cleanly and made the throw, and then it was the next player's turn, a twenty-three-year-old rookie named Luis Gonzalez. The Cuban American Tampa native had a sweet, punchy swing that was as fluid as a well-oiled front gate. Houston drafted him in the fourth round of the 1988 draft after he was scouted by front office staffer Lew Temple, who later became an actor and appeared on the TV show *The Walking Dead.*

Gonzo played in twelve games for the Astros late in the 1990 season, and in 1991 he was looking to play regularly and establish himself in the bigs. He'd been pegged primarily as a third baseman in the minors, but he also spent time at first base and left field. Was there a spot for him?

Ping!

And then it was back to Ken, who was seen as an Astros cornerstone on some days and trade bait on others. Ken's shoulders and knee were better again, for now, but he also needed to make better, healthier decisions. If he didn't, he could look around camp and guess his outcome, the same fate as Larry Andersen, Bill Doran, Dan Schatzeder, Bill Gullickson, José Tolentino, Juan Agosto, Rich Gedman, Terry Puhl, Franklin Stubbs, Glenn Wilson, Danny Darwin, Dave Smith. . . . All of those players had left through trades or free agency since late in the 1990 season. The 1991 Astros were a sea of unfamiliar faces—new arrivals and rookies, along with a handful of holdovers from the end of the Hal Lanier era: Caminiti, Biggio, and Gerald Young in the field, along with fading pitcher Mike Scott and mound mate Jim Deshaies.

The most recent salary dump was slugging first baseman Glenn Davis, who thought he was worth $5 million a year. Owner John McMullen, looking to sell the Astros, didn't want to pay that much money to the entire *team*, let alone one player (Houston's salaries totaled $11.5 million in 1991, a major league low).

So Davis was shipped to Baltimore, and in return the Astros got three promising young players: pitchers Pete Harnisch and Curt Schilling, and outfielder Steve Finley, who had played winter ball in Puerto Rico with Ken a few years earlier. It was a steep cost for the Orioles—you never know what will come from trading prospects. Sometimes they fade out. And sometimes they become All-Stars and World Series heroes, and you kick yourself for giving them away before they could do it for your team.

The former Orioles farmhands were all in camp. Schilling, a Red Sox draft pick like Bagwell, was now on his third team, a temperamental pitcher who hadn't figured out how to tap his inner potential yet.

The Astros also had a former University of Arizona basketball player, Kenny Lofton, a member of the 1988 Final Four team, at spring training in 1991. Lofton was still learning how to play the outfield, occasionally taking a bad first step or two, but he was speedy like a cheetah and could leap over a wall—his athleticism made up for any deficiencies in his game. He could hit, too. He batted .331 to lead the Florida State League in 1990, along with 62 stolen bases.

The Astros weren't going to be a good team in 1991. Maybe not in 1992, either. But some of these guys would turn into solid players. The key was uncovering which ones were worth holding on to, and then keeping them together.

Crack!

Ken smashed a solo home run and rounded the bases, and through his first four spring training games he was hitting a sizzling .727, eight hits in eleven at bats. He'd finish the spring batting .406, Ted Williams territory. He'd never played with this much urgency. After years of enduring trade rumors and struggling with his confidence and battling addiction, he wasn't giving up his position without a fight. *Life's all about competition*—that was his realization nearly a decade earlier as a college freshman—and here he was, locked in an all-out competition with a challenger he appreciated and respected.

This Bagwell guy was on the quiet side and friendly, not a rah-rah type, someone like Ken who let his effort and output do the talking. They had a lot in common. Ken wanted to challenge Jeff the way Jeff was challenging him. They started working out together. Ken wanted the guy who could help the team the most to get the third base job. Maybe they could both help the team somehow.

"We both want the same thing, and that's for this team to be successful," Ken said. "Despite what people are saying about this team, I'm looking forward to this season and what it holds for us."

Whoosh!

With Glenn Davis out of the mix, first base was open, and Mike Simms had the inside track. Simms made his debut in 1990 and batted .308 in limited duty. The Astros were hopeful that they had their first baseman of the future. The SoCal native was six feet, four inches tall—a wide frame for an arm like Ken's.

With Davis averaging 29 home runs over the previous five seasons, Houston was looking for a first baseman with pop. Simms had that. He bopped 39 home runs at Single-A Asheville in 1987, and another 20 at Double-A Columbus in 1989, and 13 dingers at Triple-A Tucson.

Simms was the favorite to get the first base job. And then, at the worst time, his bat went cold like freezer meat. José Tolentino was also getting a look, but, what if . . .

Caminiti was raking at third base, and he had the strongest arm and steadiest glove of the three, but Bagwell (.326 batting average, two HR) was also having a strong spring. Gonzalez, meanwhile, hit .377 with five home runs and drove home the winning run in three games. Manager Art Howe considered how he could get all of them into the lineup. Bagwell *could* play third at Tucson, but why not see if he could play first in Houston? Before Howe proceeded with his reimagined infield, he wanted to know that Bagwell was at least six feet in height, so he had strength coach Gene Coleman measure him.

"Well, I am six feet tall," Bagwell told Coleman.

"When are you six feet tall?"

"When I stand on the base, I'm six feet tall."

Oh. OK. Coleman went back to Howe and told him, "Hey, he's six feet tall." With the height issue brushed aside, Bagwell—who actually stood closer to five feet, ten inches tall—began working with Bob Robertson, a former major league first baseman coaching in the Astros system, and spent the last few weeks of spring training learning his new position, from cutoff responsibilities to foot positioning on throws to holding on runners. He played first base for the first time in an "A" game on March 28 in Bradenton, against the Pirates, going 3-for-4 (he'd go on to hit .400 with one home run, along with a few errors, as a first baseman). Gonzalez dabbled at first and third before settling in at left field, learning how to follow the ball and put his body behind his throws. *Life's all about competition*, and Ken fended off challenges from two players who would go on to collect a combined forty-five hundred hits and crush more than seven hundred home runs in their major league careers.

* * *

One of the most important Astros players of the early 1990s hit only eleven career home runs. But Casey Candaele could play almost anywhere on the diamond. Second. Short. Third. All three outfield positions, too. And he was really damn funny.

The pint-sized Lompoc, California, native, acquired in a 1988 trade with Montreal for catcher Mark Bailey, was a .250 career major league hitter, meaning he didn't even have the highest career batting average in his family. That honor went to his mother, Helen Callaghan Candaele, who batted .256 in five seasons for the All-American Girls Professional Baseball League during the 1940s. His mother taught him how to play baseball and fostered his love of the game.

As the losses piled up for Houston, Candaele helped keep the mood light. He was known to take batting practice naked on Sundays—he thought it brought him luck. Another time, he gave an interview impersonating Bagwell, telling the unknowing reporter that major league baseball was too easy: "I'm just thinking there's gotta be another league I need to go to, because I'm just tearing this one up." (He let the reporter in on the joke before it ended up being a story in the next day's newspaper.) He was known to ride a tray down the center aisle during team flights, a sport affectionately known as "airplane skiing."

"Every second of the day, you never knew what Casey was going to do. But it was always going to be funny," Art Howe said. "He would do anything and everything to win a ball game, and he was of smaller stature, but he was tall as far as we were concerned with the way he played the game."

"We got delayed in Montreal because the entry people asked Casey if he had anything to declare, and he said he was proud to be an American," Astros head strength and conditioning coach Gene Coleman said.

"You would see him in spring training on the dance floor at one of those nightclubs. We'd go out and drink beer. And he was a surfer dude from California, and he was the funniest guy. But he was also one of the guys that I respected along with Kenny, because Casey got the most out of what he had," said pitcher Rob Mallicoat. "He couldn't find a starting spot, so he just became really good at doing a lot of other things. But he was someone who kept you on your toes."

Casey and Ken had an effortless friendship, a fierce and loyal bond. One time, Astros broadcaster Bill Brown was talking on an internal video feed between innings of an exhibition game, and the feed was being broadcast in the clubhouse. Candaele entered the game at third base. Brown was kidding with his partner. "Casey can't play third," he said. That was the extent of it. But Ken heard the line. And he was fuming. After the game, Houston GM Bill Wood called the broadcaster over and asked about the quip. Brown apologized to Candaele. "When those guys got on that airplane, they were staring daggers through me," Brown said. "It was a big deal because Casey was the type of guy that everybody loved, and they wouldn't let him be insulted in any way. So I learned my lesson."

Casey and Ken's bond was lasting and true, even if it got Ken in trouble with Nancy sometimes. She made Ken sleep on the sofa for three nights when he came home with a tattoo on his calf. Ken and Casey had talked about getting inked, and following a day game against the Cubs in 1991—and after a little liquid courage—they went to a tattoo parlor. Candaele got a "Fighting Irish" logo and his mother's initials tattooed on his back.

"Ken got an ugly panther on his calf," Candaele said. "He actually had that redone after a while. It looked like he had a big bruise on his calf, but he had it redone so it turned out to look good.

"We weren't real popular with our wives when we came home from that trip."

The friends got matching Chinese friendship tattoos in spring training a year or two later, a reflection of their connection. Sometimes on the road they would spend their mornings lying in bed together, watching TV and talking. "We were that close and comfortable enough with our friendship," Candaele said.

As Ken became one of the longest-tenured Astros players, he grew to be enmeshed in the Houston community. Local fans like Andy Comeaux saw Ken as a superhero, for both how he played and how he treated others. Comeaux, who battled cystic fibrosis throughout his life, attended Astros games through the organization 65 Roses—and found himself frozen in fear, nervous to talk as his baseball card heroes had come alive. "Caminiti looked about as scary as you can get to a ten-year-old kid," Comeaux said. "But he was the most personable, put his arm around you, talk to you about everything, and that really stuck with me."

* * *

After fighting off the toughest positional challenge of his career, and one a lot more satisfying than his battle with Cory Snyder on Team USA years earlier, Ken spent the first half of 1991 with an average in the .240s. Spring training Ted Williams was hitting more like Earl Williams, a serviceable super-utility player during the 1970s. Ken was still getting comfortable hitting left-handed: He batted .310 from the right side, but only .213 lefty in 1991.

Ken spent hour after hour working with Rudy Jaramillo, a hitting Svengali who became Houston's hitting coach the previous season. After his own career topped out in Double-A, he became a hitting sponge, absorbing lessons from anywhere he could gather them, including from Ted Williams. He worked on drills with the players to help them with muscle memory. He also reinforced positive imagining—something that could certainly benefit a player like Ken who lacked confidence. All the work and struggle involving Ken's opposite-side swing made him wonder if it was time to give up the switch-hitting experiment and just hit from the right side. The decision was a difficult one. Switch-hitting made Ken an ultimate threat . . . but the threat didn't mean so much when he wasn't producing. Still, giving up switch-hitting would mean losing an edge.

And Ken wasn't one to take the easy road, even if the road he was traveling was *really damn hard.*

While Ken was having mixed success, that Bagwell guy was taking flight.

The rookie led the team with 15 home runs (Caminiti and Gonzalez finished right behind him with 13) and batted .294 on his way to the Rookie of the Year Award. The Larry Andersen trade was already looking like a steal. Combined, the three players competing for the same third base job ended up hitting more than half of the Astros' home runs in 1991. The team's power numbers would have been better if the height of the Astrodome's outfield walls hadn't been raised, an equalizer for opposing teams with more pop in the lineup. The pitcher-friendly dimensions cost the Astros, as a team, possibly 25 home runs during the season. Balls that would leave other parks were hitting the wall and turning into doubles and triples. Houston hit 52 home runs on the road and only 27 at home, 9 of which were hit by Ken.

* * *

Of all Ken's home runs in 1991, none meant more to him than the one he hit in a July 6 game against the Reds. The game itself was forgettable, a nondescript summertime jaunt between two teams that would finish twenty games back in the standings, but it was special to Ken because of who was there: Kendall Marie Caminiti, Nancy and Ken's first daughter, all of three weeks old.

Nancy went into labor on Sunday, June 16. Ken and the Astros had arrived in Montreal for a series against the Expos, and by the time he found out, and despite Astros traveling secretary Barry Waters's best efforts working the phones, it was too late to get a flight out that night. Patty Biggio, wife of Ken's teammate Craig, was Nancy's labor coach, and Kendall was born at 6:17 a.m. on Monday, June 17. Patty and Nancy had become close—they founded and cohosted the first Astros wives' fundraising gala, dubbed "An Evening of Stars," in 1990—and Patty was there for Nancy whenever times got tough, true friends like their husbands had become.

Ken flew back to Houston and held his daughter. . . . *Wow.* He was a father, and in that moment everything was perfect. . . . *Wow.* This, all seven pounds and eight ounces of her, this was everything.

At Kendall's first game, Bagwell struck first, drawing a two-out walk in the fourth inning, the first Astros batter to reach base against pitcher Jack Armstrong. Gonzalez followed with a double to left-center to score Bagwell, and then Ken drove the ball to right field. Was it fair or foul? Fair or foul? The ball clanked off the foul pole—home run—and Ken jogged around the bases.

"I looked up there as I crossed home plate, and [my wife and mother-in-law] were just coming down the aisle," Ken said. "I got the ball for her to keep. She may not know what it's about now, but I'll be sure to tell her."

CHAPTER 13

LONG ROAD

Hal Newhouser couldn't help but be excited by a player he was scouting in Kalamazoo, Michigan.

Newhouser—affectionately dubbed "Prince Hal"—knew baseball. He was one of the league's premier pitchers of the 1940s and enshrined in Cooperstown in 1992 after being selected by the National Baseball Hall of Fame's Veterans Committee. After his playing days ended, Newhouser became a scout, and he spent years crisscrossing Michigan looking for talented players. While scouting for Houston, he found a shortstop named Derek Jeter who was graduating high school in 1992, and wouldn't you know it, the Astros held the first pick in the June amateur draft.

Jeter's swing was smooth as silk. Newhouser gushed about Jeter in his reports, claiming the infielder was "going to be the anchor and the foundation of a winning club."

But with owner John McMullen streamlining costs and trying to unload the team, and salaries for draft picks climbing, Houston couldn't worry so much about drafting the best player—it needed to focus on drafting the best player *the team believed it could sign.* And while Prince Hal was adamant that the Astros should spend everything it could and draft this Jeter kid, Houston took a liking to a college player: a California-raised third baseman who brought a football mentality to the diamond, was spending his summer playing with Team USA, and looked pretty badass with his eyes hidden behind a pair of Oakleys.

Come to think of it, Phil Nevin had a lot in common with Ken Caminiti. The Cal State Fullerton product was potentially more affordable than Jeter, who threatened to attend college at the University of Michigan if he didn't get a suitable offer. Jeter had other options beyond turning pro. Nevin did not.

And the thinking went that Nevin, as a college player, was more polished and would probably reach the major leagues before a high school shortstop. The Astros were scouting a number of other prospects, and they also considered outfielders Jeffrey Hammonds and Chad Mottola. But inevitably the conversation kept returning to two players: Phil Nevin or Derek Jeter?

And those two players sparked a conversation about two other players, Brien Taylor and John Burke. In the 1991 draft, Taylor, an eighteen-year-old pitching prospect from Beaufort, North Carolina, used that college excuse—and some hard bargaining from his mother, Bettie, a crab sorter, along with advice from superagent Scott Boras—to rake in a then-record $1.55 million from the Yankees. They initially offered $850,000, and Taylor told them no until they offered a price that was sufficient for him and his mother.

Boras was also offering advice to Burke, a University of Florida right-hander selected sixth in the 1991 draft. The Astros scraped together a $360,000 offer for his services, but that wasn't going to be enough, especially after Taylor signed for SO MUCH MONEY. Burke was looking for at least $500,000. So instead of signing with Houston and turning pro, Burke returned to college, waited one year until Houston's rights to sign him expired, then reentered the draft, getting selected twenty-seventh in 1992 by the expansion Colorado Rockies (for slightly less money than the Astros had offered him one year earlier, albeit twenty-one spots later).

The failure to sign Burke was indicative of Houston's draft difficulties with first-round picks and its money-saving ways. If the Astros drafted Jeter with the number one pick, then failed to sign him . . . that would be embarrassing. And while Nevin was seen as the more affordable option, he also had a winning pedigree, carrying his team to the College World Series. Against Prince Hal's fervent wishes, Houston on June 1, 1992, selected Nevin with the top pick. Jeter slipped to the Yankees at number six, a partnership that would result in five World Series rings, 3,465 hits, enshrinement in Cooperstown. . . . Prince Hal quit his scouting job in disgust. He was nearing retirement age anyway, but seeing his team pass on Jeter was the final straw, the last insult in his Hall of Fame career. Not that Nevin was a bad choice—he ended up playing twelve years in the majors. It's just that Jeter was so good for so long.

"At that time, there were financial constraints that were in place in preparation for the upcoming sale of the club," scouting director Dan O'Brien said. "We liked both players. Ultimately you have one selection, and we made ours, and as they say, the rest is history." Drafting Nevin instead of Jeter was one of a handful of decisions that would haunt Astros fans for years.

During the 1991 off-season, after Biggio was finally on board with moving from catcher to second base, Houston found itself needing a backstop—while also flush with outfield talent. So the team traded away soon-to-be superstar centerfielder Kenny Lofton in a deal that brought them catcher Eddie Taubensee.

And near the end of spring training before the 1992 season, reliever Curt Schilling was pitching poorly, but he was out of options—the team couldn't demote him. But the front office couldn't justify keeping him on the roster, so Schilling—who'd become one of the premier pitchers of his generation and among the gutsiest performers in postseason history—was shipped away.

Passing on Jeter stung the most. *If* the Astros had drafted and signed Jeter in 1992, and *if* it had kept its infield of Bagwell, Biggio, and Caminiti intact, and *if* those players' stat lines had remained the same during the 1990s . . . a lot of *ifs*, yes, but those four players combined for 26.2 Wins Above Replacement in 1997, just a shade under the all-time records of 27.9 and 26.9 by the "$100,000 infield" of the 1912 and 1913 Philadelphia Athletics consisting of Stuffy McInnis, Eddie Collins, Jack Barry, and Frank "Home Run" Baker.

Patience and money were potentially all that separated the Houston Astros of the 1990s from having the best infield in modern baseball history—the very two things in short supply as John McMullen looked to sell his team.

* * *

The team's drafting of Nevin marked the beginning of the end of Ken's tenure with the Astros. They both played the same position. And while Houston tried Nevin at outfield and shortstop, the more likely scenario saw him taking Ken's spot at third base in a few seasons, and Ken playing for another team.

It represented the latest round of trade speculation for Ken. He'd been the subject of trade rumors since entering the league and, in 1991, had to fend off challenges from Jeff Bagwell and Luis Gonzalez to hold his position.

Nevin rubbed the Houston players as too cocky. But instead of viewing Nevin as a threat, Ken took the young hotshot under his wing. He bonded with Nevin like he did with Bagwell a few years earlier. May the best man win. . . .

"You're going to take my job someday. You're going to do it the right way," Ken told the number one pick. He ended up inviting Nevin to stay at his house for three weeks during the off-season so they could work out and hit together, a chance for Ken to show Nevin the ropes of what it meant to be a major league player.

"He just had a way of making me feel important," Nevin said.

* * *

While Ken's mentorship of Nevin—something he'd do for numerous young players—was a meaningful experience for the Astros' top pick, not all his lessons for teammates turned out to be helpful. Just like the older players had done for Ken when he reached the majors, he went out of his way to give Eddie Taubensee a greenie in 1992 when the catcher needed a pick-me-up—a gesture that resulted in a yearslong addiction for Taubensee.

For Taubensee, getting greenies became as casual as someone bumming a cigarette off a coworker during a smoke break. "He was the guy who introduced me to what amphetamines were. I was young; I never heard of these things. I just mentioned one day I was tired. And he said, 'Hey, take one of these.' So I took it," Taubensee said.

"I felt like I could run through a brick wall and I wasn't tired. . . . I thought, wow, I could use one of these again. So it just became something that I thought I needed to play the game in the major league level, to get up and get moving for a ball game, when in reality I didn't because I never did before.

"That was my addiction. For a few years when I was with the Astros, I thought that I needed it. Apparently, it was performance-enhancing, but I always tell people it didn't enhance my performance, because it made me so jittery, so wired, and I was so aggressive, my stats went down big time."

Likewise, Ken needed substances to help him get up and come down from games. The concoction that helped keep Ken on the field became known as a "Caminiti cocktail," a mixture of pain meds and anti-inflammatories to help dull the pain—but those drugs would also make him feel sluggish and sleepy, so he'd counteract that by adding greenies to his pre-game drinks, and then maybe down a couple of cups of coffee. After games, he would need to drink a six pack to come down from the high, or sometimes he'd mix OJ with vodka, but the pain would inevitably come rushing back.

* * *

The Republican National Convention needed a host site in 1992, and McMullen was happy to offer up the Astrodome. But the agreement didn't just cover the convention from August 17 to 20—it stretched from July 27 to August 23, at the RNC's request. The deal was reached without input from Major League Baseball, a violation of the league's bylaws. The Major League Baseball Players Association, nonplussed by the prospect of its Houston players being effectively homeless for nearly a month, filed a grievance against the owner (who agreed to donate $125,000 to different causes to make the grievance go away).

The twenty-six-game road trip only worsened fan sentiment about the out-of-town owner whom newspapers ridiculed as a "Yankee Carpetbagger" and "New Jersey Devil," off the hockey franchise he also owned.

To Bill Wood and Art Howe, the hatred against the owner was misguided.

"I liked John a lot," Howe, the Astros manager from 1989 to 1993, said of McMullen. "You knew exactly where he was coming from. He wanted to win. Just because he wasn't there all the time, he lived up in New Jersey, doesn't mean he didn't want to win."

Wood said that working with McMullen was "a challenge," but that the owner "had no hidden agenda." The owner might call the GM six times a day—he was more interested and invested in the team than people realized. But he was an easy media target, and he didn't get proper credit for the successes that occurred under his guidance, such as the 1986 division championship or the development of a Venezuelan academy that led to the discovery of players like Bobby Abreu and Richard Hidalgo. "Part of that was John's fault because of his style, and he would probably tell you the same thing, but by the same token, he would say F 'em," Wood said.

As the long trip was set to commence, it was announced that McMullen had lined up a buyer for the team: Texas grocery magnate Drayton McLane. A local owner! Who promised to spend money! The $115 million deal, which took effect after the season, brought new enthusiasm for the Astros. The future was bright.

But even with a new owner entering the fray, an agreement was an agreement, and the Astros were forced to embark on a twenty-eight-day, twenty-six-game road trip, the longest in modern baseball history. The trip had some parallels to Ken's time with Team USA in 1984—a bunch of younger players coming into their own. Three games in Atlanta, one off day, four games in Cincinnati, two in Los Angeles, a bus trip south to San Diego to play four games, three in San Francisco, a four-game series in Chicago, an off day to come home and do laundry, followed by a three-game trip to St. Louis and finally three games in Philadelphia. More than nine thousand miles of travel.

The high jinks began almost immediately. During the off day in Cincinnati, July 30, Ken went to the movies with Casey Candaele, Luis Gonzalez, and outfielder Pete Incaviglia. When they returned to the hotel, Candaele messed with the elevator's stop button for about ten minutes, a herky-jerky ride that scared the hell out of the other players. Gonzalez tried to call 911, while Ken "tried to pry open the doors like King Kong," according to a report by writer Tony DeMarco.

"Casey was mostly laughing. When we got to his floor and the door opened, he ran out laughing like crazy," Incaviglia said. "I thought Caminiti was going to break him in half. Gonzo was too busy having convulsions. It really was pretty funny."

As the trip continued, a teammate bought a blow-up doll for pitcher Pete Harnisch, and the doll was seen on the Astros bench when the trip reached Wrigley Field.

There were rubber snakes and rubber rats, cow milking, a trip to see a nuclear sub in San Diego. The players took team psychologist Fran Pirozzolo's son out to buy him new clothes—the major league treatment.

Ken hoped he didn't have to use the $150 in laundry money allocated to him. "Whenever I get hits, I don't wash my socks or cup and holder," he told Kelly Candaele, Casey's brother, a filmmaker who spent time with the pair while they stayed in Los Angeles. Ken and Casey, travel-weary, tried to pump each other up.

"Rev it up, Case," Ken said.

"That's what I'm about to do," Candaele responded.

"Rev it up, Case."

"That's what I was born to do."

The Astros did rev it up during the road trip, going 12–14—one win away from a .500 record. Up until the cross-country trek, Houston in 1992 hadn't completed a single road series with a winning record, going 13-27. After that road trip, Houston had a winning record on two of the season's final three road trips and went 9–6 away from the Astrodome to finish the 1992 season with a .500 record, at 81–81.

"It brought us all together. If you didn't like each other, it was going to get exposed. We got along, and we became a cohesive unit after that," Gonzalez said.

"It sent a message to the guys that hey, we can win on the road. We can hold our own. And from that point forward, we started playing much, much better when we went on the road—and for me, I thought that was a turning point for our team," Howe said.

The Astros seemed poised to finally break out. The kids, as it turned out, could play, and they had a new owner willing to spend money. The players picked one another up, paying attention to their teammates' efforts. "I see ya," they'd say to each other as they came off the field—I saw how far you went for that ball, I saw you hit the cutoff man, instant affirmation from the people whose opinions mattered most. "It was more important to the guys than forty thousand people standing and cheering," said Pirozzolo, the team psychologist. "It was a crazy, positive group of people that loved each other."

And teammates loved Ken. Their elder statesman, all of twenty-nine years old, batted a career-high .294 in 1992—.289 from the left side, .303 from the right. All of the effort with hitting coach Rudy Jaramillo was paying off. Ken was finally finding consistency at the plate. But his bruising style of play was getting noticed around the league.

In a September 18 game in Atlanta, Ken was on third base and teammate Pete Incaviglia hit a soft fly ball to shallow right field. David Justice jogged in to make the catch and threw home when he recognized Ken tagging up. As Justice's ball tailed downward, first baseman Sid Bream cut off the throw in the infield grass and tossed it to catcher Greg Olson, who caught the ball a half step before Caminiti arrived.

"I felt the ball from David was going to short-hop Greg Olson, so I cut it real quick and threw home, but it's slower to do it that way. And when I did that, Greg wasn't able to protect himself," Bream said.

As the ball settled in Olson's mitt, Ken had his shoulder lowered, preparing to crunch bones. Olson's right leg was tucked underneath him. Ken slammed through the catcher, a lit stick of dynamite that sent Olson tumbling backward, then up and over until the catcher flopped facedown on the dirt with his arms at his sides. He somehow hung on to the ball, but as he glanced at his leg and winced in pain, the game didn't matter all that much. Olson was out. His season was over—the collision left Olson with a broken leg and dislocated ankle. His career was never the same again. The hit was legal within the rules of the game at the time (it would be banned decades later).

"I had to go in hard—that's the only play—but I didn't want to hurt anybody," Ken said later. But deep down, Ken was hurting, too. He'd been hurting for a long time.

CHAPTER 14

EARTHQUAKE

The room was rattling like a freight train. It was 4:57 a.m.

Something long buried shifted far below the earth's surface on June 28, 1992—the 7.3-magnitude Landers earthquake struck one hundred–odd miles outside of Los Angeles. The right lateral strike-slip earthquake was the largest to hit the area in decades and ripped a forty-three-mile scar in the earth. Astros players and personnel—in town to play the Dodgers—were jolted awake.

But where others were asleep when everything started moving, Ken was still up drinking. He sprinted down the steps like he was being waved around third base and the throw was coming in, a close play at the plate . . .

The aftershocks kept coming. Ken rose to the occasion that day, tying his career high with four hits. But just as when the earthquake struck, Ken's world was shifting underneath the surface, and he couldn't control it anymore.

* * *

The tremors usually started on the fourth day.

When the Astros went on road trips, Ken drank pretty much every night—but when he came home, he tried to stay sober. *I'm going to quit*, he'd tell himself, but by day four, his hands would shake. His body was struggling with alcohol withdrawal after so many years of heavy drinking.

He put parameters around his drinking, using booze as a motivator and reward. He'd go three-for-four and drink to celebrate, because he earned it, or go 0-for-4 and try to wash it away and drown his sorrows. If he went drinking, he convinced himself, he'd have to focus even harder the next day. But it's tough to focus when you're foggy and groggy. He struggled to concentrate, swinging at bad pitches and booting plays in the field that he should have made. He was giving whatever he had left at the ballpark each day, but falling short of the player he could become.

Ken's teammates were worried. He was such a *nice guy* . . . you couldn't help but pull for Ken. You wanted to help him and hug him and let him see what he meant to you, how special he was. A group of Astros players—a rotating cast that included Biggio and guys like Pete Harnisch or Luis Gonzalez or Steve Finley, along with Fran Pirozzolo—would take turns deciding who would confront Ken to ask him if things were OK and try to keep him on the right path.

"He had these periods of disappearing. The guys cared about him. . . . Somebody would be nominated to be the interventionist," Pirozzolo said.

"He wouldn't speak to you for the next two weeks. I'd do it very gently, and start it with baseball, saying, 'Y'know, you don't seem to be seeing the ball too well.' And the conversation would shift to alcohol or amphetamines, stuff like that. . . . Whatever was happening was swept under the rug until it was a problem."

Addict is a heavy label to toss around haphazardly, but it was becoming clear to his friends that Ken was an addict, someone whose need to use chemicals was superseding his baseball career and everything else in his life. The fact that he was still playing at such a high caliber despite everything he put into his body was a testament to his talent and determination. Drugs and alcohol have undercut many successful baseball careers—players like Don Newcombe and Billy Martin and Sam McDowell and Bob Welch and Steve Howe and Darryl Strawberry and Dwight Gooden. . . . A similar pattern was emerging with Ken. At a time when teams weren't drug-testing players, with the players' union taking a hard-line stance, there was only so much a team could do with a player battling addiction. GM Bill Wood called Ken into his office during the 1993 season in hopes of getting through to the third baseman. "He would just look at me and deflect: 'Bill, I do not have a problem. I'm telling you, there's no problem whatsoever.'

"He was slipping. He would come to the ballpark not in the best of condition. And this is kind of what brought it to our attention," Wood said. "He would still go out there and bust his tail and give you 100 percent effort and play a good ball game. And that probably convinced him that he could keep doing this, that it wasn't going to slow him down, that he could have his cake and eat it, too. I look on that with a lot of regret that maybe we didn't find a way, a word, a level of sincerity, perhaps, something that maybe you feel like you could've reached down and done one more thing."

Manager Art Howe tried, too, during that blurry 1993 season. The team was ready to start winning again—Houston's first legitimate chance at the playoffs in four years—and Howe was more worried about Ken's health than he was about Ken's impact in the lineup.

"I had a meeting with him and tried to tell him that we'd give him some time off to try to get himself straightened out. As far as I was concerned, I'd tell everybody he pulled a hamstring, take a couple of weeks, and go someplace and get yourself cleaned up. He didn't want any part of it. That's where the denial comes in," Howe said. "That's what I tried to offer him. But he wouldn't do it."

Friends on other teams tried to help, too. Tom Pagnozzi, a teammate of Ken's during winter ball in Puerto Rico during the late 1980s, recognized his friend had a cocaine problem and brought it up.

"You've gotta be careful with this stuff," Pagnozzi said.

"I've got it under control," Ken responded. End of discussion.

* * *

The Astros opened 1993 brimming with optimism. After enduring the abyss of a 97-loss season in 1991, the team improved to 81–81 the following season. The rebuild was over. Now it was time to start winning.

Houston had a new owner in local grocery magnate Drayton McLane, who wanted to make his splash and opened the purse strings. Much like his predecessor, John McMullen, who made local son Nolan Ryan baseball's first million-dollar man in 1979, then later came to regret it, McLane spent big on two Texas pitching products: free agents Doug Drabek and Greg Swindell. Former Astro Kevin Bass also returned, providing veteran presence.

The Astros opened 1993 out of the gate early, having a 14–8 record in April and holding on to the division lead on May 10, at 19–12.

Pitcher Darryl Kile, with his wicked curveball, was masterful. He made his first All-Star Game and won fifteen games that year, none more significant than on September 8 when he no-hit the Mets. And Biggio and Bagwell were their usual consistent selves, each hitting 20 home runs and serving as the emotional leaders of the team.

But the Giants, behind temperamental free agent signing Barry Bonds, and Atlanta—with its triumvirate of aces in Greg Maddux, John Smoltz, and Ken's minor league nemesis Tom Glavine—were too tough. Atlanta and San Francisco both won more than 100 games. Houston's record was 85–77—a distant third, but the Astros' best finish since 1989.

There was a lot to be excited about. But what was wrong with Ken?

As the team's longest-tenured player, Ken should have been coming into his own and building off his successful 1992 season, when he batted a career-high .294. He turned thirty years old in 1993, with a growing family (his and Nancy's second daughter, Lindsey Lee, was born on August 14, 1993). But instead of finding stability, he was drifting. His average was .218 in mid-May, and his power disappeared in the middle of the season—he went two months, from June 6 to August 7, between home runs, a stretch of 173 at bats in 46 games. The Astros wanted to help Ken however they could, to bring him calm and support. But their attempts weren't working. The rumblings were becoming more frequent.

Near the end of the 1993 season, Jeff Bagwell confronted Ken about his off-the-field issues. The slugging first baseman had, with Biggio, become a team leader, the face of the franchise. It wasn't easy for Bagwell to confront a mentor and friend, but he was worried.

"I resented it. I wanted to kill him," Ken said.

But deep down, he knew Bagwell was right.

* * *

Ken quit drinking for eighteen days.

He endured the tremors, the shaky days. This was the toughest player in the game. If he could grit through a separated shoulder or bum knee, he could quit drinking all by himself, too.

His sobriety lasted until teammate and friend Gerald Young got married in the Pittsburgh area. Young and Caminiti had both seen their careers uprooted by addiction, and if you're around the people with shared addictions, you're bound to fall back into the same habits.

The wedding was too much for Ken. After eighteen days sober, he spent three days backsliding.

Back in Houston, Ken grappled with failure—he'd failed at sobriety just like he'd failed his teammates and his family. . . . Buried by self-hate and negativity, he found himself flying down the freeway, driving drunk, "tears streaming down his face, not caring if he lived or died," as *L.A. Times* writer Ross Newhan later put it. Ken made it home that night. But it was clear he needed real help. He couldn't face this alone anymore. He reached out to former NBA player John Lucas, who'd endured cocaine addiction and later opened a treatment center in Houston.

There, everything would come out, the things Ken was holding inside for so many years.

* * *

Kenny hated waking up to an empty house.

The emptiness made him feel alone and vulnerable, the way he had felt all those years ago as a boy on Cordoy Lane. Kenny was in middle school when the things he couldn't talk about began. His sexual abuser was an older male. His family had no idea.

It happened multiple times. It was their little secret. So Kenny kept quiet. Silence was the safe, easy choice. The Caminitis weren't known for talking openly about things—remember, Kenny grew up without even knowing what his father did for a living—and if his dad could keep quiet about war or work, Kenny could hold on to his secrets, too.

Then there was the fear of what would happen if his secret got out, the fear that people would consider him lesser than, diminished, *gay* . . . which he wasn't, but that wouldn't stop guys from messing with him if they found out.

No, Kenny was going to let his actions do the talking. He would hit the hardest and drink the most and be your best friend and act the craziest and laugh it all off like it was no big thing. In some ways, for him, everything else was no big thing. After you've done things you can't talk about, you find yourself drawn to doing other things you can't talk about. You compartmentalize, walling off aspects of your life to different people until everything becomes a giant maze. You get better at disappearing, at blending into the background, at lying, at making it seem like everything is under control when, in fact, nothing is. You try to please everyone, because it might mean they'll spend less time focusing on you.

Instead of talking about his abuse, Kenny buried it as deep as he could. When the shame resurfaced, he would use drugs and alcohol to try to anesthetize his inner pain. The high momentarily made him numb before all those other feelings came rushing back and he felt alone and vulnerable and shameful and dirty all over again.

The identity of Kenny's abuser and pattern of abuse he endured remain unclear. So many years have passed. . . . Those who may know the truth haven't spoken publicly about it. Until now, no one has spoken publicly about Kenny's childhood abuse.

He spent years trying to escape, but eventually he couldn't run from his secrets anymore. The things he couldn't talk about were consuming him.

The secrets finally started spilling out when Ken went to rehab, a broken man trying to fix the broken boy inside. He would continue telling pieces of his story privately over the course of the next decade as he tried to quell his inner turmoil. During rehab stints at two different facilities in late 2001 and early 2002, Ken confided about his being a victim of childhood sexual abuse, three fellow patients said years later. In rehab, Ken wouldn't be judged for his trauma and truth. Everyone else was struggling, too.

"There was a conflict with him being an athlete and being around guys and being a guy's guy, but having this shame associated with what had happened," said J. Hutton Pulitzer, who befriended Ken while they attended The Meadows of Wickenburg in Arizona together. "He dealt with that by suppressing it, but he found the alcohol could help him just blow through it and get to the next game, the next performance, or just kind of became an escape for him."

An attorney who represented Ken in 2004, Terry Yates, declined to go into detail about the type of trauma Ken endured, citing attorney-client privilege, but said that childhood trauma was at the center of Ken's addictions. "He had things happen to him when he was younger," Yates said. "We all have baggage, I guess. Things happen to us in our lives and people cope with them in different ways. I just don't think he could ever cope with it without using drugs. Drugs and alcohol are what he fell back on to anesthetize the pain he had. He just never found another way to deal with it."

According to the Rape, Abuse & Incest National Network, childhood sexual abuse victims are about four times more likely to develop symptoms of drug abuse and PTSD as adults, and about three times more likely to experience a major depressive episode.

Ken's first rehab stint, in 1993, helped him bring the walls down for the first time and face the truth. It forced him to open up about the things he couldn't talk about. In rehab, he learned that the truth would set him free—but the truth could also be painful for those around him.

He was forced to discuss his infidelities with Nancy. . . . Those details were difficult for his wife to stomach. But Nancy recognized the context of the disclosure. They both remained committed to making their marriage work, and Nancy served as an emotional rock. Ken reached a better understanding with his parents, too. They'd been through so much over the years . . . them being stern, him pushing them away. They visited during his rehab facility's family week, and they talked and cried, and left with a strengthened relationship and better understanding of each other. They couldn't protect their boy all those years ago, but now they were going to hold him tight through the aftershocks.

CHAPTER 15

STRIKE, YOU'RE OUT

Ken stood in front of his teammates and coaches, and the tears flowed as he poured out his heart, speaking about his addictions and not playing to his potential.

This was a new Ken. A different Ken.

A secure, open, clear-minded Ken. An accountable Ken. A healthier Ken. This was the version of Ken that his teammates had hoped to see more of. Sure, it was fun to party with the old Ken, and there was a sense of loss for some that those days were over, but more importantly, after years going down a dark path, Ken was walking in the light.

Ken became a born-again Christian after leaving rehab, something he'd considered for years and embraced in his sobriety. He also attended Alcoholics Anonymous and Narcotics Anonymous meetings, learning how normal his problems were. Free of substances, Ken poured himself into building his soul and body, spending the off-season working out and adding muscle.

He couldn't talk about everything surrounding his addictions. For the public, Ken settled on the truth that he was a recovering alcoholic—that was more palatable than some of his other problems and wouldn't implicate his teammates. He did have a problem with drinking, and he was done with it. He was done with cocaine and speed and painkillers, too. He'd messed up so much, with his beloved Nancy at the top of that list. But he'd let his teammates down, too, and he was devoted to staying clean and making things right.

Ken surrounded himself with clean-living people. He bonded with Andy Stankiewicz, a straitlaced, soft-hitting shortstop. Their lockers were next to each other in spring training, and Stankiewicz was drawn in by the *realness* of Ken. This guy was as genuine as they come, no air, no ego. People warned Stankiewicz about Caminiti, his reputation casting a large shadow, but Stankiewicz saw only the good in him. Andy served as Ken's roommate on the road, someone to keep an eye on Ken and ensure he wasn't disappearing at night.

"It's in that quiet time, that time alone, that those demons begin to pop up. So they asked if I wouldn't mind rooming with him, and I was like, 'Heck yeah, of course. I'd love to,'" Stankiewicz said. Sometimes the friends sat and talked. Other times they watched movies or played cards. "I tried to wrestle with him, and he would spin me around like a rag doll, and he'd throw me across the room," he added.

A sober Caminiti found himself with a new perk: meal money. He was used to spending his daily food stipend on booze. He also found himself sleepless and restless, awake sometimes as early as six in the morning. "Call me. I'm up if you want somebody to talk to," Astros coach Matt Galante told Ken, and Ken would call Galante every once and again, and they'd walk around or grab breakfast.

"He was fighting it. It's no question he fought," Galante said.

* * *

The Astros experienced many changes that off-season. GM Bill Wood and manager Art Howe, leftovers from the John McMullen era, were gone. They were replaced by Bob Watson—the first black GM in major league baseball history—and a firebrand skipper named Terry Collins who'd bounced around the minors as a player and coach in the Pirates and Dodgers systems before finally getting a shot to helm a major league team. Once again, Ken was playing for a first-time manager. Collins was a lit fuse, liable to explode whenever his players made a mistake. In that way, he was similar to Art Howe's predecessor, Hal Lanier, whose shouting can still be heard echoing around whatever's left of the Astrodome locker room. That kind of presence can motivate or melt a player. Ken was past that point of worrying *too much* . . . but Collins's approach in 1994 bothered him. He didn't like having to think about getting yelled at for screwing up. There was a way to rip a guy respectfully. Collins hadn't learned that yet.

"Terry's personality and our team personality didn't match as much. If something happened on the field, Terry would kind of fly off the handle at times. 'How did this happen? How did he not catch this fly ball?'" Astros third baseman Chris Donnels said.

That first season, critics say, Collins also had a tendency to cozy up with the team's best players, Biggio and Bagwell, and all but ignore some of the bench players, making guys feel slighted. He leaned on his favorites too much. He talked to the guys who didn't need the help.

"He came in saying he was going to be a communicator, talk to every player every day, and we're going to be close-knit, and the opposite was the case," said Fran Pirozzolo, Astros' team psychologist. "He would never talk to anyone. He would wander around during BP, and he'd talk to Bagwell and Biggio. I'd tell him, 'They don't need you. Those guys are going to the Hall of Fame. This other kid hasn't hit in a month, and he's worried about going back to Tucson. He needs you.'"

Collins has acknowledged mistakes in the way he managed the Astros, and critics are quick to note the maturity Collins later showed in managing the Mets to the World Series.

The Astros also had new uniforms and a new logo, another way for Drayton McLane to put his stamp on the team he now owned. Gone were the rainbow striping and caps with an orange star. The new duds featured a blue and gold color scheme, with the H on caps featuring a tail—shooting stars.

The new-look Astros—in the newly created National League Central Division with the Cardinals, Cubs, Pirates, and Reds—opened the 1994 season on April 4 at home against the Expos. Houston's broadcasters keyed in on the results of Cammy's off-season workouts.

"He's really beefed himself up this season, and it's all muscle," announcer Bill Brown quipped during the game.

"It's all in the right places. He's in the best shape he's ever been in," Bill Worrell responded.

Despite the new muscle, the new Ken started 0-for-5 as the game wore on into the twelfth inning. In the top half, new Houston reliever Mitch Williams, reinforcing his nickname of "Wild Thing," got two quick outs before imploding, allowing five straight batters to reach base—including two bases-loaded walks—to give Montreal a two-run lead and the hometown crowd someone to boo.

New Astros? The letdown felt the same. But then, in the bottom half, Houston rallied, getting two runners on base for Bagwell, who singled home a run. Luis Gonzalez whiffed, caught looking for the second out, which brought Ken up to bat against pitcher Denis Boucher.

Ken dug in, kicking craters into the batter's box dirt and taking his practice swings. Ready. Boucher threw the first pitch up in the zone, and Ken pounced, driving it to left-center. Off the wall! The weight lifting was paying off. Steve Finley and Jeff Bagwell raced home for the improbable win, and Ken started walking off the field, victorious, when he was mobbed by his teammates. The fans stood and cheered, and the new Ken emerged from the scrum with a . . . smile. The old Ken didn't have a lot to smile about, but dammit, baseball could be fun when you were winning and clear enough to appreciate it.

Despite the lifestyle changes and Opening Day heroics, Ken still had a slow start to the season—on May 1 he was batting .197 with only two home runs. By that point, the trade rumors started swirling again. . . . That's bound to happen when you're making $10.9 million over three years. During the off-season, Houston was considering trades that would have sent him to Minnesota for Shane Mack or to the Mets (in a three-way trade involving the Blue Jays), as well as the Padres, the Angels, and the Red Sox. The Phillies wanted him badly, too, if the price was right. . . . Moving Ken would have gotten his salary off the books and cleared room for prospect Phil Nevin.

But then Ken's bat got red-hot. He batted .372 for the month of May, with 6 home runs and 21 ribbies on the strength of a 14-game hitting streak, and suddenly his batting average was back up to a very respectable .292, to match his usual Gold Glove–caliber defense. In fact, it was his best season in the field since that breakout year 1989, when he put the National League on notice that he was the league's best pickpocket, taking sure hits out of players' grasp.

Chris Donnels, Ken's backup in 1993 and 1994, became skilled in noticing Ken's idiosyncrasies—Donnels was always ready in case Ken was too injured to play, especially involving his shoulder. "After he'd get the out, he'd throw the ball around the infield, and he'd kind of have his left elbow tucked down to his side. The throw would come back in, and his left elbow would never leave his side, and he would just kind of reach out for the ball," Donnels said. "Playing on that AstroTurf in Houston was not very beneficial for your body. He would never say anything to anybody about it, and he wouldn't get much treatment in the training room, but everybody knew. It was something that was not pleasant for him."

Astros strength and conditioning coach Gene Coleman noticed Ken moving his right arm between pitches, too. "He'd make these spectacular plays and then you would see him between pitches, he was holding his right arm out, his throwing arm. He would bring it up shoulder height, a little bit higher, and put it down two or three times between every pitch," Coleman said. "And I asked him one time, 'Hey, what are you doing?' And he said, 'I got to make sure it still works.' He was in that much discomfort."

But the pain hurt so good. He was finally playing for a winner—by the end of May, the Astros were in first place. They'd spend the summer no worse than second place, jockeying back and forth with Cincinnati for the top spot in the National League Central.

* * *

Caminiti got hot right around the time he started wearing a goatee, the first time he'd worn facial hair with Houston. John McMullen wanted to be like the New York Yankees, and since the Yankees banned facial hair, the Astros banned it as well during the early part of Ken's career.

Of course, a lack of facial hair wasn't going to turn any team into the Yankees. The Yankees were the Yankees because they *won*, while the Astros were more well-known for playing inside a domed stadium on plastic grass. Or for trading their best players away. Or coming *this close* to winning. Or wearing orange-striped uniforms. If a guy wanted to grow a mustache—some did, such as 1980s mainstays Phil Garner and Glenn Davis—it couldn't go past the corners of his mouth.

The facial hair ban continued until 1994, under owner Drayton McLane, when Wild Thing complained. Mitch Williams was the quintessential edge-of-your-seat, biting-your-nails-to-nubs type of pitcher. He'd get the save, more often than not, but he would litter the basepaths with runners to get there. He saved forty-three games in 1993 to rank among the league leaders. But he's most remembered for the save he didn't get, on October 23, 1993, against the Blue Jays in Game 6 of the World Series, when he served up a championship-clinching home run to Toronto outfielder Joe Carter.

Wild Thing showed up to spring training in 1994 with a beard, and the Astros weren't pleased. *Shave it.* Williams came back the next day with his cheeks shaved but not his chinny-chin-chin. *Please shave it?* Williams eventually ditched the beard, but after meeting with McLane, he was given the OK to grow it back. And with that, Houston's era of clean-shaven baseball came to a bewhiskered end.

It was Williams's only positive contribution to the team that season—Wild Thing lived up to his nickname, walking more players than he struck out and compiling a 7.65 ERA in twenty-five games before getting his walking papers on May 31. But the Astros players, freed of their clean-shaven ways, put down their razors and started looking wild themselves. Caminiti grew a goatee pretty much overnight and became a scruffy face for the new-look Astros. Luis Gonzalez tried to grow a goatee, too, but it came in "terrible," he said, thin and patchy. Steve Finley went with the stubble of a model in a hair salon manual, trendy and affable. Reliever Todd Jones tried a Fu Manchu—a long, thin mustache pointing downward. Doug Drabek—who wore a mustache in Pittsburgh when he won the Cy Young Award as the league's best pitcher in 1990—grew a neatly trimmed beard-and-mustache combo. Kevin Bass's goatee came in dark and thick, and he wore it proudly to show the younger players what facial hair was supposed to look like.

Two players did not participate: Craig Biggio, because he couldn't for the life of him grow a beard, and Jeff Bagwell, who didn't grow his hair beyond a shadow in 1994. But he'd participate in the coming years.

As for Ken, he felt like he played better with the goatee. Maybe some of that was superstition—hell, if he wasn't going to clean his underwear or jockstrap after a good game, why shave? But there was also a ruggedness to it. At one point during the season, he trimmed too far and ended up having to shave off the goatee, and he fell into a slump. GM Bob Watson urged him to grow it back.

"It's you. And you're doing good with it," Watson told him.

It's you. His goatee was a suit of armor, a cloak of masculinity. It represented the new Ken who was saying his prayers and going to AA meetings and getting sleep and doing the right things and signing autographs for the fans and hitting home runs in bunches—the scariest-looking nice guy in baseball.

The league was taking notice. Ken was a foxhole guy, and Jim Fregosi, the Phillies' manager, liked foxhole guys. Because Philadelphia won the National League the previous year, Fregosi got to pick reserves for the All-Star Game. Matt Williams was the league's runaway starter at third—he was hitting home runs at a Maris-like clip, and got more than 2.2 million votes from fans, but for his third base reserve, Fregosi looked down the ballot and selected Caminiti, who was ranked fifth in voting behind Bobby Bonilla, Terry Pendleton, and Tony Fernandez. Ken was one of a team-record five Astros selected for the game, along with Biggio and Bagwell, starter Doug Drabek, and reliever John Hudek.

Ken found out about the selection after Houston's 12–6 win against the Cubs on July 3, a game in which he hit two home runs: one a traditional over-the-fence blast against Mike Morgan, and the other inside the park off Dan Plesac, when outfielder Sammy Sosa couldn't come up with the ball after it bounced into the corner in right field, and Ken scampered around the bases. The accolades gave Ken a chance to talk more about his journey—a major milestone after he'd made significant changes in his life.

"I was always worried about what people were thinking about me. You know, did he make an error because he was out drinking last night? Now I don't care. I know I did my best. That's a great feeling. I have nothing that dictates how I play," he told the *Houston Chronicle*'s Neil Hohlfeld.

"It's not the drinking the night before, not staying out until five in the morning and being hung over. It's just clean living.

"I don't have the shakes anymore. If I do bad, I just say, 'I'll get 'em tomorrow.' I don't have to worry about how I would have done if I felt better."

One catch: The All-Star Game was being held in Pittsburgh, the place where Ken had relapsed the previous October after trying to stay sober on his own. And there would be no Andy Stankiewicz staying with him, no sober roomie to keep him company. Ahead of the game, Ken was honored to be noticed as one of baseball's best players. "Seeing a lot of my peers, guys I look up to, kinda just following their footsteps now, eyes open, ears open, mouth shut kind of attitude." Before the game's start, Ken took his place along the first base line and was introduced with his fellow All Stars, touching the bill of his cap and scanning the crowd as his name was announced. Ken Caminiti was officially one of baseball's best players.

He entered the game on defense in the seventh inning, with Biggio at second and Bagwell at first—three-quarters of the Astros infield—along with Cardinals icon Ozzie Smith playing shortstop, and Hudek on the mound.

The National League rallied to win the game. Braves first baseman Fred McGriff hit a ninth-inning home run to tie the game, and Padres batting leader Tony Gwynn scored the winning run after hitting a single in the tenth and racing home on Moises Alou's double. Wouldn't it be fun having a guy like Gwynn getting on base ahead of you. . . .

Ken should have been on top of the world that night. But instead, he was thinking about getting high. He could taste and smell crack cocaine, his cravings pulling him, a potential side effect for long-term drug users who quit. He called Nancy. "I gotta get out of here, I can't stay in this room," and she told him to stay, *please stay*, don't go in the elevator, just stay on the phone, stay where you are, it's going to be OK. He stayed in that night, but the urges continued to brim under the surface, liable to overpower him at any point.

Joe Tuschak noticed that Ken needed a friend in Pittsburgh, and he was happy to help. Tuschak worked as a driver in Pittsburgh for Tom Reich, Ken's rough-and-tumble agent. So when the Astros played in the Steel City, Joe would drive Ken around. After one game at Three Rivers Stadium in 1994, pushing midnight, Ken asked Joe to take him to an AA meeting. Joe crossed the river and, ten minutes later, arrived with Ken—and went inside to support the ballplayer.

Hi, I'm Ken. I'm an alcoholic.

Hi, I'm Joe, I'm a friend of Ken's. I'm not an alcoholic.

They ended up staying for about an hour, and when the collection basket came around, Ken threw in a handful of money.

"I feel a lot better that I came here," Ken told Joe. Ken talked to Joe about his wife and daughters, and he went back to the hotel and called Nancy and called it a night. He called Joe the next morning asking to go to breakfast, so Joe took him to one of his favorite breakfast places, a greasy spoon where the waitresses wore bobby socks and six-egg omelets were on the menu—"They put so much stuff in there! It was unbelievable," Joe said—and all the waitresses couldn't help but drown in Ken's eyes.

* * *

As Ken was keeping his addictions at bay, and as Houston remained in the playoff hunt behind the MVP-caliber play of Bagwell, the baseball world was facing a standoff between the owners and players.

The owners—perpetually looking to raise profits and suppress player salaries—wanted a hard salary cap. But the players' union wouldn't budge, wishing to maintain the current salary system. The sides remained far apart, and the Major League Baseball Players Association set a strike date of August 12, 1994.

Ken, serving as a player rep for Houston, participated in union meetings, showing solidarity with his fellow players across the big leagues.

Notably, when Ken went to rehab after the 1993 season, he had his teammate Chris Donnels pick up player rep duties. "All of a sudden, the strike stuff starts happening, and he goes to rehab, and I got sucked into serving as player rep," Donnels said. "I gave him a lot of crap about it."

Baseball was experiencing a dream season—Williams was on pace for the single-season home run record, Gwynn was batting close to the mythical .400 batting average, and teams like the Expos and Astros and Yankees had their eyes on the playoffs after suffering through lean years. But this was about the future, preserving players' rights to earn as much money as they could on the free market.

The last day before the strike, the Astros found themselves tied with the Reds. Win against the Padres, and Houston would take the Central Division lead. Lose, and Houston would be half a game back. Ken had three hits, but the Padres had a lot more, and San Diego won the game 8–6.

The strike began on August 12, and everyone was hopeful it would be resolved in a few days, or a few weeks, but when it wasn't, on September 14, the season was canceled.

No playoffs.

No World Series.

It was a disappointing time for Astros players hoping for a chance at October glory.

"That was the first time I was on a team that had a shot at making the playoffs," said Astros outfielder Mike "Tiny" Felder. "And I had no idea it would be the end of my career."

* * *

The offseason showed up fast, leaving Ken extra time to tinker with his growing car collection and build up his body. While visiting World's Gym in Houston, Ken met a trainer named Blake Blackwell. As the story goes, Ken was carrying an over-the-counter nutritional supplement and looked like he needed help.

"You want to take that stuff the right way?" Blackwell asked Caminiti, according to a 1997 interview the trainer gave to the *San Diego Union-Tribune*. "Let me start working with you on your diet."

Blackwell, stocky and chiseled, was a former football linebacker at Steven F. Austin State University—he was on the 1988 and 1989 teams that reached the I-AA playoffs behind quarterback Todd Hammel and running back Larry Centers, who both went on to have long pro football careers. Blackwell got into training as a way to stay in the sports world, and a client like Ken opened up new opportunities for him.

* * *

In seeing the end of the 1994 season washed away, Astros owner Drayton McLane looked to shed salary—the team had cost him $12 million each in 1993 and 1994, and having postseason ticket sales and merchandise wiped out didn't help. His mandate to the front office: Keep us competitive while saving money. Ken, who was on the hook for $4.5 million in 1995 as the Astros' longest-tenured player, was worth trading—his trade value had never been higher from a player value standpoint following his All-Star selection, and if Houston kept him through 1995, all they'd see is a compensation draft pick.

Steve Finley, the criminally underrated center fielder, was another player the Astros hoped to move. GM Bob Watson started taking trade offers, and the Padres were interested. GM Randy Smith, the son of former Houston GM Tal Smith, hammered out the basics of a trade with Watson, and the father and son ironed out the trade further over Thanksgiving dinner. By late November or early December, the trade was all but set—a twelve-player blockbuster deal that would send Caminiti, Finley, Andújar Cedeño, Roberto Petagine, Brian Williams, and a player to be named later to San Diego for Derek Bell, Doug Brocail, Ricky Gutierrez, Pedro Martínez (no, not *that* Pedro Martínez), Phil Plantier, and Craig Shipley.

Padres president Dick Freeman said that when Smith started outlining the potential trade with him, "I reached in my desk and pulled out a legal pad, drew a line down the middle, wrote 'Houston' on one side and us on the other. And he started naming off the players to me. And of course, I was taken aback by some of the names."

But there was a catch: San Diego had a new ownership group coming in led by John Moores, a Texas-based software mogul. In fact, Moores had randomly met Ken at the gym that off-season.

Moores was assembling his leadership group, which would include former Orioles executive Larry Lucchino, and the Padres decided to wait until the new ownership group came in to announce the trade, so the sides kept the deal a secret for weeks—and somehow, news of the trade didn't leak to the media.

"Holding the deal as well as keeping it quiet, that was a real challenge because there were enough people that knew that I would never have guessed that it would be able to be kept quiet until the ownership change took place, but it did," Freeman said. "And of course, the new owners got to announce it as though it was a deal that they had done."

Ken finally learned of the trade on December 29, as he was preparing to spend the day with his family at Lake Tahoe. He spoke to Randy Smith and the Padres' new manager, the former catcher Bruce Bochy. They sounded excited to have him on the Padres.

In the days before the trade, as he expected to be moved, Ken became emotional when thinking back on his time in Houston. Biggio and Bagwell had his back. They'd become like family to him. There's nothing he wouldn't do for them. But they weren't running the team.

"I just wanna go where I'm wanted," he said. "I haven't felt wanted in Houston for a long time."

CHAPTER 16

NEW BEGINNINGS

With the strike still ongoing in early 1995, major league teams fielded spring training rosters full of replacement players—has-beens, non-prospects, and never-weres. The replacement players were seen by established major leaguers as picket-crossing scabs, but the truth was murkier: A lot of them crossed only because they weren't sure when they'd see this kind of money again. Forgive Padres manager Bruce Bochy if his mind drifted away from the imposters in front of him to his actual team, the team he thought could compete in the National League West.

The gravel-voiced Bochy was a military brat as a kid, a studious sort with a size 8 noggin and, after a chemical accident at eighteen while refinishing furniture, white eyelashes on his right eye. He wasn't a great major league player (a .239 average, 26 career home runs), but he hung around a while, a catcher who saw the game from a lot of angles. After his playing career ended in 1988, he managed in the Padres system and served as the team's third base coach in 1993 and 1994 under then manager Jim Riggleman. From the third base box, he struck up friendly conversation with Ken during Padres-Astros games and got to see Ken's defensive prowess up close.

Their friendly conversation picked up after the strike officially ended on April 2 with no real resolution—the players and owners reverted to the parameters of their previous contract. The "real" Padres reported to Peoria, Arizona, over the next few days. In those rushed weeks before the season started on

April 23, Bochy started to meet the man behind the goatee and scowl, and was struck by his vulnerability.

"As tough as this man was, as badass as he came across, he needed support. He wanted affirmation. He needed you to be in his corner," Bochy said. With his new manager, Ken discussed his early Astros days, when he'd make an error and manager Hal Lanier would be flipping out from the dugout. "He said he didn't want the ball hit to him. . . . He felt so much pressure. And as tough as this guy was, you think that wouldn't have fazed him, but he wanted to be loved. He wanted to be accepted by everybody in a good way," Bochy said.

"I'm glad that he told me that story. Because as a manager, you can't help solve a problem unless you identify it.

"It resonated with me that this man, as tough as he is, he needs you in the corner and then Cammy was just the same: He was a foxhole guy. And if he knew that you had his back, trust me, he had your back. And he showed that many times for me."

If Ken's time with the Padres was going to be successful, if he was going to play to his potential, he needed help. He wanted to re-create the things that went well in Houston—friends like Biggio and Bagwell, mentors like Billy Doran, a supportive manager in Art Howe, and an attentive roommate like Andy Stankiewicz—and avoid the problems that eroded his self-esteem: a less than supportive front office and manager tirades.

Under the collective bargaining agreement at the time, Caminiti could have roomed alone, but it wouldn't have been good for him. He wasn't ready for that yet. Caminiti asked a group of his new teammates during spring training, and Scott Livingstone, a Texas-born infielder, volunteered. Livingstone was a solid influence for Ken.

His friends and mentors Bagwell and Biggio were back in Houston, but San Diego had a future Hall of Famer of its own in Tony Gwynn, the game's best pure hitter since Ted Williams and a member of the team since 1982. Gwynn was credited around the league for his meticulous use of videotape to study opposing pitchers. "Caminiti comes to the Padres and approaches Gwynn and asks him how to be a better player. And Gwynn said, 'When we go to spring training, just follow me and do everything I do.' And nobody worked harder than Gwynn," said Barry Bloom, a reporter who's covered the Padres since 1983. "So that's what Ken did."

Gwynn and Caminiti were set to play with a core of talented players like starting pitchers Andy Ashby (12–10, 2.94 ERA) and Joey Hamilton (a hard-luck 6–9, but a 3.08 ERA) along with closer Trevor Hoffman, acquired from the expansion Florida Marlins when San Diego traded away Gary Sheffield in 1993. A converted shortstop, Hoffman was starting to become dominant with the help of his changeup after fellow reliever Donnie Elliott taught him a new way to grip the ball in 1994.

Another player on the team was outfielder Melvin Nieves, who Ken had befriended as a teenager in the winter of 1988 during Ken's time playing for Mayaguez. "He took me to Ron of Japan in Chicago, which is like a really nice teppanyaki, Benihana-style restaurant, very well-known in Chicago. Ken wasn't a guy that would speak a lot, very intense, but when he approached you, we would have great conversation," Nieves said.

For catcher Brian Johnson, Caminiti was someone you could go to for advice if you were dealing with personal issues. "He was kind of a soft, big brother–type guy that would help you. It was especially great in times of need," Johnson said.

Ken wound up with his locker situated right outside Bochy's office, and he became a clubhouse enforcer, someone who would do anything for the team. In 1995, that meant going with Gwynn to talk with Bochy about an issue they were having with a teammate. Ken had never embodied the right leadership role in Houston's clubhouse. Teammates loved his on-field intensity, sure, but they could never fully trust him off the field because of his substance abuse problems. He was going to do things differently this time. He was going to be a model of dependability, the best teammate.

* * *

Ken's new franchise was doing things differently, too, with a new ownership group in place. San Diego fans were doubly hurt—once by fire sales during the early 1990s, and then by the strike that wiped out the 1994 season.

Owner John Moores and president/CEO Larry Lucchino got to work making inroads with the community. Former Orioles employee Charles Steinberg was brought on as executive vice president of public affairs to aid in those efforts.

"We needed to really build bonds in the community. We were in a strike, and the previous administration had been a catastrophe with the unpopular fire sale,"

Steinberg said. "There were twenty-eight teams back then, and the Padres that we inherited ranked twenty-eighth in core categories: lowest revenue, lowest season ticket base, lowest tickets sold, and worst won-loss percentage. And Larry said to me, 'How bad can we mess this up? The stone's already at the bottom of the hill.'"

A central focus for those community inroads came with Padres Scholars, a program in which the team and players both cosponsored scholarships for middle school students—twenty-five students would get $5,000 scholarships. That meant the players would need to raise about $60,000, and Moores would match that. The front office pitched the plan to three players at first—Tony Gwynn, Brad Ausmus, and Steve Finley—and all three were on board. Finley went around with a yellow legal pad, tracking donations from his teammates.

"Put me in for $10,000," Ken told him.

The players raised their money, and Padres Scholars was a go. John Flores was one of the first students selected for the program. Each student was paired with a player, and Flores was matched with Caminiti. The student was struck by Ken's personality, not just at the stadium but through other get-togethers, too. Ken could have had an ego. But to Flores, Ken genuinely cared about him. "Throughout that first season and the multiple seasons afterward, they had other events and I would see him, and he'd ask how I'm doing or what was new in my life," Flores said. "He was a really nice guy, a caring guy."

* * *

Bochy, ahead of their strike-shortened first season together, said that Ken was "the best third baseman in the history of the Padres." But despite the platitudes, Ken's miscues started with the first ball he fielded as a member of the Padres. Ken's old team was playing his new team, just as they had the last game before the strike. Nine of the players involved in the off-season blockbuster ended up playing in the 10–2 Astros win. In the first inning, Houston's new outfielder Derek Bell hit a chopper to third base that Ken lost in the lights—he struggled picking up the ball because of the glare created by the fading sunlight filtering into the upper deck of San Diego's Jack Murphy Stadium, later known as Qualcomm Stadium.

He never had that problem at the Astrodome. . . .

The errors picked up from there, a mix of fielding mistakes and bad throws. He'd been known to miss his throws at times throughout his career—it happened during his minor league days, and then early in his major league career, whenever he had to think about it, but his work with Astros team psychologist Fran Pirozzolo and the steady receiving of Jeff Bagwell at first helped his throwing troubles go away.

But Eddie Williams and Roberto Petagine were not Bagwell, who carried Ken's deep trust and was skilled at scooping the ball. Ken did a lot of soul-searching trying to figure out the answer. He spoke on the phone with sports psychologist Harvey Dorfman. . . . Hell, if Harvey could help Braves pitcher John Smoltz, maybe he could help Ken, too. Retired Padres player Garry Templeton gave him some tips. So did Graig Nettles, the defensive standout who played on the "Bronx Zoo" Yankees teams of the late 1970s, and who now was serving as San Diego's third base coach.

The slide bled into his hitting. Ken started the year tattooing the ball, but his bat cooled, and by June his average was hovering in the .260s. For a while, as the errors and outs mounted, Ken considered the season "my most frustrating year ever." Ken was still learning how to deal with his emotions without using substances to blur them. He was facing reality—cold, sober, plain reality—and that was still new and different for him.

Despite the errors, Ken was still making his knock-it-down, throw-him-out types of plays that he was known for, and stealing away would-be hits. In a June 3 game against the Expos, Ken put on a clinic at third base, fielding bunts and snaring liners, grabbing grounders to his left, spinning around and snapping the ball, beating the runner by a step—a one-man highlight reel.

But Montreal pitcher Pedro Martínez was twirling a gem of his own, throwing nine perfect innings and matching fast-working Padres pitcher Joey Hamilton, zero for zero. Martínez kept Ken off-balance and frustrated at the plate. After a fifth-inning strikeout that extended his hitless streak to fifteen at bats, Ken balanced the bat sideways on top of his helmet, looking for a moment like he'd snap the wood over his head, but then just leaving the bat there, befuddled, before putting it on the back of his neck and walking back to the dugout. The following at bat, with the perfect game intact, Martínez threw inside to keep Ken off the plate, then kept Ken guessing with a pitch up—what would have been ball four, but Ken feebly waved at it before turning around, raising the bat one more time, and finally snapping it over his leg.

June 3, the date of Pedro's sort-of perfecto (spoiled by a tenth-inning double, though the Expos still won, 1–0) and Ken's fielding clinic, was notable for one other reason for Ken: It was the same day that perennial Gold Glove winner Matt Williams went down with a season-ending foot injury. Williams played only about half the season, leaving the door open for someone else to win the Gold Glove at third base.

Little by little, Ken's fortunes started to change. In July, he was back in Houston for the first time as a visitor. It was good to see his pals Jeff and Craig again; he missed playing with them. But it was also special for him to forge his own path. He liked the atmosphere in San Diego better. He was at peace. The team had a winning atmosphere around it.

While in town, he was invited to a function at Damian's restaurant, a chance for the Italian Sports Hall of Fame of Houston to honor him. A thank-you of sorts. A chance to say goodbye that hadn't been afforded by his trade. Astros broadcaster Milo Hamilton served as master of ceremonies, recalling the plays that made him say, "Holy Toledo, what a play!" Neil Hohlfeld of the *Houston Chronicle* spoke, too, followed by Matt Galante, Ken's beloved infield coach. And then they presented Ken with a gold trophy featuring a glove and two baseballs, just like the defensive award he'd been denied during his years with the Astros. The trophy was inscribed, "In recognition of and appreciation for your 'golden' seasons with the Houston Astros." Ken got choked up as he discussed his time in Houston, and tears flowed throughout the room. "This is where I started. The Astros gave me a chance. I have a lot of friends here, and the fans were great to me. My heart will always be here." Caminiti later placed the trophy in his daughters' room, something dear to his heart. If the National League wasn't going to honor him, he had the next best thing.

The errors decreased further when Bochy started playing Livingstone, Ken's road roommate, at first base. A converted third baseman who Ken trusted? Yes, this was familiar to him. With a friend manning first, Ken felt free to rear back and fire without that nagging fear that he had to make the perfect throw. The cannon was still there, with its aim restored.

But more than errors, Ken's 1995 season was defined by power. Ken started hitting the ball out of the park like never before, as though he had found the proverbial fountain of youth.

Where was his power coming from?

CHAPTER 17

GETTING A BOOST

Dave Moretti made the trips to Tijuana alone.

Bringing his childhood friend along would have caused a scene—like it did one time they visited a Tijuana mall together during Christmastime, when the mall Santa took off his beard to take a picture with Ken while children watched, crestfallen.

San Diego was about twenty miles away from Tijuana, and all Moretti had to do was go to a pharmacy and ask for the drugs he needed. Sometimes the pharmacist would say yes. Other times, they'd make Moretti go to a doctor and get a prescription, a simple process that might involve a $25 payment to the doctor. And then Moretti would go to pharmacies with his prescription in hand and get his orders filled.

Moretti would get his drugs legally in Mexico, put them in the car and drive back across the border, and that was that. Every time he made the trip, he risked the threat of arrest. But to Dave, Ken was worth the trouble.

They had been through a lot together, dating back to the early 1970s, when their older brothers played Little League together. Their friendship ebbed and flowed over the decades. Ken was an asshole sometimes, and Dave was stubborn as a rock. He wasn't afraid to call Ken out if something gnawed at him, like when he got wind of Ken's college partying. But Dave was also sensitive and caring and accommodating. He wanted to make Ken proud and see his friend succeed.

Some of Moretti's motivation was born out of his own faded baseball dreams. He had the talent and drive to become a pro pitcher, but those dreams died when Dave blew out his arm pitching for a summer ball team in high school (he later played college ball as a hitter), and at age sixteen, Dave got involved with bodybuilding. He started working night shifts at California Gym in 1981, when he was a high school junior. The job allowed him to connect with body-builders and learn about workout routines and techniques . . . and yes, steroids, synthetic derivatives of the male sex hormone testosterone.

"That's where I started to learn about the different steroids, the side effects, what they do, and what body types are going to respond to certain steroids," Moretti said, sitting in his California home as his pet rottweiler snored at his feet.

Moretti went on to study chemistry and became a competitive body-builder, entering the world of spray tans and endorphins, learning how to sculpt his body by eating this and injecting that and lifting heavy metal a bunch of times. By the mid-1990s, Moretti had been exposed to steroids for more than a decade. He was smart about where and how he obtained them, ensuring they were made in sterile environments and contained the proper ingredients. But for Moretti, there was no big stigma about using them—he wasn't Ken's only childhood friend who felt the same way—and he was happy to talk to his friends or other people he trusted about steroids. He was a walk-ing repository of knowledge.

Ken and Dave discussed steroids multiple times. The conversation picked up in 1991, Moretti said, after a fellow major league player on an opposing team gave Caminiti a package of steroids. Moretti researched the drugs and got back to Ken.

"I told him it was fake and to throw it away," meaning they weren't made under proper conditions, Moretti said.

Ken followed the advice and trashed the drugs, but his fascination with taking them didn't go away. In 1993, in pursuit of more power, Ken and Astros teammate Chris Donnels discussed steroids and considered whether they were worth taking. "You see guys having success with it, and it was more of a curiosity sort of thing," said Donnels, who began researching steroids on the computer and reading about them in medical journals. "If it could help you play better, then it was something I'd want to know more about." Both decided against using steroids at the time.

But in 1995, Caminiti approached Moretti about another package of steroids he'd been given, just like he had four years prior. Once again, Moretti advised Ken not to take the pills. Moretti's roommate studied the package and came to the same conclusion.

"At that point, I told him, 'If you seriously want to do this, do it right. But you need to really consider it and think about it, take some time, and let me know, and we'll talk,'" Moretti said.

Soon enough, Caminiti was reapproaching his buddy.

"I'd like to try some and see how it feels," Caminiti said.

Moretti said he started Caminiti on an eight-week cycle of pink pills labeled *testosterona* that he obtained at the walk-up pharmacies in Mexico. Ken's use of steroids was known by several of his Padres teammates and numerous baseball colleagues—an open secret he divulged in clubhouse conversations and over steak dinners.

Former catcher Brian Johnson, an anti-steroids advocate, said Ken was open about using. "It wasn't in a glamorous way or a look-at-me way, and it really wasn't in a self-deprecating, ashamed way, just kind of matter-of-fact: *Hey, that's just the way it is.*"

Caminiti also opened up to Bip Roberts, a fleet-footed utility player whose twelve-year career included stops in San Diego and Cincinnati. "He was very honest about it," Roberts said. "As a teammate, I knew exactly what was happening. . . . He was one of the only guys I knew [was using], and that's because we were cool like that. And I loved him. You know, I just looked down and said, 'Well, that's your thing, you do your thing, man.'"

Phil Garner, a second and third baseman during the 1970s and 1980s affectionately nicknamed "Scrap Iron" for his relentlessness and grit, confronted Ken about steroids after hearing rumors Ken was using them. Garner had faced his own crossroads after undergoing back surgery in 1988 as his career wound down. He researched steroids to see if they could help him get back on the field. "In the end, I decided not to do it, not for any high and mighty, moral reason," Garner said. "I didn't think it would be good health-wise later in life."

Garner—who managed the Milwaukee Brewers during the mid-1990s before guiding the Astros to a pennant in 2005—approached his conversation with Ken from a place of personal knowledge. "He was quite honest about what he was doing, and I was actually stunned," Garner said. "I told him on several occasions, 'This is the kind of stuff you need to not do. You don't wanna do this, Cammy, it's not good for your health.'"

"In the short-term, damn right it makes a difference. But in the long-term, this stuff kills you."

* * *

Ken's play during the second half of the 1995 season was hard to ignore. While Ken was generally a strong finisher, nothing could have predicted the half season he had at the plate. Across July, August, and September, Ken batted .316 with an OPS (on-base plus slugging percentage) of .947. Up to that season, his career stats in those categories were .260 and .705, respectively.

His numbers were punctuated with pop. Ken slammed nine home runs in September, three more dingers than in any other month of his career. The blasts came in bunches and from both sides of the plate. On September 16 against the Cubs, Caminiti, batting lefty, deposited a Steve Trachsel pitch over the fence in right-center field for a 2-0 first-inning lead, then went deep from the right side against Cubs reliever Larry Casian in the seventh. The following day, he hit two more jacks, one from the left side and one from the right, fueling a 12-4 Padres win.

On September 19, he achieved the feat again—taking the Rockies deep from the left and right sides. His second home run was a 379-foot smash to left field against Colorado's Bryan Hickerson, giving Ken a career-high 8 RBIs and extending San Diego's lead to 14-4. The crowd erupted as Caminiti rounded the bases to the beat of "The Hey Song," continuing to cheer until he took a curtain call.

Doo-doo-doooo . . . Hey!

With the home run against Hickerson, Caminiti became the first player in major league history to homer from both sides of the plate in the same game three times in a season. He accomplished the feat in four days.

Doo-doo-doooo . . . Heyy!

"I'm not trying to hit the balls out," Caminiti told reporters after the game. "I really can't explain what's happening. It's just a combination of things—being lucky, getting the pitch, having lefty after righty. The guys behind me are hitting well right now, too, so they're giving me pitches.

"I think when I try to hit a home run, they don't come. I'm just as relaxed as I can be up there."

Ken had spent the bulk of his career trying to catch up, attempting to overcompensate for his rugged lifestyle. Now, the game was slowing down. Pitches looked like beach balls. He was finally the team leader he wished he could have been during those dark seasons in Houston.

Doo-doo-doooo . . . Heyyy!

After the season was over, aided by the visibility that came from his strong year at the plate and Matt Williams's injury, Ken won his first Gold Glove. Never mind that he ranked dead last in advanced defensive stats among National League third basemen, or that he racked up twenty-seven errors. . . . He finally got the defensive award he should have won six years earlier. Steroids equaled power equaled stats equaled reward.

The steroids worked. He'd have to use more of them next season.

* * *

Ken was far from the only player juicing in 1995. *Los Angeles Times* sportswriter Bob Nightengale wrote an article about steroids that season in which Padres GM Randy Smith estimated that 10 to 20 percent of players were using steroids, and San Diego star right fielder Tony Gwynn bemoaned the uncertainty about who was and wasn't using. "It's like the big secret we're not supposed to talk about, but believe me, we wonder just like the rest of people. I'm standing out there in the outfield when a guy comes up, and I'm thinking, 'Hey, I wonder if this guy is on steroids,'" Gwynn told Nightengale.

"I think we all have our suspicions who's on the stuff, but unless someone comes out and admits to it, who'll ever know for sure?"

Bud Selig, then baseball's acting commissioner, suggested that a lack of evidence made it hard for Major League Baseball to crack down on steroids. "If baseball has a problem, I must say candidly that we were not aware of it," Selig told Nightengale. "It certainly hasn't been talked about much. But should we concern ourselves as an industry? I don't know. Maybe it's time to bring it up again."

Despite Selig's seeming naivete, performance-enhancing drugs, or PEDs, had been a part of professional baseball since at least the '80s—the 1880s, that is. It all started with juice from crushed dog and guinea pig testicles. James "Pud" Galvin, baseball's first three-hundred-game winner, received injections of a substance obtained from animal testicles, a process known as Brown-Séquard Elixir, in 1889. One day after receiving his injection, Galvin took the mound for the Pittsburgh Alleghenys and guided the team to a 9–0 win against the Boston Beaneaters. Instead of being vilified, Galvin was adored for taking such extreme measures.

"If there still be doubting Thomases who concede no virtue of the elixir, they are respectfully referred to Galvin's record in yesterday's Boston-Pittsburgh game. It is the best proof yet furnished of the value of the discovery," the *Washington Post* wrote in 1889.

The elixir, as it turns out, was literal and figurative junk science—it didn't work. Any supposed gains were likely the placebo effect. Galvin, baseball's first known PED user, entered the National Baseball Hall of Fame in 1965. His plaque hangs in Cooperstown next to the one honoring Red Sox slugger Ted Williams.

Players used various performance enhancers throughout the 1900s, mainly amphetamines known by an assortment of colorful names—pep pills, uppers, red juice, and greenies—pick-me-ups to endure the bumps and bruises and travel and pounding of playing 150-odd games across six months. Stimulants were everywhere in the game. Some teams supplied them to players. Hank Aaron, the longtime career home run leader, admitted to seeking a pharmaceutical boost during a slump in 1968. "I was so frustrated that at one point I tried using a pep pill—a greenie—that one of my teammates gave me," Aaron wrote in his autobiography, *I Had a Hammer*. "When that thing took hold, I thought I was having a heart attack. It was a stupid thing to do, and besides that, I shouldn't have been so concerned about my hitting in the first place."

Scientific possibilities exploded with the synthesis of anabolic-androgenic steroids during the 1930s (anabolic means "muscle building," while androgenic means "male"). The drugs offered the promise of increased masculinity and strength, youth and vigor, in pill or injectable form. Anabolics fulfilled the vision of the Brown-Séquard Elixir—rejuvenation through what the mad scientist called the "spermatic glands"—without the messiness of crushed animal testicles.

Steroids were soon being used for athletic purposes by Russian weight lifters and Chinese swimmers and East German track-and-field athletes . . . track-and-field athletes from around the world, actually, side effects be damned.

The International Olympic Committee banned steroids in 1975 and began drug testing athletes. "Ever since Eve gave Adam the apple to improve his performance, people have been searching for other ways to improve their performances," Dr. Daniel Hanley, a U.S. member of the IOC's Doping Commission, said in 1976.

By the late 1960s and early 1970s, anabolics had made their way to baseball, with a handful of users estimated on each team. The game was reluctant to embrace muscle and weight lifting. Muscle-bound players were thought to break down easier and be less nimble. And some of the game's greatest home run hitters, such as Hank Aaron and Willie Mays, were lithe and lean.

By the 1980s, the underground steroid culture full of pills and needles and powders trickled further and further into baseball. One of baseball's earlier admitted users of anabolic steroids, outfielder Glenn Wilson, said he acquired drugs from a friend during the 1984 off-season and spent that winter lifting heavily. The drugs appear to have worked for Wilson—he put up his best offensive numbers the season after using steroids, stroking 24 home runs and driving in 99 runs, and made his only All-Star team. Wilson said that beyond the physical boost, steroids gave him newfound confidence in the batter's box.

"Before steroids and I face Nolan Ryan, I'm shaking in my shoes. After taking steroids, facing Nolan Ryan is like facing my son throwing batting practice," Wilson said.

One team, the Oakland Athletics led by sluggers Mark McGwire and José Canseco, became the face . . . er, biceps of baseball's changing physique. Canseco, a tan, handsome native of Cuba, enjoyed supermodels, Ferraris, and turning on fastballs. He became, in 1988, the first player to hit forty home runs and steal forty bases in a season.

McGwire—the bashful, soft-spoken All-American USC first baseman who largely let his bat do the talking—had played with Caminiti in 1984 on Team USA ahead of the Olympics. Since that time, he'd continued to mash, filling out his six-foot, five-inch frame and setting a rookie record with forty-nine home runs in 1987. The teammates, nicknamed the "Bash Brothers," pounded their forearms together after home runs, a ritualistic display of masculinity. They were exciting and fun, Adonises in green stirrups.

They were also juicing, and it wasn't a well-kept secret, especially where Canseco was concerned. As the 1988 season wound down, the *Washington Post* columnist Tom Boswell, appearing on the CBS program *Newswatch*, called

Canseco "the most conspicuous example of a player who has made himself great with steroids."

When Red Sox fans taunted Canseco, chanting *Ster-oids! Ster-oids!*, he smirked and flexed his biceps to the crowd.

The month after Canseco's playful muscle flex, Congress passed the Anti-Drug Abuse Act of 1988, the first significant federal regulation of steroids. Two years later, the Anabolic Steroid Enforcement Act of 1990 made some anabolic steroids Schedule III controlled substances, denoting certain health benefits and less potential for abuse than street drugs such as cocaine but the potential for physical and psychological dependence.

The laws sent anabolics further onto the black market—meaning they were frequently being produced in unsanitary facilities or shipped from overseas. Steroids bought on the black market might be counterfeit, lacking the steroid listed on the label. Some don't have an active ingredient. Others are low-grade or contaminated.

* * *

Major League Baseball finally did *something* about steroids in 1991: It added the drugs to its banned substance list. Commissioner Fay Vincent wrote a memo that mentioned steroids: "Illegal drug use can cause injuries on the field, diminished job performance and alienation of those on whom the game's success depends—baseball fans. Baseball players and personnel cannot be permitted to give even the slightest suggestion that illegal drug use is either acceptable or safe. It is the responsibility of all Baseball players and personnel to see that the use of illegal drugs does not occur, or if it does to put a stop to it by the most effective means possible."

Players who wanted MLB's crackdown on steroids ended there. There was no testing, penalties, or rehabilitation for players who used them. Drug testing would need to be approved by the players' union. MLB's memo amounted to self-righteous finger-wagging—a bunch of toothless, empty words.

By that point, federal investigators were cracking down on a steroid distribution ring that ensnared several players, including the "Bash Brothers." But because the players were buyers and not suppliers, the FBI didn't expose them, deciding instead to alert Major League Baseball.

MLB, when confronted with information about their players using steroids, did nothing. Steroid testing was briefly considered by the owners but not pursued—as MLB and the Major League Baseball Players Association negotiated before the 1994 player strike.

"We tried to warn 'em," said retired FBI agent Greg Stejskal, the lead investigator of the steroid probe called "Operation Equine." Stejskal alerted a senior MLB official in August 1994 about PED use in baseball. The response: "We kind of know about it, but there's not really much we can do because the players won't let us test," Stejskal said.

Major League Baseball gave players who used steroids no reason to stop. Some players began taking supplements such as creatine, an enzyme found in red meat and seafood that produced results similar to those of anabolics. The supplement was all the rage during the 1990s, muddying the line between legal and illegal, and offering the perfect cover as players used steroids to grow bigger and bigger.

Players who wanted to get the *good* stuff, to stay safe from the wave of counterfeit or fake drugs and avoid raising any alarms, needed someone they could trust and someone who understood the science behind steroids.

Someone who was quiet and dependable and who wasn't interested in the spotlight.

Someone like Dave Moretti.

* * *

Clop, clop, clop.

Brrr . . . Brrrr . . . Brrrrrr . . .

Mmmmmmmm! Mmmmmmmm! Mmmmmmmm! Mmmmmmmmmmm! Mmmmmmmmmmm!

The MRI machine hummed and purred, a chorus of beeps and jackhammers and power drills.

Arizona, the spring of 1996, and Ken's shoulder was acting up again.

The shoulder had been acting up since his high school football days, and then his 1984 season at San Jose State University, when he separated it trying to run through UC Berkeley catcher Bob Liebzeit, and it continued to bother him throughout his pro career, including in 1992 when he separated it again.

Pitchers sometimes paused on the mound so Ken, stationed at third base, could readjust his shoulder joint.

Ken hit the weight room hard following the 1995 season, working to gain more muscle. But he ended up doing direct shoulder lifts and damaged the weakened shoulder, Moretti said.

Ken tried to grit it out in spring training, but something wasn't right, so he got the MRI. A slight tear was found on his rotator cuff, the tendons and muscles surrounding the shoulder joint. He was told he could keep playing, but any further damage could end his season.

It took four regular season games for him to sustain further damage.

He was playing in Houston, his old stomping grounds. April 6, sixth inning, bases full of Astros, and left fielder Derrick May batting against Padres pitcher Scott Sanders. May hit a flare to the edge of the infield, and Caminiti, backpedaling, jumped and whirled to his left, extending his arm perpendicular to the ground and somehow gloving the ball before landing in a crumpled heap on his injured shoulder.

Cammy had the wherewithal to throw out the lead runner, Brian Hunter, at the plate. But instantaneously, he felt a "sharp, sharp pain." The shoulder got hot and eventually went numb. He played through the numbness, and in the thirteenth inning, with the score knotted, Caminiti came to bat with the bases loaded and hit a grand slam to lead the Padres to an 8–4 win—the third grand salami of his career.

The slight tear was now a full-blown rupture, leaving Ken's season in doubt.

"He was playing without a supraspinatus muscle in his shoulder," Padres strength and conditioning coach Dean Armitage said. "That meant he couldn't initiate his arm and lift his catching arm unless he swung his arm up or pushed it up with his other hand." The shoulder was injured again on April 20 against the Braves, when he tried, futilely, to snare a double down the line by Atlanta second baseman Rafael Belliard, and later as he slid headfirst trying to steal second base. He extended both arms during the headfirst slide, but as he popped up from the bag, Caminiti held his left arm tight and steady against his chest as if it were in an invisible sling. "It kind of takes a little fun out of the game when you've got to play with this kind of crap," he said after reinjuring his shoulder. "The game is still a lot of fun, but I just wish everything was all right."

Ken received a cortisone shot on May 1. By that point, the rupture wasn't expected to worsen, and the pain would eventually dull.

The Padres staff—namely Armitage and trainers Larry Duensing and Todd Hutchinson—worked on Ken's shoulder, focusing on maintaining his range of motion. Armitage relied on a stretching technique known as proprioceptive neuromuscular facilitation, or PNF, "to strengthen his muscles higher up and down low. So you were working the muscles all around that. We're working on the other rotator cuff muscles. I mean, that was going to be a deficit all year."

But there was another way he could build muscle strength, too.

* * *

Before Dave Moretti started his friend on a steroid regimen in 1996, he said he had Ken consult with two people: Ken's wife and a doctor. Nancy would have to know about this, especially if Ken experienced any side effects such as "roid rage," nosebleeds, sexual dysfunction, or back acne.

"I'm not going to have you lying to your wife after the struggles you've had," Moretti said he told Caminiti.

"He talked to Nancy about it. She was concerned about it. She was concerned about him cheating, some of the moral aspects of it, and she was concerned about his safety. She asked me about it, and I told her, 'My suggestion is you guys should see a doctor and get his advice on it.'"

Nancy initially said she would support the plan if the doctor signed off, Moretti said. But after the doctor gave the go-ahead, she backtracked. She was a nurse, and someone who stuck to the rules. She couldn't go along with this.

This was wrong to her.

The disagreement created further friction for the couple. After weathering Ken's addictions and indiscretions, Nancy and Ken found themselves moving in different directions. Nancy was with the girls in Texas, a de facto single parent while Ken was playing ball in California, or at this charity event, or that autograph show. . . .

Despite Nancy's objections, Ken and Dave ended up moving forward with a PED regimen following a phone call.

"I'm going to retire," Caminiti said.

"What do you mean, you're going to retire?" Moretti responded.

"I just can't play like this. I'm not helping my team. I'll retire and have the surgery, get back healthy, and I'll sign on."

"Ken, you can't do that. You have two daughters."

"I'm not gonna sit on the bench and watch my teammates play. I'm not gonna watch them go through the everyday grind of the season while I'm sitting there getting paid millions to watch them play baseball. . . . I'm not going to do it."

Moretti feared that a long layoff, coupled with feelings of helplessness and doubt, could prove disastrous for Ken and cause him to backslide on his sobriety. So he devised a three-pronged drug regimen to keep Ken on the field: testosterone to maintain muscle; nandrolone, also known as Deca-Durabolin, to help calm the joints and tendinitis issues ("WD-40 for the joints," Moretti calls it); and human growth hormone, or HGH, a hormone produced by the pituitary gland, to build strength around the damaged shoulder.

Moretti was familiar with the first two from his years of bodybuilding. He had firsthand knowledge of how well they worked. HGH, meanwhile, wasn't cheap or readily available—a cycle came with a $7,500 price tag. Moretti obtained it through a doctor friend in northern California.

The drugs worked well enough to keep Caminiti in the lineup with his torn rotator cuff.

"That combination of things kept him strong enough, and kept the shoulder from not getting worse, and it actually started to regenerate tissues in there," Moretti said.

With the new drug regimen, Ken couldn't hide his steroid use. HGH needs to be refrigerated after opening, so Ken was known to use a mini fridge on road trips. Anyone who peeked into his fridge would learn the truth.

* * *

And then there was that one game. . . .

Caminiti had given himself a shot in the leg following Moretti's guidance, and the area where he administered the shot bruised. Moretti was watching the Padres on TV, and Ken was at second base rubbing his bruised leg.

"During the game, I called him. 'Please call me when you get this message,'" Moretti said.

After the game, Ken called his friend back.

"You were just televising to the whole nation that you're taking steroids," Moretti told him.

"What do you mean?"

"You're out at second base rubbing your leg!"

"Well, it was bothering me."

"Anyone who has taken a shot in the leg knows what you were doing. Do you realize that?"

"OK. . . . Well, it bruised up on me."

Caminiti lied about the bruise to the team's training staff, saying he was playing with his daughters and tripped and hit his leg on the corner of a coffee table.

Sure. . . .

Moretti considered pulling Ken off injectables and tried to make sense of what went wrong.

"Did you reuse a needle?" he asked.

"I don't think I did."

"Are you making sure the old and new needles are separated?"

"I don't know. . . . I think it was when I was on the road."

"OK, let's go over this again." Moretti walked his buddy through the steps one more time: *Find your hip bone, walk your fingers down, find the area where you would hit the muscle properly without having issues. . . .*

CHAPTER 18

LEGEND

The ball screamed down the line like a tired toddler: *waaaaaaaaaaaaaaaaaaaa!*

Ken would normally dive with his arm fully extended like Superman in flight. But with his bum shoulder, he had to improvise. He dove to his right with his glove curved toward the ground. Even mid-dive with his bad shoulder, he somehow had the glove in just the right spot to snare the ball, then tucked his arm toward his body in an upside-down U.

But now what?

Given his clunky dive, Ken collapsed over himself as his momentum carried him toward foul territory, his legs coming up above his chest. He had to get the throw off. But standing up would take too long, so he rolled into a sitting position with his butt smack-dab in the center of the foul line. He lunged and, with his body drifting into foul territory, fired a strike across the diamond some 130-plus feet away, beating the Marlins runner, Greg Colbrunn, by three steps.

It was the best play of a career filled with them. And maybe the most improbable. This was a few weeks after he damaged his shoulder, and two days after he reinjured it. Two days! He made the play on April 22, 1996, not even knowing how his shoulder would hold up. With the injury so fresh, he was still adjusting to playing with it and finding angles at which he could safely dive.

The physicality . . . the knowledge of one's own body . . . the ability to adjust due to an injury . . . the improvisation . . .

This play was infield artistry.

After making his career-defining play, Caminiti—unable to properly lift his left arm—grasped his hat with his right paw and slipped it back on his head, put his head down, and jogged off the field. Inning over.

"Ooh, that was pretty good," he said after seeing video of his play following the game.

"I knew I did something good but I didn't know how good," he said later. It was good, all right. Pretty soon, the Padres had children doing their best Ken Caminiti impressions by sitting at third base and making their hardest throw from their butt as he stood watch, giving them high fives.

* * *

The Padres over the off-season tinkered and tooled, getting under the hood and further rebuilding the team.

Gone was Randy Smith, the GM who acquired Caminiti and Hoffman and Finley and Ashby—Smith could no longer work with cunning, callous president and CEO Larry Lucchino. "It was just a difficult working relationship," Smith said. "It's up to ownership to determine the path they want to go down. But I think the baseball decisions primarily should be made by the baseball people."

Lucchino got things built like Oriole Park at Camden Yards, and by golly, he was going to build a winner with the Padres, and while he was at it, get a new ballpark approved because this multipurpose stadium, whether you wanted to call it Jack Murphy Stadium or Qualcomm Stadium or the Q, wasn't going to cut it for the Padres in the long term. The leftover staffers from the previous administration were sent packing, one after another.

Smith was replaced by Kevin Towers—a former Padres pitching prospect who had teamed with Bochy at Triple-A, and who'd been involved in scouting. If Lucchino was a guy people were liable to dislike, Towers, or KT, was the exact opposite, the kind of guy everyone liked, a proud man who believed in his decisions with conviction, thus his eventual nickname: "Gunslinger." The kind of gambler who'd hit, and hit, and hit. Sometimes he busted out. But with Kevin Towers, things were always interesting. For Towers, loyalty was a form of currency, and for a lot of reasons, the GM and the third baseman forged a close bond, just as the third baseman had done with the manager and owner.

"In all my years in the game, nobody played the game harder than this guy," Towers said in a February 2015 interview. "Nobody cared about team and teammates more than he did."

Following its turnaround season, San Diego wanted to make a big splash. After Ken's contract was agreed to in principle with a handshake before being finalized in November 1995—three years, $9.5 million—he spent the off-season trying to woo his buddy Craig Biggio to join the Padres. He almost succeeded, but Biggio ended up re-signing with Houston. Instead of making one big splash, the Padres made a bunch of little splashes, signing center fielder Rickey Henderson and infielder Craig Shipley and pitcher Bob Tewksbury, and trading Bip Roberts to Kansas City for first baseman Wally Joyner, a steady, sturdy clubhouse jokester who happened to be Towers's college roommate and a great defensive first baseman. Tim Flannery, a scrappy Padres player from the 1980s, became the team's third base coach and saw in Ken a kindred spirit, recognizing an emotional depth in Ken that was easy to overlook. Flannery played rock and folk music when he wasn't in a baseball uniform.

The Padres brought on other guys that spring training, bit players who became close with Ken, too. Rob Deer was an all-or-nothing—often nothing—free swinger, leading the American League in strikeouts four times during the late 1980s and early 1990s. But when he connected, the ball went a long way.

Before one spring training game against the Giants, Deer connected a shaving cream pie with Ken's face, a prank that quickly went haywire—he thought it was whipped cream. "It was a foot and a half thick of just shaving cream," Deer said. "Nobody would do it, but they knew I would get him, because we had that kind of relationship." Deer stalked his prey. Ken was standing near the dugout doing an interview. "I smoked him right in the eye," he said.

Ken laughed it off, and they got a towel to clean him up. But about twenty minutes before game time, Deer still didn't see Ken. "It worried me," Deer said. "So I go in there, and he's lying on the trainer's table, and there's three trainers and two doctors above him, and they've got this wash. . . . They've got his eyes open, and they're pouring this stuff in his eyes. And he's just in pain. It looks like someone poured acid in his eyes. I felt terrible."

The game started, and Ken didn't really have a chance to warm up, and he wore bullpen coach Brady Little's number 22 jersey as they cleaned his number

21, and he was wincing and squinting—but still smashing the ball anyway. He hit a home run that game. Ken's teammates ragged on him, calling him "one eye" for a week afterward, but it came out of admiration and reverence. If he could play through a shaving cream pie to the face, what else could he play through?

Deer and Ken discussed the inevitability of their careers winding down.

"I'd like to be able to put in twelve years and hang it up," Ken said.

"You say that now, but just wait," Deer said. "They'll have to rip this uniform off of me."

Deer and Ken, along with pitcher Richie Lewis—a phenom at Florida State who roomed with multisport star Deion Sanders, and later bounced around the majors—all adrenaline junkies, made a loud entrance to spring training by riding their motorcycles into the clubhouse.

"We decided we're going to ride our Harleys in," Lewis said. "When you pull in, everything is concrete. You could drop a pin and it breaks glass, it's that loud. Of course, Cammy isn't scared of nothing, and Rob Deer joined us, so all three of us, we just pulled in like a four-foot-wide entrance to the clubhouse, and Bochy's office is the first door on the right, and we just rode our bikes in there."

* * *

Ken's injuries were piling up early in the 1996 season.

On April 12, the week after damaging his shoulder the first time, he left a game against Atlanta in the second inning with a strain to his right hamstring while running the bases.

During an April 16 game against the Rockies, Ken tried to catch a blooper by Larry Walker and injured his hip. "I wish it was my shoulder, because that already hurts," Ken said after the game. "I've got so much to deal with now."

Ken was somehow playing through his injuries. At the end of April, he was hitting .343 and the Padres were 17–10. But other injuries popped up. . . . He missed one game in early May after getting a cortisone shot, then missed three due to an abdominal strain (he had to nag his way into the lineup) before missing three more. The abdominal/groin issue, a strain of his inguinal ligament, left him doubling over in pain.

"I don't think I can change my style of play. I don't want to change. I feel like I'd be hurting the team if I did," Ken said.

On May 19, Ken reaggravated his ab/groin strain. He only played four innings. And then he didn't play for a while. The DL was a possibility.

Ken pleaded to stay on the active roster. *The trainers and doctors don't know my body like I do.*

The team wanted a backup plan in case Caminiti was unable to play—the DL assignment could be retroactively set. He could sit and rest for another week, and heal up, and be ready to play again.

That insurance option was veteran infielder Mike Sharperson, best known for playing with the Dodgers. He was on that 1988 team that won the World Series. Sharperson, a respected pro, was making the most of his stint at Triple-A Las Vegas, hitting .304 and serving as a mentor for teammates like Padres prospect Homer Bush.

"He taught me how to understand what realistic success looked like," Bush said of Sharperson.

After Bush broke his leg and was placed on the sixty-day disabled list, the Padres kept the spot on the forty-man roster open for Sharperson. If Ken couldn't play, Mike Sharperson was the perfect person to fill in. Later that week, as Caminiti remained out of the lineup, a team rep told Sharperson to fly to Montreal to meet up with the team, just in case.

Mike Sharperson had gotten the call—again.

He prepared to fly out on May 25. But he never made it. Early that morning, Sharperson was driving on a highway when he missed a turn and ended up losing control of his vehicle, which flipped. Sharperson, who was not wearing a seat belt, was ejected, and he later died during surgery. He was thirty-four years old.

Sharperson's death sent the Padres spiraling. The team went 6–18 soon after his death, going from first place with a five-game lead to as low as fourth place in the NL West. Caminiti's gutsy but ineffective play didn't help. With his potential fill-in dead, Ken's calls to keep playing won out over the team's suggestion of the DL.

But despite Ken staying in the lineup, his productivity spiraled. From June 12 to June 22—a span of eleven games—he went 3-for-43, a robust .070 batting average and OPS of .270, with no home runs or runs batted in. During that stretch, his batting average dropped from .314 to .268.

Through the season's first seventy-five games, he had only eight home runs.

Ken was far from the only injured Padres player that season. Tony Gwynn was battling a frayed Achilles tendon, Wally Joyner broke his thumb, Andy Ashby endured shoulder problems. . . . No one had the range of injuries that Ken did. And yet he kept on begging and pleading his way into the lineup. He kept playing through every type of pain.

Statistically speaking, the low point of the season for Ken came on June 22 against the Cubs. The teams both jumped out of the gate early, scoring four runs in the first three innings. The game stayed 4–4 for nine more innings, until the twelfth, when Chicago scratched across a run on a Ryne Sandberg single to take the lead. With two outs in the bottom half of the inning, Padres catcher John Flaherty slammed a home run to deep left field off Turk Wendell to tie the game again. On to the thirteenth. And fourteenth. And fifteenth. In the fifteenth inning, both teams again traded runs.

In the sixteenth inning, Chicago scored three times, the output punctuated by a two-run bomb by Brant Brown. San Diego faced its final chance. Steve Finley opened with a walk and stole second. Up came Caminiti, who struck out against Rodney Myers, pitching in his twenty-second career game. Ken finished the game 0-for-7.

After one strikeout during the putrid series against Chicago, he bit on his bat as he walked back to the dugout. Dave Moretti recalled Chicago broadcaster Steve Stone ripped into Caminiti during one of his hitless games against the Cubs, stating on the air that Ken should change his approach at the plate if he wanted to stay in the league. Moretti was listening and told his friend about the insult.

"Ken was not too happy when I told him of that," Moretti recalled. "But as a good friend can do, I knew how to get him angry in the right way."

Ken had a chip on his injured shoulder. And he would soon start hitting. The home runs began coming again on June 26 and 27, and the Padres swept the Giants to move back into first. . . . San Diego would spend the rest of the season oscillating between first and second place, never staying long in either spot. More telling than the home runs were the walks. Ken collected eight over a four-game stretch in early July, a hint that he was staying patient at the plate. Pitchers usually exploited his aggressiveness, getting him off-balance by chasing bad pitches. Ken felt like he was letting his team down by taking free passes—he grabbed his lumber to hit the ball, not to jog to first—but patience meant pitchers would have to throw him better pitches. He wasn't going to swing at junk. They'd have to do better.

With Ken's bat coming around, and after the Giants' Matt Williams was hit by a pitch, Caminiti was named to the All-Star team, a last-second addition. "I kind of feel undeserving," he told the *North County Times*. "Someone had to get hurt before I was picked." Ken still believed Williams was the game's "premier third baseman. . . . if I can keep up with him, I'm doing pretty good."

Ken asked his manager whether he should attend the game, but Bochy said sure, why not, so instead of resting, Ken packed his bag and headed for Philadelphia, becoming a second-time All-Star. Lots of players make the All-Star Game a first time, but if you make two of them, no matter if Matt Williams got hit on the wrist or not, it wasn't a mistake or a fluke.

And Ken proved that when he came to the plate in the sixth inning against Texas Rangers pitcher Roger Pavlik. Hitting lefty, Ken paused with his hands near his body, scrunched in as though he were jacketless and huddling for warmth in the cold. He prepared himself as the pitch came and uncorked, driving the barrel through the ball. *Crack!* The ball exploded off his bat, a mammoth blast that bounced off the upper deck facade in right field. Pavlik shook his head as Ken scampered around the bases. The National League won. Game MVP honors went to Dodgers catcher Mike Piazza, a Pennsylvania native. Piazza and Caminiti would spend the rest of the season trying to one-up each other.

After one of the All-Star Game workouts, Ken got on the bus to go back to the hotel, where he met Greg Vaughn, the Brewers' slugging outfielder.

"We really didn't know each other at that time," said Vaughn, who'd spent his career playing in the American League. Interleague play would begin the following season, so at that time, other than spring training, the All-Star Game, and World Series, American and National League players didn't cross paths unless they changed teams. "We started talking, and we just sort of hit it off. 'I love the way you play.' 'I love the way you play—you play the right way.' We were sort of like fans of each other."

* * *

The Padres opened the second half at Colorado, and a clubhouse issue bubbled into view. Pitcher Tim Worrell was miffed to get bumped to the bullpen, and instead of talking to his manager about it, he decided to talk to the media.

"It's a bunch of manure," he said. "I didn't pitch myself out of the rotation, I got taken out."

Worrell suggested that Bochy may have been motivated to make the move because Worrell was arbitration-eligible. Bochy was pissed.

Worrell arrived to the ballpark the next day to find the contents of his locker dumped on the ground in the manager's office, courtesy of Caminiti. "I've been reading about what you want to do. I guess you're the manager now," Ken told him. "So I figured if you're the manager now, you might as well dress in the manager's office." Worrell, sheepish, didn't have much else to say.

Another time that season, Padres broadcaster Ted Leitner remembers, Rickey Henderson—*the baseball immortal Rickey Henderson*—failed to slide into home plate and got tagged out. "And by the time he gets to the dugout, Ken's in his face," Leitner said. "I asked him later, 'What did you say to him?' And he said, 'That better never happen again,' and Rickey said, 'OK, Cammy, we're good. We're good.'"

If Ken wasn't the teammate that he could have been during his Astros years, he was going to be the perfect teammate now, someone who spent his waking breaths helping his fellow players wring out every ounce of effort and demand more of themselves. He usually didn't have to say much, only give you a stare. That's all it took.

Every Padres player, whether you were a baseball legend or bullpen arm, was on notice: Ken Caminiti was watching to make sure you weren't dogging it or messing with this team.

"He was a joy to watch play, and probably one of my favorites because of the type of person that he was, the type of guy that Boch and I could always lean on. You didn't have to worry about policing the clubhouse because you had him in there. He was gonna make sure that things are done the right way," Towers said.

Ken's agent Tom Reich—someone who was never afraid to use four-letter words or fists to settle an argument—said it best: "Caminiti was the nuts and testicles of this team."

Through July 31, Ken was batting .308 with 17 home runs—a solid stat line, given his injured rotator cuff, but nothing atypical. That day, the Gunslinger made a trade for Ken's friend from the All-Star Game, Vaughn, who became the team's new cleanup hitter. Vaughn also soon became Ken's roommate in San Diego.

"I was staying in La Jolla at the Hyatt, I had the penthouse, but I was always meeting him for lunch. His family was out of town, so we would always meet for lunch and then after games, 'OK, let's grab a bite to eat,' and then all of a sudden he's like, 'Why do we keep doing this? Why don't you just move in with me?'" Vaughn said. "That's how it evolved, and we just became like besties, as they put it."

While Vaughn struggled at the plate after his trade, his presence meant Ken would get pitches to hit. Ken, with added protection in the lineup, went on a prolific tear.

It's easy, now, to look back and credit Ken's success to S-T-E-R-O-I-D-S, as though pills and needles alone made him great in 1996. Steroids certainly helped him finish a season strong, a boost during the long season.

You ask Ken's Padres comrades, and they offer a range of perspectives on whether they knew he was using steroids. Ken wasn't really *hiding* anything.

"He'd say, 'Don't worry about my swing, it'll be all right Friday.' And sure as shoot, man, Friday he'd have some stuff in his locker, boxes of stuff, and boy, he'd start swinging that bat again," hitting coach Merv Rettenmund said. "If they're just in boxes in his locker, everyone else knew it, too."

Bochy said that at the time, he wasn't aware of Ken's use of steroids.

"He was doing what he thought was the best thing for himself to become the best player that he could be. He was relentless with his workouts. And back then, the radar for steroids was not up, and these guys, they were just so into weight lifting and getting stronger," Bochy said.

But Ken's success resulted from other factors than just steroids. For one, he had the potential, under the right circumstances, to carry a team—just consider his 1986 season in Double-A, when he batted .346 over the last two months of the season, with 9 home runs (compared to 3 in his first 76 games) and 41 RBIs.

By the time August rolled around, Ken was getting more comfortable playing with the torn rotator cuff. The injury meant Ken couldn't overswing with the top half of his body, a tendency when he got overaggressive at the plate. He'd swing violently when leading with his upper body, tying himself in knots. With the torn rotator cuff, he couldn't generate the power to overswing. The injury required him to rely on his hips, his true power center, to drive through the ball.

Crediting steroids alone, as though they help some middling underperformer become *Ken Caminiti*, discredits the other things Ken had in his corner in 1996. Sobriety meant he wasn't running hard at night. He was allowing his body to rest. He had a manager in Bruce Bochy who believed in him and wasn't cursing him out and throwing gear from the dugout, and a first baseman in Wally Joyner with a suction cup glove who could handle his throws, and teammates who supported him, and a team that was in the race, and a city that adored him, and he wasn't the subject of any trade rumors, and he felt wanted and secure in a way he never did while playing for the Astros.

Beyond those things, Christianity helped keep him centered. Ken pursued Christianity during the first few years of his major league career, a way to "make the Christian guys on the team look at me a little different because I was running hard, going out after games, and stuff like that," he told journalist Jane Mitchell of Channel 4 San Diego for her in-depth profile series *One on One* in 1997.

"It wasn't until 1993 when I actually got down on my knees and said the prayers, and watched the little things happen through my prayers, that I really started noticing the difference and seeing how He works. That was my big deal [in 1996], and I tell a lot of people, the way I went about my job was, before every anthem or during the anthem I was on my knees and telling Him to look after my family, and I was going to play as hard as I was going to play, and whatever happens happens. And I'm going to hang my hat up and know in my heart that I did my best. And that's all I could have asked for myself."

* * *

The Padres had to get creative because of politics.

Just like four years earlier, the Republican National Convention in 1996 was sending Ken's team on the road. Bob Dole and Jack Kemp were coming to San Diego. While the RNC ended up not using Jack Murphy Stadium, the NFL's Chargers needed the stadium for a preseason game. Instead of scheduling a doubleheader, team president and CEO Larry Lucchino thought outside the box and looked outside the country.

"We've got the ocean on one side, the desert on the other side, Anaheim to the north, and the Mexican border to the south, and Larry thought, correctly, we should embrace Mexico to a much larger degree," said longtime Padres employee Andy Strasberg.

So it was decided that San Diego would play three games against the Mets in Monterrey. La Primera Serie was the first MLB regular season series played

outside the continental United States and Canada. The players used special
balls with green and red stitches for the series. They'd be playing at Estadio de
Beisbol Monterrey, which opened in 1990 and seated more than twenty-one
thousand fans.

Ahead of the trip, the Padres gave players a list of tips:

Avoid drinking water straight from the tap, due to the microbes—they
could make you sick.

Avoid swallowing water when you take a shower.

Avoid eating food washed in the local water, like salads.

"They had a list of things you could eat and couldn't eat, and they gave us
pills to take every day. One of the things on the list was don't eat any vegetation
that grows in the ground," Ken said. The salad lover forgot to pay attention to
the tip.

The series began August 16 with the Padres tied for first place. Fernando
Valenzuela—the Mexico native who took baseball by storm in 1981—was on
his last legs with San Diego, and he got the ball in the first game, the native
son returning to his homeland. When the team's bus arrived at the hotel in
Monterrey, about fifty fans were waiting. The Padres stars started coming
off—Gwynn, Caminiti, Finley, Hoffman—"and nobody's paying attention
to them," said sports radio host Jeff Dotseth. "All of a sudden, Fernando
Valenzuela starts coming off the bus, and you start hearing the crowd going,
Toro, Toro (El Toro, "the bull," was his nickname), and you look at the smiles on
the faces of Caminiti and Finley, all these guys realize this was for Fernando,
and they pick up the chant, so here are all of Fernando's teammates, *Toro!
Toro! Toro!*"

Valenzuela pitched into the seventh inning and got a standing ovation
when he left the game on his way for the win.

Ken came up in the fifth inning against Mets pitcher Robert Person, and
National League president Leonard Coleman was in the broadcast booth. Person,
tiring, tried to sneak a pitch down and in against Caminiti, who mashed the
ball to the back of the right field bleachers and almost clear out of the stadium.

Broadcaster Gary Thorne asked Coleman about the league-wide power
spike moments after Ken's blast. "You liking the offense?"

"I think the offense is good for the fans," Coleman responded. "Obviously,
with so many guys having such great years, I think it provides a lot of excitement,

and the game is for the fans and fan reaction to it has been very good, so once again, we're pleased with that."

Here was the president of the National League, moments after a steroid-fueled player obliterated a baseball, talking about how much fans enjoy the power and how the league was "pleased with that." The connection couldn't have been more obvious. Baseball, the monolithic Major League Baseball, the power brokers of the league, weren't going to wonder too hard about where the power was coming from, even if it was because the players were doing something they shouldn't. The fans liked it. And fans equaled money. And money was good, especially after the 1994 strike washed out the World Series and corroded fan support.

For Game 2 of the series, played the following night, Ken went 2-for-4 with a walk as the Padres lost 7–3. Back at his hotel room following the game, he started to feel sick. At first, he didn't know what was wrong. His stomach was doing somersaults. His forearms, calves, and hamstrings cramped.

As it turns out, Ken had eaten salad, failing to follow the food instructions the team had given to each player before the trip. And now he was paying the price. Food poisoning—Montezuma's revenge. After a sleepless night, much of it spent in the bathroom, Ken was back at the ballpark white as a sheet and badly dehydrated. Bochy was in his office when the team's assistant trainer, Todd Hutchinson, and team doctor Jan Fronek put Ken on an adjacent table, using a coat hanger for a makeshift IV.

"He can't play," Hutchinson told Bochy.

After one bag of solution, Caminiti "started focusing a little better." So they gave him another bag. All the while, Bochy saw no way he was going to submit a lineup card with Caminiti's name on it.

As game time approached, Bochy prepared to walk with his lineup card to home plate. He still didn't see how his third baseman was going to be ready for game time.

"I'm going down, Kenny, maybe we can use you later in the game," Bochy told him.

"Hold on," Caminiti responded, following his manager.

"Cammy, just stay there," Bochy told him.

"Hey, I'm good. I'm good."

"Cammy, I can't put you in there."

"Look at me, I'm telling you—I feel great. I just needed some IV."

Bochy paused.

"Sure enough, he talked me into it," Bochy said.

The team planned to keep a close eye on Caminiti. He slipped on his uniform just before 4:05, game time. He stepped onto the field and ran two sprints.

The sun was beating down, and Hutcheson was putting eye black "stickers" on Finley's cheeks. Caminiti yelled to "Hutch" for a Snickers, the gooey chocolate bar featuring peanuts, caramel, and nougat. But given the noise from the cheering fans, Hutcheson misheard Ken and brought Caminiti a batch of the eye black stickers.

"Not stickers. I said Snickers," Caminiti told Hutcheson. Ken quickly got his candy bar and scarfed it down.

Leading off in the second, Ken stood outside the left-handed batter's box, his helmet bill pulled nearly over his eyes. He inhaled and exhaled, his breathing labored.

He grimaced as he stepped into the box and set his bat.

Paul Wilson delivered, and Caminiti swung through the first pitch, late. Strike one.

A short walk and a deep exhale and Caminiti was back for the second pitch, a ball outside. One and one.

He leaned his bat against his leg and adjusted his batting gloves, barely stepping out of the batter's box—why expel any extra energy? The next pitch was another ball. Two and one.

Ken wiped his nose, spit, and dug in.

This was going to be the pitch.

Wilson threw over the plate, and Caminiti pounced—a laser beam. The ball climbed over the infield and kept carrying, settling into the left-center stands. Caminiti, half an hour after being strapped to an IV, had just hit a home run. He took a slow trot around the base paths. He wasn't showing up Wilson—he simply couldn't run any faster due to his weakened state. He stopped running before reaching home plate and walked across, taking the thirty-odd paces from home plate to the dugout with his hand on his left hip.

There, Bochy and his Padres teammates smiled and laughed. Some IV fluid and a Snickers bar, and Ken went from death personified to hitting a home run.

He came up again in the bottom of the third with two runners on. Wilson delivered a fastball on the outside corner for strike one.

The second pitch was a ball outside.

The sweat dripped off Wilson's nose. Caminiti had been battling sickness and dehydration, but now Wilson's stomach was in knots.

Wilson threw the ball down and in, and this time Ken smashed it to right-center . . . get up, get up, get up, and it was gone, to give the Padres a 4–0 lead.

As Ken rounded third, he stuck out his tongue at coach Tim Flannery, their usual routine, but this time he wasn't playing—he was gassed.

The crowd celebrated Ken's accomplishments with noisemakers and "the wave."

He came up once more in the fifth. During the at bat, Thorne discussed the IV solution Ken had received before the game.

"Is that legal?" broadcaster Ralph Kiner asked.

"It's medically appropriate," Thorne responded, laughing.

"'Cause I'll start taking it if it's all right," Kiner said.

"Just a little solution to fight off the dehydration. Lotta water. Probably some sugar."

Ken, wincing and squinting in the batter's box, worked the count to 3-and-2 before striking out. He swung and missed, and the momentum carried him three steps outside the batter's box—he had to pause to steady himself from falling over. Another long, cautious walk to the dugout, and Caminiti's day was over, the legend forever forged.

He received another liter of IV fluid after playing and signed autographs for an hour.

"I don't know what happened," he said after the game. "Actually, I didn't think I touched the ball."

Ken's teammates, awed by his performance, started playfully requesting Caminiti's treatment, IVs and Snickers, themselves.

Ken's tear continued after the team returned home: He hit a grand slam the following day against Montreal's Pedro Martínez as part of a six-RBI output; then, two days after that, on August 21, he hit two more home runs to key a series sweep over the Expos. He'd already surpassed his career high for home runs in a season with more than a month left.

The Padres, starting with Ken's "Snickers game," won ten of eleven games to build a two-game lead over the second-place Dodgers. After Ken showed his teammates how far he would go to play—and playing through food poisoning was a step beyond the shoulder or hamstring pulls or abdominal issues—it forced them to dig deeper, too.

Ken would have fought to play that Snickers game regardless of the importance—he was pulling similar exploits playing winter ball in Puerto Rico under manager Tom Gamboa—but the playoffs being *so close* gave him extra motivation. The Dodgers entered that fateful August day with a one-game lead over the Padres. But there was more than a month left in the season, and seven games left between the two teams. Ken was certainly motivated to overtake Los Angeles, given that he'd played 1,200 major league games without reaching the playoffs, and this was his best chance to get there.

There was always something deeper with Ken, a desire to keep playing no matter how much pain he faced, affirming his belief that *life's all about competition*. That drive inspired the sweetest performance of his career.

* * *

An article on August 22 by Bernie Wilson of the Associated Press cemented a new nickname for Caminiti.

Fans call him "Scary Man" because of his intense stare, his linebacker's body and what he can do to a baseball.

Ken Caminiti, San Diego's Gold Glove third baseman who's too tough to sit, might be something else—MVP candidate.

Scary Man? The man was a teddy bear under his persona . . . but Scary Man it was.

After Ken's exploits in Mexico started getting attention, the Padres' two media relations assistants, Shaun Rachau and Theo Epstein—yes, *that* Theo Epstein—spent more and more time focusing on a campaign to help Scary Man win the MVP Award. Which was kind of humorous, since Ken hadn't won the league MVP award in high school, college, or his minor league days, or even gotten a single MVP vote during his major league career.

Mars, the maker of Snickers, called. They wanted to talk to Ken's reps. A full-page ad in *USA Today* followed, and then an article in *Sports Illustrated* by reporter Tom Verducci that featured a photo of Ken on a customized motorcycle that renowned designer John Covington of Surgical-Steeds in Scottsdale, Arizona, had created for him.

"That whole Snickers situation hit nationwide," Rachau said.

Epstein was twenty-two years old that summer, a prodigy who'd spent three years interning with the Orioles before Lucchino recruited him to work with the Padres. Rachau was perplexed by his colleague's plan to go to law school and jump over to the baseball operations side. *What was in his head?* Rachau wondered. Epstein had something figured out. Before he led the Red Sox and Cubs to world championships and became one of the most widely respected executives in baseball, Epstein was writing Padres game notes and arranging player interviews.

"You could see in that guy that there was more to come down the road," Rachau said.

The same could be said for Ken, who kept on hitting. For the month of August, Ken batted .344 with 14 home runs and 38 RBIs, and an otherworldly OPS of 1.271 on his way to winning league Player of the Month honors.

The Padres were in first place, and Ken was playing baseball like never before.

His exploits only made San Diego fans adore him even more. Ken's love affair with Padres fans that summer was torrid and raw. It wouldn't last forever—these things never do—but it was so alluring and passionate, burning hot like a blue flame.

"With what he did in Mexico, but just the way he played the game, diving for balls, playing hurt, and of course what he did with the bat and the glove, they just fell in love with him," Bochy said. "Tony Gwynn is Mr. San Diego, but this was Cammy's time, and they absolutely adored him. I mean, he had everything. He was a strong, tough, good-looking guy that gave it his all. He left everything on the field, and the fans appreciated that."

Ted Leitner, longtime Padres broadcaster, agreed. "I've never seen a player connect like that to the fans and vice versa, ever. And no Padre, not even Tony Gwynn, did that," he said.

Leitner remembers hearing stories of season ticket holders who would call the ticket office to ask if they could move their season tickets from the first base line to the third base line. "And the ticket guy has heard this nine times that week. So he'd play along and say, 'Well, is there a problem with your seat, something wrong?' 'No, to be honest with you, I just want to be close to Cammy and watch him field and have that seat that I have on the first base line on the third base line.' And that happened a lot," Leitner said.

James Hayashi helped set up public appearances for players and first met Ken in 1996. They remained friends during the rest of Ken's playing career. The role allowed Hayashi to recognize Ken's popularity compared to other San Diego sports icons—from his teammate Tony Gwynn to football icons like Junior Seau, Dan Fouts, and Kellen Winslow. For a while, "Ken was the biggest athlete San Diego's ever seen," Hayashi said.

To Hayashi, though, Ken lacked self-awareness—he never quite understood why he was so popular.

"We were at a public appearance and a woman was there, she was probably in her early twenties. And she walked up to get something autographed by him. And she was shaking. I think she might've been crying.

"After she walked away, Ken was like, 'What was that all about?' I was like, 'Ken, do you realize you're like a sex symbol in San Diego?' And he looked at me, and I always remembered because whenever you said anything that he didn't understand, he always had this weird grin, and that was the first time that I understood that he didn't understand how big he was in San Diego."

But there was so much more to the fan interest than simply Ken's looks. The fans loved his heart. Ken was Patty Cahill's favorite. They got formally introduced through her godfather, Astros great Jimmy Wynn. Patty was a season ticket holder with seats along the third base line in 1996 because of Ken. "It was all about the team for him," she said. "He wanted to succeed as a team. He didn't like the individual accolades."

The next year on Opening Day, inspired by Ken's home runs in Monterey, she passed him 162 Snickers bars, one for every game of the season.

"They were all different types of Snickers. I had Easter Snickers bars, the Fun Size, I had Minis Size, I had the normal size, King Size. I asked one of the ushers if he could bring it to Cammy, and Cammy's like, 'Who is this from?' And he's like, 'Patty.' And Cammy smiled. 'She's done so much for me already.' And when the usher came back and told me that, I'm like, what? I've done so much for him? He's done so much for me! And it was just really sweet that he said that," Cahill said.

Amy Schneider has run a support group for teens with cancer, Some of My Best Friends Are Bald, or SOMBFAB, since the 1990s. At the height of Ken's fame, the teens wrote a letter to Ken about his Snickers game in Mexico. Ken attended a meet-and-greet with the group, and the teens read their letter aloud. "And the sweet thing is, he cried," Schneider said. "He was deeply touched and very, very nice to the kids."

His fans included children of his teammates, like pitcher Bob Tewksbury's son, Griffin. "His Padres jersey was number 21; he had a locker in the house that we rented in San Diego that had Caminiti on it. He imitated his batting stance from both sides of the plate. And whenever he came into the locker room, he ran to Cammy's locker first and not mine," the pitcher said.

"I just idolized him. He's a lefty hitter, I was a lefty hitter, he was a righty thrower," said Griffin Tewksbury, who was five at the time. "My dad was a pitcher, but I remember when I was younger, it was all about hitting and home runs, and he just had this big male persona I was drawn to."

The singular nature of stardom, and how uncomfortable it made Ken feel, started to become clearer after he got his own song—a parody of the dance sensation "Macarena" by Glenn Erath, a local radio fixture who was known for coming up with San Diego–inspired lyrics to popular songs. Erath admits to writing the lyrics in "maybe a half hour or an hour." But the song resonated for fans.

> Hey, there's a man that we know him Caminiti
> He can dive, he can slide, and he's piling up the ribbies
> The MVP playing here in our city
> Hey, Caminiti

Ken would sometimes hear the song—they played it one time during a Padres game—or a restaurant might play it when he stopped by. He wasn't used to being singled out like this.

* * *

As the season entered its final month, the M-V-P chants became louder. Every time you checked the box score, it seemed like he was picking up two or three hits, or hitting a home run, and that doesn't account for the Gold Glove defense or leadership. . . . He even received support from Dodgers manager Bill Russell, whose catcher Mike Piazza was also having a good season.

"To me, I think Caminiti is obviously the leading candidate," Russell told reporters on September 19. "If you're going to be objective and you're not allowed to pick one of your own players, he gets my vote."

After Piazza complained about the perceived slight, Russell met with the catcher and later clarified that "Mike Piazza is the MVP for me." Piazza believed, according to his book, *Long Shot*, that Dodgers broadcaster Vin Scully was also overenthusiastic in his support for the Padres third baseman.

Piazza had a great season in 1996: 36 home runs, 105 RBIs, a .336 batting average, and .985 OPS.

Caminiti hit 40 home runs, drove in 130 runs, batted .330, and had a 1.028 OPS.

Advanced stats such as WAR (wins above replacement) show Caminiti with 7.5 offensive WAR for the season, compared to 6.4 for Piazza, meaning Ken's bat was worth one more win for the Padres than Piazza's for the Dodgers.

In terms of overall WAR, three National League players topped Caminiti in 1996: outfielders Bernard Gilkey and Ellis Burks, also having career seasons, and Giants superstar Barry Bonds, who topped all position players with 9.7 WAR.

If anyone had a gripe about Ken being named the MVP, it was Bonds, not Piazza. (Bonds would win seven MVP awards during his career; Piazza received MVP votes in nine seasons but never won the award on his way to the Hall of Fame.)

But Bonds and Piazza weren't sentimental favorites in 1996. They didn't have the season stories Ken did—the torn rotator cuff, the throw from his butt, the Snickers game, overcoming addiction.

However, before MVP voting was finalized, the players needed to finish the season. The Padres against the Dodgers for a three-game series in Los Angeles. San Diego was two games behind LA in second place.

All the Dodgers had to do was win one of those games, and the division title was theirs. The loser was in the mix for the wild card as the league's best second-place team.

The Dodgers were six outs from winning the division title on September 27, and Ismael Valdéz was dealing, scattering five hits for the game's first seven innings.

Top of the eighth. Caminiti was leading off the inning. He worked the count to 2-and-2. Ken had seen the ball well throughout the game—he already had two singles and a walk—but now he was scuffling, fouling off Valdéz's offerings to stay alive.

As he started digging back into the box, a paper airplane sailed from the stands. Ken called time. *Breathe.* Made some shadow swings. Dug back in.

The next pitch sailed in, and Caminiti sent it flying—beyond center fielder Chad Curtis's reach for a home run.

Tie game.

"A shot of Vitamin Cammy, right in there at the right time," Padres broadcaster Ted Leitner called the home run.

The crowd reacted with a smattering of boos, then quickly grew silent. The celebration would wait. The Padres' bullpen kept the Dodgers at bay. Doug Bochtler in the eighth inning, Tim Worrell in the ninth.

In the top of the tenth inning, the score still knotted at 2, it was time for another shot of Vitamin Cammy. Steve Finley started the inning with a single, and Cammy came up against Antonio Osuna, making his seventy-second appearance of the season.

First pitch, ball one.

Second pitch, ball two.

Third pitch, ball three.

The fourth pitch was a fastball in the strike zone, and Caminiti was waiting for it, lacing a shot into the left field corner. Finley danced around the bases, and Caminiti had a double, and the Padres had the lead, and they wouldn't lose it.

After a Wally Joyner walk, Padres shortstop Chris Gomez singled to left field, scoring Caminiti. Los Angeles outfielder Todd Hollandsworth tried to get Joyner at third and ended up overthrowing the ball, allowing Joyner to score to make it 5–2 Padres. The game ended with Piazza grounding into a double play.

Dodgers fans headed for the exits, the champagne stayed on ice, and the plastic sheets in the home locker room came down. Game 1, Padres.

Game 2, the Padres fell behind again—by the third inning, it was 2–0 Los Angeles, and Hideo Nomo, who'd clinched the division against San Diego the season before, was in a groove, keeping the Padres scoreless through five innings.

This time, it was Steve Finley's turn. The other big star in the Astros-Padres mega trade in December 1994, Finley had found a new level of success in 1996, hitting .298 with 45 doubles, 30 home runs, 22 stolen bases, and a .885 OPS. If not for Caminiti, Finley might have gotten more MVP attention.

Finley led off the sixth by depositing Nomo's pitch beyond right field for a home run. The Padres had life. Caminiti followed with a single, as did first baseman Wally Joyner, and then it was Chris Gomez's turn.

The soft-hitting shortstop, who had had a key extra-inning hit the game before, struck again, doubling down the right field line and scoring Caminiti. Tie game, 2–2.

Worrell—who begrudgingly accepted his bullpen assignment after grappling with Bochy and Caminiti earlier in the year—was masterful, allowing only one base runner and one ball out of the infield over two innings of work.

The score was tied in the eighth inning, and Dodgers pitcher Darren Dreifort got two quick outs when second baseman Jody Reed came to bat. Reed—who spent his best years with the Red Sox—was on the tail end of an eleven-year big league career, the type of player who understood the size of the moment and the importance of every at bat. Even if he only batted .244 in 1996, he wasn't going to waste this chance. And he didn't, singling to keep the inning going.

That brought up the pitcher's spot. Bochy turned to Greg Vaughn, Caminiti's new friend and roommate, to pinch-hit. The outfielder had struggled after getting traded from the Brewers, but he was true here, hitting a single to make it first and second.

Top of the order—Rickey Henderson. The best leadoff man in baseball history worked a walk to load the bases, chasing Dreifort.

Mark Guthrie came on to pitch. He'd be facing "Mr. Padre," Tony Gwynn, the team's only mainstay from the last playoff team in 1984, and the best pure hitter in the game. Gwynn settled into his stance, worked the count to 2-and-1, and did what he did best—slicing a single through the left side of the infield, past the outreached glove of diving shortstop Greg Gagne, to score Reed and Vaughn.

The Dodgers tried to muster a rally. Second baseman Eric Karros opened the ninth inning with a double to right field, but Karros would not advance—San Diego's all-world closer, Trevor Hoffman, struck out three batters to seal the win.

Game 2, Padres. The Dodgers' celebratory champagne was still on ice, and now the teams were tied atop the National League West, 90–71, with one game left to play. The winner would notch the division title and face the St. Louis Cardinals, winners of the Central Division. With Montreal eliminated from contention, the loser would wind up with the wild card, the honor for best second-place team, and travel to Atlanta to play the juggernaut Braves, defending their World Series title from the season before.

But Ken wasn't content with a wild card berth—the Padres didn't celebrate.

"We're gonna win this thing tomorrow, because they're going to answer the phones Western Division champs, not wild card team," pitcher Bob Tewksbury, who was starting the final game, remembers Ken saying in the dugout the day before. "And I was like, 'Yep, got it, thank you. I'll do what I can do, Cammy.' And so I hardly slept a wink that night."

Despite the lack of sleep, Tewksbury pitched well in Game 162, keeping the Dodgers scoreless in seven innings of work. Dario Veras followed with three innings of scoreless relief. But the Padres weren't scoring, either. LA starter Ramón Martînez was pulled after one inning to keep him fresh for the playoffs, and the Dodgers bullpen matched the Padres, inning by inning, zero by zero.

San Diego nearly broke the shutout in the eighth, when pinch runner Doug Dascenzo was thrown out at home trying to score from second on Finley's single; then, after Caminiti was intentionally walked to load the bases, Vaughn popped out to end the threat.

The top of the eleventh opened with Finley hitting a single to center against Chan Ho Park. The Padres were in business. Caminiti battled back from 0-and-2 with a single of his own through the right side of the infield, with Finley moving to third. The lead, and potentially the game and division title, were ninety feet away. But next was the pitcher's spot—Bochy had done a double switch in the eighth inning and used Vaughn's spot in the lineup for the pitcher.

The Padres needed a pinch hitter. Sometimes, as a manager, you go against statistics and logic and let your gut guide you. And that's what Bochy did in Game 162, in the eleventh inning, with the division title on the line. He went with Chris Gwynn, Tony's younger brother, who'd teamed with Ken on Team USA more than a decade earlier. By 1996, Chris was a seldom-used pinch hitter in his brother's shadow. Chris, since July 19, had one hit—a 1-for-19 cold streak that saw his average dip to .169. As a pinch hitter, he was batting .135—seven hits in fifty-two at bats. But Chris Gwynn was a veteran, and he'd played parts of seven seasons for the Dodgers, including 1995, after which he was granted free agency.

The Dodgers didn't want him anymore. And here he was, with two men on and a bat in his hand. Park delivered.

"He threw me a changeup, and I saw it," Gwynn said. "So I put the bat on the ball."

The ball rolled all the way to the wall in right-center, scoring Finley and Caminiti. It was the final swing of Chris Gwynn's regular season career, and *oh doctor*, what a swing it was.

Three quick outs later, the Padres were celebrating on the Dodgers' field and in the clubhouse, spraying the champagne, carried to the division title by a man who played the entire season with a damaged shoulder.

As Ken stood in the locker room, victorious, playoff-bound for the first time, with beer seeping into his eyes, his teammates broke into a chant: "M-V-P! M-V-P! M-V-P!"

* * *

Mark Webb and Will Vince, two of Ken's San Jose friends, were in town for that series against the Dodgers, along with Mark's father. Ken set them up with tickets, and afterward he invited them to meet him at Morton's Steakhouse in Beverly Hills, where Ken and Nancy were hosting a dinner with about ten of Ken's Padres teammates. They had a private room.

The singer Rod Stewart was there with his then wife, Rachel Hunter, and Stewart stopped by Ken's table to say hello. The artist LeRoy Neiman was at the steakhouse that night, too.

Webb remembered Ken's contentment that night. "He was buying Dom Perignon, didn't touch a drop, and he had this ear-to-ear smile. It was Kenny at his best. He was sober, he was proud. It was a wonderful, wonderful feeling," Webb said.

* * *

After a champagne-soaked celebration in Los Angeles, the Padres traveled to St. Louis to face the Cardinals in the first round of the National League playoffs.

Back to business.

Todd Stottlemyre, the brother of Ken's former minor league teammate and the son of his former Astros pitching coach, got the start for St. Louis. Ken was also close with Cardinals catcher Tom Pagnozzi, his former winter ball teammate in Puerto Rico in 1988–89.

But this was Ken's year, and he was expected to carry that momentum into the postseason. He got an early chance in the first inning. Stottlemyre gave up a double to Tony Gwynn and then hit Steve Finley with a pitch. One out, potential MVP coming up to bat. But Stottlemyre evidently didn't get the memo about Caminiti's magical season. He fooled Ken with an upstairs slider, and Ken swatted at the air, coming up empty. Strikeout. Wally Joyner's ground ball wound up in Luis Alicea's glove, and the Padres' rally was snuffed out.

The Cardinals then took a 3–0 lead off a three-run homer by Gary Gaetti.

After Rickey Henderson countered with a homer of his own in the sixth inning, Ken came up with Tony Gwynn on base—a chance to tie the game.

Stottlemyre went inside-outside-inside-outside, and with the count 2-and-2, he went outside again with a sinking pitch down and away, and Ken waved at it, coming up empty.

Ken came up again in the eighth inning with Steve Finley on base. The pitcher was Rick Honeycutt.

Ken batted right-handed, and Honeycutt got two quick strikes. He threw his third pitch in the dirt, and Ken, off-balance, swung and came up empty for a third time, all with a runner on base. After 1,238 regular season games without a taste of the postseason, Ken needed a game to get the nerves out.

"I was a little aggressive. I tried to do too much," he admitted later.

* * *

Game 2 followed two days later.

After a second-inning strikeout, Ken came up again in the fifth inning, leading off against Andy Benes, his former Padres teammate. The Cardinals were leading 1–0, and the Padres still didn't have a hit.

After two strikes, Ken stepped out of the box and collected himself.

Breathe. Breathe.

He went back to shortening his swing, the tactic that had worked so well throughout the season. Benes pitched the ball inside and up, and Ken was on it, lifting the ball over right fielder Brian Jordan and into the stands. What slump?

With one swing, the Padres were back in the series. But the Cardinals stayed one step ahead of San Diego, and behind a three-run double by Ron Gant, along with some crafty baserunning by Brian Jordan, St. Louis scraped out a 5–4 win to take a 2–0 series lead.

* * *

Game 3 represented San Diego's first home playoff game in twelve years.

But as the game wore on, it became a battle of one-upmanship between two players who wouldn't quit: Caminiti and Brian Jordan.

Ken hit a home run in the bottom of the third, and the home team built a 4–1 lead.

But again, St. Louis answered, clogging the basepaths with runners and taking a 5–4 lead in the seventh inning.

The score stayed that way until the bottom of the eighth inning. Ken led off against Honeycutt.

Ba-da-da-da-da-ch!

The opening beats of Jimi Hendrix Experience's cover of "All Along the Watchtower" announced the hero's arrival, and the crowd erupted.

The hour was getting late on this night—October 5, 1996. Afternoon sunlight acquiesced to dark and artificial brightness. Win-or-go-home baseball for San Diego. One run down.

The right spot. The right time. The right guy.

"Watchtower" faded out, and the slugger dug in, ticking and tocking the bat with his wrists before cocking it in the ready position. He glared toward the mound, his eyes piercing into the pitcher's inner Little Leaguer.

The outcome was a foregone conclusion—the forty-two-year-old meatball tosser against the hottest player in the league.

First pitch, called strike.

The second pitch was a hanging curve—the kind of fat stuff you're advised not to throw to this guy. *Hit in the air to deep center . . . back goes Lankford, back to the fence . . . this game is tied.*

Bedlam among the palm trees.

The slugger glided around the bases, all the hurt momentarily diminished. The opposing pitcher stared at the outfield in disbelief, as if the wall was somehow to blame. Teammates filtered out of the dugout to honor their savior. The crowd broke into "M-V-P" chants, growing louder for effect. The tech guy blasted electric guitar, trying to prolong the moment.

And you wish you could pause time and keep things just as they were, with Scary Man nearly willing his team to another comeback victory, the fans forever clapping, the music lingering for a few more notes.

Baseball seasons are measured by Octobers, and Caminiti's life followed suit.

With the game knotted and Trevor Hoffman on the mound, Ron Gant walked, and then it was time for the Cardinals outfielder with ice in his veins, Jordan.

Jordan took ball one and ball two, and Hoffman regrouped, attacking the zone. Fouled back for strike one, fouled off for strike two. Jordan took a ball inside for ball three—full count. Jordan fouled the next pitch out of play on the third base side. Hoffman looked in for the signal and shook off his catcher. He came set. Pitched.

Jordan put wood on the ball, and it kept rising. Rickey Henderson jogged to the warning track and found the wall, preparing to jump, but the ball was out of reach—gone.

Jordan's chain jangled around his neck as he circled the bases. The Cardinals were up 7–5 in the top of the ninth.

Bottom half, last chance for San Diego, and Ken was slated to be the fifth hitter.

Wally Joyner flied out to start the inning, and Rickey Henderson singled to left field and moved to second. St. Louis cared about the potential second run, not the first. Tony Gwynn was next. He'd singled in his last at bat. But not this time. He lined out to shortstop.

Two outs. Scary Man was on deck, gripping his bat barrel in preparation for doing more harm.

Jordan was worried what Caminiti might do with one more at bat.

"I was in right field saying, 'We cannot let Ken get up to the plate. We gotta get this out.' And that's, that's how I truly felt, because I knew if he would've had another opportunity, he would have done something big," Jordan said.

But Steve Finley lofted the first pitch he saw to the outfield, giving Caminiti a front-row view as his team's season ended, the emotions swinging from enthusiasm over what could be, to desolate, cold finality.

He ambled back into the dugout, watching with those soul-crushing eyes as another team celebrated on his home field.

Even in defeat, the home fans cheered—thankful for what the team and its biggest star meant to them. But a nagging feeling hung over the stadium. You wished Caminiti had one more chance for glory.

CHAPTER 19

PLANES, SPRAINS, AND AUTOMOBILES

The doctors sliced open Ken's shoulder, and it was a blown car engine, the parts junked and out of place from all the over-revving.

Days after the Padres' season ended, the bill from the mechanic came due. The surgeons, Dr. Lewis Yocum and Padres team physician Dr. Jan Fronek, found more damage than they expected. Tendons were torn. Cartilage was shredded. Bone spurs jutted out. Ken had "a complete tear near the top of the rotator cuff," Fronek said, as well as a tear in the glenoid labrum, the ring of cartilage located below the rotator cuff.

"Part of my rotator cuff was torn completely and retracted—retracted so long like a rubber band out in the sun too long, and it had become brittle," Ken said.

They also found lots of scar tissue and muscle growth due to the human growth hormone, steroids, and strength exercises that had helped Ken stabilize the damaged shoulder. The surgeons had to split Ken's deltoid—"the only good muscle in the whole damn shoulder," Ken said—and from there, they performed multiple procedures, reattaching and sanding down and scraping away and rebuilding the shoulder. As if that wasn't enough, his biceps tendon was also torn. Tears of the supraspinatus tendon are often the result of heavy lifting and falling on your outstretched arm, and Ken did both at the start of the season, meaning he played like this, with his left shoulder mangled and threadbare, for six months, and even if he claimed the pain deadened, it's still stunning to consider what Ken endured to play the 1996 season.

It was estimated that recovery from surgery would take five to nine months, but even five months was a rosy view, the best-case scenario. According to that timeline, Ken could expect to miss the start of spring training and probably the first month of the regular season as he got back into playing shape. But Ken wanted to be ready to go on the first day of spring training and in the lineup on Opening Day. With Ken, everything was fast, even his recovery timeline.

That recovery process did not include steroids. Catherine Ondrusek made sure of that. The physical therapist worked with Ken up to three times a day to help him return to form following his surgery. Before Ken began his rehab, the doctors and Ondrusek warned him that using steroids during his recovery could do lasting damage and potentially derail his career.

"The doctors were very, very adamant, and so was I, that before he healed, if he did [steroids], the muscle was going to literally rip everything back out from the bone," Ondrusek said. His friend and admitted steroid supplier, Dave Moretti, also confirmed that Ken did not use steroids that off-season. Ken limited his workouts with his trainer Blake Blackwell during his rehab, too. The wrong exercise or lift could undo months of progress. If he wanted to be ready for spring training, he had to do *everything* he was told. The margin for error was tendon-thin.

Ondrusek initially approached her role in Caminiti's rehab with skepticism. Years earlier, she had babysat for some of the Astros players, and through brief glimpses of his booze-fueled postgame behavior, she anticipated he would be a difficult client who wouldn't follow her commands. But she encountered a different side of Ken following his surgery. "He did everything I asked him to do," she said. "His dad spent several weeks with him when he first came home. They actually drove back across the country when he got out of the hospital, even though he was only a few days out of surgery."

At the beginning of the process, Ken couldn't move his arm. Getting dressed and applying deodorant became adventures that required angling against a wall. But Ondrusek used her skill, and Ken's willingness, to naturally speed up the rehab, pushing his shoulder just a little bit more each session. She would space out their sessions around his errands and try to stimulate his body to heal. Eventually he became able to throw a small medicine ball or begin using arm weight machines. He followed every one of Ondrusek's orders.

During those months of rehab, Ondrusek jokes, she saw more of Ken then she did of her infant daughter. Through her work with Ken, she gained a different perspective about him. "The man I knew was a fabulous family man, and really struggled with trying to find the balance to be a dad," she said. "Baseball's a hell of a sport on a family."

Ken's family added a new member that off-season: another daughter, Nicole. She had her daddy's eyes, those lovely eyes.

* * *

The results of the Most Valuable Player voting was announced on November 13. Twenty-eight writers voted. And all twenty-eight listed Ken Caminiti first. Ken hadn't garnered a vote in any other season, and now he was the fourth unanimous MVP in National League history, joining three Hall of Famers: Orlando Cepeda, Mike Schmidt, and his buddy Jeff Bagwell. His rival, Dodgers catcher Mike Piazza, finished second, and Barry Bonds came in third.

"I got picked MVP for doing my job, basically," he said.

Ken was the emotional choice. He had the best story, from the dehydration and Snickers game in Mexico, to his blistering second half, to his leading the Padres to the division title on the last day of the season, to his playing the entire year with a torn rotator cuff. It was his year. If the award had been given on stats alone, Barry Bonds would have been the runaway pick—his 42 homers and 129 runs batted in were in line with Ken's 40 and 130, but Barry also had a league-leading 151 walks. Bernard Gilkey of the Mets and Colorado's Ellis Burks also had statistically stronger seasons. But the Giants and Mets were 90-loss teams, and the Rockies finished in third place behind Caminiti's Padres and Piazza's Dodgers. And voters of the era showed a pattern of taking the award's name literally, selecting the player whose team wouldn't have reached the playoffs without them.

Ken Caminiti's 1996 season was a fairy tale, an aberration. Sure, he was an All-Star-caliber player and a Gold Glove fielder, but there was nothing from his first nine major league seasons that hinted that a season of this nature was possible, other than maybe his strong finish to the previous season when he was mashing from both sides of the plate. And usually, players' best seasons come in their late twenties or early thirties. Ken, at thirty-three, was on the outer bands of a player's expected prime.

The greatness of Ken's 1996 season becomes clear when setting it against players of the same age. Ken's on-base plus slugging plus, or OPS+—which measures each player against a league average of 100, and adjusts for league and park factors—was 174, meaning his season was 74 percent better than the league average. Against all other players' age thirty-three seasons, Ken's OPS+ was tied for the ninth best ever at the time, behind Babe Ruth (206), Lou Gehrig (190), Honus Wagner (187), Willie Stargell and Johnny Mize (186), Dan Brouthers (179), Rogers Hornsby (178), and Harmon Killebrew (177), tied with Ed Delahanty, and ahead of Willie Mays (172). With a smart steroid program and an otherwise clean lifestyle, Ken Caminiti in 1996 performed like an inner circle Hall of Famer.

* * *

The MVP award came with notoriety and obligations for Ken in the years ahead. Like in 1997 when he appeared at Collector's Corner II, a card shop in Los Gatos located a ten-minute drive from his childhood home, for an autograph signing. The local boy had made good. Proceeds from autographs, $5 for children twelve and under and $10 for everyone else, benefited the baseball program at Leigh High School, his alma mater. And one of Ken's unused bats was raffled.

"He was not egotistical, was not arrogant, very humble and polite," said Mike Wasserman, the card shop owner and, later, an official for Santa Clara County. "And his choice was to help promote his high school program that helped get him to where he was. So I'm sure it went to buying equipment and things for the team."

The person sitting next to Ken at the show, helping him cycle through the gathered fans, was none other than Dave Moretti, his friend and steroid supplier. Moretti was wearing a checkered short-sleeve shirt. In photos from the event, you can see Moretti and his shirt in the corners of images.

* * *

Everything was going well for Ken. A new baby, a new award, a new shoulder. And that February, he wound up receiving two more awards: ESPYs for best baseball player and best baseball play for his throw from the seat of his pants against the Marlins. The show was held in the Big Apple, a chance for Ken to be celebrated across the sports and entertainment worlds—the guy who had spent years missing out on Gold Gloves was going to be honored in front of Muhammad Ali. And *Baywatch* actress Yasmine Bleeth. And Dennis Hopper. *Sports Illustrated* cover model Tyra Banks would read his award. The moment—the celebrity, the scope, the nervousness, everything—was too much for Ken. He could play third base in front of forty thousand people a night without any problem, but this was a roomful of somebodies, a roomful of people who were accustomed to a world that he wasn't. A roomful of people watching *him*. So when a fellow baseball player handed him a glass full of vodka, what else was he going to do but bring the glass to his mouth and take a sip? Everyone was having fun, and he would, too. "I thought I could go ahead and sneak a drink. Told the bartender to make me a vodka drink but make it look like ice water," he described it years later. "I drank about a hundred of them."

A lot of people in the league watched out for him, but players didn't always pay attention to Ken's problems or weren't aware of them. He was the toughest guy in the league, but his toughness made people overlook his weaknesses. And with one sip, three years, three months, and eight days of sobriety were over.

* * *

The pickup barreled down Interstate 10 in western Texas. Ken Caminiti drove his Chevrolet "dually" with his trainer Blake Blackwell sitting in the passenger seat. Both were excited for the chance to build off the magic of 1996. Ken hoped to play a healthy season and carry his Padres back to the playoffs. Blake wanted to make Ken strong again while building his own connections in baseball. When people credit you as the trainer who helped Ken Caminiti become *Ken Caminiti*, when you're name-dropped at the ESPYs, you're worth listening to—and the Padres were inviting Blackwell to spring training camp to discuss the popular supplement creatine.

The whole thing was a bit of a charade. Many of Ken's teammates and friends knew it was steroids, not creatine, that helped him become an MVP-caliber player. But why ruin the illusion?

On the way, his pickup broke down twice. "I was about ready to throw it off the road, hitchhike and get a flight, and tell my wife I totaled my truck," said Ken, whose truck problems caused him to report to Padres camp one day later than he'd hoped. Even with the truck breakdown, Ken was back about four months earlier than expected following his shoulder surgery.

The fact that he was in Peoria, Arizona, to start spring training was stunning. The baseball world was expecting Ken back around the All-Star break. As a counterpoint, the reigning American League MVP, Juan Gonzalez, would miss the first month of the season with a torn ligament in his thumb. Ken had to sustain major repairs of his shoulder, and he was ready to go.

Catherine Ondrusek's plan had worked perfectly. Still, Ken felt weak. He was used to weight lifting to add strength and muscle during the off-seasons. He was months behind on his strength. With Moretti in Arizona, too, he had two men with him who could help him regain strength. His trainer Blake Blackwell helped Ken with his lifting while mentoring Padres players like Greg Vaughn and Craig Shipley on creatine use. Although Moretti said he wanted Ken to ramp down his usage of steroids in 1997 to "doing a single oral steroid or an injectable water base that was mild to the system," he said Ken was interested in getting bigger—he wanted to look a certain way.

"I was trying to keep Ken happy and keep him from overdoing it," Moretti said.

In addition to the steroids provided by Moretti, Ken also started carrying around legal supplements provided by Blackwell like milk thistle and cat's-claw in a black goodie bag. Ken began touting the legal supplements in interviews, highlighting their bodybuilding and health benefits.

"The [legal] stuff in the black bag was Blake," Moretti said. "Sometimes he would have his steroids in there, and sometimes he wouldn't." (Blackwell did not respond to multiple requests for comment.)

For Moretti, all of the legal supplements were unnecessary, since Ken was already taking steroids. "If you're taking testosterone, you don't need all that crap," he said. Moretti believes creatine in particular slowed Ken down. "That caused his hamstring issues, because Ken's hamstrings were always tight. He always had tight calves and hamstrings, and they would pull on his hips, pull on his lower back. It would give him back problems. When those muscles are tight, it pulls on the glutes and the lower back, and it strains everything. I finally got Ken to stop using it. I had to scream at him and kind of wake him up."

Blackwell and Moretti were two men who had differing approaches about what was best for Ken's body.

* * *

A player contacted Ken after the 1996 season—he was interested in learning about Ken's steroid regimen. Ken reached out to Moretti.

"He was asking me about this stuff. I told him what I did. I don't remember all the stuff you told me! I don't wanna mess the guy up. Do you mind if I have him call you?" Ken asked Moretti.

"All right, I'll talk to him."

The player called, and Moretti gave him the same advice he gave Caminiti: Take a blood test, and make sure what you're taking is real.

"Well, can you get me something?" the player asked.

"I guess," Moretti responded. And that's how it picked up, with the MVP sending fellow players to his childhood friend for their steroid needs. Moretti ended up helping pitchers and hitters, stars and scrubs.

Lots and lots of them. Fifty? One hundred? Two hundred? Too many to accurately count.

Part of that was on purpose—plausible deniability. Moretti didn't want to know. Because if he knew everyone he worked with, and then he got caught . . . Sometimes he would give Ken steroids on behalf of a teammate. Or a client would ask about an unnamed outfielder or a relief pitcher, and Moretti would consider the player's body type and match him with a regimen that would help for his positional needs. He'd ask for enough money to cover his costs and then a little bit extra—that way he could maintain supplies and not be tapped out in case a shipment got lost.

One of the players Moretti worked with was Richie Lewis, who teamed with Ken in spring training with the Padres in 1996. The pitcher—standing five feet, six and a half inches tall—was rehabbing from Tommy John surgery entering the 1997 season after appearing in a career-high seventy-two games the year before.

"I absolutely busted my tail to get back," Lewis said in a 2019 interview.

Lewis was the best collegiate pitcher in the country during the mid-1980s, a Florida State flamethrower who pitched as hard as he lived. Lewis was overused at FSU, so by the time he reached the pros, his most commanding performances were already behind him.

Lewis made his major league debut with the Orioles in 1992 and, after getting selected in the expansion draft, spent the next three seasons with the Florida Marlins. (The Marlins, in drafting Lewis, passed on another reliever, a Panama-born Yankees prospect named Mariano Rivera.) Lewis bounced around the league. Baltimore. Florida. San Diego for spring training. Detroit. Respected but not a star. Someone who had to scrape and claw and hustle to make the team, then make smart pitches to stay.

Following his surgery in 1996, Lewis recognized that a long recovery might mean the end of his career. "It's either poop or get off the pot," he said. And Lewis wasn't ready to get off the pot.

Moretti had a lot in common with Lewis. Both were on the short side of six feet. Moretti had endured his own arm injury during his teen years in San Jose. They became friends.

Moretti was happy to help Lewis, he said, supplying him with Deca-Durabolin, or nandrolone, along with Winstrol (stanozolol), a white injectable fluid you need to snap with your wrist because it separates when sitting, and pink Dianabol tablets. Lewis recalled that the steroids were "all about healing," a way for him to bounce back from his injury and build strength.

Lewis had Moretti inject him. "I didn't want to mess the injection up," Lewis recalled. "I'm not a nurse or doctor." They met up when Lewis pitched for the Oakland A's Triple-A affiliate, the Edmonton Trappers of the Pacific Coast League.

Midway through the season, Lewis was released by the A's, signed by the Reds, and assigned to the Triple-A Indianapolis Indians. Moretti wanted Lewis to stay strong, so he sent a package of those pink Dianabol tablets addressed to Lewis at the Indians' home park, Victory Field, 501 W. Washington Street, Indianapolis, IN 46225. Moretti used a house around the corner for the return address, just in case the package got intercepted.

This package did get intercepted—by the Indians' front office staff. The shipment was delivered to the stadium but ended up getting thrown away, Lewis and a front office employee both independently confirmed more than twenty years later.

Lewis grew heated as he tried to explain to the employee how important his "vitamins" were. Eventually, "I kind of blew it off," Lewis said, and soon after, on the strength of a 0.76 ERA in twenty-one appearances for Indianapolis, he got called back up to the big leagues. "It's another example, in my opinion, that they knew what was going on," Lewis said of Major League Baseball's willful ignorance about PEDs.

"Other than that, I never really took them. I know some folks that just took 'em to see if they could get better with them. Mine was rehabilitation. I felt like I was living on borrowed time."

* * *

The Padres kept the training wheels on for Ken at the start of spring training. He didn't take BP from the left side right away, and he didn't swing a bat in the team's first six games. Bochy, as much as one can, made sure Ken wasn't diving in the field until the team felt confident in his progress. Telling Ken Caminiti not to dive was like telling a fish not to swim. But the last thing they needed was for him to go all-out in a meaningless game and undo an entire off-season of rehab.

However, those instincts were hard to break. . . . In one game, the Cubs' Shawon Dunston hit a shot down the line, and Ken did what he always did—he dove. "But the moment he left the ground, you knew that he knew it wasn't wise," Don Ketchum wrote in the *Arizona Republic*. "Caminiti tucked the shoulder and rolled as the ball went past for a double." He'd play a few games, then have a few games off, not pushing things too hard. The Padres needed him in September and October, not February and March. Bochy wanted Ken to let him know if he had any discomfort, which Ken did. He didn't have to prove anything to anybody.

He got his first hits in a "B" game against the Mariners on March 3; his first home run didn't come until March 13 off Anaheim's Mark Langston, a fellow San Jose State product. Ken hit five bombs that spring, and he collected hits in bunches.

On March 7, he met with Dr. Lewis Yocum, one of the doctors—along with team doctor Jan Fronek—who had performed his off-season surgery. The following morning, set to be Ken Caminiti MVP Day, he awoke with soreness and ended up getting scratched from the lineup. The doctors didn't want to rush his return. If he missed a few games, no big deal.

Ken met with Dr. Fronek on March 28, days before the start of the season, in hopes of getting his final sign-off. Fronek wasn't keen on Ken returning. . . . He was approaching this from a pragmatic place, a place where it didn't matter if Ken was back on the field on Opening Day, or April 9 against the Pirates, or April 20 against the Reds. Fronek's suggestion: Sit out a little while. Maybe a few more weeks. Maybe the first month. What was the rush?

But Ken wanted to play now, he was ready, and after all the rehab sessions with Catherine Ondrusek, after using Opening Day as his North Star for half a year, he wasn't going to back down. He met with Bochy and Dr. Cliff Colwell, a member of the team's medical staff, and they left the decision up to Ken, which is why he was in the lineup on April Fools' Day against the Mets, as he'd hoped since going under the knife. He went 1-for-5 with a single and an error in the field, and San Diego beat the Mets 12–5.

The next day, Ken hit his first homer of the new season and scored a key run in the twelfth inning as San Diego won again.

Ken was back.

And he wanted a raise. He wanted to stay in San Diego for a while.

Ken had the ninety-ninth-highest salary in baseball during his MVP season—$3.275 million—which was less than half of the $6.6 million that Matt Williams raked in playing third base for the Giants. Other third sackers making more than Ken included Gary Sheffield, Robin Ventura, and Travis Fryman. AL MVP Juan Gonzalez brought in $7.425 million.

It's the nature of baseball. Players often have their best seasons and then get paid for past performance.

Ken entered 1997 looking to negotiate a contract extension, something that would keep him in San Diego long-term (he was under contract through 1998). But the talks didn't go very far. The team offered Ken an extension of $5 million for both 1999 and 2000; Ken wanted $7 million, a salary in line with Williams's. But owner John Moores didn't think any player was worth $7 million, and the talks reached an impasse and wound down without a resolution.

"I know what the market value out there is, and I don't need to be on top, but I need to be treated fairly," Ken told the *San Diego Union-Tribune*.

* * *

When the Padres traveled to Hawaii to face the Cardinals early in the 1997 season—another first for a major league regular-season game, just like Mexico the year before—he showed the fans a lot of himself, taking infield and batting practice shirtless. His muscles glistened and bulged, his shorts were a size too small, his chest was a thicket of hair, his hat was on backward. This was what a *man* was supposed to look like.

The Padres video team captured footage of Ken shirtless, and pretty soon it was playing on the scoreboard during home games at Jack Murphy Stadium, set to the Paula Cole song "Where Have All the Cowboys Gone?" Ken with his shirt off was pure sex, and women *loved* the video.

"That video was probably by far the most popular video that we ever did," said Padres videographer Chase Peckham.

"When the video board guys would put up a video of him working out on a hot day, he would do it without a shirt, and you could hear the girls scream. He was truly a rock star," Padres marketing employee Andy Strasberg said. "They loved him shirtless, but he was absolutely, without question, a fan favorite for different reasons with different segments of the fan base—guys, gals, and kids. All for different reasons." Ken and his teammates got a kick out of the video, especially Wally Joyner. "Whenever they showed that picture of me in Hawaii in 100-degree weather, hitting with my shirt off, Wally started taking his shirt off. Every time," Ken said.

No one seemed to consider the subject matter of the song: a dissatisfied wife holding the household together while her man struggles to make a living and drinks too much and doesn't give her enough attention. "I will raise the children / If you pay all the bills," Cole sang, and she might as well have been singing for Nancy, who was back in Texas building a cocoon around her and the girls while Ken was in San Diego doing his best Duke Wayne impression, ready to raise hell and rally his men.

* * *

Ken had girlfriends throughout his career, but there was one in particular during his playing days whom his agent Tom Reich didn't like.

They started dating in 1997, and the girlfriend became a more and more visible presence, his concerned friends and multiple people around the Padres say.

Ken was lonely. . . . With Nancy and the girls in Texas, he started spending more and more time with the girlfriend, and giving her money from his autograph signings, and leaving her tickets for Padres games. Ken was drifting in other ways, drinking and smoking a little weed sometimes, thinking he could handle it, even though the people who knew him best recognized he couldn't. There was never *a little bit* for Ken Caminiti.

As the 1997 season continued, Padres players started noticing little changes with Ken. Like the beers on the team bus or plane trips. . . . After all he'd done for this team, if he wanted to sip on a beer, who was going to stop him? Ken's reputation on the field made him almost unapproachable off it. During his Astros days, when he was running ragged, he was still a twentysomething who hadn't begun to tap his full potential. Now he was a thirtysomething who was among the most respected and feared players in baseball.

"I remembered on a plane flight that Cammy went to the back of the plane, and I wasn't spying on him or anything like that, but I kind of turned around and saw that he had a beer in his hand and thought to myself, 'All right, something's a little different here,'" catcher John Flaherty said.

Pete Smith, a former Braves pitcher who came up with the likes of John Smoltz and Tom Glavine, joined the Padres in 1997 and struck up a friendship with Ken. Caminiti assigned Smith an important job. "You're in charge of the beer," Ken told him. "Make sure we have beer on the bus." Ken didn't want to be seen lugging it around, but Smith didn't have the same concerns. Ken would sit in the back of the bus drinking, and Smith was there to help, passing him cans. "It was kind of a joke between us. I was the one bringing it, and he was the one drinking it," Smith said.

Smith wasn't fully comfortable helping Ken . . . but it wasn't like Ken was showing up drunk to the ballpark or doing anything inherently reckless.

As Ken was experiencing changes in his personal life, the accountability structure around him was also shifting. Guys would come and go from the Padres, and the guys who could stand up to Ken and watch out for him might get replaced by guys who wouldn't be as motivated at keeping him sober. In 1997, Ken's roommate on the road at the beginning of his Padres days, Scott Livingstone, was traded to the Cardinals (in return, the Padres got the stand-up Mark Sweeney, someone who connected deeply with Ken).

And Greg Vaughn, now an established Padres player following his midseason 1996 trade, had his own place on the beach—he didn't need to room with Ken anymore.

Ken's buddy Dave Moretti did his best to help Ken, staying with him for weeks at a time, but he didn't travel on the road with Ken, and the girlfriend sometimes did. The girlfriend's presence forced Ken's friends to have to juggle his lies, and that wasn't fair to them, and it especially wasn't fair to Nancy. Girlfriends are common in the game. Players might have different partners in different cities—a woman in Chicago or Florida who you might visit when you were in town—but those relationships were narrow in focus. This had different stakes, and it was all going to blow up. Nancy wasn't going anywhere. Not now anyway. But she would always do whatever she could to protect the girls, and eventually she had to protect herself, too.

* * *

Despite the hints that things weren't the same for Ken, brightness still shone through in his good deeds and thoughtfulness.

Early in the 1997 season, the Padres decided to launch a new initiative, a fundraiser in honor of Cindy Matters, a Padres fan who died of cancer. Matters's favorite player was Brad Ausmus, and Ausmus and other players recorded a video for her in 1996, and she threw out a first pitch before one of the team's games. Now the Padres wanted to do *something* more . . . and team officials decided on a pediatric cancer program as a way of honoring Matters's life. Michele Anderson, Padres director of community relations, discussed the initiative with players.

When she approached Ken, he had his game face on—that *stare*. "He had an intensity about him, but sometimes I couldn't always tell if he's hearing me," Anderson said. Ken didn't say much to Anderson, and she wondered if maybe this program wasn't right for him.

The next day, he saw Anderson and called her over.

"I've really been thinking about this, and I decided I want to donate my bike. I think that would get some excitement," he told Anderson.

He had heard Anderson the day before—"he was simply trying to formulate the best way that he could respond to it, and he was really excited about it and energized," she said. "It touched him, and he just needed a little time to figure out the best way to help."

He was always looking to help his friends. Bench coach Rob Picciolo didn't have a cell phone, and he showed up at the clubhouse one day to find a phone on the folding chair at his locker.

"Where'd that come from? Did everybody get one?" he asked.

Nope—Ken bought it for his coach.

"He's a tough competitor, and he's going to do everything he can to beat you. But this guy was a Teddy bear," Picciolo said.

Will Cunnane was in the majors in 1997, a twenty-two-year-old trying to find his way. Early in the season, during one of the team's road trips, the pitcher was wearing his one suit, because he was a rookie and that's all he had. "Hey, we're going shopping," Ken told him.

"How come?" Cunnane asked.

"I'm sick and tired of watching you wear the same suit over and over and over again," Ken told him. So when the Padres traveled to Miami to play the Marlins, Cunnane got a phone call at nine in the morning. "Meet downstairs, we're going shopping," Ken told him. There he found Caminiti, Joyner, Henderson, and Vaughn. Next thing Cunnane knew, he and his teammates were at some brightly colored building complex, and he was being asked what he wanted to eat. "He'll have what I'm having," Ken said, which turned out to be chicken marsala. "I get a tape measure around my legs, from the crotch to the foot, around my waist, shoulder. Two hours later, we had suits, we had shirts, this and that and the other," Cunnane said.

Cunnane glanced at the price tag: $2,200 a suit, "and he got me two," he said. "I was like, 'Is this what the big leagues is really like?'"

* * *

Despite sputtering through the first three months of the season trying to regain his form, Ken was voted the starting third baseman for the National League All-Star team. The shoulder recovery meant he was still weak when batting lefty—he needed to get his strength back, which would take time—and a hamstring injury sent him to the DL, sapping his ability to drive the ball with his legs like he had the season earlier.

But the fans adored Ken. He got the nod for the game, held at Jacobs Field in Cleveland, even though he had the worst stats of any starting player, with only 6 home runs, 35 RBIs, and a .247 batting average. Fellow third baseman Matt Williams was in the American League after being traded to Cleveland, and up-and-comers Chipper Jones and Scott Rolen were still emerging, making Ken the most well-known National League player at his position at the moment. So 1,438,736 circles next to his name were punched out on ballots, about 300,000 more than for Chipper Jones.

He was representing the Padres along with outfielder Tony Gwynn, the immortal hitting machine selected to start; outfielder Steve Finley, chosen as a reserve; and their manager, Bruce Bochy, nabbed for the NL's coaching staff.

Ken's back was bothering him, but that didn't keep him out of the lineup . . . although he inexplicably wore the wrong uniform for the game. Every player on the National League squad—coaches, pitchers, and hitters—wore their gray uniforms for the game. Not Ken. He ended up wearing a blue Padres alternate. He also nearly missed his spot for introductions. Ken jogged out of the dugout, his steps choppy like he was running through tires, and smiled as he high-fived his friends, his buddies razzing him and cheering him on. Just about every person along the line had a connection with Ken. The National League's manager, Bobby Cox, had scouted Ken as a minor leaguer and tried to trade for him, to no avail. Leading off for the NL was his Houston buddy Craig Biggio. Hitting second was his current teammate Gwynn. Third was Barry Bonds, the guy with the best stats in 1996. Fourth was Mike Piazza, the star Dodgers catcher who'd been envious of Ken's MVP heroics. Fifth was Jeff Bagwell, the Astros masher who'd competed against Ken for the third base job in 1991, only to shift to first and become one of his closest friends. Rockies outfielder Larry Walker and Ken, a decade earlier, were two of the top prospects in the Double-A Southern League, and they spent the ensuing years playing against each other. Ray Lankford, batting eighth, smashed a liner off Ken's cheekbone in 1993. Reds shortstop Barry Larkin, his teammate on Team USA in 1984, was elected to start but didn't play. In his place was Atlanta's Jeff Blauser, who was born in Los Gatos and played college ball at Sacramento City College before reaching the majors a few weeks ahead of Ken.

Backup players standing down the line included his former Astros team-mates Kenny Lofton and Curt Schilling, two breakout players Houston traded away too soon, along with pitcher Darryl Kile, who the Astros had smartly kept, a good, kind man with a lethal curve.

Ken's first at bat was against that tall, lanky USC pitcher Randy Johnson, who'd become the nastiest pitcher in baseball, eighty-two inches of heat and fury. The ball was rocket artillery coming out of the Big Unit's hand, so you were just happy to hit it, which Ken did—he grounded out to short to end the second inning, and grounded out against Detroit's Justin Thompson in the fifth, and that was that.

* * *

As Ken watched the Rocky Mountains out the window, the sky full of bands of amber and purple, he couldn't help but think about the future.

Nancy and the girls were here, in Padres owner John Moores's private Challenger jet, along with Bruce Bochy and Tony Gwynn and their families, on their way to connect with the team in Denver to start the second half of the season. The first half was shit—the reigning division champs were in fourth place, thirteen games back at 38–49—but anything could happen. Ken could feel his bat heating up again, just like it had in his MVP season. . . .

As the plane approached its destination, Ken watched the runway. *Wow, that's neat*, he thought. Everything seemed so steady and normal—until it wasn't.

"And all of sudden it went sideways and the wing almost hit the ground," Ken said. A wind shear, a sudden difference in wind speed or direction, jolted the twelve-seater sideways. Quick action by pilot Ken Rogoff kept the plane from crashing, narrowly averting a devastating tragedy for a sport that still mourns the crash deaths of stars Roberto Clemente and Thurman Munson during the 1970s.

"If the pilot makes a slip, a half-second wrong decision, we're all over that pavement," Ken said later.

Rogoff remained humble about his efforts. "It was a freak thing that happened. Luckily, everyone was OK," he recalled decades later, not wanting to say much more.

For Caminiti, the near disaster made him reflective. Life is short and fragile. It can be taken away at any time.

"It puts a new perspective, for right now on me, about life," Caminiti said. "You've just got to enjoy yourself, because you never know."

Ken was enjoying himself on July 10 against the Rockies and emergency starter John Burke to begin the second half. They could have been teammates, Caminiti and Burke, but the pitcher declined to sign with the Astros after being drafted in 1991. So now they were on opposite sides of the field, and Ken was unburdened of care: *See the ball and hit the ball.* Quilvio Veras and Tony Gwynn reached base in front of him. Burke worked the count to 1-and-2, but Ken pulverized the next pitch, sending it to the upper deck in Coors Field 465 feet away, near purple-painted seats representing one mile above sea level. He batted in the fourth, again with two men on, and worked the count to 2-and-0 before smashing the ball off the right field foul pole.

It was his first multihomer game since the playoffs against the Cardinals the previous season. With his two-homer, six-RBI outburst, Ken was putting the National League on notice: I'm *really* back. "My problem is I try to swing too hard," Ken said. "Today, I had rhythm and timing. Rhythm and timing are everything. If you don't have timing and rhythm, you're going to try to muscle everything."

Once again, over the second half of the season, Ken was magic—15 doubles, 20 home runs, 55 RBIs, .331 batting average. But the Padres never turned the corner, finishing in last place in the division and a franchise-worst 4.99 ERA. It was frustrating to fall short of expectations. But after he'd endured so many wasted seasons in Houston, Ken was happy to have expectations. This team had the talent to go far in the playoffs. . . . Ken could feel it. The Padres had a strong core of talent. It just needed an ace to take it over the top.

CHAPTER 20

TG

Tony Gwynn had the best laugh. It rumbled from deep inside of him, *he-he-he-he-he-he*, hoarse and raspy like a squeaky wheel, and whenever he laughed, you couldn't help but laugh yourself.

The laugh was disarming, as pure and perfect as his swings on singles through the "5.5 hole" between shortstop and third base.

"TG" did a lot of hitting and laughing during his years with the Padres. Chuckles and base hits helped to overshadow some of the frustrations he endured along the way—seeing many of his best years wasted on dead-end teams, as well as the heaviness of his eight batting crowns. Because he was so good at hitting, and such an established player, he was thrust into a team leadership role that he didn't necessarily seek out the way that his teammates Ken Caminiti and, later, reliever Trevor Hoffman did.

Ken built a rapport with Gwynn during their first season together, shadowing the hitting guru. But over their years as teammates, signs of friction started to brew between the two superstars, multiple people connected to the Padres say. Many of the issues dealt with the players' differing styles in communicating and approaches to their roles with the team. Ken privately grizzled to friends that he thought Gwynn was costing him RBIs with his conservative baserunning in 1996, which is statistically true—that year, Gwynn's extra bases taken percentage, a measure of a runner's ability to take more than one base on a single, or more than two bases on a double, was 26 percent, the lowest for a full season in his career and a significant departure from his 45 percent career average—but such criticism fails to take into account how much pain Gwynn was enduring due to an injured heel and frayed Achilles tendon.

Ken enjoyed going out to eat with teammates to steakhouses, sitting down for two or three hours and opening up. He invited Gwynn out on a number of occasions, Ken's friends say, but Gwynn preferred grabbing food and taking it back to his hotel room. He was more of a homebody, a lone wolf where camaraderie was concerned.

"I don't think Tony cared about being a leader. And part of that was that Tony didn't run with the guys," longtime Padres broadcaster Ted Leitner said. "Tony got done, went to his room, watched videotape; if Alicia [his wife] was on the road, they would be together and have room service or go out to dinner. And Tony didn't drink. Tony didn't run with the guys, and Ken did all that. And so sometimes you get a bad rap that you're not a leader or that sort of stuff, because you don't do what everybody else does. Tony's leadership was magnificent from the standpoint of *this is how you work*. This is how you have a work ethic. This is how you prepare every single day."

Ken also became frustrated after Tony, on multiple occasions, insulted his friends or had them removed from the clubhouse without discussing it with him first.

One occasion occurred at spring training in 1997, when Ken's childhood friend Dave Moretti had a broken toe. Ken wanted a Padres staffer to drive Moretti in a golf cart to a back field where he was filming a commercial, Moretti said, but that plan was nixed when Gwynn started complaining about it. "He doesn't need to drive you, you can walk. You're strong enough, you can walk," Gwynn said, according to Moretti. Later, when Ken found about the situation, he was "steaming mad," Moretti said.

Another incident involved David Indermill, known as "Detail Dave" because he would spend games cleaning players' cars, making them spotless inside and out. Indermill—who first connected with Ken and befriended his teammates through him—was in the clubhouse one day, and Gwynn complained, and the next thing he was gone. "I got eighty-sixed out of there because of Tony. And Ken was so pissed because I was his boy," Indermill said. His ban continued for years after both players retired.

In terms of the clubhouse issue, Bruce Bochy sides with Gwynn. "Tony did the right thing. You know, you're not supposed to have friends in the clubhouse, and I think Cammy at first was upset, but hey, I think he saw that Tony did what he would have done, too," the manager said.

Tony had a deeper reason to be upset with Ken, too. Gwynn was one of the players who sounded the alarm on steroids in baseball in 1995, only to have his teammate use them on his way to becoming a power-hitting superstar—success that momentarily made Ken a bigger fan favorite in San Diego.

Following their careers, after Ken's steroid use became widely known, Gwynn penned an interesting column for ESPN, writing, "Although I still love the guy, knowing he took steroids—at least during his MVP season in 1996—taints what he accomplished as well as baseball's integrity. As a former teammate who was on the field working alongside him, it is disappointing to know Caminiti was doing something to enhance his abilities."

And by 1997, Ken was starting to fall back on his addictions again. . . . The other shoe was inevitably going to drop. Tony—who'd tragically endured the cycle of addiction playing out with teammates like Eric Show and Alan Wiggins—simply wanted one more chance to win after so many listless summers. "Tony didn't like to be a leader in the clubhouse," said beat reporter Barry Bloom, who became close with Gwynn. "As he became older, he ended up having that foisted on him, and he just never wanted to do it. And he didn't have patience with people. He turned very quickly with watching Caminiti doing what he was doing."

Whatever feelings they harbored internally, those close to the star players saw nothing but reverence between them outwardly. That includes Chris Gwynn, Tony's kid brother, who got the key hit to help the Padres win the division in the last game of the 1996 season. "I think it was mutual respect," Chris Gwynn said of the relationship between Tony and Ken.

The stars supported each other publicly, expressing excitement that they got to play together.

"A human highlight film," Gwynn called Caminiti.

Ken gave Tony's praise right back. "Tony's the man. He's Mr. San Diego. Those are some heavy shoes to fill when you've got one of the greats saying that you're a good player," Ken told journalist Jane Mitchell.

Ken and Tony were complicated, imperfect, special people who, even if they had minor squabbles along the way, found some of their greatest successes together. Tony got on base, and Ken hit him home. The formula would take the Padres far.

CHAPTER 21

CAPTURE THE FLAG

The Padres were ready to roll the dice.

Despite the first-to-worst turn in 1997, San Diego featured the core of a winning ball club. The outfield, with Tony Gwynn in right, Steve Finley in center, and Greg Vaughn in left, had the potential to generate lots of runs. Corner infielders Ken and Wally Joyner could carry the team and provided veteran leadership. Quilvio Veras and Chris Gomez were steady at second and short, and Carlos Hernández had pop in his bat at catcher. Closer Trevor Hoffman anchored San Diego's bullpen. Hoffman would enter games to the AC/DC song "Hells Bells," and from the first guitar chords to the final out, everything was electric.

But the rotation was missing something. An edge. The kind of intensity Dave Stewart possessed during his playing days. He was a guy you didn't mess with, someone who owned the mound, and the plate, and your mind—he may have been one of the few baseball figures with a more menacing glare than Ken. After Padres pitching coach Dan Warthen was fired at the end of the 1997 season, GM Kevin Towers decided to fill the role from within the front office—Stewart was already serving as a special assistant for the Padres, and now he'd pick up coaching duties, too. Stewart's task: Make the Padres pitchers *own* the games they started. Make every pitch count. And make the opposition fear you. Improve on the previous year's 47–62 record, 4.98 ERA, and 933 innings pitched, or about 5.75 per start.

He set the intensity level from the first day of spring training, making sure the pitchers did extra running. They needed to be better conditioned. That would cut down on the injuries and help them go deeper in games.

"They were a good group of guys that were anxious to learn, and they were also anxious to compete," Stewart said.

It helped having a true ace, a number one starter, someone who could go toe to toe with the other team's best pitcher. Someone who could neutralize a Maddux or Smoltz or Martínez or Johnson or Mussina. The Marlins happened to have just that kind of ace in Kevin Brown and were in a liquidation sale, just like your local furniture store—everything must go—after winning a surprise World Series. The thirty-two-year-old Brown went 16–8 during the 1997 season, then outdueled "Mad Dog" Maddux and "Gretzky" Glavine in the playoffs with ice in his veins.

The Marlins fielded offers for Brown, who had one year left on his contract. The Mets were a possible destination, but San Diego offered three prospects (one of whom was Derrek Lee, a first baseman who went on to have a solid career). Having Brown allowed the Padres to move Andy Ashby and Joey Hamilton and Sterling Hitchcock back in the rotation. Between Brown and Stewart, the Padres had a new tone and depth and mandate: Win now.

Brown, a ground ball pitcher who started tinkering with a forkball that spring, would also be tossing in front of an infield that featured the reigning Gold Glove third baseman three years running. But it would be a little while before Ken got to play behind the Padres' new ace. Ken was still recovering from surgery on his right patella tendon, and while he expected to be ready for spring training, he ended up missing the first nine spring training games and finally got a pinch-hit at bat (he grounded out to first) after pleading his case to Bochy. He was tired of watching his teammates play without him.

"I talked my way in," he said.

Soon enough, Ken was easing back into his spot in the field and lineup, and he was mashing: flirting with .400 and hitting homers in consecutive games. But even though his bat was heating up and his team seemed built for a deep playoff run, something wasn't right with Ken. He was surly and withdrawn, less available, less open. He'd make plans, then disappear. He spent more time alone. He was becoming someone you couldn't quite trust to do the right thing.

The woman he was dating in 1997 was still in the picture, and he was gravitating more and more to the wrong people and pulling back from the teammates and friends who revered him, putting up walls and acting more and more like the old Ken from the early 1990s.

"We could see his mood changes. He was much more irritable, much more reclusive. He just wasn't quite the same guy. I thought a lot of it was because he was down on himself 'cause he wasn't quite putting up the same numbers, being the same player; he was having a hard time handling that," Bochy said.

For Bochy, and others, you'd ask Ken how he was doing. *I'm fine*. You didn't expect him to tell you the truth, but you wanted to ask anyway because you cared.

Friends like Dave Moretti expressed their concerns to Ken about his backsliding.

"I know I sound like a nag, but these people aren't healthy for you. They're just not," Moretti told him.

"I know who I am. I'm OK. I know who I am," Ken responded.

"I know who you are, too, but I also know that sometimes we can't fight addiction and we can't fight weakness. Sometimes you get yourself in a situation, and you can't fight it."

The more Ken felt like a screwup, the more his inner critic screamed at him, the more self-fulfilling it all became. He felt like he couldn't do anything right. Which is why after the 0-for-4 games he'd spend extra time signing autographs, because he felt like he owed the fans *something* after letting them down.

In his bad times, he couldn't figure out how to quiet his self-hate. But when he faced innings of insults from a heckler at a game at Peoria Stadium in that spring of 1998, Ken couldn't block it out. And he wouldn't let it rest. This was personal. It tapped into something deep. After Ken was pulled from the game, he showered and changed and sat down in the stands right next to the heckler.

He didn't say a word.

For three.

Long.

Minutes.

After what felt like an eternity of silence, he turned to the now-quiet heckler. "Do you know who I am?"

"Yeahhh, I know who you are," the man told Ken.

"I don't come to your job, screaming at you about what you do wrong. So why did you come here and do that to me?"

Ken recounted the story soon after it happened to his friend James Hayashi, who was at the stadium that day. "That guy was scared shitless," Ken told him.

Hayashi noticed Kevin Brown standing near Ken, keeping a close watch, and wanted to know why. *Because Kevin Brown thought I was going to kill the guy.* This time, the ace was backing up the Gold Glove third baseman, instead of the other way around. As Ken stood, his mission of making the heckler feel two inches tall complete, nearby fans erupted in applause.

Recounting the story, Ken was "I think more proud of himself at how much he scared the crap out of the guy by not saying anything," Hayashi said.

* * *

The most bittersweet season of Ken's career began with the ace on the mound and the offense taking a big lead. By mid-April, an eight-game winning streak cemented the Padres' status near the top of the league. The team had so many weapons. In an April 10 game against the Arizona Diamondbacks, one of two expansion teams in 1998, San Diego fell behind 4–2 and was down to its final out with Greg Vaughn on base. But Mark Sweeney and Quilvio Veras both walked to load the bases, bringing up Steve Finley, who took reliever Félix Rodríguez's pitch up and out for a two-out walk-off grand slam, the kind you dream about when you're playing backyard baseball as a kid.

The season started as a dream for Ken, who homered in four straight games in April and had six home runs in the season's first twelve games—the same output he had for the entire first half of the season before.

But while he was crushing the ball, Ken was secretly hurting, physically and emotionally. Before an April 18 game against the Pirates, he was pained by an ingrown toenail—so he ripped it out with a pair of pliers. Roughly an hour later, he was hitting a single in his first at bat of the game, then torpedo-ing through second baseman Tony Womack to break up a potential double play. He played ten innings that day he ripped out his ingrown toenail, and the Padres won 7–5.

On April 22, Ken drove home the game-winning run in the fourteenth inning against the Cubs, helping the Padres to a 15–4 record—the best start in franchise history. But as the calendar turned to May, Ken was headed in the wrong direction, mired in an 0-for-15 slump.

The Padres were playing at Miami's Pro Player Stadium in early May when a clubhouse attendant found Bochy. "Cammy's outside. He wants to talk to you," the attendant told the Padres manager. Bochy walked outside the clubhouse and looked around. No Ken there. . . . He eventually found the toughest man in baseball outside in the parking lot, in the 100-degree heat, bawling.

"He was balled up in a corner by the fence there," Bochy said. "He was just kind of breaking down weeping. And then I realized that we've got some serious issues here."

Bochy consoled Ken. "He was looking for help. He wanted help and he knew he needed it and he didn't battle this," the manager said.

"And so what the club did is it put him on the disabled list to get him some help and send him home to his family in Texas. So we just gave him a break from baseball to try to get him right. He went home to Nancy and the girls, and I talked to him at some point there, and he seemed so much better, like he was doing well, and eventually he came back."

The Padres told everyone Ken's left quad was acting up, and it was, but it wasn't the real reason he wasn't playing. They could have attributed the absence to any physical ailment: knee, shoulder, abdominal, leg, wrist, arm, back. . . . The parallels between Bochy's tearful conversation with a shattered Ken in 1998 and the surly response Ken had had five years earlier with Astros manager Art Howe—in which Howe suggested the very thing the Padres ended up doing with Ken, sending him home and covering it up, and Ken said no—speak to Ken's recognition of what he was up against. He knew trying to bury this and move on wouldn't work. He couldn't lie and tell Bochy he was OK this time.

* * *

With Ken out of action, his buddy Greg Vaughn provided punch in the middle of the lineup. Vaughn, who roomed with Ken after his trade to San Diego in 1996, was left for dead by the Padres as his average in 1997 neared the so-called Mendoza Line, .200, that separates bad from really bad hitters. He was still getting accustomed to the National League, and never could get comfortable platooning with Rickey Henderson. . . . The Padres decided to ship the slumping left fielder to the damn Yankees for Kenny Rogers and Mariano Duncan, but a rotator cuff injury showed up on Vaughn's physical and the Yanks voided the deal. Now Vaughn was effectively unwanted by two teams. But by working on vision exercises and getting hitting tips from Tony Gwynn, and getting to play every day, Vaughn was hitting the ball again, and hitting it hard—he knocked 12 homers in May, with a .330 average.

The Padres went 11–9 during Ken's absence. He returned to the team in Houston, of all places, his old haunt. He'd spent parts of eight seasons playing in the Astrodome, and here he was back again in imposter's clothes. The May 23 game started pretty much like his major league debut a decade earlier, when he made one play after another at third base before showing off the lumber. Ken cleanly fielded grounders by Derek Bell and Sean Berry in the bottom of the first. Then, in the top of the second, he lined a double to left field and scored the game's first run three batters later. He singled in his second at bat. San Diego was up 3–2 until the bottom of the eighth, when Berry homered off Dan Miceli to give the Astros the lead. In the top of the ninth, with Quilvio Veras ninety feet from home, Caminiti came up with two outs to face fireball closer Billy Wagner. A chance to be the hero.

Ken struck out looking to end the game.

"When he came back, he looked fresh, he looked close to the old Cammy," Bochy said. "But it was a matter of time before he was right back running through that cycle again."

The cycle was painful. It was bad enough when Ken was using alcohol and drugs, but piling steroids on top of his substance abuse made him a different person, difficult and moody. Near the latter part of the season, he was back to using cocaine again, a shell of the person and player he'd been during the height of his Padres days a few seasons earlier. His body and spirit were breaking down.

He felt like a failure, which only drew him further and further into his addictions. . . .

And yet, you hoped he could turn things around, rip the IV out of his arm and go hit a home run like he did in Monterrey. He made you believe that he could do it, even when things turned bad.

Throughout that 1998 season, his Padres colleagues did their best to remember the Cammy of summers past, everything he'd done before, and kept their fingers crossed that he could jump-start the engine again. Without his efforts, this team wouldn't be in this position. His strong 1995 season had established a foundation for the team that set the stage for his epic success in 1996, which caused the Padres to get Greg Vaughn and start thinking big, and gave the team hope that it could wash away its frustrating 1997 season, which motivated the Padres to gamble and trade for Kevin Brown, and without any of that . . . who knows?

Despite the struggles, Ken had battled back, again and again. If he was in uniform, if he was on the field, you could never count him out. Broken bones, torn rotator cuffs, ingrown toenails, bad knees, bad back, hamstring pulls, abdominal strains, addiction—he was going to keep fighting, no matter what he was facing.

But Ken was on the back end of thirty-five now. And after spending years pushing himself beyond the limits, of burning the candle on "both ends and in the middle," as his Astros teammate Rob Mallicoat said, Ken's body and spirit began pushing back more forcefully. Bochy tried to preserve Ken as much as he could, subbing him out of games late for defensive replacement Ed Giovanola. But Ken took that personally, because he took a lot personally, and he wasn't one to be OK watching others play in his place.

"It's the worst," he said. "Because when you're struggling that bad at the plate, you can still save the game with a great play in the field. I haven't made many of those this year."

* * *

While Ken's return gave the Padres an emotional lift, the team was sputtering, losing four of five in early June to fall to second place behind the Giants and Barry Bonds, quietly having one of his best seasons—37 home runs, 122 RBIs, .303 batting average, 130 walks, 1.047 OPS, *walked intentionally with the bases loaded.* But no one was paying attention to Barry Bonds in 1998. Instead, they were focused on Mark McGwire and Sammy Sosa, who were forging a two-man traveling homer show.

The single-season home run record at that point, Roger Maris's sixty-one, was set in 1961—an expansion year (welcome, Senators and Angels) in which the season was extended from 154 to 162 games, causing some traditionalists to affix an invisible asterisk to the accomplishment, as if it didn't mean as much. Now, 1998 was another expansion year (Diamondbacks and Devil Rays), and in time there would be an invisible asterisk added to Mac's and Sammy's feats, too.

The Padres and Giants entered June 12 tied for first and beginning a three-game series against each other. In the first game, the Giants jumped to a 3–2 lead behind a Bonds homer (of course), and Ken came up to bat in the seventh with a runner on second and hit a double to tie the game. He got the job done, and San Diego opened it up from there, scoring seven straight runs for a 10–3 victory. (Ken was intentionally walked his next at bat.) Joey Hamilton and Andy Ashby handcuffed Giants hitters for the rest of the series, and Trevor Hoffman closed the door for the sweep, part of an eleven-game winning streak that saw San Diego advance its division lead to five and a half games.

The Padres wouldn't trail in the division for the rest of the season.

Even though Ken was struggling in 1998, he was still hitting the ball hard—his 29 home runs that year were his second-highest career total, behind his MVP season. But his batting average, .252, was the lowest for any season since his blurry, drug-addled 1990 campaign. Where in 1996 and 1997 he was one of the league's best second-half hitters, he all but disappeared down the stretch in 1998, batting .237 in August and .177 in the season's final month.

And based on defensive wins above replacement, or dWAR, Ken was the worst regular third baseman in the league in 1998, with -1.0 dWAR (Jeff Cirillo led the league with 2.0 dWAR, followed by Scott Rolen, Vinny Castilla, and Matt Williams).

But Ken still had the potential to wow you on some nights. Like on July 12, when he battled left wrist and elbow pain—Bochy considered sitting him—to smash three dingers, driving in five runs. The win stretched the Padres' division lead to seven games.

Or August 25, when he endured back pain to club two home runs (one against his former Astros teammate Curt Schilling) as San Diego topped the Phillies 5–3.

But those nights were becoming less and less frequent.

* * *

The Padres players did so much together—they legitimately enjoyed one another's company. They golfed. They went out to eat. They were a family.

"That team was so close, we could get on anybody anytime during that time. Even Cammy, 'cause you couldn't always understand him when he started talking," Greg Vaughn said. So they named Ken "Cousin It" because of the way he mumbled. Vaughn was "Hootie," due to his resemblance to Hootie and the Blowfish lead singer Darius Rucker. "I had T-shirts made up," Vaughn said. Tony Gwynn was nicknamed "Gary Coleman," Kevin Brown was "Beetlejuice," and coach Rob Picciolo was dubbed "Gilligan" after Bob Denver's character on the TV sitcom. Steve Finley became "Woodstock" due to his long hair, and Joyner became "Mark Messier," due to his lack of hair.

After Wally Joyner shaved his head, some of the players started touching their bald heads together. "Before the games, we just all had a special handshake or something. We'd touch heads or rub heads," Vaughn said, adding, "Wally is one of the funniest human beings you'll ever meet in your life."

As if the Padres needed more personality in 1998, on June 20 they acquired Jim Leyritz in a trade with the Red Sox. Leyritz, a catcher and utility player who carried the inauspicious nickname "the King" (bestowed by Yankees icon Don Mattingly), had an ego like a hot-air balloon, liable to float away if it wasn't held down by ropes and sandbags. Leyritz had a funky stance—he'd keep his front leg stiff while twirling the bat pre-pitch like he was spinning rain off an umbrella—but whenever the stage was largest, when the lights were brightest, he delivered.

Case in point, American League playoffs, 1995, Yankees-Mariners, Game 2, when his home run in the fifteenth inning won the game for New York. Or the 1996 World Series, Game 4, with the Yankees down 6–3, Leyritz took Mark Wohlers into the bullpen to tie the game, which New York would win 8–6. The Yanks didn't lose again. He was a good guy to have on your team if you expected to play into October.

In Leyritz's first game with the Padres, he drove in three runs. He also happened to have experience catching pitcher Sterling Hitchcock, a fellow Yankees product who had bounced between the bullpen and rotation earlier in the year. Bochy pulled Leyritz into his office to see if the King could catch Hitchcock. "I can catch him with my eyes shut," Leyritz said, and with that, he was catching Hitchcock every fifth day.

As the King reconnected with Hitchcock, the normally outspoken Leyritz (by his own judgment) spent the first month adjusting to the clubhouse. "I've never been one to shy away from trying to be one of the leaders, but I also have to watch my space here, because I don't want to disrupt the ship that's going pretty well," he said of his trade to San Diego. His personality and swagger would come through in time. After he lost a bet to bald-headed first baseman Wally Joyner, Leyritz began shaving his head, too, one more element beyond his 10-ton cowboy hats and car muffler–sized belt buckles that screamed *loud*. The King was the brashest backup catcher in baseball, but he could back up all the talk. You'd bring him on because you wanted to win, then tire of his oversized personality, then ship him away and immediately miss him. Which made him a perfect fit for a team entering uncharted territory.

* * *

George Arias was a monster for Triple-A Las Vegas in 1998, batting .308 with 36 home runs and 119 runs batted in, in 114 games. Arias played third base. And Ken, struggling with off-the-field issues that were becoming increasingly obvious to the Padres, was in the final year of his three-year contract. If Arias could perform in San Diego similarly to the way he played in Triple-A, it would make Ken expendable. The Padres could let Ken walk as a free agent when the season was over. As much as everyone loved Ken—and they did—Arias was cheaper and younger and came with less baggage.

It benefited Ken to see Arias fail. But like Ken did with his potential replacement in Houston, Phil Nevin, he took Arias under his wing, inviting his understudy to stay with him when Arias got called up in August.

"He never viewed it as a threat," Arias said. "He's just that kind of a guy who cares. He just has an unwavering generosity in him." Arias saw Ken's mentorship as a once-in-a-lifetime opportunity. "I talked to him about hitting, I talked to him about playing defense, and I picked his brain. I really wanted to be a great defender, and a lot of the advice that he gave me helped me win a gold glove in Japan," Arias said.

Ken was open about lots of things with Arias, including his use of steroids. Arias asked Ken why he took the drugs, and Ken discussed his desire to keep his family secure, which was certainly one element of it, but to Arias, Ken's using the drugs went deeper than that. "There's that inner appetite that we have, and sometimes we have to go to the extreme just to try to fulfill those needs," Arias said of Ken's steroid use.

Ken was always devoted to helping his teammates reach their potential and passing along his lessons, even when he was in a rough patch—focusing on others allowed him to spend less time worrying about his own failures. He was doing *something* right. He had value in service to others, the ultimate teammate and helper and guide.

One time on a team flight, Wally Joyner and Andy Ashby and Vaughn and Ken were playing cards, and Arias was walking back to go to the bathroom.

"George, sit down here and play for me," Ken told Arias.

"I'm not gonna play for you," the understudy responded, and he went to the bathroom. On his way back to his seat, Ken grabbed Arias.

"Play for me," he said.

OK. . . . Arias ended up sitting down and playing against the vets, and winning.

"Attaboy, half for me, half for you," Ken told him.

After Arias got called up, he had a used CJ7 Jeep, just something to help him get around. He was driving Ken one day.

"George, this is a piece of junk. I've got an engine for you," Ken told him.

So two weeks later, Ken informed George that his engine was ready, and where to drop off his Jeep for installation—and now Arias had a 350 small block in his CJ7. "I ended up nearly killing myself in that thing because of the power, the force behind it," Arias said. But Ken thought the power suited Arias.

"George, that's what I'm talking about. Now you can drive around looking good," Ken told his friend.

Even though Ken and Arias were close, Ken shielded his friend from some of the things he was doing. Some nights, Ken would drop off Arias at the house, and then he'd take off with other friends as his addictions and nightlife took more and more of a hold.

* * *

If one game captured the Padres' resilience in 1998, that never-count-them-out mentality, it was on September 12 against the Dodgers. San Diego was listless, and Matt Luke, the Dodgers' left fielder, was playing the game of his career, driving in five runs to pair with an Eric Karros dinger to make it 7–0 Los Angelinos in the fifth inning.

But Wally Joyner hit a solo homer to make it 7–1 in the bottom of the fifth, and Greg Myers and Andy Sheets reached base behind him, and Chris Gomez doubled to left to make it 7–3, and then in the bottom of the sixth, the Padres went station to station to make a mess of your scorebook and take an 8–7 lead, and the bullpen shut the door, and the Padres were your 1998 National League West champions.

The players celebrated in the clubhouse and then streamed back onto the field to celebrate with the fans, all 60,823 of them, or however many were left. Ken, his hair soaked in sweat and champagne, hugged and celebrated with teammates. It was a rough year, but this was what it was all about. Reaching the postseason.

* * *

Ken's knees and back and hip flexor were bothering him heading into the playoffs.

Over the final few weeks of the season, Bruce Bochy gave Ken a few days off, hoping to keep his third baseman rested. Bochy also put Arias, Ken's backup, on the roster in case Ken couldn't play. The team went with only ten pitchers for the Division Series, and wouldn't you know it, Ken's current team was facing his old squad, the NL Central champion Astros. Houston won a franchise-record 102 games that season.

It was a season to roll the dice, and Bochy was hedging his bets in case his third baseman couldn't play. He also had his ace—Kevin Brown—taking the bump in Game 1 against Houston's own rental arm, Randy Johnson, who was 10–1 after being traded from Seattle. Johnson and Brown traded zeroes until the top of the sixth, when San Diego loaded the bases with no outs—Gwynn doubled, Vaughn and Caminiti singled—and then it was time for the King, who lofted a fly ball to center to score Gwynn and give the Padres a 1–0 lead. Vaughn homered in the eighth to make it 2–0.

Ken had some nice defensive plays during the game. But by the ninth inning, all of Brown's effort was nearly undone by Ken's struggles at third base. Bill Spiers led off the inning with a drive to third base, but Ken couldn't come up with it—his feet looked like they were stuck in hardening concrete as he flopped on the turf. The ball skirted past him to left field for a leadoff double.

After Trevor Hoffman got Derek Bell and Jeff Bagwell out, it was Moises Alou's turn. He hit a grounder to third. Ken leaped to his right, frog-like, to grab the ball on the third base line. But he struggled to get a good base underneath him. He balanced on his right knee and stuck his left leg out like a bike's kickstand to hold himself up, then chucked the ball. . . . It nearly hit Spiers as it trickled across the infield, away from Joyner at first base to score the runner. Hoffman got the next hitter, Carl Everett, to fly out to center to secure the 2–1 win, but with his mobility diminished, Ken was becoming a defensive liability for the Padres.

* * *

As the calendar turned to October, the King, Leyritz, came alive.

San Diego was down 4–2 in the ninth inning of Game 2. Ken singled, and with two outs, Bochy pinch-hit for Wally Joyner. The King would face Astros closer Billy Wagner. Leyritz, down to his final strike, took Wagner the opposite way, a laser down the line. If it was fair, the game would be tied. The King took a few steps down the first base line and twisted his torso to the left, trying to will it fair.

Being that this was the King's month, he got what he wished for—home run! This was exactly why the Padres traded for him. While the Astros rallied to win in the bottom half, the Padres felt confident. They'd beaten the Big Unit at the Astrodome and had home field advantage as the series moved to San Diego.

* * *

Ken saw his pitch. Top of the seventh in Game 3.

And he *just* missed it. Batting lefty against Houston's Scott Elarton, Ken skied the ball to the heavens, high enough to bring rain and for Astros infielders Biggio and Ricky Gutierrez to both call for the ball and try to catch it, running into each other (Biggio gloved the ball). Leyritz was next. Tie game. October. The pitch was down, and the King golfed it to left. Back . . . back . . . another home run, his second in two nights, after hitting four dingers in sixty-two regular season games for the Padres. Leyritz came back to the dugout yelling and pumping up his teammates. The fans were charged up, and he and Joyner had reason to tap their bald heads together, and the Padres would take a 2–1 series lead.

The Big Unit was up next for Houston. San Diego countered with Sterling Hitchcock in Game 4. Johnson's team hadn't lost consecutive games he started since July.

Leyritz never hit Johnson all that well during his career—a .111 career batting average.

But the King came up against Johnson to lead off the second inning. Johnson was a scary man to face. His 100 mph heater could go anywhere and destroy anything in its path, birds included. Standing on top of the mound, the six-foot, ten-inch Johnson appeared nine feet tall.

And Leyritz felt as tall as Johnson stood. The King worked the count and Johnson battled back: full count. Leyritz put wood on the ball, and it went a long way. The King left the building. The fans erupted, sixty-four thousand strong. After the King crossed home plate, his teammates gathered at the corner of the dugout to congratulate him, and Ken gave Leyritz a high five and patted him on the back. The King was hot—he knew what that felt like. Ken's time was going to come soon.

In the sixth inning, as a matter of fact. Ken prided himself on picking up on Johnson tipping his pitches—the pitcher would grip the ball and hold his glove differently based on what he was planning to throw. Not that it helped Ken much—how do you hit a blur? That was always the problem with the Big Unit: He was damn near unhittable. But Ken enjoyed knowing what was coming.

He knew what was coming during his sixth-inning at bat. The game was tied 1–1, and Vaughn was on second base. Ken chopped the ball to third base. Astros third sacker Sean Berry came up with the ball and threw to first, but the sure-handed Bagwell couldn't handle it, and San Diego was up 2–1. The Padres wouldn't trail again, and the champagne flowed after the game. For the first time since 1984, the team made it to the National League Championship Series.

And they'd be facing a Braves team that won a franchise-record 106 regular season games. No big thing.

* * *

The Padres endured a two-hour rain delay and seven innings of John Smoltz, and somehow had the lead, so closer Trevor Hoffman was on the mound to close out Game 1 of the NLCS. Hoffman got one out and walked stocky left fielder Ryan Klesko. The next hitter, catcher Javy López, singled to left field, putting runners on first and second . . . but Klesko inexplicably kept running to third.

Rubén Rivera, on for the injured Greg Vaughn, threw the ball to Ken, but he couldn't come up with it—instead, Klesko matched his face with Caminiti's shoulder and wound up with a bloody nose. With a runner on third base, the next hitter, Andruw Jones, lifted a fly ball to center, and suddenly Atlanta had new life, coming back against a near-automatic closer. Hoffman's appearances in 1998 usually went, in this order: "Hells Bells," three quick outs, high fives. This time, the game would go to extras.

In the tenth, Ken came up to bat against Braves rookie pitcher Kerry Ligtenberg with the score knotted at 2–2. When Ken came up in the first inning with two men on, he didn't even take the bat off his shoulder. Between that and the misplay on the Klesko tag, it was obvious he was hurting.

Ligtenberg wasn't hitting the strike zone to start the at bat—Ken worked the count to 3-and-0, then took one strike to move to 3-and-1.

The pitcher did not want to lose this hitter, who was in a 2-for-18 slump, especially since the King was on deck, and the King had haunted Atlanta in postseasons past. Better to throw Ken your best pitch, so Ligtenberg did. Fastball down.

And Ken answered with his best swing, driving the ball to left-center. Andruw Jones jogged toward the wall, but he ran out of room, and the ball landed about ten rows up. What a time to dial up a moment. . . .

"I was seeing the ball good. My timing was back. And I felt good. It was big," Ken said after his game-winning home run. It was very big. And it reflected Ken's grittiness, a chance to remind people of the player he used to be. After Kevin Brown outdueled Tom Glavine in Game 2, going the distance and scattering three hits in a 3–0 Padres win, San Diego found itself up 2–0 and returning home. The World Series was in the Padres' sights. But Atlanta wasn't ready to fold just yet.

* * *

The King wasn't going to back down, even if he was facing home plate collisions and balls flying at him.

Game 3 of the NLCS saw Atlanta take a 1–0 lead in the third off Sterling Hitchcock, who was coming into his own in the postseason. But the Braves failed to push across another run due to a phenomenal play at the plate when left fielder John Vander Wal threw the ball home and Leyritz hung on to tag out Walt Weiss. Inning over.

The next time the King came to the plate, Atlanta pitcher Greg Maddux plunked him. A little payback, eh? The Padres came alive in the fifth inning, when Hitchcock singled past a diving Weiss—his dives just weren't working out this day—and with two outs, Steve Finley doubled home the pitcher. Tony Gwynn was up next. . . . No way Maddux was pitching to Gwynn, who batted .429 against him during his career. And that meant Ken's turn to hit. Ken sliced a single up the middle to score Finley, and the cheering washed over him. He was getting it done, somehow. And after a 4–1 victory over Maddux and the Braves, Ken's Padres were one step away from the World Series.

After Atlanta won Game 4, the stage was set for another round of heroics from Ken in Game 5. One win away. . . .

First inning, John Smoltz on the mound . . . someone Ken would face in seventy-seven regular season plate appearances without a home run.

Finley was on first base. . . .

Smoltz delivered a ball off the plate, and Ken drove the pitch to the opposite field. . . . The ball kept climbing. . . . Klesko raced to the wall and jumped . . . but it was out of his reach, creeping over the wall and landing amid the palm trees for a two-run home run.

The fans were electric, and Ken pumped his fist to the crowd, a moment of pure joy that captured the energy and vibrance of Ken's successes in San Diego. With lucky breaks like these, the Padres were going to clinch the pennant at home, and Ken was going to be the hero—but Atlanta's Michael Tucker drove in five runs—three on an eighth-inning homer off Kevin Brown, pitching in relief—as Atlanta squeaked past the Padres 7–6.

Two days, a cross-country flight, and another strong outing from Hitchcock later—along with a five-run sixth inning—Ken and the Padres were National League champs. "I can't describe what it feels like. All I know is that I have been living for this moment," Ken said after the Padres clinched the pennant.

CHAPTER 22

FALLING DOWN

Ken's body was failing him by the time the World Series rolled around.

And his marriage was coming apart at the seams, too.

Things between Ken and Nancy started going sideways before Game 1 in New York against the Yankees, before the moment Ken had been waiting for his entire career. Nancy wasn't stupid. The girlfriend he'd started seeing the season before was still in the picture.

Ken had been spiraling again in his sobriety, too. After experiencing his breakdown in the early part of the 1998 season, Ken's drug use intensified near the end the year.

Nancy was mad, and she was sad, and she was concerned. . . . She was worn out. Worn out from trying to hold their family together while her husband's problems intensified.

They could talk about it further after Game 1. Ken had a game to play.

* * *

During introductions ahead of Game 1, the Yankees Stadium faithful rained down boos and vitriol on the Padres players.

All until Jim Leyritz, the King, was announced.

Yankees fans couldn't forget his previous heroics for the Bronx Bombers.

But after the King tipped his cap—he wrote the number 39 on it for New York's Darryl Strawberry, who was getting treated for colon cancer—the boos resumed for Padres first baseman Wally Joyner.

"I must've done something," Joyner said as he walked down the baseline. "We had the edge, then we lost it," Caminiti said.

* * *

As Ken strode to the plate for his first World Series at bat, he resembled a guy looking to pick a bar fight. Fast walk. Crisp outfit. The goatee. A scowl to size up the competition.

He had someone he wanted to drive home. A single would give the Padres the lead, but getting to second base, third base, or home would be preferable. His teammate, Quilvio Veras, who ran faster than an overflowing creek, was on third base, ninety feet away.

Two outs, top of the first inning.

Batting right-handed, Ken performed his usual pre-pitch routine, kicking the dirt with his back cleat, then flicking the bat at waist level, shadow-swinging with a metronome's precision—tick-tock, tick-tock, tick-tock—before positioning the bat over his shoulder and setting his hands.

Yankees pitcher David Wells delivered the first pitch, a looping curve high for a ball.

The barrel-shaped power pitcher—whose exploits off the field, such as drunken all-nighters, no-holds-barred interviews, and a tendency to strip in public, were almost as notable as those on it, and that included a perfect game months earlier—focused in.

Wells didn't want to fall behind in the at bat, especially with Jim Leyritz, the King, on deck. The pitcher got the signal from his catcher and fired a fastball on the outside edge of the plate. In his best times, Ken could take the pitch and drive it the opposite way. But these weren't his best times. These weren't even good times or adequate times for Ken. He swung meekly, well late, unable to pick up the pitch. Ken's timing was off . . . and with one swing, everyone knew. He couldn't catch up to Wells's fastball. Or anyone else's, for that matter.

Wells tried to exploit his rival's weakness, peppering the outside corner with fastballs. Caminiti might as well have been swinging a feather duster.

With two strikes the crowd rose, cheering on Wells to get the strikeout. Caminiti exhaled, trying to collect himself. Kicked the dirt, shadow-swung, set his hands. The fourth pitch of the at bat, Caminiti finally made contact, slicing the ball foul to right field, late again.

On the next pitch—another fastball on the outside corner, of course—Ken's bat splintered. The batboy came out with two pieces of lumber. But another piece of wood couldn't fix his problems.

The crowd stood and cheered once more, anticipating the inevitable. With Caminiti guessing fastball, the colorful pitcher tucked an off-speed pitch inside, right underneath Caminiti's flailing swing.

Strike three. Inning over. Threat averted.

* * *

The Damn Yankees took a 2–0 lead, but the Padres tied the score in the third inning on a homer by Greg Vaughn, who'd been in line to be traded to New York the season before, only to have him fail a physical and return to San Diego.

In the fifth inning, Tony Gwynn strode to the plate. Mr. Padre deserved this opportunity more than anyone—he'd endured every up and down since the team last played in the World Series in 1984. Gwynn had toured Yankee Stadium's Monument Park during the workout day before Game 1, soaking in the building's history. Just like Ruth or Mantle or DiMaggio, Gwynn was a player for all time.

And against Wells, Gwynn rose to the moment, slashing Wells's pitch off the facing of the upper deck.

A home run.

For the game's best pure hitter.

You can't predict baseball. . . .

On the next pitch, Greg Vaughn hooked a ball inside the left field foul pole, his second home run of the night. It was now 5–2 San Diego. Wells was lost, and Kevin Brown was pitching for San Diego, and the crowd was quiet.

* * *

On to the seventh, and Kevin Brown was gassed.

He'd been battling a flu bug that was making its way through the Padres' pitching staff. Brown allowed two runners to reach, and then his night was over. Bochy called on reliever Donne Wall to face Yankees second baseman Chuck Knoblauch.

Wall struggled to find the strike zone on the first two pitches.

On the third, he wished he hadn't.

Knoblauch cracked the pitch to left, and the ball sailed into the left field stands. Tie game. The Yanks had life. The stadium erupted. Bedlam in New York.

Mark Langston followed for San Diego.

New York loaded the bases with a single by Derek Jeter—the superstar shortstop the Astros passed on drafting in 1992—and two walks.

First baseman Tino Martinez was the hitter, someone who'd struggled in the postseason for New York, batting .184. But sometimes the Baseball Gods smile down at you, and after Langston's 2-and-2 pitch split the strike zone three ways, umpire Rich Garcia, seeing something no one else did, called the pitch a ball.

New York had another strike, another chance, and you never, NEVER give the Yankees extra opportunities in October.

Tino became the Bambino on the next pitch, hitting a grand slam to right. A 5–2 Padres lead had been turned into a 9–5 Yankees advantage. The Padres managed to get only one more run.

* * *

Following the Game 1 loss, Ken looked dejected in the locker room, exhaling loudly during a postgame interview: *Pffffffft.*

"It's a tough one to swallow, definitely," he said. "But it's the World Series. Anything happens. We just gotta come back tomorrow."

If only Ken had taken his own advice. After the game, back at his hotel room, Ken and Nancy had a tearful conversation about the direction his life, and their life, was taking. Nancy was putting an end to whatever he had going with the woman he'd been seeing since the previous season. "He called me after the game from the bathroom telephone in his hotel, and I could hear Nancy yelling, screaming, and crying, and it broke my heart," said Ken's lifelong friend Dave Moretti. "On one hand, I felt for him, and then on the other, look what you did, you dumbass." Nancy had weathered the storm of Ken's issues before, but she was done putting up with his straying now. Ken was going to have to make major changes if their marriage was going to last.

* * *

Game 2 came down to two plays—one that was made, and one that wasn't.

In the top of the first, with two men on base and two outs, Wally Joyner drove to ball to deep right field. Yankees outfielder Paul O'Neill drifted back, toward a wall sign promoting the Wiz electronic stores, and he grafted himself onto the wall to make the catch, ending San Diego's threat without a run.

O'Neill came to bat in the bottom half and poked a grounder to third that tailed toward the line. Caminiti—not expecting the ball—backtracked toward the edge of the grass. The slow-footed O'Neill ambled up the line. Caminiti reared back and fired, failing to set his feet, rushing his throw. Joyner tried to stretch his frame another few inches and snare the ball out of the clouds. He got his glove on it, but it trickled away, and with it went the Padres' hopes. Knoblauch scored to make it 1-0. After a Bernie Williams groundout, Chili Davis hit a bouncer up the middle, just beyond the reach of a diving Chris Gomez: 2-0. Tino Martinez—the unexpected second-chance hero of Game 1—singled, and the Yankees' third baseman, Scott Brosius, singled to left field: 3-0. All runs unearned. The Yankees scored three more times in the second and once more in the third—7-0, and it felt like San Diego was just digging a deeper and deeper hole.

* * *

By the ninth inning, the game was out of reach: 9–3 Yankees. Two outs, and it was Caminiti's turn at bat. His hitting had started coming around—he hit a double the previous at bat—and despite the deficit, he remained in the game. With the bases empty, Caminiti was trying to hit a six-run homer, swinging violently.

As Caminiti made one off-balance swing after another, he began grabbing his groin. Another injury. Bochy and the team trainer came out.

"I'm fine," he told them. They persisted, and so did Ken. "I'm fine."

So Bochy and the trainer went back to the dugout, and Caminiti continued to flail away until he was frozen by a Jeff Nelson pitch down the pike. Strike three, cue "New York, New York," two-nothing Yankees.

The Padres sat in the dugout, soaking in the scene. What was there to say?

* * *

The Padres were down, but not out, for Game 3, especially with the team's hottest pitcher, Hitchcock, on the mound. New York was countering with David Cone.

The game remained 0–0 into the sixth, when Hitchcock keyed a three-run rally with a leadoff single. But his sprinting on the basepaths tired him out, and the next hitter he faced to lead off the seventh was New York's third baseman, Scott Brosius.

Where Ken was one big muscle pull, Brosius was loose and limber, lifting a ball into the palm trees to make it 3–1. Three batters later, Chili Davis hit a grounder between shortstop and third base, the type of play Ken had made a thousand times before, but this time the ball trickled past his glove.

"You cannot convince me Ken Caminiti is healthy," broadcaster Joe Buck said following Ken's error.

As the game continued, the fates of the third basemen began to juxtapose each other more and more. The thirty-two-year-old Brosius was in his first season with the Yankees, after spending the first seven years of his career with the Athletics. He wasn't a flashy player, but he could rise to the occasion, and he did in his next at bat, in the eighth inning, with Hoffman on the mound and San Diego hanging on to a 3–2 lead.

With two men on base, Brosius lifted a ball to center that kept going, beyond the 405 sign, and there went San Diego's chances. Brosius danced around the base paths into October glory.

Ken's enduring image from the World Series would come in the bottom of the eighth against that other Hall of Famer closer, Mariano Rivera.

The Qualcomm Stadium faithful cheered, and "All Along the Watchtower" played over the speakers, but this wasn't the Ken they knew.

The first pitch was a cutter down and in, and with Ken's legs failing him, his swing was all upper-body torque as he shifted on his feet in a herky-jerky manner. After he took a ball, the subsequent pitch was in a similar spot as the first one, down and in, and Caminiti put wood on the ball—sending it ricocheting into his left leg. He crumpled to the ground, rolling on the dirt, pausing for a moment before hopping up. The trainer didn't bother coming to check on him. . . . What was the point? He was just going to say he was fine, even though he was far from it.

He walked in a circle. Gathered himself. Stepped back into the box.

By this point, he was playing through every type of pain imaginable . . . the physical: his knee and groin and hip and whatever else . . . the emotional: his marriage . . . his addictions. . . . He was going to play no matter what, and this was no matter what. This was so far beyond Monterrey with his IV bags and Snickers bars. Even with the Snickers game, he was ready to tap out after five innings. . . . He knew when to say enough. Here, he was inadvertently undermining his team every time he swung the bat or touched the ball, but for anyone asking, he was *fine*, end of story, no more questions. He was going to keep going, because he didn't want to think about the alternative—the reality that things were going to be different at the end of the season, that he wasn't going to be back in San Diego. He had something special here. But then he got cocky about his sobriety and let the wrong people in, and his addictions flared up, and his play suffered, and his life became a mess again.

After the World Series ended, Ken was going to become a free agent—for the first time in his career—but he still had something to prove. To himself, to the fans, did it even matter anymore? He wanted to show the Padres something. And he wanted to hang on for a few more games because everything was going to change, and he wasn't ready for that.

Ken stepped back in the box against Mariano Rivera, who was coming into his own as the best relief pitcher in major league baseball history. Rivera waited for Jorge Posada's signal, came to a set position, and threw a fastball up.

Caminiti—swinging out of his shoes, all upper body—teetered like a spinning top, winding up on his ass. Brought to the ground. Humbled.

After the game, he camped out in a phone room in the clubhouse for more than half an hour, then went to a players' lounge, according to the *San Diego Union-Tribune*, avoiding the media and staying away from his locker.

* * *

Game 4 felt a lot like Game 3, with the Padres staying close and the Yankees finally pulling away, with Ken twisted in knots by Andy Pettitte's pitch and falling down, with Brosius—the series MVP—securing a key hit, with the Yankees bullpen keeping the lead intact.

The final score was 3–0.

Following the game, the Yankees celebrated another championship, while the San Diego crowd stuck around to cheer on its team. Ken and the other players filtered back onto the field to thank the fans for their support.

The Padres had vanquished the Astros and Braves, then faced a Yankees team that won more games than any other team in any other season.

This was a special Padres team.

And the shame of it was that everything was soon going to change for Ken and the Padres.

CHAPTER 23

MOVING ON

The fans lined the San Diego sidewalks, fifteen deep in some spots, to get a glimpse of their heroes. A chance to say thank you. The Padres fell four wins short of the ultimate prize, but you wouldn't realize it from the turnout and fervor. Players waved from open convertibles, and marching bands played, and baseball balloons floated overhead.

The parade was festive and merry. Almost every player was there: Gwynn and Finley, Vaughn and Brown, Hitchcock and Hoffman. But the player who deserved the most credit for putting the team into position to make a run for the pennant—Ken—wasn't. Without a playoff berth in 1996, Ken's MVP season, the Padres might not have felt comfortable taking a risk trading for Kevin Brown. And without Kevin Brown, the Padres weren't winning the pennant.

After the World Series was over, Ken headed home to Houston to piece his life together. He wanted to be in San Diego. But given the embarrassment of the World Series and how beat up he was . . . he just wanted to hide. And his marriage needed work. His sobriety, too. Both of those things were cratering. Now Nancy would be calling the shots. They'd been through so much. This was his last chance to make things right before she left for good, she told herself, and she meant it this time.

If Ken had his choice, he'd probably re-sign with the Padres. He felt wanted in San Diego. The manager and front office and owner and players still loved him; they always would. But Ken needed to be protected and kept in line. Maybe Nancy could move out to San Diego full-time. . . . That could go a long way toward keeping him in check. The Padres, if they were going to bring Ken back for 1999, needed some assurances that his personal life was secure.

But Nancy didn't want to uproot—Nancy wanted Ken to come home to Houston and sign with the Astros. She'd built a life with the girls there. He could play with his old friends Craig Biggio and Jeff Bagwell again while being a better family man.

Nancy called on Ken to disconnect from those she deemed negative influences. Who could blame her? Ken was surrounded by enablers and hangers-on, and he wasn't doing a good job of saying no. Someone needed to say no.

So Ken's girlfriend was gone. Nancy decided Dave Moretti was out, too. Moretti had run afoul of Nancy with his supplying steroids to Ken, and after everything went down in 1998, he was an easy target. As far as Nancy was concerned, Dave bore part of the blame for Ken's descent, too. Ken flew to San Jose after the 1998 season ended and called Dave soon after he arrived.

"Hey, I'm in town," Ken told him.

"What are you doing?"

"Can we meet?"

Suuuuure. . . . They ended up talking for five minutes or so. Ken told Dave that he was focused on repairing his life and marriage, and that they'd have to cool things off for now. Dave understood the stakes. He just wanted his friend to have a stable, steady life. They'd be in touch. Dave could still send Ken packages of steroids through the mail.

* * *

Even though Ken and the Padres considered a reunion, a few things had to happen first. For one, the team hoped to re-sign other free agents like ace pitcher Kevin Brown, who was poised to get a big raise from his $4.5 million contract. Steve Finley's contract was up, too.

And then there was the stadium vote. If San Diego voters approved Proposition C on November 3, the team would get a new stadium—a ballpark of its own—and ensure that it stayed in the area for decades to come.

Team officials suggested that passing Prop C could help the team re-sign its key players . . . but in the meantime, Ken filed for free agency, meaning he could field offers from any team.

The Padres ended up making a verbal one-year offer to Ken at $3 million, a pay cut from the $3.5 million he made in 1998. Other teams were willing to offer more. Like the Tigers. Detroit GM Randy Smith had orchestrated the twelve-player trade that brought Ken to San Diego four years earlier. Smith wanted to establish a winning culture on the Tigers, and he couldn't think of another player who could do that better than Ken.

Detroit wanted to sign Ken to a big contract: three years, $21.5 million.

"It was a young team that needed to learn how to be gritty, how to win, how to be team first. And I thought that his personality would help us mature and grow. I knew the talent, because of the injuries, had declined some, but he was still a guy whose intangibles brought a lot," Smith said.

Ken was flattered by the offer, but he wasn't motivated by money the way most players were. He had enough for a secure life for his family, and that was that. And Detroit was a long way from home.

Brrrrrrring! Brrrrrrring!

On a Sunday afternoon during the off-season, Astros owner Drayton McLane's phone rang.

It was Ken. Ken had never called McLane personally like this before. "I want to become a Houston Astro," Ken told the Astros owner, making his pitch.

"Well, Ken, we know you've been struggling. . . ."

"If you bring me back, that will not be a problem again," Ken reassured him.

McLane remembers their talking for about thirty minutes. After they ended the call, McLane got another call. It was Craig Biggio, Ken's longtime teammate and friend and the team's most established star alongside Jeff Bagwell.

"If you bring back Ken, Jeff and I will take care of him," Biggio told the owner. And that was good enough for McLane and the Astros, which offered Ken a two-year deal worth $9.5 million. It was what Nancy needed. Despite his union's frustration at him taking a hometown discount, Ken ended up turning down the Tigers and choosing the Astros. Ken was going home again.

"I'm sure a lot of the big-time ballplayers are going to be laughing at me and saying I messed up the market," Ken said. "But you can take a look at the market; I didn't mess it up. I'm not going to worry about what anyone else has to say. I only worry about my own happiness and what's best for my family."

Houston was entering this recoupling with eyes wide open. Team officials were well aware of Ken's addiction issues, between his earlier problems with the Astros and recent issues with San Diego, and the steroids weren't a big surprise, either. According to strength coach Gene Coleman, the team wanted to insert language into Ken's contract forbidding him from working with his personal trainer, but the wording was never added.

After signing with Houston, Ken remained bitter about the way his contract negotiations had been handled by the Padres. In particular, Ken singled out president and CEO Larry Lucchino.

"Larry Lucchino has no people skills. He's the money man. He'll do anything for money. It's around the whole clubhouse. Larry puts a damper on things. A lot of people there are unhappy," Ken told Bloomberg News Service.

For Lucchino, who did not respond to multiple requests for comment, the criticisms came with the job. "I'm sorry Caminiti feels that way, but he's entitled to his opinion. But the last time I looked, winning popularity contests from agents and players wasn't part of the job," he responded at the time.

There was some truth to Ken's statements. Someone had to be the money man. What was left unsaid: the Padres had ample reasons to let Ken sign elsewhere. His struggles might have been mostly hidden from the public, but they were no secret to Lucchino and others with the team. Ken's return to Houston was announced at superstar pitcher Roger Clemens's charity softball game, held at Rice University, which pitted a team of major league stars, the MLB Bombers (plus former president George H. W. Bush), against a top-flight fifty-plus softball team, the Houston Texans. Astros broadcaster Milo Hamilton was lending his voice to the game, and *Holy Toledo!* What an exciting development.

* * *

Larry Dierker was excited to have Ken play for him. As a pitcher, Dierker was one of the team's first homegrown stars during the 1960s and 1970s, before transitioning to broadcasting. The Hawaiian shirt–wearing Dierker made witty comments from the booth and seemed to have a good feel for when to make a move. And when Terry Collins was canned after the 1996 season, the Astros made Dierker their next manager.

Dierker was a calmer presence in the clubhouse. He was especially sharp managing the pitchers—he taught the starters to go deeper in games, to pitch with intensity. That effort would galvanize in 1999 with three pitchers having solid seasons. Dominican-born Jose Lima identified his starts as "Lima Time," and Lima Time was usually a fun time, especially when Lima was hitting his spots with his pitches. Astros pitchers Mike Hampton and Shane Reynolds were also coming into their own.

The broadcaster turned manager had spent years around Ken, getting to know him through functions and golf outings.

"I didn't hang out with the players when I was a broadcaster, but I felt like we were pretty good friends. So when Ken came back and I was the manager, the first time he walked through the door I shook his hand and went to give him a big hug, and he just kind of shrugged it off," Dierker said. "I thought, 'That's weird.' I thought we were pretty close. I was trying to show him how glad I was to see him and how much we wanted him, and he was being almost defensive about it. Looking back, you see some signs that things weren't right that you didn't really make much of at the time."

He wasn't the same guy he used to be. And despite some familiar faces, these weren't the same Astros, a team of up-and-coming talent looking to scrape to respectability.

After four seasons away, Ken rejoined the Astros hoping to help Houston to its third consecutive National League Central Division title. The 'Stros, led by his friends Biggio and Bagwell, had finally broken through to the postseason but hadn't been able to advance past the first round of the playoffs. The 1998 Houston team was probably the best in franchise history, especially after picking up Seattle Mariners ace Randy Johnson at the trade deadline. "We were all like kids the night before Christmas" when the trade was completed, Astros utility player Bill Spiers said. "All of a sudden the deal gets done, and we couldn't even sleep." The Big Unit went 10–1 with a 1.28 ERA and four complete-game shutouts in eleven starts for Houston, and the Astros finished the regular season with a 102–60 record, but then Ken's Padres team, behind their own rental ace Kevin Brown, squeaked past Houston, and the Astros were left to wonder, yet again, what it would take to break through.

It helped having young talent, and the Astros had that in outfielder Lance Berkman and closer Billy Wagner. Berkman, a Rice University product, was a Swiss Army knife at the dish, someone who could work a walk or smash a double or crack a homer with machinelike precision. Berkman made his major league debut in 1999, the beginning of a fifteen-year career, and he quickly connected with Ken.

Ken bonded with Billy Wagner, too. The Astros closer was a rocket strapped onto a scrappy five-foot, ten-inch frame. "Billy the Kid" fell out of a tree and broke his right arm as a boy growing up in Virginia, and while his natural right arm was healing, he taught himself how to throw left-handed, and that left arm took him to the height of the baseball world. Ken and Billy met when Ken was playing for the Padres. Billy the Kid had heard so many stories about Ken from his buddies Craig and Jeff, so they got to talking one day around the batting cage before a Padres-Astros game, and Billy the Kid was struck by Ken's warmth and intensity.

"He was a close talker," Wagner said. "He was big, bulky, spoke quietly. You really didn't know what he was thinking when he was looking at you.

"As a young player, you felt like, 'I don't want to say anything inappropriate because he might rip my head off.'"

For younger players like Billy the Kid, Ken and Jeff Bagwell cut an imposing presence, two players who didn't need to say a word—*speak softly and carry a big stick*, as Teddy Roosevelt's mantra went. "You didn't have to hear what they were thinking, you could feel it, because when they looked back, you knew when you'd done something wrong or inappropriate or you weren't pulling your load," Wagner said.

* * *

Craig Biggio tried keeping an eye on his buddy.

This was *Ken*. They went way back, longer than any of their other teammates. They'd do anything for each other. Their families were interconnected.

During spring training, Biggio was living in the same condo complex as Ken, and Biggio's agent Barry Axelrod was also staying with him. Axelrod, like his client, also lobbied for McLane to bring Ken back—the agent was close with the Astros owner.

They'd go out to dinner, Ken and Craig and Axelrod, and things seemed steady.

"We'd come back, time for bed, and Craig would get up, peek outside. . . . Cammy's car was gone," Axelrod said. "We would do our best to get him home and safe and sober, and then he'd just make those decisions. You try that hard to help someone and you think you're making progress, and then they make that decision. Man, it's tough."

Craig *tried*. He tried really, really hard. But as Ken's addictions piled up, there was only so much Craig could do to help his friend. Same went for Jeff Bagwell and so many other players.

Even if Ken's friendships with Biggio and Bagwell weren't quite the same, the trio still remained connected—to the fans, they represented the team's heartbeat. It was only fitting that they appeared together on a box for Houston's Triple Play, a honey nut toasted oats cereal produced by Famous Fixins. The box shows Ken holding an upside-down Astros helmet filled with the solid torus-shaped cereal. Bagwell and Biggio are on either side of Ken, holding spoonfuls of the sugary snack.

The cereal box came together through the efforts of Rick Licht, an agent and attorney with an eye to entertainment ventures. Licht began representing Ken near the end of his Padres days, and pretty soon a futuristic, musclebound Ken was starring in a comic book called *Super Sluggers* that showed him, Barry Bonds, Mike Piazza, and Ken Griffey Jr. serving as intergalactic peacekeepers.

As Craig and Jeff reached their wits' end trying to help Ken, Rick picked up more and more of the slack. Maybe he could help Ken. He was going to try his best.

* * *

After his return to the Astros, Ken wanted a roommate again—it brought him a sense of stability. He ended up choosing Russ Johnson, a twenty-six-year-old infielder and pinch hitter who'd played in twenty-nine career games heading into the 1999 season.

If Ken was seeking out an accountability partner, Johnson wasn't it. What could Russ Johnson say or do to rein in Ken Caminiti? Ken saw in Johnson another young player to mentor, another Phil Nevin or George Arias.

"Whenever I met him, he wanted me to be a roommate with him for a while. They don't even have roommates in the big leagues. You don't have roommates, you got your own room. And I went in there and his comment to me was, 'You're gonna keep me straight.' And I kinda laughed at his comment, because I was probably wilder than he was at that time, you know? And I was thinking to myself, 'I'm going to keep *you* straight, dude?' I said, 'I'll try.'"

Johnson did try, but Ken liked to drink, and he was generally fun and upbeat when he drank around Johnson, a notable change from his usual stoic demeanor—"very talkative and personable and a totally different person," Johnson said. "It was a different side of him that you never saw, so it was almost like an unlocked door of who he really was."

But Johnson was yo-yoing up and down between Houston and Triple-A New Orleans in 1999, meaning he wasn't always around to keep Ken straight.

Ken's 1999 season started slowly. He hit two home runs the first month, and while his batting average bounced between .275 and .300, he never really got going. For one thing, he was back to playing in the dungeon known as the Astrodome, now in its final season of use. Houston would move into a new ballpark the following season, an open-air park that presented better opportunities for hitters: Enron Field, named for the then-flourishing energy and securities company that served as corporate sponsor. After thirty-five years, it was time for the Astros to move on from the "Eighth Wonder of the World," a facility that bears some responsibility for all the wear and tear on Ken's body "The turf is hard, the mound seems so close, and it's really hard to pick up the ball. None of us are shedding a tear over leaving this place," Ken said.

Beyond home turf, Ken also had problems of the pharmacological kind that year. His sure and steady steroid supplier from previous seasons, Dave Moretti, was on the outside due to Nancy's off-season edict. Dave devised a plan to send Ken packages on the road.

"There was a particular series where—I had it timed out—I knew if I sent it at this point, he would get it at 12 p.m. on a particular day, I knew Ken was leaving the next day at noon, so there was a twenty-four-hour window," Moretti said. "Ken ended up leaving and never called to tell me that he didn't get the package. I checked the tracking number, and the package had arrived when Ken was still in the hotel. For some reason, it never got to him, and I had addressed it to his fake name, K. Callan. I don't know why he used that.

"So I called him. 'You need to talk to whoever handles this for the Astros, because it's there.' The guy ended up getting the package for him."

As it turns out, a hotel employee noticed the package and gave it to Barry Waters, the director of team travel. "The hotel forwarded the package to Waters, who opened it and found glass vials containing a white liquid that he believed to be anabolic steroids and pills that he believed to be vitamins," according to what is commonly called the Mitchell Report, an investigation into steroids in baseball that came years after Ken's baseball career ended. "Waters did not deliver the vials to Caminiti, but believing incorrectly that there was no policy requiring him to report the incident, he did not report the matter to anyone else with the Astros or to the Commissioner's Office."

With Moretti lacking a safe way to send Ken shipments, it marked the end of his days supplying his childhood friend with steroids, a partnership that had helped Ken reach the upper echelon of the baseball world. Dave continued supplying other players with steroids for another year or two, but his heart wasn't in it anymore—he was ready to move on.

"I was actually going to stop it earlier, but guys were calling, and I kind of felt bad. Because it would always start out the same way: 'What can you tell me about this?'

"They all had questions. They wanted to know. You're talking about a time when there wasn't a whole lot of truth out there."

But even if Moretti wasn't supplying him steroids anymore, Ken still needed his fix. He needed to look and feel strong. He'd have to find his drugs elsewhere.

* * *

Due to baseball's indifference about drugs, Ken and other players had a symbolic green light to use whatever substances they wished, and during Ken's second stint with the Astros, that meant GHB, or gamma hydroxybutyrate, a depressant known as the "date rape drug." Ken had dabbled with it during the mid-1990s in tab form—it was seen as a weight-lifting drug. Ken would drink a solution containing GHB before games, and it gave him a beer-like buzz without filling him up or giving him beer breath. His body had taken a beating, and he found himself anxious at times, and the GHB helped him mellow.

David Indermill, one of Ken's friends from San Diego, was in Houston visiting Ken in 1999 when he found out about Ken's latest substance du jour. They were in the Astrodome hours before a game when Ken discussed GHB and asked if Indermill wanted to try it.

"If you say it's like a beer buzz without drinking the beer . . . ," *sure,* Indermill said.

Ken took a small bottle of GHB—he kept them in his locker—poured the solution into the bottle top, then poured one capful each for himself and for Indermill, stirring the GHB into orange juice. This was the Caminiti Cocktail 2.0, new and improved, his solution to dull his pain and nerves ahead of games, so he could be *loose.*

"After you do this, go to the stands and buy yourself a beer," Ken told his friend. So Indermill did, and he experienced a mild buzz, *no big deal,* it just felt like he'd been drinking for a few hours.

The next night, Ken had a drink ready for his friend.

"Is it the same as yesterday?" Indermill asked.

"Yeah," he told Indermill with a wink and a glimmer in his eye.

Indermill drank the solution and did the same thing as the day before—bought a beer and found his seat.

"I couldn't drink because I felt so weird," Indermill said. "I felt myself going in the fetal position and passing out." He remembers Nancy and the girls arriving. "I'm sweating bullets, and I'm afraid to talk to them because I'm freaking out inside my head." He remembers waking up to a camera lens in front of his face—one of the team's videographers. "They found me, passed out, and put me on the Jumbotron."

Hours later, he confronted his friend.

"Ken, what the hell?"

"It was pretty good, huh?"

"No, you dick, why would you do that? How many did you put in there?"

"I put like two," double the dose of the previous day—playing fast and loose with a central nervous system depressant that, taken in large doses, can be deadly. Mixing GHB with alcohol intensifies the chances of overdose.

"I guess he kind of pulled a prank on me," Indermill said. "He didn't hurt me, it was just his way of messing with me."

* * *

It was a fluky play, an overlooked line in the box score: "SB—Caminiti (5)." Ken reached base with an RBI single on May 21 against the Giants, but when he tried to take the extra base with a steal, he strained his calf.

"He grabbed his leg as he neared the base and slid around shortstop Rich Aurilia's tag to complete the steal, but limped off the field," the Associated Press reported.

The injury was initially classified as day-to-day. Ken had played through everything imaginable, what was a calf injury? His leg could be falling off and he'd be asking into the lineup. Ken would work with the training staff and ice and wrap, patch himself together, and get back on the field in no time.

But this injury was a bit more problematic, a tear, and Ken was placed on the fifteen-day DL. Despite the injury, Ken continued working out and traveling with his teammates. Idle time and bad feelings weren't a good mix for Ken. He needed to keep busy.

Biggio and Bagwell worried what might happen if Ken remained at home with his time and his frustrations and his thoughts, and backup third baseman Jack Howell decided to take Ken under his wing and keep an eye on him. Howell would stay in an adjoining hotel room to Caminiti's, hoping to embody a role similar to the one that Andy Stankiewicz and Scott Livingstone had played for Ken years earlier. Howell didn't drink and had led baseball chapel when he was with the Angels earlier in his career. "I could be the guy who just said, 'Now let's just go back and put on ESPN and just sit around and talk,'" Howell said.

The Astros were facing the injury bug in 1999. Lots of players went down with strange injuries. Outfielder Moises Alou fell off a treadmill before spring training, tearing his ACL, then inexplicably reinjured the knee in a bike accident with his son as he was getting close to returning with the club.

As the season wore on, besieged by injuries, Houston was pressed to field infielders at all three outfield positions.

But nothing could have prepared the team for June 13. That day, the Astros had a 4–1 lead following a sixth-inning grand slam by Derek Bell. It was the eighth inning, and Jeff Bagwell was getting ready to bat, when the umpire told him to wait. Something was happening in the dugout. Something serious involving Astros manager Larry Dierker. One moment coach Matt Galante was talking with him about which pitcher to bring in for the ninth inning, and after Dierker mumbled a response, he collapsed and started shaking violently. Galante screamed for a trainer, and there he was, and paramedics arrived from center field. Dierker was attended to as he continued to shake, then restrained and taken away by ambulance. A hush grew over the crowd. Astros players gathered near the dugout, bowing their heads. Pitcher Jose Lima cried. The game was suspended. Everyone was too rattled to play.

They initially feared a tumor. As it turns out, a bundle of blood vessels in Dierker's brain had become malformed—a condition known as a grand mal seizure, also known as a generalized tonic-clonic seizure. As Dierker underwent and recovered from brain surgery, Galante, the longtime assistant, guided the team, going 13–14 as interim manager with Dierker's number 49 jersey hanging in the dugout. The Astros' first-place lead shrank due to a hot streak from the hard-charging Reds, but after Dierker's brush with death, baseball didn't seem to matter quite so much.

Dierker returned to the dugout on July 15. Scars curved around his skull like the seams and stitches of a baseball, but here he was, back in action.

He returned before Ken, who was placed on the sixty-day DL after he tried running and the calf "blew up the next day." An apparent day-to-day injury had turned into a two-month disappearing act from the lineup—a normal recovery process for a more moderate calf strain, but a long time on the shelf for Ken's usual play-no-matter-what style. After Dierker returned to the Astros, teammate Carl Everett turned to Ken in the dugout and didn't hold back his feelings: "We've got a guy that took less time coming back from brain surgery than you did from that pulled muscle." By late July, Caminiti was running again, hoping to begin a rehab assignment in the minors. "I'm dying to get back on the field, start playing, earning my money. I'm way too competitive to sit around for as long as I have."

He reported to Nashville, where the Triple-A New Orleans Zephyrs were playing the Sounds. It was his first time playing in the minor leagues in eleven seasons. The calf remained sore—by the fourth or fifth inning he would start feeling it—but he was back on the field.

But with the team back in New Orleans, Ken's off-the-field problems were bubbling over.

New Orleans isn't a good city for a recovering addict. And there was no Jack Howell to keep watch over him, and there was no Russ Johnson, either.

During the August 13–15 weekend, after playing a game against the Las Vegas Stars, Ken wound up at Bruno's, an iconic college bar located near Loyola and Tulane universities. There, he encountered Sean Cassidy, a law school student who tended bar but on that night was shooting pool. Cassidy eyed up

Caminiti. Here was someone with lots of money, someone who would be up for a challenge. "Let's play some pool, and maybe I can get a couple dollars off the guy," Cassidy recalled. But somebody informed Ken of Cassidy's racket, which made Ken suspicious—this after he'd given someone else money to buy drugs for him, only to see the money disappear. They ended up playing some pool, and Ken was drinking, and he reassured an older fan who'd recognized him that his ragged days were a thing of the past, that he had things under control. *Everything's good.* For a while that night, things were good, but Cassidy and his friends were sitting near the flap of the bar, the hinged part of the counter that goes up and down, and they were marveling at the baseball star as they talked among themselves. "We were being juveniles," Cassidy said, "coming up with what we could say to Ken Caminiti right now that would really piss him off."

You throw like a girl.

Your wife's hideous.

"We were just kind of chuckling to ourselves and laughing." Ken was maybe twenty feet away. "None of it was to his face, not even close, but we were laughing, and probably somebody turned and looked at him while we were laughing, which indicated to him that we may have been laughing at him.

"And then he charged. He charged us. He's like, 'What the fuck are you guys talking about?'"

Some Tulane baseball players were there and broke things up before it turned physical. But Ken was yelling, "and we were scared to death, quite honestly, because he was a very intense fellow," Cassidy said.

Things settled down, and Ken left through a side door that was normally locked from the outside. A friend of Cassidy's was coming through the door to start his shift, and someone said something funny to break the heaviness, and people laughed, and Ken turned around, standing at the side door, and Cassidy's friend didn't know any better—*hey, it's Ken Caminiti!*—so he let Ken in, and Cassidy said Ken charged toward him again before being held back.

"I promise you I was not egging this dude on," Cassidy said.

Eventually the mood did calm down, and Ken apologized: *Sorry, I kinda lost my head.* "No problem, Meat," Cassidy said, using the nickname from the baseball movie *Bull Durham*, and things were cool after that, and Ken offered to buy a round. They wound up at a different bar together and drank until three or four in the morning, at which point Ken was off to get some drugs, maybe cocaine or ecstasy. That next day, as Cassidy and his friends were nursing hangovers and recovering from a long night, still in their boxers, Caminiti was back in Houston, ready to continue his major league career.

* * *

Ken's buddy Casey Candaele was hanging on with Triple-A New Orleans in 1999, and assistant GM Tim Purpura remembers watching the team take batting practice. Candaele sat down next to Purpura.

"Do you guys have, like, a head doctor?" Candaele asked.

"You mean like a chief doctor, a number one doctor?" Purpura said.

"No, a doctor for your head."

"Yeah, we've got a very good one. Why?"

"I'm really worried about Cammy."

"Yeah . . ."

"I'm just afraid that he won't last five years after he's out of the game; he's going to be dead."

This wasn't the same Ken they knew. He was gruff and short and edgy. Purpura said that during Ken's second tenure with the Astros, the team tried to help him through its Employee Assistance Program, a chance to provide Ken with independent, confidential counseling services. The Astros weren't blind to the fact that he was struggling—Houston re-signed him knowing full well that his addictions were liable to flare up, and he carried a lot of respect and love within the team. They wanted to help Ken. But the team could only do so much.

* * *

Ken was walking in the tunnel in Shea Stadium a week after returning to the Astros, and he approached someone he knew through the baseball pipeline: Kirk Radomski, who worked for years in the Mets clubhouse and who'd been supplying players with steroids.

"You got a minute?" Ken asked.

Sure, Radomski said, and there in the tunnel they talked about Anadrol, the steroid Ken had begun taking in 1999 after he stopped receiving his PEDs from childhood friend Dave Moretti. Anadrol made him feel superhuman but also wreaked havoc on his body.

"I asked him if he had the shits a lot, and he said, 'Yeah. Once in a while, I taste blood in my mouth.' Yeah. . . . It burns holes in your stomach. Even in short periods, it happens," Radomski said.

"He was taking it on and off the whole entire season. He liked the way he felt."

Anadrol, also known as oxymetholone, is sometimes prescribed for people with anemia and HIV/AIDS to help them maintain or gain weight. It can be hazardous to the liver if taken over long stretches and is known to cause nausea, diarrhea, upper stomach pain, and rapid weight gain in the face or midsection.

Radomski warned Ken about Anadrol's toxic nature. He mentioned how other third basemen were taking Deca-Durabolin and testosterone—the exact drugs Moretti had been supplying Ken during his Padres years.

"A lot of these kids nowadays don't even know what Anadrol is because there are so many things out there that will give you all of those benefits without the side effects," Radomski said. "In the '80s and '90s, it was all about size. That's it. Now, people are more conscious about their health. They want to feel good and look good. Back then, they just wanted to look good; they didn't care how they felt. Ken, he said he had some guys that he knew that were big weight lifters, and that's why they recommended it."

Moretti would see video or pictures of Ken and could recognize that his steroid use was becoming dangerous—but Dave was out of the picture, and Ken was back in Houston, where his trainer Blake Blackwell could help him get bigger, which Moretti said was always Blake's plan and something Ken had wanted.

"There's no way his body, his frame, should have been that big," Moretti said. "Ken played his best baseball when he was 195 to 200 pounds, that's it. When he was at that weight, his hips were quick, his hands were quick, his feet were quick, he was dynamite. He could move on the field, he could steal bases, he could do it all. Once he got over that weight, it was too much for him, and his frame couldn't handle it.

"At 200 pounds, his size-32-waist Levis were big on him. The guy had a physique that was incredible. But he always wanted to be a monster, to look like a bodybuilder."

Moretti reached his breaking point during 1999 when Ken had one of his hangers-on contact Dave and ask for steroids. "I'm not doing that anymore,"

Moretti told him. "Tell Ken I'd like to talk to him." But Ken didn't call. And the childhood friends drifted apart.

"It just went bad," Moretti said.

"At that point, I wanted to respect Nancy's wishes. I wasn't feeling good about any of it."

As Ken and his longtime steroid supplier became estranged, and as Ken began getting his steroids elsewhere starting in 1999, the signs of his overuse started coming into focus—the Faustian bargain of his use of PEDs. The drugs worked really, really well when he used them properly. But then he stopped using them properly.

According to the National Institute on Drug Abuse, the misuse of anabolic steroids has been known to increase irritability and aggression, can come with other mood and behavioral effects due to hormonal changes, a higher likelihood of anxiety, major mood disorders, and depression.

Ken suffered from all of those things, as suggested by his actions, the concerns of those close to him, and his public and private disclosures. He was more irritable and surly, case in point his aggressive nature at the New Orleans bar during his rehab assignment.

He was anxious, which was the reason he cited for taking GHB before games.

He became increasingly depressed, he admitted in the years ahead.

And his body stopped producing testosterone on its own, forcing him to start receiving hormonal injections as his playing career was coming to an end.

* * *

Ken was a welcome addition to the Astros lineup when he returned from his calf injury.

On August 20, against the Marlins, he took a Ryan Dempster pitch out for a home run in the third inning. The Marlins pitchers hosted a wind farm walk-a-thon, striking out a total of 21 Astros batters but also giving 17 free passes (Jeff Bagwell was walked six times) before Ken came up in the sixteenth inning and hit another homer, this time off Jesús Sánchez, to give Houston the long-awaited W.

Ken was seeking redemption on August 31 against the Mets. Jose Lima was coasting, in line for his eighteenth win—LIMA TIME!—and the

Astros were up 2–0 with two outs in the eighth inning, when Mets shortstop Edgardo Alfonzo hit a ground ball to Ken, but Ken threw the ball away, allowing Alfonzo to reach base. E5. *Dammit.* He squatted on the turf, wishing he could drill a hole and climb inside, as he yelled at Lima, "Pick me up, Jose! Pick me up!"

John Olerud, the sweet-swinging first baseman, was up next. Billy the Kid was warming up in the pen, ready to face Mets catcher Mike Piazza, Ken's former divisional nemesis from his Dodgers days, who was on deck. Larry Dierker had a decision. Lima was on three days' rest. Dierker took a walk to the mound to consider his options, then kept Lima in to face Olerud—which backfired on the first pitch, when Lima left the ball up, and with one swing of the bat, Olerud was jogging around the bases and the game was tied. *Dammit.*

The Astros faced Turk Wendell in the bottom half. A superstitious reliever, Wendell brushed his teeth in between innings and wore a shark's-tooth necklace and number 99 before it was fashionable for baseball players. Hell, it was a superstitious game, why not embrace it? Wendell walked Biggio with one out, and the hit-and-run was on with Matt Mieske hitting, but Mieske swung through it, and Biggio scampered back to first. Still at bat, Mieske doubled to make it second and third, and it was Bagwell's turn until the Mets called for a free pass—the Mets gambled and walked Bagwell to pitch to Caminiti with the bases loaded.

You don't underestimate Scary Man, and Ken made them pay—for doubting him, for his letting Lima down, for every goddamn thing. Wendell grooved a 1-and-1 fastball that didn't have enough oomph, or maybe too much oomph, but either way it was a goner: grand slam.

When he reached the dugout, there was Lima, treating his third baseman like a punching bag with a flurry of celebratory hooks.

"He's a strong man," Lima said. "I hit him about twenty times. It's like hitting Mike Tyson."

"My chest is all bruised up," Ken said. "But that's a good thing. I like it. Now I gotta go into the weight room and build it back up."

Two games later, at the Big O in Montreal, Ken was back at it, homering twice as Mike Hampton also won his eighteenth game—Lima and Hampton were both pacing the league. The 8–1 victory over the Expos kicked off what would become a twelve-game winning streak as Houston ran its division lead over second-place Cincinnati (with its key off-season acquisition, Ken's Padres teammate Greg Vaughn, anchoring the middle of the lineup) to four games.

But the Reds weren't going away easily, and the Astros were facing threats from all sides, even the outfield stands. That's where a fan came from during a September 24 game in Milwaukee, attacking right fielder Bill Spiers—a former college football player—and leaving Spiers with a bloody nose, a welt under his eye, and whiplash. The Astros raced to help Spiers, kicking the fan and getting him away from the utility player. The incident rattled Houston. How couldn't it? They ended up losing the next three games, setting up a two-game series with Cincinnati, which found itself with the same record as the Astros.

In the first game, on September 28, the Reds were starting Pete Harnisch, Ken's buddy who spent some of his best years playing for the 'Stros after coming over in the Glenn Davis trade. Houston was countering with Lima, his wins now up to twenty games, but this one was very much not Lima time, with the Reds jumping to a 4–1 lead in the third inning before both teams turned off the offensive faucet and the game ended that way. The Reds were in first place. The division lead was gone.

For one day. On September 29, the teams reached the same score but in reverse, with Ken driving in two of the Astros' four runs.

A tie atop the division at 95–54 with three games remaining. The Astros would face the Dodgers at home—did the schedule makers purposefully make sure Ken's season ended every year with Los Angeles?—while Cincinnati was facing the Brew Crew in suds town. The division winner would secure a playoff spot, while the second-place team could either wind up with the wild card (the Mets were lurking with 93 wins) or go home for a long, lonely off-season.

The first game didn't go the Astros' way. The Dodgers jumped out to a 5–0 lead against Shane Reynolds, while LA pitcher Eric Gagne—eventually a lockdown closer—got the start and held Houston scoreless for six innings. By the time Houston scratched across a run in the eighth inning, the game was already out of reach. Ken got the silver sombrero with three strikeouts. But a walk-off win by the Brewers kept the division tied. The Mets, meanwhile, won 3–2 to pull within one game of the Astros and Reds.

Houston bounced back in the second game—LIMA TIME!—with the animated starter winning his twenty-first game, 3–0. The game was scoreless until the sixth inning, when Biggio took a Chan Ho Park pitch deep and gone, 1–0; then Houston scored twice more in the eighth inning when Spiers hit a bases-loaded single. The win gave the Astros sole possession of first place, as Cincinnati lost again, and a Mets win coupled with a Reds loss meant those teams were tied for the wild card lead with one game left.

Game 162.

Mike Hampton, with his 21–4 record, took the hill on three days' rest for Houston, potentially playing in its final game at the Astrodome.

The Astros stayed patient against the Dodgers and Robinson Checo, pitching in the sixteenth and final game of his major league career, while Kevin Brown, the ace the Dodgers signed over the off-season, didn't pitch during the series with his potential twentieth win out of reach. Sorry, Mets and Reds.

In the bottom of the first, Stan Javier, Bagwell, and Carl Everett all walked, and then it was time for Ken to follow suit—a bases-loaded walk to bring home the first run. Houston's next hitter, Daryle Ward, found a more economical way to get the runners home, driving a double to right field. After one more batter (and a walk at that), Checo was replaced by Matt Herges. Six straight batters had reached base, and four runs were in, and only one of those batters put the ball in play.

Herges stopped the bleeding for a while, until the third inning, when Ken came to bat again. All the years Ken had played in Houston, it was without a taste of the postseason. . . . He was still in the minors in 1986, and the 1994 team was poised to play in October when the strike wiped out the playoffs. All he wanted was to reach the playoffs with Jeff and Craig. He thought about them when the Padres clinched in 1996—how sweet it would be, how much Bagwell and Biggio would enjoy this feeling, how much they deserved to play meaningful baseball. The Astros' Killer Bs did that in 1997 and 1998 (Ken's Padres squeaked past the Astros their second year in the playoffs), but here they were on the cusp of doing it together, making some final memories in this felt-covered cavern.

Herges fired, and Ken smashed the pitch, sending it to deep right field. Home run. As it turned out, it was the final regular season blast in the Astrodome, and one more reason to celebrate the 9–4 win. After 162 hard-fought games, after enduring injuries and brain aneurysms and unruly fans, the Astros were back in the playoffs. The crowd erupted, and fireworks rained down from the Astrodome roof. As the Houston players piled on top of one another, Caminiti and Bagwell hugged, a deep bear hug that said everything words couldn't.

A postgame celebration featured players from Houston's past who Caminiti used to play with—icons like Nolan Ryan and Mike Scott and José Cruz and Phil Garner. And Willie Nelson was on hand to perform. But it wasn't time to end the Astros' party, or turn off the Astrodome lights, just yet. The playoffs loomed.

Despite clinching the division, the Astros had to wait to find out who they'd be playing next—the Mets and Reds ended up tying for the wild card. The victory by New York meant that Ken and the Houston Astros would be facing the Braves, with its troika of aces along with emerging starter Kevin Millwood, who won eighteen games and was positioned as the Braves' next superstar pitcher.

On the offensive side, Atlanta was led by third baseman Chipper Jones, the league's MVP that season, along with center fielder Andruw Jones, who represented a perfect blend of glove, speed, and smash.

Here was Ken's chance to dispel the October demons of the previous season, when he was broken and battered, falling down and overmatched, during the Padres' World Series run. The game remained airtight for the first eight innings, with the Astros clinging onto a 2–1 lead. Braves reliever Mike Remlinger found himself in trouble, surrendering a walk to Matt Mieske and a single to Stan Javier. Bagwell got a free pass to load the bases—no way Bobby Cox was going to let Bagwell beat him—with the hope that Carl Everett could ground into an inning-ending double play. And Remlinger had been hot in 1999, going 10–1 with a 2.37 ERA in 73 relief appearances. Everett kept hacking away, scraping, and golfed a low looper to center fielder Andruw Jones, who had one of the best arms in the game. But what the hell. . . . Mieske tagged and sprinted home, and the throw was off-line, giving the Astros a 3–1 lead.

Up came Ken with men on first and second and two outs. Remlinger delivered, trying to get ahead of him, but the pitch caught too much of the plate, and it was up. Ken didn't miss, lifting the ball where no one would catch it, a few feet beyond the wall in left-center. Knockout blow. For the Braves, still smarting from Ken's dinger off Kerry Ligtenberg the prior postseason, his three-run blast felt like lightning striking twice. With the win, the Astros were up 1–0, and Ken's bat was molten magma.

But that was the problem in Game 2: No one else on the Astros was hitting. Ken smashed another homer (Kevin Millwood tried to pitch away and ended up throwing over the middle of the plate . . . big mistake), but it was the team's only hit. Millwood was masterful, facing two batters over the minimum, striking out eight as he recorded the game's first playoff one-hitter since the Lyndon Johnson administration.

Even so, the Astros had gone into Atlanta and come away with a split. And now they were headed back to the Astrodome, to make a few final memories before saying goodbye.

In Game 3, Houston jumped out to a 2–0 lead against Tom Glavine, Ken's nemesis dating to their minor league days. Ken hit a first-inning single to score Biggio, and then three batters later, longtime Astros catcher Tony Eusebio walked with the bases loaded to score Bagwell.

Mike Hampton kept the Braves at bay until the sixth. He got two quick outs, but then Bret Boone singled and Chipper Jones walked, and up came Brian Jordan—the same Brian Jordan who three seasons earlier had waged a tug-of-war with Ken in the National League Division Series, hitting the decisive home run to help the Cardinals advance past Ken's Padres. They were both on different teams now, but this series also would focus more and more on Jordan and Caminiti.

Because Jordan, the former NFL player, came alive in October, and he did against Hampton, hitting a three-run blast to put the Braves in front 3–2.

In the bottom of the seventh, the Astros tied it back up on a Bill Spiers RBI single.

Remlinger, who Ken homered off two games earlier, was on, and he walked Bagwell to load the bases to face Ken. The count went to 3-and-1. Another ball meant a run. Remlinger went with his best pitch. "I had to throw him a fastball down the middle," he said. Ken fouled it straight back, *just* missing it, the type of foul ball that's so scorching, you can smell the bat wood burning. "I came back and threw a changeup, and struck him out," Remlinger said.

The threat was averted, but the teams continued playing with fire.

On to extra innings. After the Braves had a runner at third base in the top half of the tenth inning, but came away with nothing, the momentum started to shift. You could feel it. This was the Astros' time. The time to break through. The time to dispel the Braves.

Bagwell led off the bottom of the tenth with a walk, and Ken followed with a first-pitch seeing-eye single to right field. Jose Lima paced in the dugout, wearing his hat folded with the bill standing up like a shark fin, occasionally hitting the dugout railing with a bat out of nervous excitement. *Whatever helped.* . . . Stan Javier was next, putting down a bunt, but pitcher Russ Springer hesitated, declining to make a throw, so the bases were juiced with no outs.

Braves reliever John Rocker raced to the mound facing a world of trouble. The defense was in—the only play was at home plate. Everett hit a chopper to first base that Ryan Klesko fielded cleanly, and he threw home to force out Bagwell.

Next was Eusebio, who took the first pitch for a strike. He hit the second pitch up the middle, on the shortstop side of the dirt surrounding the bag. The ball was destined for the outfield, fated to secure Houston the win. Braves shortstop Walt Weiss, who had entered the game as a defensive sub in the seventh inning, dove in desperation like a soccer goalie trying to stop a penalty kick—the ball was all but past him, forcing him to angle toward the outfield as he dove. "When it hit my glove, I was shocked," Weiss said. "And it was hit so hard on that old turf that they used to have in the Astrodome. It was like playing on an indoor-outdoor carpet."

Eusebio's ball nearly knocked off Weiss's glove, a Mizuno model that he used throughout most of his career—it was so gnarly, his Oakland teammate Mike Gallego called it "the Creature." By the 1999 postseason, "the Creature" was all but falling apart.

The ball snow-coned in "the Creature" and popped out, landing directly in front of Weiss. As Ken charged down the line, Weiss grabbed the ball, steadied himself with his glove hand, turned almost 360 degrees, and threw, off-balance, in the vicinity of the plate, where catcher Eddie Pérez was stretching to catch the ball, his toes keeping contact with home plate ahead of Ken's arrival. Somehow, someway, Walt Weiss had made the most improbable play. Ken charged through home plate, tripping on Peréz's leg, and tumbling over his feet.

The Braves got out of the inning, and Brian Jordan plated two runners in the twelfth inning, because of course he did, and the Braves pulled out a win as narrow as the webbing of Walt Weiss's glove. Decades later, Braves and Astros players remained stunned that Weiss was able to make the play.

Billy Wagner: "We had done so well, and to see Walt Weiss make that play, you just cringed."

Houston pitcher Scott Elarton: "That play right there kind of broke our backs. We felt like we had some momentum going, and then Walt Weiss pretty much single-handedly took the wind out of our sails."

Braves manager Bobby Cox: "I thought it was through, I thought it was over, that's that. That play was one of the best I've ever seen."

After the game, amid the commotion in the Braves clubhouse, Weiss got a phone call. It was Ken. "I just want you to know that's the greatest f-ing play I've ever seen in my life," Ken told him. "That was a devastating loss, but I had to call and tell you that."

The Astros' season ended one game later, with Ken putting the finishing touches on a stellar postseason series. In the four games against Atlanta, he batted .471 (8 for 17) with a 1.526 OPS, hit three of the team's five homers, and drove in more than half of Houston's RBIs. But Biggio batted .105, and Bagwell .154, and the Braves had Brian Jordan, and Walt Weiss's glove. The party was over for the Astros, and it was time to turn off the lights on the team's 1999 season.

CHAPTER 24

WARNING SIGNS

The early exit from the 1999 playoffs gave Ken time to catch up on other things.

Like hunting.

So on October 20, instead of wrapping up the National League Championship Series against the Mets, which would have awaited Houston had the Astros beat the Braves, Ken was in southern Texas, preparing a deer stand in a tree. But he leaned out too far and fell, fracturing three vertebrae in his back.

Another off-season, another long road to recovery.

He called on an old friend, physical therapist Catherine Ondrusek, who'd helped Ken recover following his shoulder surgery three years earlier. That experience had gone beautifully, Ondrusek recalled. Ken did everything she asked—including not using steroids—and because of their efforts, Ken was in the Padres Opening Day lineup in 1997, returning to action months ahead of schedule.

This time around, Ondrusek was saddened to find a different person than the man she knew, someone who was impatient and not following the steps his body needed to recover as he abused steroids and other substances.

"He wasn't clean. He wasn't cleaning himself back up at that point," she said. "Treatment relies on the body to be its own best advocate. When you're mixing other things in that are greater than the body can tolerate," recovery is difficult.

His body was like one of the cars in his garage—every now and again, it purred like old times, but more and more, it wound up broken down and collecting rust.

* * *

His buddy Jeff Bagwell was a little nonplussed by how he found Ken in 2000 spring training: clean-shaven. Nancy liked him that way during the off-season. When they'd spoken months earlier, Ken and Jeff both agreed to grow the bushiest facial hair they could. Bagwell held up his end of the agreement, making himself look like a lost member of ZZ Top, his bushy red beard long enough that you could grab it (not that anyone would—you don't tug on Superman's cape, and you don't tug on Baggy's goatee, either).

"The deal was that Caminiti and I were going to do it during the off-season—and he forgot to do his," Bagwell said. "So I got stuck with it and said, 'The heck with it, I'm just going to keep it.' It's something different."

* * *

Dave Matranga was trying to survive.

The Astros draftee was in his first minor league spring training in 1999, playing in A-ball—the lowest rung on the pro baseball ladder—when a 94 mph pitch sailed high and struck his helmet. After receiving treatment, he went to sit in the trainer's room and rest. There, he found Ken, who himself was getting treated for an injury or recovering from a cold. The rookie and the vet spent hours talking.

"He took an interest in me right away, and he didn't big league me," Matranga said. "He just seemed like a real genuine guy."

Ken supplied his protégé with gear—a glove, bats, shoes, a box of batting gloves—and they stayed in touch throughout the season. After the minor league season ended, Dave was driving from Florida home to California with his wife, and Ken suggested they stay for a few days with the Caminitis in Houston. Soon enough, Ken was asking the minor leaguer to room with him the following spring training. *Yes, of course*, Matranga said.

The arrangement concerned Astros leadership. Matranga would show up for workouts and face questions and raised eyebrows. *So, you're rooming with Cammy. . . . What's that like?*

For Matranga, the experience was eye-opening. Ken was honest with his young friend—he talked about his heavy drinking during his high school days and nursing minor league hangovers, street drugs and steroids and everything in between. He wanted Matranga to learn from his mistakes. He wanted him to recognize the lessons he wished he had learned all those years ago.

"He was open about his steroids use with me. It wasn't something that was hidden. He was very quick to protect me from it," Matranga said.

Ken warned Matranga to stay on the right path. *Hey listen, man, this isn't a road you want to go down*, he said. *You can make it without using. I've just fallen into this vicious cycle, and I can't really get out of it.*

Even as Ken wanted more for his young friend, he was struggling in his own life. He looked like a pro wrestler, hulking and bloated from his overuse of steroids. He needed to have a monster season in 2000—the Astros held the option on offering him a third season of the hometown discount contract he signed in November 1998. Have a great season in 2000, and Houston would offer Ken a one-year option at $5.5 million.

If Ken had a bad season, the Astros could buy out the final year of the contract for $500,000. And then maybe he'd retire.

"I don't want to play anywhere else. I started my career in Houston, and it would be nice to end it in Houston. In my mind, this was my last contract. I'd like to play next year, I think. But I don't know for sure," he told the *Houston Chronicle.*

"We'll see how this year goes. I'm going to have a whole bunch of fun, let my hair down, and play as hard as I can play. Hopefully, if I'm healthy, everything will work out."

During his time in Florida at spring training, Ken would have friends come over. Some were old baseball teammates like Wally Joyner or Casey Candaele, or his buddy in San Diego who helped with autograph signings, James Hayashai. They cared about Ken's health and wanted the best for him.

But other people were meeting with him, too. . . . Ken tried to shield his roommate from some of his other guests that spring. "If there were people who came over to the apartment that he didn't want me to be around, he was quick to tell me, 'Hey, dude, I need you to go to bed early tonight. There's some people coming over tonight that I don't necessarily want you to be around,'" Matranga said.

So Ken went off and did the wrong things with the wrong people, and sometimes, Matranga would get glimpses of Ken's world spiraling. Like the time he was meeting Ken and Craig Biggio after practice at Texas Roadhouse on Highway 192 in Kissimmee. He followed Ken to the restaurant, and Ken pulled up in his loud truck and parked, and Dave waited for Ken to get out of the truck. Maybe he was on the phone? But the stereo was blasting through the windows. . . .

Dave got out and checked on his friend, and there was Ken, in the driver's seat of his loud truck with the stereo blasting and the windows rolled up, asleep.

"I'm, like, what the heck is going on right now? Is he OK? Did something happen to him? Did he have a heart attack?" Matranga said.

"I don't know what had happened the night before, I don't know what he had done. I wasn't aware if people came over, if he was up all night doing things that he shouldn't have been doing and didn't get any sleep. . . . He was at the park that day and showed up for work. I couldn't get his attention. I tried to knock on the window. He didn't do anything."

A concerned Matranga went inside and found Biggio, the Astros star who'd had the longest friendship with Ken of any major league teammate, dating back more than a decade.

"That's just sometimes what Ken does. You just gotta let him go, and he'll wake up when he wakes up, and maybe he'll come in, and maybe he won't," Biggio told Matranga.

"We've all tried to help Ken. I know you're sitting there and you're with him and you want to reach out to him and help him. Trust me, we've all been in your shoes, and you're just a young pup. . . . I've been doing this for a long time. All these guys have tried, and it's one of those things where nobody can get to him; he just wanted to fight it by himself."

* * *

Ken's fortunes in 2000 mirrored those of his team: optimism dashed by turmoil.

Houston was hopeful for a fourth straight NL Central title to celebrate its brand-new ballpark. But its spring training was marred on the night of March 12, 2000, when two robbers entered a room at a Holiday Inn where minor leaguers were staying and held five players at gunpoint. The players—Morgan Ensberg, Derek Nicholson, Keith Ginter, Michael Rose, and Eric Cole, all twenty-three or twenty-four, along with Ginter's girlfriend—didn't think they would survive. A sixth player, Aaron Miles, twenty-three, was robbed in an adjoining room. One of the players was able to free himself and called the front desk, which called 911. While one of the men jumped and escaped, the other man wrestled with Miles for control of his gun and bit the second baseman before being shot by police.

The incident jarred the players for years afterward.

And it put a cloud over a team that was set to move into a new ballpark that was named Enron Field after the Houston-based company bought a $100 million, thirty-year license for the naming rights. (The following season, the scandal-plagued company declared bankruptcy, and the Astros bought back the naming rights in 2002.)

The new stadium was a big adjustment from the outdated Astrodome, which was the ultimate pitcher's park. But in 2000, Enron Field—which featured flourishes from other historic ballparks, such as a ramped hill in center field, an outfield flagpole that was in play, and a train—was problematic for reasons other than its name.

Since construction on the ballpark finished shortly before the season, most of the players hadn't seen it before coming back from spring training.

So the Astros didn't have long to prepare for its quirks. Like the prevailing wind that blew out to left-center during the early part of the season, before the roof closed due to the sweltering heat.

"In April, we tried to keep the roof open whenever we could because the weather was nice," Astros manager Larry Dierker said. "So we started to see that season off, and it was kind of like "The Star-Spangled Banner"—you know, the rockets were red glaring all over the place, the balls were flying out of it like rockets."

Enron Field soon had a nickname: ten-run field, representing the number of runs the Astros were giving up each game as the team stumbled to last place.

"It was like playing in Yellowstone and then being moved into a shoebox," closer Billy Wagner said. "It was a whole different setting of how everything in your perspective looked. I mean, a 3–0 pitch in the Astrodome, hey, I'm throwing it on the outside part of the plate and seeing how far he can hit it, and chances are it's just going to the warning track and you're out. You had to be a better pitcher at Enron than you had to be anywhere else at that time, because for me as a fly ball pitcher, now you're playing in a very small park except for one spot. It was different. I had to learn how to pitch in that ballpark."

The Astros had new pinstriped uniforms that season to reflect the team's new home. Ken would have a habit of staring at himself in the mirror before games.

"Cammy would come into the weight room every night just before the anthem. And he would walk in, and we had these full-length mirrors, and he would turn around with his back to the mirror, look over his shoulder, look me in the eye, and say, 'Do these stripes make my ass look big?' He would laugh and walk out, every night," strength coach Gene Coleman said.

* * *

Ken and Raymond Martin bonded over loud, fast vehicles. Martin, a stock car racing legend, had a need for speed just like Ken, and even with their roughly twenty-year age gap, they became good friends. They ended up teaming together on an NHRA pro stock truck team, with the idea of Ken getting behind the wheel once his playing days were over.

Ken grew close with Raymond's wife, Linda, and daughters, Mystic and Jordan—they came to view each other as extended family members, especially when Ken would bring his girls around. The Martins didn't see Ken's star power or baseball success; they saw a kind man you had to lean in to hear because he could speak so softly. And they also recognized how much trouble he had saying one word: "no."

"If someone called him and needed money, needed a vehicle, needed anything, he could not say no . . . people quickly learned about that and absolutely took advantage," Mystic said.

* * *

Ken came to the plate on April 15, 2000, in his return to San Diego as a visiting player—this was his first time playing here since departing the Padres after the 1998 season. He missed playing at the Q in 1999 due to his calf injury. But here he was, playing in front of the fans who adored him so much—and each at bat, he faced a smattering of boos.

The booing intensified in the ninth inning, after he hit an RBI double off buddy Trevor Hoffman, then was pulled for a pinch runner in San Diego's 5–3 win.

Ken initially brushed off the negativity, but later he admitted that it bothered him.

"It was a sad day for me," he told the *Union-Tribune*'s Tom Krasovic.

"The way they turned on me in San Diego, I don't want anything to do with that place."

Padres owner John Moores was so bothered about the booing, he sought out Ken to apologize. The booing was a reflection of fan frustration with the team's fire sale following the World Series run. Kevin Brown signed with Los Angeles, Steve Finley joined the Diamondbacks, Greg Vaughn was traded to the Reds, Ken returned to the Houston Astros. . . . Ken's departure was a lot more complicated than Brown's, which was fueled by money.

"I really felt I left it on the field when I played there. I have a lot of great memories of just learning who I was there," he said. "I just felt so good when I was there with my teammates and everything. I didn't expect to get booed. I didn't expect to get a standing ovation. But I expected to get some cheers. I might have heard a couple in my first at bat, but after that, it was predominantly boos.

"It just hurt, because I played hard. I'm just happy my wife wasn't in the stands."

* * *

Through the season's first few months, he was batting well over .300 with 15 home runs—carrying over his hot hitting from the end of the 1999 season.

But the ticking clock, the passage of time, was a constant for Ken. He was on the back end of his career. You could try to keep Father Time at bay, and steroids were a means of Ken trying to counteract the aging process, but the end comes for every player. Ken reflected on that reality ahead of the 2000 season. "It's getting tough just getting up every morning. This definitely could be my last year. I never used to come into camp just wanting to stay healthy, but that's where it is. As I get closer to thirty-seven, it gets harder to do this," he said.

"I'm going to play hard, not hold back. If I get hurt, so be it."

Ken was always hurt, so the bumps and bruises and strained hamstring weren't a surprise. But on June 15 against Colorado, Ken was facing Kevin Jarvis. The pitch came in, and he swung, and he felt something in his wrist *pop.*

He dropped the bat. Picked it up. Took a practice swing. Nope.

"I hope it's not serious. Then I'll be back in a couple weeks," he said wishfully.

And if it's serious? "If it's serious, I'm done. I am retiring."

As it turns out, the injury was serious. And Ken wouldn't be back playing for the Astros in a couple of weeks . . . or at all. A ruptured tendon sheath, a likely by-product of his steroids overuse. Ken underwent surgery on June 19, with an expected return in eight to twelve weeks.

But during Ken's time out of the lineup, he continued to spiral, his addictions worsening. Idle time left him wallowing in his failures and connecting with the wrong people. People who didn't have his best interests in mind.

Baseball gave him structure. He had no structure now.

And he was drifting further away from Nancy. They ended up separating in 2000, leaving Ken living apart from his family.

"Ken's good at hiding things. But when he was hurt, you could see the depression," she told the *Dallas Morning News*'s Evan Grant in 2001. "You could feel it."

By mid- to late August, Ken was taking grounders and batting practice in hopes of returning by September 1. But his actions were growing increasingly inconsistent. Things came to a head during Houston's series at Shea Stadium against the Mets on August 28–30. Ken was supposed to be working out with Astros strength coach Gene Coleman.

"He kept missing the bus, and he would take a taxi and come in late," Coleman said.

During one of the games against the Mets, bench coach Matt Galante went to check in with Ken. He wasn't on the bench. "I went down into the locker room to find him. He was kinda sleeping on a couch," Galante said.

The coach went to wake up the player. "I looked in his eyes, and I said, 'No, go back to sleep,'" Galante said. Ken wasn't right. Galante mentioned it to Dierker and also talked to Ken's close friends Craig Biggio and Jeff Bagwell. "We gotta get him help, he's in trouble," Galante said he told Biggio and Bagwell. "You could see it in his eyes."

Word about Ken's behavior filtered to the Astros' front office and manager. "The general manager came to me, and my philosophy to the player was, and it didn't make a difference who it was, I'm going to protect you every way I can, but I'm not going to lie for you. So the general manager came to me and said, 'Has Cammy been showing up and working out with you?' And I said, 'No,'" Coleman said.'

After the Astros returned to Houston, Dierker called Ken into his office.

"What's the deal? You wanna play or not?" Dierker asked him.

"I can't," Ken said. "Because I want to, but . . . I have this clause in my contract that activates for next year, and I'm afraid if I don't play well, then I won't have a contract for next year."

"Cammy, that's ridiculous," the manager said. "Everybody here knows what you can do; we just want to see if you're healthy. . . . If you come in and get twenty or thirty at bats and don't even get a hit, and go out in the field and make a bunch of errors, if you just look like you're moving well, and your injury is healed, we're not worried about what you do."

The Astros were out of the playoff race by September, but the team was trying to finalize its plans for 2001. Ken's return to the lineup could show the Astros' front office that he still had something left in the tank—or serve as a de facto tryout for any team that wanted to sign him in the off-season.

Ken's indecision and hesitation were concerning to Dierker.

"There was something behind that. There was an insecurity. He knew that whatever was going on in his life and in his system beyond the injury was what he was afraid of, more than the fact that he wouldn't get a contract the next year," Dierker said. "Whatever he was doing, it blurred his thinking to where he had some fear. And that's the last thing anyone would have ever associated with him."

As the team decided what it would do with Ken, he sought out Coleman about ten minutes before the start of one of the team's games.

"Hey, I understand that you told them that I haven't been working out," Ken said.

"Yes, that's true," Coleman told him.

"I understand. You didn't rat me out. But let's go out to the outfield and run."

"Cammy, it's ten minutes before game time, and you're on the DL."

"Yeah, but I want them to see that I'm committed," Ken told him. So Ken went out on the field moments before the national anthem and ran sprints, his last fleeting moments connected to the team that had drafted him in 1984.

At the same time Houston leadership was growing increasingly concerned about Ken's well-being, his wife, his father, and his trainer Blake Blackwell staged an intervention on September 2.

Ken sulked, of course, but he eventually agreed to check back into rehab. This time, he'd go to the Smithers Institute in New York—the same city where his backslide into addiction began three years earlier with a sip from a glass, and the site of his biggest professional failure in the World Series, a city that would become intertwined with Ken's story.

* * *

Ken's second stint in rehab gave him a chance to reflect on the man he wanted to be and everything he had.

For the first few weeks, he battled a fever.

"They couldn't figure it out. They had to take blood every other night. They'd wake me up at three in the morning to take my blood," he told the *Fort Worth Star-Telegram*'s T. R. Sullivan. "I went through blood, sweat, and chills for so long I was miserable. But I was in a great place. I was in the place I needed to be in. I never felt like that. I always felt like I could take care of myself."

Ken faced a range of emotions in rehab: "everything negative and then, eventually, everything positive," he said.

And it was there, in rehab, that he met Maria Romero.

* * *

Maria Romero grew up fast.

Hardscrabble Brooklyn, New York, can do that. She started dating Robert Silva as a teenager—their families lived nearby and had known each other over the years—and they had a baby, Robert Jr., born in 1988, but she and Robert Sr. split up after he got locked up for drugs.

She ended up having two more boys over the next decade, and she was working at a bodega as a bookie, running numbers from behind the glass wall and scraping to get by, but she had a drug problem herself, and she needed to get clean to be there for her sons, and that's how she met Ken.

Ken saw something of himself reflected in Maria. And three boys . . . He saw need and recognized he could help. Ken and Maria shared a connection.

Maria's oldest son, Robert Silva-Romero, first met Ken at the Smithers clinic in 2000 when visiting his mom. He was a Yankees fan. He'd watched Ken a few years earlier falling down in the World Series, and here Ken was, befriending his mom.

After Ken and Maria completed their stints in rehab, they stayed in contact, their connection blossoming into something more. Was it love? Desire? The need not to feel judged? When Ken was around Nancy, it reminded him of his failings. With Maria, Ken felt needed, like he didn't have to explain himself. Ken was broken. Maria was broken, too. Maybe they could be broken together.

Of course, getting involved with people you meet in rehab is discouraged. It amplifies the likelihood of a backslide. Rehab is a chance to work on yourself, to diminish distractions and find your new you.

After Ken and Maria completed their stints in rehab, Ken visited with Maria and met her family—her youngest, Mikey, was less than one year old at the time, and Ken held the baby. Maria was having problems scraping together rent money, and she and her mother ended up getting into an argument, so Ken stepped up, and the next thing Maria knew, she and the boys were living in East New York, in Brooklyn, a middle-class neighborhood.

Ken could help Maria. But Ken was ready to continue his major league career, too. He wasn't ready to end his career on such a sour note.

CHAPTER 25

OLD DOG

As Ken's yellow Labs played outside the clubhouse, it should have been obvious that the 2001 Texas Rangers season would go to the dogs.

Ken brought Casey and Candy—named for his Astros teammate Casey Candaele—with him to spring training at Port Charlotte, Florida. Clubhouse manager Zach Minasian went to Home Depot and bought stakes and wire so the dogs could run around. His assistants spent the spring playing with those dogs, feeding and cleaning up after them, in addition to their usual baseball duties.

The dogs, and the addition of the free agent third baseman, were a sideshow act for the actual circus: Alex Rodriguez, baseball's $252 million man. During the off-season, the Mariners superstar shortstop had signed the largest contract in pro sports history, a ten-year pact that brought media attention, fan interest, and expectations.

Expectations of October glory. Expectations that a moribund Rangers franchise was finally going to be a winner. With the $252 million man in town, the thinking went, all you needed were a few spare parts: a few pitchers off the free agent scrap heap, and a well-worn third baseman who could use some TLC and a new home.

The Rangers—the team that missed drafting Ken in 1984—did their due diligence before signing Ken. GM Doug Melvin and Dan O'Brien, who knew Ken from his days in the Astros front office, met with him. "We sat down and had a very, very candid conversation about where he was at in his life and his expectations and what he could anticipate from the next step in his career,"

O'Brien said. "And he was very forthright with us and basically wanted the opportunity to continue his career." Scout Rick Schroeder and hitting coach Rudy Jaramillo, Rangers personnel from Ken's past, also vouched for his character.

The contract had stipulations and outs built in: Ken would be required to regularly undergo drug tests to ensure his sobriety. One failed drug test, and he was gone. If Ken was on the roster on August 15, the next season's contract would automatically kick in.

But it was an opportunity, and after his rocky 2000 season, opportunities like this couldn't be overlooked. The full contract would potentially cover three years and pay $20.9 million. And if his game remained steady, he'd be with the Texas Rangers until age forty-one, the uniform number he ended up wearing during 2001 spring training in Port Charlotte (he switched to his usual 11 a few games into the season).

Port Charlotte was a solid place for Ken, a quiet town that afforded him a chance to steer clear of the nightlife scenes of other spring training locations. While star players like the $252 million man were liable to rent a helicopter and fly to Miami or Tampa, Ken was content in Port Charlotte with Casey and Candy. Maria, who Ken had befriended in rehab months earlier, also visited him.

"There was absolutely nothing to do in Port Charlotte," said Matt LaBranche, the head of the Rangers spring training operations in 2001. "It was just a small town that happened to have a major league spring training team there."

The Rangers facility wasn't ready for the A-Rod circus. The team held a press conference with Rodriguez at the start of spring training, and LaBranche ended up renting speakers from a local karaoke store and setting up the speakers and a table on top of the dugout, with media members spread out in the stands along the first base line.

"I just remember thinking, 'Oh my God, please don't make this little karaoke machine break right in the middle of this press conference,'" LaBranche said.

There was a lot of that with Texas that year—taking spare parts, putting them to the test, and hoping they didn't break. The anticipated lineup, while chock-full of superstars like A-Rod and catcher Iván Rodríguez, also included more creaky joints than a door hinge warehouse, with four players age thirty-five and above: first baseman Rafael Palmeiro, Ken at third, and a mix of Rubén Sierra and Andrés Galarraga, who'd turn forty during the season, at designated hitter.

Ken had never played with so many superstars around him. Sure, those early 1990s Astros teams were full of talented players, but players who were still reaching their potential. The Rangers had the opposite problem. Many of the players, especially those in the over-thirty crowd, were big on name recognition, but their best days were behind them.

Some of the players, as we'd later learn, were relying on performance-enhancing drugs. Pro wrestler physiques and personal trainers were red flags, but for George Petrides Jr., a Rangers strength and conditioning intern that spring, the prevalence of PED use became clearer when he helped document players' weight and body fat. Petrides started working with the team in early March, a few weeks after players first arrived, and some had lost 15 to 25 pounds during that time, he said. The weight fluctuations were uncommon for players who weren't using steroids, especially those in their mid-thirties.

"I had my suspicions," Petrides said.

Ken was committed to staying strong physically and emotionally. For some away games that spring, Ken could be seen sitting on the bus beside a man who wasn't a part of the team: a therapist. A chance to talk through his problems. Between the dogs and the therapist, it was out in the open that Ken was dealing with some issues. Ken's new teammates embraced him. He was stoic and quiet, letting his work ethic do the talking.

"You sort of wanted to learn as much as you could from him, soak up all of his knowledge," said Rangers outfielder Gabe Kapler. "When you looked in his eyes, it was very intimidating. He's staring right through you, but in a very warm way and engaging and kind way."

He still had the Look . . . along with a balky, aching body and a swing that wasn't coming around. At one point in spring training, he fell into an 0-for-30 slump. He knocked on manager Johnny Oates's office and talked to his new skipper, explaining how it usually took him a little while to knock the rust off.

"Don't worry. Don't let what's going on bother you, because this is the way it is every spring. I get maybe three or four hits every spring," Ken told his new manager, a sensitive, patient, God-fearing man. "I'm in there, trying to get myself in shape, see a lot of pitches. Sometimes my swing doesn't come through all of April."

Ken—who was still adjusting to a new slate of pitchers and the American League's different style of play—believed his bat would come around in time. But time was one thing in short supply for the 2001 Rangers. The other was pitching.

The American League West in 2001 was tougher than tree bark. Despite losing the $252 million man, the Seattle Mariners were somehow *better*, especially after adding Japanese star Ichiro Suzuki, a Chuck Yeager–fast slap hitter who used his first name on the back of his jersey instead of his last name. Second baseman Bret Boone, in the midst of a dramatic later-career resurgence, was poised to have a breakout season. Seattle's pitching staff was solid, led by Freddy García, Aaron Sele, and Jamie Moyer.

The Oakland Athletics were also formidable, with slugging first baseman Jason Giambi and a triumvirate of stud pitchers: Tim Hudson, Mark Mulder, and Barry Zito.

The Rangers had a stock of middle-of-the-rotation starters like Rick Helling, Doug Davis, and Darren Oliver, along with Kenny Rogers—the lefty pitcher, not the singer—which was fitting, since the team was out of aces.

From there, the rest of the staff and the bullpen were stocked with past-prime middle relievers and reclamation projects. You spent $25 million on one guy, and you start cutting corners elsewhere. The 2001 Texas Rangers were a gaudy mansion with a stunning facade and no working bathrooms. Nice to look at but not very practical. And things started to back up pretty quickly.

"You can't just put a bunch of talent together in pieces and think that you're going to ignore the team aspect of these pieces," said Bo Porter, an outfielder with the Rangers in 2001.

The $252 million man and company opened the regular season April 1 against the Blue Jays at Puerto Rico's Hiram Bithorn Stadium. The game served as a homecoming for Iván "Pudge" Rodríguez and Toronto's Carlos Delgado, native sons who'd made the island proud. A-Rod went 2-for-4 with a throwing error and also slipped on the seam of the turf at shortstop. Ken also took a tumble while fielding a ball in the third inning. He added two hits in the losing effort, batting seventh—seventh!—and playing in Puerto Rico for the first time since winter ball in 1988–89, when he was still trying to establish himself as an everyday player.

The Rangers' home opener April 3 against the Angels provided a glimpse of Ken's potential impact with the team. Texas entered the ninth inning with a 3–2 lead, but reliever Tim Crabtree loaded the bases without getting an out. Glenallen Hill came to the plate, a crafty hitter who'd won a World Series with the Yankees the previous season. Hill and Caminiti had been crossing paths since their Southern League days in 1986, and now they'd cross paths again.

Crabtree got ahead of Hill, 0-and-2, and after Hill fouled off a fastball, Crabtree threw a sinker with one outcome in mind: Get Hill to ground the ball to Caminiti. Hill did exactly that, and Ken fielded it cleanly and threw home, getting the runner and starting a 5–2–3 double play, Caminiti-Rodríguez-Palmeiro. Crabtree got the next hitter out to secure his shaky save, and the $252 million man and his teammates were in the win column. After the game, Ken came up from behind his new teammate and gave him a bear hug, a smile as big as Texas across Ken's face. Winning was fun.

But lots of losses followed.

The Rangers finished April in second place in the AL West with an 11–14 record. Seattle, meanwhile, raced to a 20–5 start, meaning Texas was nine games back after one month of the season. The gap widened in the weeks that followed. On May 4, with the Rangers 11–17, Johnny Oates resigned as manager, replaced by Jerry Narron.

Things kept going downhill.

Ken injured his shoulder—a partial tear. He decided against finding out the extent of the injury. He was going to keep playing either way.

On June 16 against his old club, Houston—nearly one year to the day after his ruptured tendon sheath—he drove a ball to right field in the top of the seventh, but as he rounded first base, there went the hamstring. Ken tried to limp his way to second base but got thrown out. He couldn't play through that injury, so he went on the DL.

With it went the end of his Rangers career.

Under different circumstances, his time with Texas could have ended differently. Ken hit nine home runs and played solid defense but was only batting .232. With the Rangers stuck in last place, there was no reason to keep him around—the team was focused on trying out its young players and finding out if they had a future. That meant Mike Lamb would be getting more playing time at third base.

The most important number was three, as in million—that's how much of the next year's salary would kick in if Ken stayed on the roster. And after you commit to $252 million and have nothing to show for it, you start holding on to your chips.

Ken knew his time was up with Texas, and he decided to walk away, requesting his release on July 2. Maybe another team could use his services. As it stood, Ken made his $3 million in base pay for 2001 and $750,000 of a potential $3.8 million in incentives.

Ken signed with Atlanta three days after his release from the Rangers.

He would be learning a new position: first base. Atlanta already had future Hall of Famer Chipper Jones at third base. What it needed was production from across the diamond. First basemen Rico Brogna and Wes Helms combined to bat .235, with 8 home runs and 40 RBIs during the early part of the season. If Ken could keep hitting, and provide adequate defense . . . which wasn't guaranteed. But for a prorated league minimum deal—$95,092—it was a safe risk.

Braves manager Bobby Cox had been keeping an eye on Ken since scouting him at Double-A Columbus during the mid-1980s. By 2001, Ken was a shell of his former self. He didn't move the same. Age and a bloated physique had robbed him of the agility and athleticism of his earlier days. But even with all his off-the-field issues and diminished ability, Ken commanded ultimate respect among his peers. Even if Ken Caminiti wasn't *Ken Caminiti* anymore, he was still someone you wanted on your team.

Playing for Atlanta reconnected him with some familiar faces, like Merv Rettenmund, his hitting coach in San Diego, who served the same role for Atlanta. His former Padres teammate Quilvio Veras was with the Braves, too. And now he'd be teaming with Brian Jordan, the former NFL player who had terrorized Ken's teams in the playoffs in 1996 and 1999.

Ken borrowed Wes Helms's first baseman's glove and got to work. He practiced fielding throws from Jesse Garcia, a middle infielder who was "ecstatic" to play with Caminiti. Garcia was an Astros fan growing up in Robstown, Texas. He loved the way Ken played, his hustle, and here he was playing with a childhood idol.

"We'd go out there early, and I'd throw balls from short. We worked on one-hoppers for him to try to pick it," Garcia said.

After joining his new team in Boston and serving as designated hitter and third baseman, Ken made his first base debut on July 12 against Baltimore. He booted the first grounder he faced, off the bat of Brady Anderson, and also struggled to pick up a shot by Chris Richard after stopping the ball. "The ball comes a lot different. It's going to take me a couple days to get used to it," he said after the game.

The problem for Ken was that he had to *think* about playing defense now. Think about the angles and responsibilities. He was never effective when he had to *think* about it. Baseball happens too quickly to *think*. As Ken learned to process the game from a new angle, his footwork at first base was stiff and clunky like timid freshmen on the dance floor at their first college party.

Atlanta was more interested in his offense than his defense, and he delivered in that capacity against the O's, going 3-for-3 with a homer in Atlanta's 6–5 win. But after that game, his bat went cold. From July 13 to 24, a span of eleven games, Ken went 4-for-35 with one double, no homers, one lonely RBI, and a .114 batting average.

He wondered if he had a place on the team.

If he should keep playing.

Maybe he should just retire. . . . No, Brian Jordan and Bernard Gilkey didn't think that was a good idea. The pair took Ken to a Chinese restaurant for lunch when the team reached Montreal. He was important to Atlanta's plans, they told him. The conversation flipped a switch. The next three games, Ken went 7-for-13 with four home runs. It felt good to be wanted.

* * *

Ken quickly found there was more to first base than simply thinking of the field in reverse. Now he was holding runners and awaiting throws from the pitcher. Shifting to a ready position as the pitch comes. Scooping throws from across the infield.

He had to learn how to catch the ball differently. Instead of extending his glove to secure the out a moment sooner, he watched the ball into his glove, bringing his "taco," as he called the first baseman's mitt, into his chest.

Bad positioning meant Caminiti was often moving to field throws—sometimes into the basepath, putting him on a collision course with runners. During an August 1, 2001, game against the Cardinals, third baseman Plácido Polanco hit a rocket to third base that was snagged by Chipper Jones, who threw to first. The throw was high, but instead of jumping in fair territory, in front of the bag, and swiping to tag the runner, Ken jumped into the baseline and smothered Polanco as he landed, turning the first base line into a full-contact tackling drill. As Polanco lay dazed on the ground, his helmet beside him, Caminiti held up his glove to show that he was still holding on to the ball. Out, indeed.

You dance in traffic, and someone's liable to get hit.

Braves infield coach Glenn Hubbard and Wes Helms had a running bet going in the dugout whenever Ken played first base: which inning he would wind up on the ground.

"He was so uncomfortable with the footwork at first base that he didn't have the smoothness of an everyday first baseman that played his whole life, so therefore he would just catch the ball and jump on you to tag you, or his footwork around the bag, he would try to stretch and wind up on the ground even though he'd keep his foot on the bag," Helms said.

It didn't help that Ken was struggling with an ingrown toenail by that point. . . . He'd hit the ball and stumble out of the box. He wanted to stay in games, but Bobby Cox would often replace him on defense or on the basepaths late in games, a chance to preserve his body.

* * *

Merv Rettenmund quickly recognized that this wasn't the same Ken he'd befriended in San Diego—Ken would sleep in the trainer's room, which told him that Ken wasn't sleeping enough at home.

The pair went fishing when the team was in Colorado. And Ken told his hitting coach something that haunted him for years.

"He would say stuff like 'I'm not gonna live that much longer.' And I said, 'Cammy, you gotta be kidding me. You have this beautiful family. . . .'

"And his thing, 'Aw, they're all taken care of. You just don't understand.' And I guess no one did understand, to tell you the truth."

Brian Jordan and Ken bonded over steak dinners—the veterans shared a deep respect. They both carried football mentalities onto the baseball field. Ken opened up to Jordan about his struggles with addiction. Jordan was shocked by what he heard.

"Ken Caminiti really, really opened up to me. I didn't expect anything. I didn't know what we were gonna talk about, but he told me about his life.

And in that moment, I just . . . I felt so sorry for him, because through all the greatness he was alone," Jordan said.

"He had a great wife, he loved his wife, she was a rock to him. She put up with everything, and was there for him. He expressed that to me. He didn't understand why she put up with him. . . . He really loved her.

"He told me about the cocaine, he told me about everything. He'd snort cocaine before games. It was just an eye-opener for me. As I listened, my jaw dropped, how he'd hang out all night getting no sleep, just go to the ballpark.

"He said he played in Montreal one day, I guess he had stayed out all night, so he did some cocaine to get through the game, and he swung so hard he just fell straight back. People thought he was dead. That's how bad it was."

* * *

The first base experiment ended on August 25. Ken's defense was a liability—his .977 fielding percentage was the worst for anyone playing so many games at the position that season—and he wasn't really hitting, either . . . so Helms was back starting at first. Ken was relegated to pinch-hitting, which wasn't his ideal role, but Cox couldn't keep putting Ken out there.

Ken started in Chipper Jones's place at third base on September 9, going 3-for-5 with two doubles in Atlanta's 9–5 win over the Cubs. It felt good for Ken to contribute amid the playoff race. The team had an off day on September 10.

The Braves, leading Philadelphia by three and a half games, were set to begin a three-game series against the Phillies at Turner Field on September 11. But all of that—the Braves, and Phillies, and sports involving bat and ball—took a back seat after hijackers brought four planes out of the sky. They slammed two into the World Trade Center towers in New York City, twin 110-story pillars that buckled under the weight and fire and force. A third plane crashed into the Pentagon just outside Washington, D.C., a broadside against the country's military force. A fourth plane, headed toward the nation's capital, crashed near Shanksville, Pennsylvania, after passengers stormed the cockpit. America was under attack.

National flights were grounded, and President George W. Bush—a former minority owner of the Texas Rangers—was resolute that America would "defend freedom and all that is good and just in our world." Major League Baseball canceled all games on that sunny, terrible Tuesday, and Wednesday, and the rest of the week, too. Baseball could wait.

The Braves, which had an off day that Monday, were already at home when the attacks happened and avoided some of the travel hiccups other teams faced with flights grounded. (Pitcher John Burkett, who had traveled to Texas, borrowed former Rangers teammate Rusty Greer's Jeep to make a sixteen-hour drive, while team president Stan Kasten had to drive from Milwaukee.)

The Braves' season resumed the following Monday, September 17, in Philadelphia. In the top of the seventh, with Atlanta down 3–2 and a runner on second base, Bobby Cox turned to Caminiti to pinch-hit against Robert Person, one of the pitchers he had homered against in his magical series in Mexico during his MVP season. But Ken didn't have any home runs left in his bat. He grounded out to second base, inning over, and was pulled from the game mired in an 8-for-54 slump.

The guy who needed to play, who struggled just watching others, was doing a lot of sitting and stewing. Ken was the kind of player who *had* to be on the field. And here he was getting bench splinters in his ass. He pinch-hit the following night, working a walk before getting the start at third base against Philadelphia on September 19 and 20. (With B. J. Surhoff also floundering, Cox moved Chipper Jones to left field and Ken to his natural spot at third base.) In the September 20 game, Cox was ejected in the second, frustrated that umpire Mark Barron called a pitch to Ken a strike—he thought it should have been ball four. Ken still walked, but Cox wasn't ready to let the issue rest, and he got the heave-ho.

Even if Cox wasn't always using Caminiti the way the player preferred, Ken didn't have to worry that his manager had his back.

And then it was on to New York to play against the Mets on September 21, in the first sporting event held in the devastated city following the September 11 attacks. Before the game, the teams held a somber salute to honor emergency and military personnel that included a twenty-one-gun salute and chants of *USA! USA! USA!*

Braves and Mets players and personnel shook hands and embraced on the field before the game, an uncommon display at an uncertain time. And then, somehow, someway, ten days and fifteen miles removed from the unthinkable, it was time to play a baseball game.

In the top of the fourth inning, with two down and Chipper Jones on first, Caminiti, batting righty, squibbed a ball past diving first baseman Todd Zeile. The ball squirted midway down the right field line, and Jones didn't stop running. The throw beat Jones by at least five steps, but Mets catcher Mike Piazza couldn't corral it, and Jones scampered across home plate to open the scoring.

Ken dialed back the time machine in the bottom half of the inning. The Mets tied the game, and with runners on second and third, New York was itching to take the lead. Outfielder Jay Payton grounded a two-bounce chopper that took a scenic route to third base. By the time the ball landed in Caminiti's glove, he was more than ten feet down the line beyond the bag, and his momentum was taking him into foul ground. And Payton was fast.

Ken grabbed the ball and chucked it like a grenade with the pin pulled—get it close to the target and hope for the best—and the throw settled into first baseman Julio Franco's glove a whisker before Payton reached the base.

Ken made another key play in the bottom of the fifth, again with two runners on, again with two outs. This time, Mets catcher Mike Piazza was at the plate. Piazza worked a full count. The fans erupted, looking for a big hit. Piazza grounded to third, and Caminiti sucked up the ball, tagging the approaching runner, Matt Lawton, and doing a twirl. These old bones could still dance on the infield dirt.

In the top of the seventh, with the game still knotted 1–1, Caminiti singled to right—and was replaced by a pinch runner, Jesse Garcia. Bobby Cox liked to use his bench, and it didn't behoove the manager to lose Ken to a hamstring pull from running the bases. No one at the time could know that it was the final multihit game of Ken's career.

The score remained 1–1 until the eighth inning, when Brian Jordan doubled home a run to give the Braves the lead. Atlanta turned to Queens native Steve Karsay to pitch. The umpire's strike zone was inconsistent, and Karsay seemed to have struck out Edgardo Alfonzo a couple of times—at 1-and-2, Karsay painted the outside corner, and if that strikeout had happened, the inning would have been over. But the ump called the pitch a ball, and Alfonso kept fouling off Karsay's pitches. After a 3-and-2 ball, or was it 3-and-4, who really knows, another pitch near the strike zone, Karsay threw up his hands.

Cox moved to the top step of the dugout but didn't go beyond it. Nope, he wasn't going to get tossed right now. There were bigger things at play.

With Alfonso at first, Piazza was up next. The superstar catcher settled into the batter's box, carrying a city's hopes and dreams on his back. The Mets needed a win. The fans, after a week full of so many tears, wanted to believe in something, to feel alive again.

Karsay looked the runner back to first. Catcher Javy López called for a pitch away, but the pitch stayed over the heart of the plate, and Piazza crushed the ball into the night, a towering home run for New York City and for America—resilience in the face of unspeakable tragedy.

"For Mike to hit that home run and the crowd to be jubilant and try to maybe forget about what had happened for just a few minutes and be excited about something that a sports or entertainment piece could provide . . . it was a nice moment for what had happened," Karsay said.

As Atlanta made its march to the playoffs, Ken's bat all but disappeared again—over the season's final two weeks, he batted .120 with three hits in twenty-five at bats and only one RBI.

But it was the postseason, and Ken's bat was liable to come alive. It was October . . . and October had meant so much to Ken these past few years.

* * *

The Braves were facing the Astros—the team where Ken had spent the bulk of his career, and the team that had declined to re-sign him after his troubled 2000 season.

In Game 1, with the Braves down 3–2 in the top of the eighth inning, Ken came in to face Michael Jackson, the same pitcher he'd faced in his debut game in 1987, when he walked and ended up scoring the winning run. Keith Lockhart was on second base with a leadoff double. It was Ken's chance to be the hero. But Jackson made quick work of him, getting the strikeout. As Ken walked back to the dugout, Atlanta would quickly take the lead. Marcus Giles singled in Lockhart, and after Julio Franco reached on an error, Chipper Jones hit a home run against Billy Wagner, making it 6–3. Atlanta ended up winning 7–4.

Atlanta won Game 2, 1–0, behind Ken's longtime nemesis—and now teammate—Tom Glavine's eight-inning masterpiece (John Smoltz, working out of the bullpen, got the save).

In Game 3, Ken pinch-hit in the seventh inning with Atlanta up 4–2, hitting a fly ball to center fielder Richard Hidalgo. The Braves would add two runs to win the game 6–2, and sweep the series.

The team celebrated the playoff win. For Atlanta, the Arizona Diamondbacks, with dual ace pitchers Randy Johnson and Curt Schilling, loomed in the National League Championship Series. Amid the hubbub, Ken was called into Cox's office.

It was a closed-door kind of conversation. Cox had made a decision. A tough one. But a decision that had to be made. Ken was being left off the NLCS roster. Pitcher Kevin Millwood was being added instead.

"There's no easy way to explain that to a guy that's had his type of career," Cox said. "He was an All-Star player and had been to playoffs so many times and all that, but it just didn't work for the postseason. It was very difficult."

Ken chose not to travel with the team as it continued on to Arizona. It was too painful for him to watch, and not to play.

Brian Jordan watched as Ken was called into Cox's office. *Uh-oh, here we go*, he thought. You spend enough time in the clubhouse, and you recognize what the meetings mean. Ken left the office and sat in the middle of the clubhouse, wrapped in a towel.

"Eventually the towel dropped off, so he was buck naked sitting in the middle of the doggone clubhouse. And he had his phone in his hand, and he was just in a stare of anger. And nobody would come close to talking to him," Jordan said. "And I remember going up to him to say, 'Hey, c'mon man, get dressed, y'know, we need you there to support us.' And he looked up at me with this stare and said absolutely nothing. And I looked at him and I said, 'Look man, I want you to go, man, c'mon.' And he didn't say nothing. He just looked back down, and I was like, 'Whoa.'

"Next thing you know, we leave, he did not get on the bus. . . . With his body slowing down, it was almost like he knew he had nothing after this. It was sad."

CHAPTER 26

LOST AND FOUND

Ken filed for free agency on November 6. The market on broken-down thirty-eight-year-olds isn't usually a strong one, but Ken hoped to catch on with another team. He still felt like he had something to offer the game.

But the end of the 2001 season sent him spiraling. Being left off the NLCS roster. The potential end of his career. He wasn't wanted on his team, and he wasn't wanted in his family, living apart from his wife and three girls. Everything good in his life, it seemed, was in the rearview mirror. He had nothing in front of him.

He felt worthless. Lower than low. He wanted to disappear.

And he could just about do that at the Ramada Limited Inn on Southwest Freeway in southwest Houston. He and a few others checked into the motel on November 13.

He gave the keys to his Mercedes to Lamont Palmer. Palmer was driving the car, and authorities thought he seemed "suspicious"—that's the word they used, *suspicious*, to describe this black teen who was driving a $100,000 car, so they pulled him over and asked about the car.

It's Ken Caminiti's, Palmer said. *He gave me the car to detail it. If you want to ask him yourself, he's staying at the Ramada Limited.*

So Harris County deputies Patberg and Worley, and Detective Clark, and Sergeant Barber all proceeded to Room 2025, all the way at the end of the hallway, and as they approached, the smell of crack cocaine became stronger and stronger.

Detective Clark knocked on the door. A nineteen-year-old woman, Latoya Bowman, opened it. A man, Cedric Palmer, Lamont's cousin, was lying down on a bed.

Deputy Worley entered the room and "immediately observed the door immediately to his left being shut," authorities said. Worley walked to the door and "discovered a white male"—Kenneth Gene Caminiti—standing in the bathroom. Worley found a "used crack pipe lying in the white bathroom sink in plain view."

The bathroom contained a plastic Ozarka water bottle and Coca-Cola can used to smoke crack cocaine. Other drug paraphernalia was found throughout the room. Ken's Gucci wallet didn't contain any money—but where the money would go, "the wallet contained a heavy trace of white powder substance . . . cocaine." A stolen handgun was also found in the room.

Five years to the day after his receiving the National League's Most Valuable Player award, Ken was in the news for all the wrong reasons, the TV cameras capturing him in the back of a police car. From the highest of highs to the lowest of lows.

Ken, Bowman, and Palmer were all arrested and charged with possession of a controlled substance: less than a gram of cocaine. Ken's bail was set at $2,000. He paid and was released. Bowman and Palmer couldn't pay their bail (Palmer's was set at $15,000 due to a prior offense), and both remained jailed.

The arrest stunned the public. Ken's struggles with alcohol were well-known, but crack cocaine? And what was Ken doing with the two people in the room with him, in a seedy part of Houston? None of it made sense.

Ken had known Cedric and Lamont Palmer for some time. Bowman, speaking to the Associated Press the following month, said she only knew Ken for a few days before their arrest, and that he asked her for advice on dealing with Nancy. "He was a nice person, but he seemed to have issues at home," she said. She recalled him smoking crack cocaine. He was known in Houston's drug scene.

This was not the same guy who Ken's baseball teammates knew. Ken was the guy with the dirty number 11 or 21 uniform, but now he had a new number, his SPN (System Person Number), also known as a "spin" number—001891936.

Ken's mug shot showed him stern and forlorn, his hair mopped across his forehead, his goatee offset by days of stubble, his eyes staring forward, blank and lost. Within days, it was plastered across the internet. Three years after his World Series meltdown, Ken was falling apart in front of our eyes. Again.

Ken needed help. And he went out of state to get it.

* * *

J. Hutton Pulitzer had no clue who this handsome, goateed guy was when they met in late November 2001 at the Meadows of Wickenburg in Arizona.

The man was a good athlete—that became obvious through the pickup basketball and games of H-O-R-S-E he shared with this guy, named Ken, and another man from North Carolina. Over time, as Pulitzer bonded with his new buddy, he learned all about Ken's baseball days, along with his talent and addictions and good heart and inner turmoil.

"When you go to the Meadows, you're in for thirty days," Pulitzer said. "It's a top-to-bottom immersion, seven days a week. From the time you get up at daylight 'til the time you go to bed in the evening, it's all counseling and group stuff and therapy."

Unlike Ken, Pulitzer never got into drugs or alcohol. His PTSD was triggered by his tech company falling apart and his then wife filing for divorce. Digital Convergence Corporation had developed a device that attached to your computer called the CueCat—it was shaped like a stretching feline—with which you could scan the barcode on a publication or item, and it would take you to a website.

The device was the internet's *next big thing*, a predecessor to the QR codes popularized by smartphones in the years that followed. Coca-Cola and RadioShack and NBC all invested . . . but then the CueCat failed to take off like Pulitzer had wished, and the dotcom bubble burst. As Pulitzer was preparing a last-ditch effort to make the CueCat a success, the 9/11 attacks stunted the market and sent its developer spiraling.

"My world came crashing down," he said.

So Pulitzer went to the Meadows to fix himself, and that's where he found Ken, the nicest, most genuine guy you'd ever want to meet. Pulitzer quickly recognized Ken's desire to help others—the same qualities that his baseball teammates adored when they played with him. "With Ken, it was never about Ken. It was always about someone else," he said. It was no big deal for Ken, if someone aimed to get straight, to write a check. He had the money. He could help them."

Pulitzer and Ken spent hours talking about Ken's plans. He was thinking about getting some land out in the country and running a ranch. The girls could help in working the land, and everything would be steady and stable. "He wanted to spend more time with his girls and be out of the limelight, and he thought being in a ranch or farm setting would be really good," Pulitzer said. "He talked about either putting that together or healing things with his wife."

* * *

At the Meadows, Ken dove into his feelings about baseball, his addictions, and his unresolved childhood trauma more deeply than ever before.

Ken, in rehab, discussed his drinking as a means of silencing his inner self-judgment—reflecting a desire to quiet the voice inside and suppress the shame that lingered from the childhood sexual abuse he endured, Pulitzer said.

"One thing that was obviously a crisis and would mess with anybody's head taught him how to medicate through substances, and that just morphed into something else," Pulitzer said. "That was the tipping doorway that taught him, 'Hey, you can shut down some of these feelings.'"

And shut them down he did. For a long time.

He couldn't shut them down anymore.

Ken, through his treatment, desired to be "the person he always wanted to be but never felt he could be . . . a good guy just doing his thing, supporting his family, without a lot of expectations." The money he made was nice. It helped him provide for his family. It could help a lot of people.

While those in baseball loved Ken, warts and all, the people in rehab loved him for what was underneath those warts, the reasons behind his struggles and vulnerabilities. "We all bonded totally broken and totally exposed, so there was nothing to hide. You have these friends who know your worst warts, the kind of stuff you'd never tell anybody. The kind of stuff you'd never admit to is exactly what we all know about each other. It creates this interesting, very trusting friendship," Pulitzer said.

* * *

Cindy Popp was used to being around famous people, and as a big sports fan, she knew who Ken was, and of course he was easy on the eyes. She didn't care about any of that stuff.

"We were trying to heal," she said.

The then New York–based photographer met Ken in late 2001 at the Life Healing Center of Santa Fe, a facility nestled in the Sangre de Cristo foothills. Ken was there between December 2001 and February 2002. They were in group therapy sessions together, sharing their darkest secrets, taking a wrecking ball to the walls and the pain and the damage that had built up around them.

"I think Ken had a lot of hard things, from what I heard in my group, that were very hard for him to deal with," she said.

Every morning, Ken would make a smoothie for Cindy, and she would return the favor by making breakfast for him, friends helping each other in a time of need. Cindy bonded with another person who was attending the center at the same time, Ryan Burda—they would end up becoming a couple. Ryan, a Wisconsin native, didn't quite know what to think about the former National League MVP at first. He struggled with trust issues. But after Cindy's reassurance that Ken was a good guy, Ryan and Ken became fast friends, too.

Ryan said he and Ken weren't at the facility specifically for alcohol or other drug abuse, known as AODA; the focus was "more secondary, digging into the shit that happened to you when you were a kid.

"You're paying professionals a whole bunch of money to kinda turn you inside out," Ryan said.

Ryan and Ken both struggled, he said, with being the victims of child sexual abuse. "It was a painful thing for him. He's a tough guy, intimidating dude."

Ryan recalled Ken talking highly of his parents.

There was a set of cabins two or three hundred yards away from the center's main building where Ryan and Ken would soak in the sunshine. They learned how to bury tobacco and burn sage sticks, and over time they started stacking rocks, "almost like you were stacking wood, six feet tall, this big honeycomb rock pile."

Program participants would watch movies at night. *Gone in 60 Seconds*, the car heist flick starring Nicolas Cage, was among Ken's favorites. "He could meditate to that," Ryan said.

Ken was especially drawn to a scene early in the movie that shows the character Tumbler (Scott Caan) throwing a tennis ball against the wall as he discusses his new method for pleasuring himself. "I call it 'the stranger.' What I do is, I sit on my hand for, like, fifteen, twenty minutes until it goes numb. No feeling at all. And then I rub one out." One time when they were watching the movie, and that scene came on, Ken started sitting on his arm, acting out the joke with a glint of boyish mischief in his eye as if he were back at Lone Hill School or in the Padres clubhouse.

"He kind of got scolded for demonstrating all of that and showing us the joke," Ryan said.

Another time, the group was riding buses to go to an AA/NA meeting at a hospital in Santa Fe, and Ken was ahead of Ryan, and all of a sudden Ryan saw a guy sprinting past him, going, *Do you know who that is?* Even in treatment, Ken couldn't fully break free from his celebrity.

Cindy saw the deep work Ken was putting in, day after day, to improve himself and get things right. She saw his goodness shine through. He was a *good guy*. But rehab isn't always about being a good guy. There's a selfishness that comes with personal recovery, putting yourself first. And Ken was focusing a lot on everyone else.

"Ken was one of those people just trying to be something [for others], and I get it, but he couldn't just do it for himself, you know? And he needed to," she said.

* * *

As Ken was coming out of one of his stints in rehab, there was a point where he needed to pick a sponsor, and his racing buddy Raymond Martin agreed, so Ken moved in with Raymond's family for a while. Things were good. Things were secure.

The Martins helped Ken find a house in Baytown, a few miles from their home. Ken was going to get a fresh start. After Ken moved into his new house, Raymond stayed there every night. The Martins were at Ken's house, or he was at theirs.

"He was like a big brother to me that lived with us, and then he got his own house," said Martin's daughter Mystic.

Ken was reestablishing the healthy bonds in his life. He also returned to the Padres in Peoria—for one day, at least—to share an important message with a grieving team.

Outfielder Mike Darr, who'd played with Ken briefly in spring training in 1998 and spent the following three seasons with San Diego, flipped his Jeep during spring training. He'd been drinking and wasn't wearing a seat belt, and he and his childhood friend Duane Johnson died in the crash. Darr was twenty-five years old and left behind a wife and two young sons.

The tragedy bore similarities to Mike Sharperson's rollover crash in 1996, when he died while on his way to meet the Padres in Montreal.

Manager Bruce Bochy wondered what he could say to the team. Bochy told them to make every day count, and his hope that they could learn something from the tragedy . . . and then he yielded the floor to Ken. After hearing about the circumstances of Darr's death, Ken wanted to say something from the heart. Ken was fresh from rehab, fresh from addressing his own substance abuse issues, and he was an open book.

* * *

Ken's parents were in court with him on March 21, 2002, when he pleaded guilty to cocaine possession. He was sentenced to three years' probation. If he could stay clean, the conviction would be wiped from his record.

Visiting state District Judge Bill Hatten chastised Caminiti during the court appearance.

"You're getting a break," the judge said. "You better take advantage of it."

Under the terms of the plea agreement, Ken was required to pay a $2,000 fine, complete two hundred hours of community service (which he could do by working with youth baseball programs), submit to periodic urinalysis, and avoid all contact with Bowman and Palmer. He was also forbidden from entering bars and required to turn over his weapons.

Ken signed his conditions of community supervision with the same looping signature he used to autograph baseballs and bats and cards and photos for his fans.

"I'm not trying to get too far ahead of myself, and I'm definitely not trying to dwell on the past," he said after leaving court. "I'm just trying to move forward taking baby steps, you might say."

He was a new man looking for a fresh start. At thirty-nine, he was facing his first spring without baseball and trying to figure out what shape his life would take.

He had nothing to hide. And that was his outlook the following month when he got a phone call from someone who wanted to talk.

CHAPTER 27

THE TRUTH WILL SET YOU FREE

Jules Roberson-Bailey couldn't get past the changing bodies. Players' heads were *bigger*. Their jaws were more pronounced. This wasn't normal. Roberson-Bailey, a producer with the sports network CNN/SI, had spent half a decade covering spring training, and by 2002, performance-enhancing drugs were an obvious problem. The problem was obvious to her anyway.

The record books had been written and rewritten in recent seasons. From the start of professional baseball through the 1997 season, only two men—Babe Ruth and Roger Maris—hit sixty or more home runs in a major league season. Then in 1998, two players, Mark McGwire and Sammy Sosa, both smashed that milestone, and they did it again in 1999, and Sosa hit 64 more in 2001—the year Barry Bonds, the San Francisco Giants' otherworldly outfielder, hit 73 home runs.

All told, the top six single-season HR totals in major league baseball history were set between 1998 and 2001. And yes, expansion meant a watered-down talent pool, and ballparks were smaller, and the balls were livelier, and the bats more explosive, but the most notable change had to do with players' bodies.

Lots of people in baseball saw the same changes Jules Roberson-Bailey did, but the topic was more of a whisper. Speculation. Innuendo. It was damn near impossible to come out and accuse players of using the stuff without proof, even if the proof was visible in larger hat sizes or indescribable power numbers, or guys coming to spring training looking like they'd pop if you pricked them with a pin. Hell, during the height of the 1998 home run race between McGwire and Sosa, AP reporter Steve Wilstein was vilified for reporting that McGwire had a bottle of androstenedione, a steroid precursor, in plain view in his locker—not McGwire for using, but Wilstein for reporting. By 2002, the problem was out of control. Roberson-Bailey, who was based out of Texas, called her boss in Atlanta and asked to pursue the story.

"There is something going on," she told him.

They talked about how to best approach the topic. They needed a player who was willing to talk about his own use of steroids. A player who was open to discussing what he did, someone who was respected and trusted.

They cycled through a number of names before coming to Ken Caminiti. He'd discussed his alcoholism in the past, and given his cocaine arrest in the Houston hotel room months earlier, it was possible he had tried steroids, too. The transformation of his body throughout his career, from a skinny rookie to a muscle-bound masher, was difficult to ignore, and his late-career power spike stood out. Roberson-Bailey did her homework, getting Caminiti's cell phone number through a close contact. She called the number.

Ken answered, and Roberson-Bailey said they ended up talking for half an hour. He was in Nevada attending the Laughlin River Run, a popular motorcycle show. He seemed open to talking for her story.

"Why don't I fly out to Laughlin? Let me come out, let's talk, let's sit down, let's have a conversation. I'll come out, and let's just see where this takes us," she said.

"No, you bring a camera," he told her. "I have no trouble, I'll talk about it. I'll talk about what I'm trying to do. I'll talk about why I'm trying to stay clean."

Caminiti's motivation for talking, she said, was driven in part because he wanted teams to know that he was staying on the right path. "At the time, he had talked to a couple of teams," she said. "He was trying to get back in the game, either as a player or as a coach or manager. And I think there had been some minor interest, but I don't believe anybody was going to take that step, knowing his drug history."

Those close to Caminiti and familiar with his recovery believe his desire to talk was a direct result of his time in rehab. In rehab he had been told the truth would set him free, and that his secrets could hurt him only if he tried to bury them, as he had with his childhood trauma decades earlier.

Roberson-Bailey approached the meeting in Nevada with cautious optimism. She warned her bosses that Caminiti could change his mind at any point and the story could fall apart. But it was worth a shot. So she flew to Nevada and hired a freelance videographer, and they went to a hotel room and set up for the interview.

The Ken Caminiti who met with Roberson-Bailey was windburned, his skin the color of a worn glove from hours on his motorcycle. His face was puffy, and he wore a flannel shirt.

He wasn't afraid to talk and didn't shy away from any topics, including his use of alcohol and amphetamines and cocaine, his relapse at the ESPY awards, his mindset as a player, the pride he had playing the game the right way.

He discussed his disdain for counseling: "I go because I'm supposed to." It was tough for him, he said, to keep spilling his secrets.

He also found it difficult to watch baseball, given that he still identified as a player—it wasn't easy for him to shift to the next phase of his life, to turn the page, to move on. He fidgeted and got nervous if a game was on.

Family came up, too. He discussed the toughness his brother and father had ingrained in him, as well as his three little girls, and the difficulty that his addictions had caused them. "I know people at school give them a hard time. I know that they've had to deal with all this," he told Roberson-Bailey. "I just keep telling them, 'Daddy's sick, but Daddy's gonna get better.'"

Roberson-Bailey waited until the second half of her interview before asking about the S-word.

"OK, we've talked about your alcohol and your cocaine use, and we've talked about the amphetamines. Have you ever done andro?"

"No," Ken said.

"What about steroids?"

"Yeah."

"Were they readily available like amphetamines were?"

"I took a black market deal, and, uh . . ." he said, inhaling loudly, his brow furrowed. "It's the worst thing I did. Because I got the strength, whatever. I built the muscles up.

"I was trying to do anything to play, and I knew I was tore up. So I said, 'OK, do it, you know, just hold it together, hold it together, hold it together.' And I played that whole year, you know? And I was MVP."

As Caminiti discussed his use of steroids, Roberson-Bailey felt a rush—that *holy shit* moment as a journalist when your interview subject says something earth-shattering. "He admitted that he had taken steroids. You're sitting there as the person doing the interview, going in your head, 'Oh my gosh, he's just admitted this,'" she said.

This was THE STORY, the thing that everyone was talking about, and Ken Caminiti's words would change the conversation about performance-enhancing drugs in baseball. This was a player admitting—voluntarily, without reservation—that the steroids had helped him achieve his greatest seasons. Up to that point, guys would talk in generalities, brush off the impact of PEDs, or go off the record as a means of protecting themselves and their fellow players. The admission that would impact baseball's past and alter its future began with a field producer and a freelance videographer in a hotel room above a motorcycle show.

The interview was cordial, and Roberson-Bailey left the hotel hopeful that Ken could overcome his personal struggles. "I really rooted for him, and as a journalist you know you're not supposed to take a side. . . . You just come out going, 'Man, I hope the best for him,'" she said.

John Covington—who'd built motorcycles for Caminiti and was at the show with him—said reality started to sink in for Ken after the interview concluded that he was too truthful about what he'd done. "He was too honest with somebody he shouldn't have trusted," Covington said. "And it was sad, because he was talking all the way up there about how he's a new guy, he's got nothing to hide. *This is who I am. I'm OK with me now.* So he went and he was fresh out of this therapy and just was too open with somebody. He just didn't know who to trust again, y'know?"

The day after the interview was recorded, in the early morning hours of April 27, two rival motorcycle clubs, the Hells Angels and Mongols, got into a brawl at Harrah's Laughlin Casino, leaving three people dead. The "River Run Riot," as it was dubbed, forced a lockdown, which meant Ken was stuck inside his hotel room. Which only made him stew even more. When the lockdown was over, Ken and a buddy from Houston who'd been along on the trip ended up flying back to Texas.

In the ensuing weeks, Roberson-Bailey traveled to Caminiti's home in Baytown for a follow-up interview. But during the second interview, she said, Caminiti's mood quickly shifted. "The interview went well for the first five minutes, and I asked him some more questions about the steroids because at this point, word's out," she said. "We had crews around the country going to major league ballparks and asking teams, whether it be in St. Louis or New York—they were asking teams and players about steroids."

Midway through the interview, Caminiti had enough of the questions and ripped his microphone off. He leaned toward Roberson-Bailey, who was sitting in an adjacent chair. She didn't know what he was going to do.

"He stood up and he kicked the chair out of the way and he stormed off," she said. "At that point, we left. He was done."

Roberson-Bailey called her boss in Atlanta. She had gotten all she was going to get from Caminiti, so for her, it was on to her next story—to St. Louis for coverage ahead of Ozzie Smith's induction into the National Baseball Hall of Fame that summer. While there, she played video from Caminiti's interviews on a tape deck, cycling through the footage and logging his quotes. When she finished, she sent the log of her interviews with Ken to her boss, as well as Tom Verducci, the well-respected *Sports Illustrated* baseball writer who'd spent months trying to crack a story about steroids in baseball for the magazine. He listened to agonizing pleas from clean players seeking a level playing field.

Verducci had profiled Caminiti during that magical 1996 season, and he would be picking up the next story involving Caminiti, the coverage that began with Roberson-Bailey. As a seasoned TV producer, Roberson-Bailey didn't mind handing off the story—she simply wanted it to be told. She was more worried that a competitor (namely, ESPN) would break the story first than she was about getting publicly credited for her efforts.

"It was a big story to be a part of. I felt good about the job I did, but then I had to hand it off, and that's just how it works," she said. "Those decisions were much higher than my pay grade."

Beyond corporate synergy, there was another reason CNN/SI wouldn't break the story about Caminiti's steroids admission: It was folding. The twenty-four-hour network, which launched in 1996 as a marriage between the two Time Warner brands, was seen as a rival to ESPNews and Fox Sports Net's *National Sports Report*. Though CNN/SI broke a number of major stories, most notably a story about an Indiana University basketball player accusing famed coach Bobby Knight of choking him, it never fully found its footing, and its reduced reach—only about twenty million homes—meant weakened interest from sponsors.

CNN/SI went off the air on May 15, before the story about Caminiti ran. Roberson-Bailey was offered a job in New York City, but she turned it down—"I had a house, dogs, cars, husband. I didn't want to live in New York. I love visiting, I love going, but it just didn't fit my lifestyle at that time," she said. She ended up taking a buyout.

* * *

Verducci initially thought steroids was a "niche element" in the game, an endeavor pursued only by the José Cansecos and Lenny Dykstras, but by 2001, as the clean players kept complaining to him, the scope of the problem started coming into focus.

"Players felt like they either had to compromise their integrity, which they didn't want to do, compromise their own health because at the time there were still a lot of concerns about the effects of using steroids, or play at a disadvantage. None of those options is good," he said.

"It was no longer just the niche thing going on in the game, but it became a highly competitive thing that to keep up with the game, you really did need to use some kind of PED, or else you were behind."

Before the 2002 season, the *SI* team discussed coverage topics for the coming year.

"The biggest story in baseball is going to be the use of steroids in the game, and somebody's going to write it, and it better be us," he said.

Verducci started chipping away at the story, but he still had a ways to go. He needed someone to come forward, "someone to say that the emperor had no clothes and have their name attached to it."

And then he got the tip about Caminiti from Roberson-Bailey.

"She said, 'You may want to talk to Caminiti, because he seems like he's open to the idea of discussing the subject,'" Verducci said of Roberson-Bailey.

Verducci called Caminiti, and Ken—encouraged by Roberson-Bailey to speak to the *SI* scribe—invited Verducci to visit him in Texas. "To my surprise, he immediately said, 'Sure, fine, I'll talk to you. I'll talk to you about whatever you want to talk about,'" Verducci said.

They sat on lawn chairs in Ken's garage. "We were there for hours, and it was just a very comfortable conversation," Verducci said. "You think some guys might be a little reticent, or hem and haw a little bit, but I gotta say, the questions about his own use, he met them head-on."

Verducci asked Caminiti what percentage of players he estimated were using steroids. Caminiti guessed about half. Following the interview, Verducci said, he and Caminiti went to eat at a nearby restaurant. Caminiti, who was known by the waitresses and cooks, ordered an egg white omelet.

"This is going to be a big story, don't you think?" Ken asked.

"Yeah, it is. I'm not going to tell you otherwise. It's gonna be a big story."

"Well, I understand. And I don't care, because this is what happened. I'm just answering questions."

* * *

As Verducci worked on his story, another outlet was advancing a story that threatened to pull back the lid on steroids in baseball. On May 17, Fox Sports Net aired an interview between José Canseco and host Jim Rome in which the former Oakland A's star, alleging that he was blackballed by Major League Baseball, said he was ready to spill the beans about everything, PEDs included, in an upcoming book.

"How prevalent is steroid use in major league baseball right now?" Rome asked.

"It's more than what people think, and it's more [than] people can imagine. It's rampant," Canseco responded.

"How rampant? I mean, half the guys in major league baseball? Two-thirds of the guys in major league baseball? If you had to put a percent on it, what would it be?"

"Eighty-five."

"Eighty-five percent?"

"There would be no baseball left if they drug-tested everyone today," Canseco said.

Rome pressed the "Bash Brother" on whether he had used steroids himself.

"That will be covered in the book. Everything's gonna be covered in the book, who's involved in it, who's done it—there will be certain names in it that will shock the world," Canseco said.

"That's not a no."

As Canseco continued to evade the questions, Rome challenged Canseco's claim that nearly all major league baseball players were using PEDs.

"If 85 percent of the guys in major league baseball are doing steroids, very clearly this has had an effect on the game, to the detriment, right?" Rome asked.

"It's completely restructured the game as we know it," Canseco said.

Canseco's comments, at the time, were curious but drew mixed reactions. For one, he had an ax to grind and was looking to bring others down with him. He was always seen as a publicity fiend and a bit of a clown, someone who dated the pop singer Madonna and raced Ferraris and who, during a 1993 game, had a baseball bounce off his head and over the outfield wall for a home run. If 85 percent of players used, that would mean an average of twenty-one players on every team. *There's no way....* Who's to say Canseco was even telling the truth? How much did he know? He was also mum about his own use, meaning it was difficult to figure out what to believe. No, someone else needed to come forward, someone who wasn't interested in burning everything down. Someone who was worth trusting.

* * *

>> SPECIAL REPORT <<
STEROIDS IN BASEBALL
CONFESSIONS OF AN MVP

"At first I felt like a cheater, but I looked around, and everybody was doing it."
—Ken Caminiti

The *Sports Illustrated* cover featured two crossed syringes, forming an X atop a baseball, but it may as well have featured a live bomb with a burning wick. On May 28, 2002, in tandem with the magazine issue hitting newsstands, CNN and *SI* launched a cross-platform publicity effort, pushing the story on the network and publishing coverage online. Caminiti's quotes turned the baseball world upside down. The secret was out. Pandora's box was open.

- "I've made a ton of mistakes. I don't think using steroids is one of them."

- "It's no secret what's going on in baseball. At least half the guys are using steroids. They talk about it. They joke about it with each other. The guys who want to protect themselves or their image by lying have that right. Me? I'm at the point in my career where I've done just about every bad thing you can do. I try to walk with my head up. I don't have to hold my tongue. I don't want to hurt teammates or friends. But I've got nothing to hide."

- "If a young player were to ask me what to do, I'm not going to tell him it's bad. Look at all the money in the game: You have a chance to set your family up, to get your daughter into a better school. . . . So I can't say, 'Don't do it,' not when the guy next to you is as big as a house and he's going to take your job and make the money."

- "At first I felt like a cheater. But I looked around and everybody was doing it. . . . Back then you had to go find it in Mexico or someplace. Now? It's everywhere. It's very easy to get."

Verducci's article also contained quotes from pitchers Curt Schilling and Kenny Rogers, and outfielder Chad Curtis, who estimated that 40 to 50 percent of players used steroids—right in line with Ken's estimate. "Steroids can jump you a level or two," Rogers told Verducci. "The average player can become a star, and the star player can become a superstar, and the superstar? Forget it. He can do things we've never seen before."

A video report by Bob Fiscella, a CNN sports anchor, included a mix of Caminiti's on-camera quotes to Roberson-Bailey and off-camera quotes to Verducci—a reflection of the team effort that contributed to the story coming together. Fiscella's report led off CNN's *Wolf Blitzer Reports*, ahead of stories about the death of congressional staffer Chandra Levy being labeled a homicide, the fight against the terror group al Qaeda in the Middle East, and President George W. Bush's meeting with the pope to discuss the Catholic Church sexual abuse scandal. Caminiti's disclosure was bigger than sports. It was a national news story, a black eye for the national pastime.

Caminiti, as he was apt to do in interviews, told Verducci a handful of half-truths that ended up making it into the *Sports Illustrated* article—half-truths that would be upheld as fact in the ensuing decades. Ken said that he drove to Mexico himself to buy steroids, putting all the responsibility on his own shoulders for trips that his childhood buddy Dave Moretti now says he took on his friend's behalf.

Ken also suggested he wound up "injecting twice as much steroids as was considered normal" in 1996, causing his testicles to shrink and retract. But according to Moretti, Ken's PED use was measured and regulated during his MVP season, and following Ken's shoulder surgery, when he was working with rehab specialist Catherine Ondrusek, his body's natural testosterone production was sufficient to fuel his recovery during a time when he wasn't using steroids. After he began getting his steroids from others and taking more risks with them starting in 1999, his body struggled to produce its own testosterone, forcing him to inject synthetic hormones to meet his body's needs.

But what Ken told Verducci was close enough to the truth. And none of those hazy details changed the explosive fact that Ken was admitting, without remorse, that he had used PEDs.

Verducci's article included a passing reference to a friend in California who had supplied Ken with steroids starting in 1997, but the friend wasn't named. "Any time the conversation might have left him as a topic, he went right back to his own responsibility. So the details, the individuals—he was just not naming anybody," Verducci said.

Dave Moretti noticed the reference—Ken was referring to him. He and Ken had joked, during the height of their PED partnership, about making the pages of *Sports Illustrated*. And now they had.

Moretti said he initially feared what Ken might say about him. But Moretti's name didn't leak. And his personal concerns took a back seat to his friend's disclosure.

"I was proud of him, because I knew what he was doing it for. I knew he was trying to bring his demons out of the closet and expose them, and take away the power they had over him," Moretti said.

"I was extremely proud of him, and I thought that he did a good thing."

For Moretti, Ken's 50 percent estimate—something any person in the game had no way of knowing—was a means for Ken to defend his own use.

But Ken's disclosures were worrisome for some players. One of the players Moretti previously supplied with steroids called, panicked that his name was going to leak due to Ken talking. "I don't think so," Moretti told him. Ken wasn't naming names, and Moretti wasn't on anyone's radar now that Ken took responsibility for buying his own steroids in Mexico.

And Moretti made sure not to leave a paper trail. He didn't keep notebooks or computer files with players' names on them. "All I have is some numbers saved in my old phone," he told the player.

Moretti already took the battery out of the phone, but just to be safe, at the player's urging, he dumped the phone in a bucket of ice water, destroying whatever evidence existed of his days helping guys bounce back from injuries or make a roster or, in his childhood friend's case, transform from an All-Star into a folk hero.

* * *

Due to Ken's comments, the league couldn't ignore its PED problem anymore.

He broke baseball's *omertà*, sharing secrets from the clubhouse, and that was a cardinal sin. Not using steroids—that wasn't the issue; it was talking about using steroids.

Reaction to Caminiti's article was widespread and ranged from sympathy to scorn.

Some expressed concern for his well-being.

Some feigned ignorance.

Some criticized his motives.

Some argued that it undermined his accomplishments.

Some stated it didn't surprise them.

Some agreed with him.

Some thanked him.

Some called for drug testing as a means of cleaning up the game.

Some called him a snitch.

But Major League Baseball and the players' union couldn't ignore the issue anymore, and within three months, they struck a new deal included testing for steroids and other PEDs.

* * *

Ken tried to defend or explain himself in subsequent interviews with Dan Patrick on ESPN Radio and on Jim Rome's syndicated radio show. The crux of Ken's issues came with that 50 percent figure. That's what baseball players were griping the most about, since it implicated them.

"What's really bothering me most about this whole thing is how it got blown out of context," he told Patrick.

"I don't know if I mentioned half or not. That is something that might have been thrown in my face or in my mouth. That's not true. That's a false statement. I didn't mean half. There's a couple of people that have done it that I know of. Baseball's a pretty clean sport."

Talking to Rome, his voice weary, Ken expressed frustration with the direction and tone of the article. "They came to me wanting to talk about life after baseball, and then it turned into this whole steroid thing," he said. "I never knew the interview was going to go like that. It just got real ugly."

While Ken's conversation with Jules Roberson-Bailey began with a focus on life after baseball—that much is true—his aborted follow-up interview with Roberson-Bailey and subsequent conversation with Verducci dealt heavily with steroids.

Verducci was so worried about how Ken would handle their interview and any possible distractions that he made sure he went alone to Caminiti's house. No photographer that day. Just two men talking. A photographer came in the days after Verducci spoke to Ken, snapping photos of the ballplayer holding a bat and staring into the camera. His goatee had flecks of gray, but he still had those eyes, those piercing blue eyes.

If things were so ugly during Verducci's interview with Ken, he wouldn't have agreed to a photo shoot.

Verducci said he was open with Ken about the story's focus. While the journalist was interested in learning more about Ken's life and recovery—topics that were both included in the article—"the story was about steroids," Verducci said.

Ken's public backtracking reflected a desire to save face in the game. He'd spent his career cultivating respect with fellow players, going all-out and playing the game *the right way*. It was painful getting attacked and called a rat or a snitch for talking about something that hundreds of people in the game, from teammates to opponents to fellow users, knew he was doing. Especially for someone like Ken, who'd spent his career trying to please others.

If they only knew the secrets he'd been holding in. . . .

In private, Ken was proud of himself. He told the truth. *His* truth. This wasn't about ratting out his fellow players or burning bridges. This was about Ken's attempts to break free from his demons.

* * *

Ken and Jose Canseco's comments forced Washington, D.C., to pay attention. Within weeks, the Senate held a subcommittee hearing on steroids in sports. "Like it or not, professional athletes serve as role models to our kids," said Senator John McCain of Arizona, who requested the hearing.

The Major League Baseball Players Association had held firm that drug testing was a violation of players' privacy. But with Congress threatening to hold baseball accountable, and with a cloud hanging over the game, and amid tense talks to sign a new collective bargaining agreement and avoid a strike, the players association agreed to allow blind testing of players for 2003—the testing would expand if more than 5 percent of players tested positive. But that would never happen, right?!

* * *

Through his community service, Ken ended up working that summer at Baseball USA, a Houston-based youth park.

Ken was working baseball camps amid the fallout from his disclosures to *Sports Illustrated*. Don Keathley, a former minor league player for the Athletics and later a high school coach, remembers Ken addressing campers about the mistakes he'd made.

"He probably took at least an hour talking to the entire camp about it, and he was just very honest about some of the choices that he made and some of the lifestyle. He was just trying to tell those kids, 'Don't do what I did.'"

Keathley respected how Ken approached his time at the camp.

"He got involved, and he had a station like everybody else. If he had an infield station or hitting station or something, he did the same thing as every other coach that was working," Keathley said. "And that was kinda cool to see that."

Ken also attended a Little League camp run by a local pastor, John Gilligan, that summer. Gilligan told Ken how God had a plan for his life—and how better things lay ahead for him.

"He was wide-eyed," Gilligan said. "He was wide-eyed and fully receptive to what I was saying."

Ken addressed the children, talking about his stumbles and his faith. "If God wasn't in my life, I don't know what I'd do," he said.

Gilligan was touched by Ken's presence. He was required to be there—it wasn't like Ken was getting paid for this—and could have been embarrassed by his recent headlines. But instead, there was Ken, getting on the ground to teach the children how to slide properly on sliding pads, passionate about sharing his baseball lessons.

Gilligan tried to keep in touch with Ken after the camp was over, but his phone didn't seem to work. He would be great, and then he would disappear again, and you didn't know who he was with or what he was doing.

CHAPTER 28

RELAPSE

Aaron Crumpton considered himself a burnout while attending Leigh High School. The kind of teen who no one noticed was missing from the yearbook by senior year. His sophomore year photo sees him with a forced half smile, an ironed oxford shirt, and a messy mop of hair. At the top of the page, a saying: "The road is long . . . with many a winding turn."

Aaron's road was long and winding, and it led him to spend many nights behind bars. While Ken was going one way in early adulthood—success, fame, riches—Aaron was going the other way, an addict who was hopelessly lost.

Meth took its hold, and that was that. For a while anyway. After Ken got arrested for his DUI in California in 1989, he had to do weekend work during baseball's off-season, and there was Aaron, doing a year in jail. The high school classmates saw each other and started chatting.

"He came over to talk to me and my mom," Crumpton said.

A few years later, Crumpton got clean—and stayed clean. He'd been sober for a full decade before he had a chance encounter with Ken's brother, Glenn, in 2002.

"When you see Ken, tell him Aaron Crumpton's been clean for ten years," Crumpton told Glenn.

"Actually, he's going to be here Friday for my dad's birthday. Why don't you take him to a meeting?" Glenn told him.

Wow. Aaron Crumpton was starstruck. He'd known Ken, just like pretty much everyone else at Leigh, but they'd never been close. And Aaron was a huge baseball fan—he'd tell just about everyone he knew about his famous classmate. "First time he made it, ESPN, *Ken Cam-in-etti* . . . I was so thrilled," Crumpton said. He also loved driving motorcycles. . . . Come to think of it, he did have a lot in common with Ken. And pretty soon they hit it off, riding bikes and going to meetings and talking about life.

Aaron, for Ken's parents, represented new hope at getting Ken's life straightened out. They'd spent so long worrying about their son but could only do so much—his previous attempts at sobriety had been monitored more closely by Nancy or his teams or his agents or his handlers, and whenever they tried to get closer, he'd push away. But now those other things had taken a back seat. And they wanted to give it another shot.

"They entrusted me," Crumpton said of Lee and Yvonne. "If he was with me, it was fine. If he was with other people, they were worried.

"I took that pretty seriously, because I have a lot of respect for his parents. But that put me in a bad spot. I remember one time in his garage, he was with his dad. Ken wasn't with me the night before, and he told his dad he was with me, and I was sitting there thinking, 'I can't lie for you. I can't lie to your dad.'"

* * *

Ken was confronting the loss of everything he held dear in 2002—all at the same time.

His baseball career, the thing he singularly identified with, was over, and he carried regret that he wasn't able to walk away on his own terms. His marriage with Nancy was history. They'd been living apart, but she made things official on July 10, 2002, by filing for divorce. The reason cited: "conflict of personalities." Maybe he could win her back. . . . And now his reputation—something he'd spent so many years cultivating—was torn to shreds due to his comments to *Sports Illustrated*. As if that wasn't enough, his body wasn't working properly due to his excessive use of steroids. He needed testosterone injections. He was moody and depressed.

His life represented a series of voids. He was used to filling voids in his life with drugs and alcohol, and he was battling to avoid that path now.

But he was vulnerable.

And there was Maria, his friend who he'd met in rehab two years earlier, reentering the picture. Maria and Ken's relationship deepened, and Maria ended up moving to Baytown, Texas, with her two younger boys. Ken could help them. And having a family structure around Ken helped fill the void left by his living apart from Nancy and the girls.

"One thing I remember walking into was the game room, and there was a deer head in the wall," said Maria's youngest son, Mikey, who was about three years old at the time. "I was terrified of that deer head." But Ken had his yellow Labs, Casey and Candy, and they were fun for the boys to play with, and they'd all go to IHOP for breakfast, and Ken would order his egg white omelets.

Maria's oldest son, Robert Jr., then thirteen, initially didn't want to go. "It was country," he said. "There was nothing there!"

He wound up bouncing back and forth between New York and Texas. He'd stay with his grandmother in Brooklyn, then down to Baytown with Maria for a while, then to his father back in Gotham. When Robert Jr. did finally make his way to Texas, he said, he found stability and, in Ken, someone who was interested in helping him without being too pushy.

"He was cool, man," Robert Silva-Romero said of Ken. "He would try to spoil me whenever I was around. Every time he'd leave the house. 'Come on, you coming with me?' 'Yeah, I'll come with you.' He always wanted me around him. He used to talk to me about how drugs were bad, how they mess people's lives up, and staying away from it."

Ken would take Robert to the racetrack. For the teen, being in the car with Ken was an adventure in itself.

"He was driving his Impala, and he was doing about 90 on a curve. I was so scared. I was in the front seat, like, 'Man, does this dude even know how to drive?' He hit that curve doing about 90 miles an hour in that Impala. Freaked the crap out of me, and blew the engine, too. He had to tow it when we got to the racetrack," Robert said.

Robert said Ken let him drive his Mercedes one time. Ken asked the teen to pull the car out of the garage and put it in front of the house. "I stopped it maybe a foot and a half from the garage door," Robert said.

Ken would give Maria $1,000 at a time to buy groceries or run errands, and Maria would hold on to the money for three weeks or a month, her son said. "We grew up poor," Robert Silva-Romero said. "So Mom knew how to budget. Mom was good at budgeting money."

Ken and Maria wanted Robert Jr. to stay in Texas so, he said, they enrolled him in a nearby high school. He lasted four days.

"I stole the phone from the dean's desk when she turned her back," he said. "As soon as she turned her back, my hand moved quicker than the eye. I don't even think she remembered she even had a phone on her desk, because she didn't find out until two days later when I was making all them calls to New York, calling all my girlfriends and stuff like that.

"Those people in Texas don't play," he said. "They tried to lock me up over there." But Ken got a lawyer to represent Robert Jr., and he had to write an essay apologizing to the dean, and he was enrolled in an alternative school.

Maria couldn't handle her son, so she wound up sending him back to New York so he could live with his father. By this point, traditional school was an afterthought—he was gaining a street education. Ken's lessons and advice would only go so far.

* * *

Ken's friends and colleagues aiding his recovery were concerned about Maria's role in his life—with her in the picture, they believed it was just a matter of time before he'd use again.

"For some reason, Ken was so infatuated with this woman. When she was in Houston and he was trying to get sober and stay clean, she was always there, and not in a good way for him," said Daniel "Gus" Gerard, Ken's drug counselor.

Gerard understood Ken's struggles with addiction on a deep level—he'd seen them destroy his own pro basketball career and wreck his marriage. He recognized Ken's desire to fight through drug use like Ken battled on the baseball field, this feeling that you could come from behind and will yourself to victory. But addiction isn't your final at bat against a closer who's throwing smoke.

"When you're an athlete, you have this tremendous ego and confidence that you can do things extraordinary. That's how you get to the level he got to, because you're confident and you're arrogant and you feel like you can do anything on your own. You can accomplish anything," Gerard said. "The problem is when you have a substance abuse problem, it's very detrimental because that same mental outlook on his career as an athlete becomes a hindrance, because in order to win or beat addiction, you have to fully surrender. And with an athlete's ego, you're taught to never surrender."

Ken and Gerard discussed Maria on numerous occasions. "I don't understand. I love her, Gus. I love her, but I don't know why," Ken said.

Gerard thought that Ken needed to worry about himself and his own sobriety before getting involved with anyone.

The situation was complex. In Maria, Ken saw someone who wouldn't judge him. She had been down a dark road, too. They understood each other's pain.

* * *

Things were going OK with Ken's sobriety until the motorcycle crash.

Highway 17 near Santa Cruz is hilly and long, and like the quote above Crumpton's high school yearbook photo, it has many a winding turn. Ken was riding with a woman, a motorcycle friend of Aaron's who Ken had been seeing, and Aaron was riding ahead of them. "When we'd go out on motorcycles, he was dangerous. He was a little sketchy. A little scary," Crumpton said.

Aaron kept checking his bike's rearview mirror, looking for Ken's headlight. One of the times when Aaron looked back, he didn't see the headlight anymore.

Aaron sat. Waited. Nothing.

He turned around. . . . Ken had crashed. The injuries weren't too major, but they landed Ken at the hospital, and while there, he was given a narcotic pain reliever, and it made him feel pretty good. Pretty soon, Ken was back to using other things that made him feel good again.

"From that wreck on, it just seemed like he would pull out of stuff," Crumpton said. But how to proceed? How to keep Ken on the right path? Push him too hard and he was liable to withdraw, to put up walls, to lie.

"He was doing good, and then he'd just slip away," Crumpton said.

"He would change his phone or disappear, and then he'd admit to it and get better. It was just this cycle. You just couldn't do nothing about it."

To Crumpton and others who tried to help, Ken resembled a wet bar of soap as he battled sobriety. "If you hold it in your hand there, and let it sit, it's fine, but as soon as you start to squeeze, it'll squirt out," Crumpton said.

Since Crumpton surrounded himself with other sober people, Ken would stay away—he was ashamed. Sober people would judge him and try to help. He didn't want to be judged. He didn't want help.

In San Jose and Houston, Ken would gravitate toward high school class-mates and hangers-on who were happy to do drugs with him, people who were on roads to ruin themselves.

Crumpton was tired of the unanswered calls, so he went for a drive looking for his friend. He said he found Ken's truck at a drug house in San Jose. Aaron went into the garage. Seven people were inside, including Ken.

"What are you doing here?" Aaron asked Ken.

"These are my friends. They don't bother me," Ken said.

From time to time, Aaron would run into people in Ken's circle of drug users. *Hey, you know that baseball friend of yours? He was doing three times as much drugs as everyone else.* Yep, that was Ken. . . . he'd give someone a bunch of money and say to get a half ounce of meth for everyone else, and to get him a quarter ounce of coke. And he'd just sit there and do it, like it was a beer on the team bus, and no one was going to challenge him over it.

"He was more comfortable with lower companionship," Crumpton said. "I think the expectations were a lot lower."

* * *

In January 2003, one of Ken's urine samples came back dirty, and he was ordered to state jail for an intensive, six-month substance abuse treatment program. Judge Bill Harmon seemed unrepentant about Caminiti's backslide. "Did you see Ken Caminiti in my court today? I just sent him to jail for six months," Harmon told another probationer appearing before him in court that day, according to the *Houston Chronicle*. "Don't think I won't do the same to you if you test positive one time."

Ken was at Harris County Jail before being transferred to a state jail facility in Humble. But before he could complete the drug treatment program, it was shut down due to budget cuts.

He reflected on his time behind bars during a speech that September for National Alcohol and Drug Abuse Recovery Month.

"Just a little while ago I was in jail. You think it's never going to happen to you. You think you'll never be locked up and never be put away," he said. "That was a real eye-opener for me, walking down the corridors in prison and having people walk up and say, 'Hey, Caminiti, sign my crack pipe.'"

Ken made friends quickly behind bars. It didn't hurt that he had money—a luxury that many of his fellow inmates didn't have. "He had a commissary, and he's buying stuff for everybody. And so it was like a big playground for Ken to socialize with other people, even though he was locked up," said childhood friend Peter Morin, who remained close with Ken's brother, Glenn.

During his time in jail, Ken also received a letter from his former Padres teammate Craig Shipley. Craig was working in the Red Sox front office alongside Theo Epstein, the onetime Padres media relations staffer turned GM.

"I asked how he was doing, wondered when he got out, if he was interested in doing anything in the game. And at the time, Theo was the GM. And we talked about Cammy and reaching out to him," Shipley said.

"He responded, and I still have the letter that he sent me back."

Ken was grappling with how to stay connected to the game, and whether anyone would want him around. He'd fallen out of touch with some of his closest friends in the game, like Craig Biggio and Jeff Bagwell. His legal issues and the steroid disclosure were still fresh and painful and embarrassing.

But people still loved Ken—they would always be rooting for him, whether he realized it or not.

CHAPTER 29

GREATEST DAY

As the car approached its destination, the sweat poured down Ken's forehead.

He wasn't ready for this.

He couldn't face another round of boos.

Ken was in the back of a limo headed toward Qualcomm Stadium, known as "the Q" on September 27, 2003—the Padres' final series in the stadium he called home during four of his most successful seasons.

Dozens of former players were coming back for the festivities. The celebration would have been incomplete without him. He was the only player in team history to win an MVP award while wearing Padres brown, and he was arguably the most influential figure in generating the team success and fan interest in the mid-1990s that culminated with voters approving funding for a new ballpark, Petco Park, which would open in 2004.

Padres personnel—including team owner John Moores—made personal pleas for Ken to show up for the closing ceremonies. Ken was one of Moores's favorites. "Ken and I had dinner in Houston, and we talked a couple of times. I begged him to come back, and I was really surprised how he was so concerned that people were gonna boo him or laugh at him," Moores said.

Ken was reminded of the boos that rained down on him the first time he played at the stadium after leaving San Diego. Fans were pissed off that Ken and other players jumped ship after the team's World Series run . . . but with Ken, the reasons for leaving (family, addiction) were complicated. Money had little to do with it.

So much had happened in his life since he parted ways with the Padres: He left the Astros to go to rehab; saw his career fade away; got arrested after being found with crack cocaine in a Houston hotel room; failed a drug test and went to jail; and oh yeah, blew the lid open on baseball's steroid scandal by admitting, voluntarily and without remorse, that his greatest successes with the Padres were chemically aided.

So maybe Ken had good reason to sweat. . . . But in doing so, he also underestimated the boundless love Padres fans carried for him and the deep respect that remained among fellow players.

Padres director of community relations Michele Anderson admitted that Ken's off-the-field issues gave team officials pause in how to incorporate him into the stadium-closing celebration.

"There was some trepidation at first with how we should approach this, because it was a sensitive issue. I mean there's a point where you realize that sports do set an example to kids and that kids look up to individuals, but also teams. And so, how do you deal with that issue of substance abuse? But at the same time, he was really trying to pull himself out of it, and he was such a part of Qualcomm and our years there, that we felt like it would be a healing thing for San Diego to see him again," Anderson said.

"I don't know that we totally knew how the fans were going to react, and we wanted to do the right thing. We wanted to do the right thing for the fans, we wanted to do the right thing for what we were standing for, and to do the right thing for Ken."

Ken's agent Rick Licht urged him to go, as did his friend Aaron Crumpton, who was trying to help him in his recovery. Ken and Crumpton were in Reno together at Street Vibrations, a motorcycle festival, in the days before the closing ceremonies.

"He thought everybody hated him," Crumpton said.

After a missed flight and some airsickness, Ken was finally back in San Diego and panicking. He took the limo to the stadium with James Hayashi, a friend from his Padres days who coordinated autograph signings and public appearances. Hayashi was well connected in the San Diego sports scene, and Ken peppered him with questions.

"What are the fans saying about me? What are the Moores saying about me?" Ken asked Hayashi.

"People here still love you," Hayashi said.

"Really? . . . James, I think I should tell the limo driver to turn around."

"Ken, no, I guarantee you they still love you here."

"Are you sure?"

"Yes. John Moores says nothing but nice things about you, he never brings up anything negative about you."

"OK."

Moores's—and the fans'—adoration for Ken became clear during that Saturday's game, when the owner had Ken watch the game from his private box. Midway through the game, the Padres video team played his "Where Have All the Cowboys Gone?" video over the scoreboard, the one the fans loved so much, and then they cut to a live image of Ken.

Their cowboy was back.

And the fans erupted. A standing ovation.

Ken waved to the crowd and tapped his heart, struggling to fight back the tears. *Thank you*, he mouthed. He'd later call the moment his greatest in baseball.

* * *

The following day was the Padres' final game at the Q—a chance to be honored alongside other Padres greats during a postgame ceremony. A chance to slip on a uniform top and take the field again.

While Ken was honored and touched by the standing ovation the day before, he still didn't know what fellow players thought of him. He'd disconnected from most of his baseball friends following his arrest and steroid comments, out of fear or shame. He broke the code, and that was a heavy thing.

John D'Acquisto, a San Diego native who pitched for the Padres from 1977 to 1980, came across Ken that weekend at a moment when "nobody was talking to him." Like Ken, D'Acquisto had run afoul of the law. After pleading guilty to financial crimes, he turned his life around while in prison. So D'Acquisto felt a need to approach Ken.

"Hey, I just got out. I know what you're going through. Sit down. I need to talk to you," D'Acquisto told Ken.

"First of all, you're going to think everyone hates your guts and no one likes you," D'Acquisto continued. "You're absolutely wrong about that. Everyone loves you. They want to help you pull your life together. Let them get involved, but don't go back to the people who got you into this mess. That's the thing you have to do."

"Yeah, yeah, I know," Ken said. "That's the one thing I'm afraid of. You know that they're going to come around. . . ."

"They might, but you have to be strong enough to fight them off."

"I appreciate that, man. I really appreciate that."

The older players were warm, and asked how he was doing, and it helped him relax. *No, they didn't hate him, far from it.* When his name was announced once more, *Ken Cam-in-etti* . . . and Ken made his way to third base for a final time, the sellout crowd erupted in another standing ovation. The cheers echoed off concrete and reverberated in Ken's bones, a long-overdue chance for the fans to thank Ken and let him know how much he meant to them, a chance to see Ken at third base one last time.

CHAPTER 30

THE END

The backslide began soon after Ken's greatest day in baseball.

The following month, he was in Florida with Aaron Crumpton, his high school classmate turned sobriety guide, and a few others for a series of motorcycle events, making their way to Daytona, when Ken decided he was going to head to Tampa—that's where Maria was staying at the time. When Ken rejoined the group, "he came back up three days later, like fifteen pounds lighter," Crumpton said. "You could tell he had been on a run."

Ken was drifting.

And surrounding himself with the wrong people.

People looking to take advantage of him.

Things got so bad, Ken's attorney Kent Schaffer on a few occasions—once at his ex-wife Nancy's request—had to go to Ken's house and clear the people out of it. "There were guys sleeping on the couch, there were three or four people in the kitchen," Schaffer said. "Just really trashy people. I went over there with my investigator, this big guy, former federal agent, he just told everybody, 'Get your shit, you're leaving,' and physically kicked people out of the house."

Ken would call friends at random times, from random places, and they could tell he was high.

Ryan Burda, who'd befriended Ken in rehab, noticed his friend's phone calls becoming less consistent and coherent. "He'd call in the middle of the night, driving around, and you could kind of tell he was back on the stuff," Burda said.

Another time Ken called Burda while waiting to get a haircut. "His phone was blowing up. He was pretty stressed out."

At some point in 2003 or 2004, Ken called his childhood friend Chris Camilli from a racetrack.

"He sounded like he was in pretty bad shape. He usually wouldn't call me if he was high. But he did that time," Camilli said. "He had a lot of regrets about Nancy. . . . He knew he'd really screwed up and he did wrong, but he knew that if he could just get himself together, that she would take him back, and he seemed highly motivated to do that."

He'd lean on friends to help him cut corners on his treatment. High school classmate Peter Morin, who turned his own life around after battling addiction, wanted a similar outcome for Ken, but he recognized Ken wasn't taking his treatment seriously enough.

"I knew he wasn't done going back to jail. It didn't really scare him," Morin said. One time, Ken pulled out a slip—he wanted Morin to sign it for him so he could get credit for attending an AA meeting. "He got pissed because I didn't sign it," Morin said. Ken gave him that scowl, the same one that would intimidate his fellow players, but *nope*, Morin wasn't signing the sheet.

There would be wonderful, healthy stretches with Ken, and then he would withdraw, and those trying to keep him on the right path—like the family of his racing friend Raymond Martin—knew things weren't OK. Raymond's daughter Mystic wanted to invite Ken to her graduation party, so she and Raymond went over to Ken's house to drop off an invitation.

"When we got there that day, he was at the house, he was by himself, and there's just something wrong," Mystic said. "I could just tell that he was in a bad mood. He was very irritable, and I tried to give him an invitation, just to tell him, 'cause we hadn't really seen him in a couple of months. He had been really withdrawn. And when I gave him my invitation, he didn't even look at it. He didn't even open it, and he didn't ask what it was. And then he had no clue that I was even graduating at that moment, like he had just kind of pushed everything else away."

As Ken's addictions worsened, and as he continued to be pulled down by negative forces, the Martins had to pull back. . . . They'd invested so much energy and effort into helping Ken, but they'd been on this road with other people in their lives.

His addictions weren't letting go.

"We couldn't pull him back in," Linda Martin said.

* * *

The Padres weren't done trying to pull Ken back in.

The team wanted to build off Ken's poignant appearance with the team for the final games at Qualcomm Stadium by having Ken come to spring training in 2004. Team owner John Moores kicked around the idea with GM Kevin Towers.

"Hey, Kevin, is there anything we can do for Cammy just to kind of get our arms around him and try to help him out?" Moores asked Towers. Moores thought maybe Ken could serve as a strength and conditioning coach. Towers considered the idea. *Hmmm. . . .*

"I think he'd be good at it, but Ken's not going to be happy with a role like that with the organization," Towers told Moores. "No, it's better we bring him in the spring and put him in the coach's locker room with the coaches and have him work with some of the infielders and some of the hitters."

So it was that Ken returned to the Padres as a spring training instructor, with a focus on infielders like third baseman Sean Burroughs. There weren't any coaching positions open at the time, but if things went well with his spring training role, the Padres would create a position to keep Ken with the team on a more permanent basis.

The Padres faced public scrutiny for embracing Ken, given his off-the-field issues and steroid admission. Columnist Bill Madden of the *New York Daily News* wrote that the move showed "once more that baseball is truly the 'last chance saloon' of professional sport." Oof.

Ken ended up arriving in Peoria midway through spring training, on March 16. Just like his trip to San Diego the prior season, Ken wasn't sure how he would be received.

"I was nervous coming here," he said after arriving in camp. "You don't know what to expect. I still don't know what the hell I'm doing. Just walking around with a fungo in my hand."

He added, "I feel like I have a lot to offer."

He did have a lot to offer. Decades of playing experience. The inner drive to be great. An understanding of *every* temptation facing big league players.

Switch-hit power. One of the most electric defensive third basemen of his or any era.

The Padres' owner, GM, manager, fellow coaches, and players were all happy to see him. "It was so good to have him back," Bruce Bochy said. "Cammy's time with the Padres had earned him the right to be part of the Padres alumni for the rest of his life."

But the Cammy they encountered wasn't the same Cammy they knew and loved. Things weren't right for this Cammy. He was fidgety. Nervous. Stressed. Worried.

Maybe it was too soon. . . . He was still learning to live with the fact that his career was over, and the steroids cloud was still hanging over the game.

* * *

After Congress started sniffing around due to Ken Caminiti's and Jose Canseco's statements on PEDs, the players' union and league had to do something. Blind testing in 2003 was as close to the bare minimum as possible.

Players wouldn't be punished for testing positive, and their tests wouldn't be publicly released.

The testing was also narrow—it wouldn't catch players who used human growth hormone, or hGH, which wasn't detectable with urine tests, or steroids precursors like andro, or amphetamines.

So players, if they chose, could all switch to hGH and no one would test positive for traditional steroids, and that would be that. Two straight years of less than 2.5 percent of players testing positive, and the mandatory testing was finished.

But if more than 5 percent of players tested positive for steroids from blind testing, it would kick off expanded unannounced testing the following season.

Many players did make the switch, and it became increasingly obvious if you were paying attention. People who overuse hGH are bound to suffer from a bloated gut, protruding jaw, increased hand and foot size, and an enlarged tongue.

Some players—including a contingency of White Sox led by anti-steroids advocate Frank Thomas—considered purposefully failing their drug tests by declining to take them in order to drive the league above the 5 percent threshold.

But in the end, the sabotage wasn't needed. Even with ample advance notice and alternatives that weren't detectable on urine tests, 104 players—7 percent, well over the 5 percent threshold—tested positive for steroids in 2003, unlocking expanded testing for 2004.

Washington was paying attention.

"To help children make right choices, they need good examples," President George W. Bush said in his 2004 State of the Union Address. "Athletics play such an important role in our society, but, unfortunately, some in professional sports are not setting much of an example. The use of performance-enhancing drugs like steroids in baseball, football, and other sports is dangerous, and it sends the wrong message—that there are shortcuts to accomplishment, and that performance is more important than character. So tonight I call on team owners, union representatives, coaches, and players to take the lead, to send the right signal, to get tough, and to get rid of steroids now."

By March 2004, the scandal was bubbling over—the *San Francisco Chronicle* reported that Barry Bonds, Jason Giambi, and Gary Sheffield had received steroids from a nutritional supplement lab called the Bay Area Laboratory Co-Operative, or BALCO. While Ken didn't have a direct connection to the BALCO scandal, it felt as though every new disclosure was somehow tied to his comments to *Sports Illustrated* two years earlier.

* * *

For Phil Nevin, Ken seemed "out of his element" in spring training with the Padres. Ken's former heir apparent in Houston bounced around the league and diamond before finding a spot in San Diego, filling Ken's shoes at third base in 1999 after George Arias struggled and becoming an All-Star in 2001, on his way to surpassing Ken's single-season team home run record.

Being back with the Padres in uniform was a reminder for Ken of one more thing that was out of reach, a burner down the line just past his outstretched glove.

"I think where he was physically, he understood that he wouldn't have been able to [play], and that might've been eating at him. There were a lot of things that were taken away from him through his dependencies. And I think it was just finally becoming a reality that he wasn't going to have baseball anymore. And there were some other things in his life that he'd lost, and I think it was all coming to a head," Nevin said.

To Ken's colleagues, he didn't *look* right. "He was still pretty thick and in good shape, but his color was the first thing that got me," said Dave Magadan, a longtime competitor of Ken's who was on Bruce Bochy's coaching staff. Instead of his typical bronzed "Captain America look to him," Magadan said, Ken looked ashen and gray.

Ken wanted to make things work. But for Towers and Bochy, Ken's eyes hinted at deeper issues in his life. "He didn't have the same look in his eyes that he had when he played. It was kind of dark, hazy, just really not there, and it was really hard to see," Towers said.

Bochy thought Ken "seemed a little lost." Padres personnel tried to help Ken feel more comfortable. Everyone in the Padres camp did. "Then we heard that he had a friend or two that was there also, that was kind of leading him astray. He just didn't look the same. He just had a beat-up look about him. His eyes, everything about him, he just wasn't the Cammy that we knew."

As Ken's world was falling apart, when he seemed lost, when his friends in baseball were worried that he didn't look right, when his regress into addiction was all over his face, Maria said, their love was blossoming—Ken bought her a ring and proposed while they were in Arizona. They were planning on getting married in April 2005, Maria's son Robert Silva-Romero said.

A few days after Ken bought the ring for Maria, he was supposed to ride motorcycles with Nevin. Ken's protégé walked out of the clubhouse, expecting to find Ken, but Ken was . . . gone. He went off on his own. "I was kind of disappointed, but it seemed like he was just in a hurry," Nevin said. Ken ended up wrecking his motorcycle that day, damn near ripping off his thumb or big toe in the process—his San Diego friend David Indermill remembers Ken gloating about the injury sustained when he was popping wheelies in his flip-flops.

Given all the issues Ken was facing, Bochy wasn't surprised to find that Ken decided to leave camp. Ken was on hand April 8 for the first game at the Padres' new ballpark, along with Padres fan favorites, former president Jimmy Carter, and Bud Selig, the financially focused MLB commissioner who stood idly by as PEDs ran rampant in the game.

The Padres video team showed Ken on the scoreboard again, just like they had for the close of the Q—a chance for Padres fans to cheer in the House that Ken (and Tony, and Bruce, and John, and Kevin . . .) Built.

A few weeks later, on April 23, Ken was having a different type of exchange with his parole officer, Tracy Burns. Ken was always honest with Burns. It's one of the things she appreciated most about him. But she could usually tell when clients had relapsed—their eyes, their physical appearance, and the way they talked would tell her the truth, as it had for Ken's friends with the Padres.

As Burns told ESPN and his drug counselor Gus Gerard confirmed, Ken admitted that he'd relapsed—and asked her for help with Maria. "He said he was trying to get Maria out of his house and she would not leave," Burns told ESPN. "He was distraught, and I had to go out there and intervene." Maria and her two sons were put on a plane—she ended up receiving kidney treatment in Florida. Ken participated in treatment for his addictions at Next Step, and the terms of his probation were amended on May 11, 2004: "You are to have no contact with Maria Rodriguez in person, in writing, by telephone, via the internet, a third party, or any other means for any reason except as specifically permitted by the Court." (Maria Romero also went by Maria Rodriguez at the time.) Ken was now barred from communicating with Maria. But the amended probation order—and the threat of further incarceration—didn't stop Ken and Maria from meeting that summer, travel logs and her oldest son confirmed.

"Of course they were communicating. I even think Mom was actually staying with him at the time that he wasn't supposed to be seeing her," Robert Silva-Romero said. "I think he was staying in Florida at one point; they snuck around and went to my aunt's house out here in Florida to see each other."

On September 10, a day when the Padres were playing in Colorado and the Astros were facing the Pirates, Ken was arrested at his Baytown home after failing another test for cocaine. He made a brief court appearance days later and would spend nearly a month in custody.

Ken represented a mix of emotions to his new attorney, Terry Yates, moments of positive energy and optimism balanced out by frustration with how things had gone wrong.

"He was pretty disenfranchised from everyone at that time. By that time, a lot of his friends and family had grown tired of him or more or less given up," Yates said.

Yates foresaw Ken getting back into baseball as a mentor to younger players—he had so much to offer them, so many lessons to impart. But Ken also had visions of playing again. . . . Competition would always be in his blood.

"He still thought he could play, even in '04, which . . . I'm not going to tell a guy he couldn't," Yates said.

Ken talked to Yates about his playing days, about his family, about his inner turmoil, about his problems with addiction . . . and also his thinking about heading to Montana. There, he could work on the land, hunt and fish, and get some cold air in his lungs. In Montana, he felt, his problems would go away.

Kent Schaffer, who'd represented Ken since his 2001 arrest, didn't like the Montana plan—he wanted Ken to attend an intensive treatment program in Mississippi called COPAC.

Ken was also kicking around the possibility of eventually heading to San Diego, his friend James Hayashi said.

If Ken followed through on a treatment program and stayed clean, the Padres would consider taking him back. . . . But after his struggles as a spring training instructor, after the arrests and steroids scandal, the team wanted assurances that Ken was staying clean.

One thing that was clear to Ken: staying in Houston wasn't a solution. He knew too many people there. Too many people knew him. Too many who could take advantage of his vulnerabilities. Yes, his girls were there . . . but he needed to be clean before he got more involved with their lives again. He didn't want to bring them more problems and suffering.

Glenn flew out to meet with Ken. Sure, the brothers had their friction . . . big brother, as fiercely proud of his sibling as he was, struggled in his little brother's shadow, the way things went from Glenn and Kenny to Ken and . . . Glenn. Glenn had been the Big Man on Campus. Big brother is supposed to be able to impart insight and advice to little brother, to guide him forward in life, but what could big brother say after little brother had succeeded beyond anyone's wildest imagination and raked in more than $30 million in career earnings? What could anybody say to him?

But Glenn was going to try to say something. He was worried that his brother was slipping away. Ken could go to treatment and continue fighting the drug charge that had been lingering since 2001. By March 2005—a matter of five months—he could properly complete probation without a conviction on his record.

Ken instead wanted to admit to violating his probation and take the felony count. With more than 180 days served between jail and treatment, he could get credit for time served and move on with his life. No more monthly urine tests and check-ins with his probation officer, no more community service, no more being barred from seeing Maria or doing whatever the hell he wished.

And no more structure.

Glenn and their parents hoped that Kenny would get help and straighten things out, then he'd be free and clear to begin his life again, and maybe pick back up with the Padres in some role. Ken wasn't interested in that plan, or in listening to Glenn's message. The bar of soap had been squeezed too tight.

Ken suggested that he was a failure. A lost cause.

"Quit trying to save me, because I can't even save myself," Ken said. It would be the last thing Ken told his brother.

Ken appeared in court on October 5, decked in orange and white, the Astros' colors, but this time the colors represented Ken's orange prison jumpsuit and white undershirt, and his hands were bound in handcuffs, and his legs were shackled, and he was on "the chain" as he was paraded to court, and he hadn't had a chance to bathe or shave or brush his teeth regularly.

"It's a degrading experience," Yates said.

Ken looked sullen as he appeared in court.

Guilty.

The MVP was now a convicted felon for possession of a controlled substance.

But he'd now be a free man with his future ahead of him.

He spoke to Yates that day about Montana, the chance to get his feet on the ground, to get a fresh start.

Tracy Burns, Ken's parole officer, saw him in court that day, too. They spoke in the back of the courtroom.

"I'm going to make you proud, Tracy," he said.

"That's not what this is about—you need to be proud of yourself," she told him. "You need to take care of yourself for yourself, not for me."

When Burns thinks back to that conversation, she can't help but recognize how Ken was still trying to please everyone else.

After he was released from custody, Ken visited Schaffer's office to pick up his wallet and other items. He stayed for about an hour. He told Schaffer about his plans for Montana—fresh air, an investment opportunity.

And then he told the attorney that he planned to go to New York. With Maria.

The attorney tried to warn him against that plan. That would only lead to trouble.

"I'll go with you tonight to Mississippi," Schaffer told him.

But Ken didn't want that. Maria's oldest son had gotten into trouble, and maybe Ken could help.

Ken's friends think there was more to the trip—it was a chance for Ken to leave the world behind and disappear and maybe get high one more time, to be around people who weren't going to judge him.

So Ken, against his friends' and relatives' and attorneys' wishes, traveled to Tampa and met up with Maria, and together they flew to New York City, a place that brought out so many of Ken's struggles.

* * *

Robert Silva-Romero was going down the wrong path.

Maria's oldest son, now sixteen, had gotten locked up for possession of cocaine and marijuana—he was selling and using drugs. He got out the same day because he was a juvenile.

"I messed up my life in New York. And [Ken] went out there basically to go save me," he said.

Robert said Ken and Maria picked up the teen after they arrived in the city and took him to the Marriott hotel in Queens where Ken was staying.

But instead of focusing on Robert's issues, he said, the conversation turned into a fight between Maria and Ken over money. Ken threw a bunch of $100 bills at Maria.

"This is what you want me for?" he asked her.

"Fuck you. I don't want your money, I don't care about your money," she told him. Maria took the bills, Robert said, and threw them out the hotel window.

"You know what I did? I ran downstairs, and I was looking for the money. I only found three $100 bills on the sidewalk. I don't know where the rest of the money flew to. It was windy, so the money could have gone anywhere," Robert said. The teen, $300 richer, ended up hailing a cab and going back to his father's place. So much for an intervention. . . .

That Saturday, Maria and Ken went to her mother's house in Brooklyn.

Her mother ended up going to the hospital, and Ken and Maria snapped a cell phone picture of the two of them sitting together. Ken, wearing a plaid shirt and Robert's Philadelphia 76ers cap, stares into the camera with those piercing, dark eyes. His goatee is turning gray, and gray hair peeks from the corners underneath the cap. Maria rests her head on his shoulder.

But Ken needed to get away, and he spent part of the day apart from Maria.

Early that next morning, Sunday, October 10, Robert Silva-Romero said, Ken and his mom were fighting again.

"At four or five in the morning, he's blowing up my father's phone," Robert Silva-Romero said. Ken had been friendly with Maria's ex—they got to know each other in the preceding years. Robert Silva came out to Texas at one point with his son to visit Baytown.

But the father also had his own drug problems.

"My dad, at the time, he was using," Robert Silva-Romero said. "He was using heroin at the time."

Bits and pieces of Ken's time with Robert Sr. have emerged in various reports—a cash advance of $1,025 from American Express, a flurry of phone calls, and a cab ride to meet up with Silva's friend Angel Gonzalez in the Hunts Point section of the Bronx, a hardscrabble neighborhood.

It was after three in the afternoon, in the apartment on Seneca Avenue, as Gonzalez was out of the apartment buying chicken, that Ken emerged from the bathroom clutching his chest.

"I'm not feeling good," he said, and collapsed.

Silva administered CPR. A 911 call was placed at 3:36 p.m.

Paramedics rushed to save Ken, taking him to Lincoln Hospital.

But it was too late.

Kenneth Gene Caminiti, the National League's Most Valuable Player in 1996, who loved Nancy, adored his three daughters, lived for competition and the camaraderie of his teammates, played baseball harder than anyone and through so much pain, rode motorcycles and enjoyed tricked-out show cars, who made women swoon and men believe and children happy, whose scowl and goatee scared the hell out of you, whose laugh disarmed you, whose body seemed like it was carved and chiseled by the gods, because he looked so good in a baseball uniform or a tuxedo, whose piercing blue eyes made you feel alive, who served as a torchbearer at the hot corner, inspiring a generation of third basemen behind him, whose honesty broke the lid open on baseball's biggest scandal, who was fiercely loyal to his friends, who struggled to say no even when he needed to, who gave so much of himself and lost so much more, who tried so hard to beat his demons, was dead at age forty-one.

* * *

People struggled to make sense of Ken's death.

New York City? This news couldn't be right. . . . Ken wasn't in New York City. . . . He was in jail. . . . No, he was in Houston. . . . No, maybe he was in California. . . . *No.* . . .

Robert Silva, who was present when Ken's heart gave out, grappled with how to tell his ex, Maria, that Ken was gone. His son Robert Jr. remembers his father coming to his grandmother's apartment that day, "hysterical. He was in shock. I've never seen my dad like that," Silva's son said.

"Oh my God, I gotta tell you something, I can't tell your mother," Robert Silva told his son.

"What the hell happened? What's going on?"

"Ken just died."

"What?"

"Ken just died. I was trying to give him CPR. He came out of the bathroom, holding his chest, next thing you know, he fell down." Eventually he told Maria the same thing. . . . It all felt like some weird prank, a sick joke, but no, it wasn't a joke.

New York media members called Kent Schaffer, Ken's attorney through his legal troubles, for comment. . . . He thought the trip to New York was a bad idea, but *this?* Ken's other attorney, Terry Yates, carried guilt for years for helping Ken get out of custody, thinking he was helping Ken get started on his trip to Montana, not the Big Apple.

Many friends feared the day would come.

They wondered what more they could have done or said to set him straight. But there was a boy inside that Kenny couldn't fix.

And most of all, they were just sad.

Dave Moretti, Ken's childhood friend and later his steroid supplier during the height of his career, planned to reach out to Ken after Ken got out of jail—he wanted to inform Ken about his father's death a few weeks earlier. That night, Dave received a call from his brother Mark.

"You watching the news?" Mark asked.

"No," Dave said.

"Watching TV at all?"

"No."

"You hear about Ken?"

"No. . . . What about him?"

"He's dead."

"What do you mean, he's dead?"

"Ken died today."

"What do you mean he's dead, what happened?"

"He died in New York of a drug overdose."

"No, no, he's in jail."

"No, Dave, he died of a drug overdose today."

"No, he's in jail. I was waiting for him to get out so I could talk to him about Dad." But in the back of his mind, Dave knew it was true. He walked into the room where his wife was. She asked what was wrong. "And I just lost it," Dave said.

Roger Samuels, who'd played against Ken in youth sports and later teamed with him as a pro baseball player, glanced at the next day's *Mercury News* on his doorstep and saw the headline, "and the tears started coming down."

When Ken died, his '55 Chevy was at Keith Graves's shop. Keith's wife came out of the house at about one in the morning to inform him of what had happened. "I'm working on his car, and I didn't even know he was out of town. I had no clue he was in New York City when he died," Graves said.

Ken's minor league manager Gary Tuck was preparing scouting reports for the Yankees' ALCS matchup against the Red Sox. "I was in the food room in old Yankee Stadium, and it was like a ritual that I would do the scouting reports for the catchers by myself. I have it all laid out. . . . And somebody came in and they said, 'We got some bad news for you. Ken Caminiti passed away,'" Tuck said. He was devastated to learn Ken died within miles of the stadium. "And I cried. I cried for three years."

His old pals with the Astros Craig Biggio and Jeff Bagwell were forced to confront his death while attempting to carry the team to its first playoff series win in franchise history. Houston lost 6–5 to the Braves—the final team Ken played for—on October 10 to force a deciding Game 5 the following night. The Astros would win 12–3 to advance. But a cloud hung over the victory. Their friend wasn't there to be a part of this.

While Ken's death drew national attention, it was overshadowed by the passing of *Superman* actor Christopher Reeve, who died the same day, hours apart.

In the days and weeks that followed Ken's death, the news emerged that his friends and fans had feared. His cause of death was acute intoxication due to the combined effects of cocaine and opiates—a "speedball" of cocaine and heroin, the same toxic mix that killed funnymen John Belushi and Chris Farley.

Conditions contributing to Ken's death included coronary artery atherosclerosis (hardening of the arteries) and cardiac hypertrophy (an enlarged heart). Those conditions can be worsened by cocaine use, steroids, alcoholism, methamphetamines, familial history . . .

The manner of death was deemed an accidental overdose.

No one was charged in relation to Ken Caminiti's death. Even if someone had been, it wouldn't bring Ken back. And it wouldn't erase the fact that he'd pumped his body full of drugs for decades, some of it connected to his play, much of it street drugs meant to help him escape or momentarily soothe his anguish.

The manner and place in which Ken died, and the people he was with that weekend, reflected the randomness of life. His heart could have given out anywhere, with anyone, at any time. But it ended up happening in New York City, a short distance from where he played his first World Series game.

Ken's was one of 722 unintentional drug overdose deaths in New York City in 2004. The majority of those deaths involved cocaine and heroin.

Ken's family and friends struggled to grieve amid the national attention brought on by his sudden, sordid, tragic death. His agent Rick Licht, who'd been there through so many of Ken's struggles, who tried so hard to help his friend, was there for Ken's family in their time of mourning.

"I've been in this role many, many times in my life where things shift so badly, it becomes the rescue. Man, you're doing everything you can to save a guy from his own end," said Ken's agent from earlier in his career, Tom Reich. "Rick was fabulous in his effort."

A memorial ceremony for his baseball friends was held in Houston. Padres owner John Moores chartered a plane so dozens of Ken's colleagues with the team could attend.

Craig Reynolds, Ken's Astros teammate during his first few seasons and later a pastor, was one of the speakers. He addressed Ken's daughters directly.

"You're going to hear some really, really good things about your dad here today. And later, after you leave, you're going to hear some bad things about your dad. And when you do, remember that those people didn't know him the way everybody in this room did," he told them.

Biggio spoke that day, too, struggling to hold back the tears.

"I love you, Cammy," he said.

A subsequent private service was held in San Jose. The program cover showed two images of Ken: one of him riding a motorcycle, the other of him getting congratulated by Biggio and Bagwell after crossing home plate. The photos are offset by text:

> Dearest Ken
> Ride free
> You've made it home

EPILOGUE

The hulking, chiseled bodies sat in a row as photographers snapped away.

St. Patrick's Day 2005, and a formidable lineup was appearing before the House Government Reform Committee for a hearing on steroids in baseball.

Jose Canseco. Sammy Sosa. Mark McGwire. Rafael Palmeiro.

It was a day for excuses and denials. Canseco, without being granted immunity and facing probation in Florida, didn't want to put himself in further legal jeopardy. Sosa, after suddenly losing confidence in his English speaking, relied on a translator. McGwire—whose past included 583 home runs and that mythical 70 from 1998—didn't want to talk about the past anymore, pleading the fifth. Palmeiro wagged his finger, stating defiantly, "I have never used steroids. Period. I don't know how to say it any more clearly than that. Never."

A subsequent panel featured Commissioner Bud Selig, Executive Vice President Rob Manfred, MLBPA head Donald Fehr, and general managers Sandy Alderson and Kevin Towers.

Towers was there because of a quote he'd given following Ken Caminiti's death, how he "felt like I knew" Ken had used steroids during his time with the Padres.

Ken Caminiti's name wasn't mentioned much during the hearings. People were already starting to forget. Or they didn't know what to say. His story was too sad and too complicated.

* * *

The emotional counterpoint of the hearings in Washington came about a month later, on April 21, what would have been Ken's forty-second birthday, at Petco Park, the House That Ken Built.

The Padres decided to honor Ken with a ceremony before a game with the Dodgers. Ken's family was on hand—Nancy and the girls, Yvonne and Lee, Glenn and his wife, Debbie. Kendall, then thirteen, threw out the first pitch to Ken's close friend Trevor Hoffman, the Padres closer. Some media members criticized the Padres' ceremony, doing their best hand-wringing and pearl-clutching, as though Ken should be erased from everyone's memory simply because of his struggles. The most tone-deaf response came from Ron Cook of the *Pittsburgh Post-Gazette*: "What's next? Charles Manson Night at Dodger Stadium? Or maybe Jeffrey Dahmer Night at Milwaukee's Miller Park?" Groan. Even after Ken's death, people didn't understand what he meant to the Padres.

Ken's family, like his baseball brethren, struggled to find the right way to honor him. Glenn and Debbie started a foundation in Ken's name in 2005. There were plans for a youth center in San Jose.

But there was that stigma, and the issue of funding. . . . It was the same sticking point fellow San Jose native Roger Samuels encountered years later when he was kicking around the idea of getting a youth baseball field named after Ken in the old neighborhood. Samuels looked at a patch of dirt and uneven ground and a few oak trees, and he saw potential, a way to honor his friend, but baseball fields are expensive and come with red tape, and life has a habit of getting in the way.

People were slow to embrace Ken's memory. At Leigh High School, which counts a Manson disciple and a Doobie Brother among its former students, items related to its superstar baseball product remained hidden away in storage more than a decade after Ken's death.

Baseball's steroids cloud both tarnished and burnished Ken's reputation. As the years pass, Ken's words loom larger and larger. Who else has come forward voluntarily to talk about what they took? Who else spoke as unflinchingly as he did?

Ken's steroid use was a focus of an investigation led by former U.S. senator George Mitchell into steroid use in Major League Baseball. The report, released in 2007, highlighted Ken's "open use of steroids" in 1995, his interest in steroids in 1993 and 1994, when he discussed them with teammate Chris

Donnels, as well as the shipment of steroids meant for Ken that was intercepted by an Astros team employee in 1999.

Dave Moretti, who now admits to supplying Ken and other players with steroids during the late 1990s, remembers scanning the Mitchell Report and coming across the names of his former clients. He won't name names, even over a half decade's worth of interviews, and even if he did, so what? Baseball's steroids cloud was cultural and institutional in nature. The problem wasn't who did or didn't use steroids, but that every player had to make the choice.

The thaw toward suspected and known PED users has been gradual, and it's come with a steady drip of disclosures involving major figures.

McGwire, who denied doing anything improper for years, finally admitted in a 2010 interview with Bob Costas that he used steroids. He came clean as a means of getting back in the game as a coach.

Alex Rodriguez—Ken's teammate with the Rangers in 2001—was implicated in two PED scandals, first in 2009 through a report that he failed a blind test in 2003, and years later in the Biogenesis scandal involving a Florida rejuvenation clinic.

Red Sox slugger David Ortiz was also reported to have failed a drug test in 2003.

Since players from the "steroids era" began to retire, Hall of Fame voters have endured a yearly tradition of playing gatekeepers to an institution that has considered players' potentially chemically aided merits on an individual basis instead of against the era in which they played.

Some players who've faced steroids whispers—such as Mike Piazza, Iván Rodríguez, and Jeff Bagwell—gained entry into Cooperstown. Others, despite worthy stats, have been denied entry. Still others have been elected into the Hall of Fame without the public having any idea whether they used PEDs or not.

Meanwhile, the man whose sloth-like response to steroids in the game allowed the problem to proliferate, Allen H. "Bud" Selig, waltzed into the Hall without as much as a sideways glance, gaining entry through a trapdoor called the Today's Game Era Committee.

When Ken came up for the Hall of Fame in 2007, two voters, Rick Telander and Gwen Knapp, included him on their ballots due to his honesty about steroids.

Telander wished the Baseball Writers' Association of America had considered parameters for how it would gauge steroids-era players. "I wanted to hold a mirror up to Major League Baseball, to the writers in particular. I mean, we have to make decisions. Is Andy Pettitte—OK, he used—can we vote for him because he's a good guy? Do we not vote for Bonds and Clemens because they're such jerks, and because their numbers were just so crazy? I don't like having that responsibility, but I really believe in the Hall of Fame and I believe in people being rewarded for greatness," Telander said.

Knapp was appreciative of Ken's honesty. "Caminiti told the truth when no one else would," she wrote in the *San Francisco Chronicle* at the time. "He stands for something that should be recognized at Cooperstown, especially as the great uncertainty of the steroids generation descends on the Hall of Fame."

For players like Ken who spoke out, the truth came with heavy consequences. Ken's contemporaries have faced death threats for admitting to using PEDs.

* * *

The passage of time allows us to consider Ken's life and legacy in a different light. The country's approach to drug addiction has evolved in the years since his death, with a shift from criminalization to compassion. Harris County, Texas—facing waves of criticism for locking up low-level drug offenders like Ken—has seen success with a drug diversion program. If Ken were found with the same amount of drugs in 2021 that he had in 2001 in the Houston hotel room, his case would have likely been assigned to a special docket and he could have entered a pretrial intervention program that may have kept him out of jail.

"I can't think of a modern domestic policy that has failed worse than the war on drugs," said Katharine Neill Harris, the Alfred C. Glassell, III, Fellow in Drug Policy at Rice University's Baker Institute for Public Policy. "The mission was to achieve a drug-free America, and we haven't done that. It's come at such a great cost, both financially and in terms of the lives that have really been damaged and ruined by arrests and incarceration for drug use. And that doesn't just pertain to the individuals who were using drugs and arrested for it, but to their families and their children. Those collateral consequences really fan out into entire communities."

* * *

Ken will forever be connected to his longtime Astros teammate Craig Biggio—the pair forged the deepest of bonds.

That bond was reflected in a plot of hunting land that Biggio purchased in Sabinal, Texas, a small town between San Antonio and the Mexican border clear across the state from Houston.

Biggio and Caminiti had a previous hunting spot called Cambo Ranch, a combination of their last names, and Biggio's family decided to name the land in Sabinal Cambo Ranch, too.

It was there, under an ancient oak tree, that Caminiti's ashes were laid to rest.

* * *

Maria's world collapsed when Ken died.

Her love was gone. And with him went the financial stability he provided. Where many of the women who hovered around Ken were attracted to money and fame, Maria didn't exhibit those same qualities. She wasn't stashing money aside and getting cars or houses put in her name.

"When Ken died, my mother didn't have a penny of Ken's money. Not one penny," said her oldest son, Robert Silva-Romero. "After Ken died, we came to Florida and were living in a one-room shelter in Zephyrhills for months before my mother got an apartment."

In Florida, after losing everything, after losing Ken, Maria was able to turn her life around and achieve sobriety. To break free from the cycle.

But her son Robert—the teen who Ken visited on that awful weekend in October 2004—couldn't do the same. He continued to run with the wrong crowd. He was convicted of robbery with a gun or deadly weapon, among other charges, and served about five years in prison in Florida. After being released in 2014, he was re-arrested a few years later for the same offense.

Robert was offered a plea deal—twenty-five to life.

He took it.

His sentence is scheduled to run until 2040, when he will be fifty-one years old.

* * *

In the years after Ken's death, his parole officer, Tracy Burns, used to bring up his name to kids going down the wrong path. Ken was an example for them. A lesson. Someone who struggled the way they were struggling. But pretty soon, she would bring up the name and get blank looks.

"Now I have to use that on a forty-year-old when I see them. They're the only ones who know who he is," she said.

* * *

The Padres couldn't forget Ken. How could they?

The team in 2016 decided to add Ken to its Hall of Fame, making him the eighth player to receive the honor, blowback be damned.

Ken's ceremony came on a sun-kissed Saturday in August before a game against the Phillies, the first MLB team Ken played against decades earlier.

Nancy and the girls, now young women, were there, along with Ken's parents and other relatives and friends. It was a happy day. A bittersweet day. They gave out replica jerseys to fans at the gate, 1990s-style, white with brown pinstripes, and c-a-m-i-n-i-t-i and number 21 on the back.

Ted Leitner, "Uncle Teddy," the longtime Padres broadcaster and one of Ken's favorites, served as master of ceremonies, recalling Ken in mythical terms. "You'd never seen a player like this, a man like this," he said. "It was as if God took a great third baseman like Mike Schmidt and crossed him with John Wayne. Clint Eastwood. Charles Bronson. He was all of that, and that's not an exaggeration."

Trevor Hoffman, the Hall of Fame closer who teamed with Ken, talked about Ken's nod, his silent way of showing his approval.

Kendall, the oldest of the girls, read a statement on behalf of Ken's family. "I know my dad is up there, probably breaking a bat over his knee, because he can't be here to actually receive this honor himself, but I know he's looking down today, and he is smiling," she said as she stood next to her sisters.

* * *

The Houston Astros were shedding veteran players like skin cells and rebuilding around a young core. Again.

Much like the early 1990s youth movement, the mid-2010s Astros featured lots of talent. Second baseman Jose Altuve. Center fielder George

Springer. Shortstop Carlos Correa. A young third baseman—Alex Bregman—provided pop.

But this time, instead of trading key players away too soon, the franchise allowed the players to mature and matriculate into superstars. Houston finally broke through in 2017, reaching a stratosphere that the team had previously never reached: World Champions.

Houston toppled two teams, the Yankees and the despised Dodgers, it had long envied on the way to the title. The Astros pounced on Los Angeles in Game 7 of the World Series, scoring 5 runs in the first two innings and then coasting to a 5–1 win.

The Astros were at the top of the baseball world after fifty-three seasons of futility.

It was a moment for all the players who came before, all the guys who wore the "Tequila Sunrise" uniforms and sacrificed their knees and backs to the Astrodome turf.

It all felt too perfect, too good to be true.

And as it turned out, it was too good to be true. In the years that followed, it was revealed—following pitcher Mike Fiers coming forward to *The Athletic*—that the team employed an elaborate system in which it would decode the opposing team's pitch signals using a video monitor, then tip off the Houston batters to off-speed pitches by banging a garbage can or making other noises.

Much like Caminiti, Fiers received waves of criticism for breaking the *clubhouse code*, baseball's *omertà*.

But someone had to do it, just as in 2002 when Ken stood alone and spoke his truth and ended up taking a sledgehammer to baseball's innocence.

* * *

The House that Ken Built went a long time without hosting a meaningful baseball game.

The Padres languished, year after year, near the bottom of the National League West standings. Key players and personnel like Bruce Bochy and Trevor Hoffman and Jake Peavy flitted away.

But by 2020, a talented lineup started to emerge, led by third baseman Manny Machado—the Padres' best third baseman since you-know-who—and shortstop Fernando Tatis, Jr., whose father played against Ken.

The season was a strange one due to the COVID-19 pandemic. Fans were barred from games, and teams filled the empty stands with cardboard cutouts of people to give the appearance of a crowd and piped in fan noise over the loudspeakers.

San Diego, with a 37–23 record, secured a wild-card spot as the National League's fourth-best team. The Padres ended up playing against the Cardinals, the team that Ken's Padres had faced to open the 1996 playoffs.

Cardboard cutouts of the 1998 World Series team were placed into the seats behind home plate. The Padres were in the playoffs, and the best third baseman you've ever seen was back on your TV screen. There were Ken and Bruce and Greg and Kevin and Trevor and Tony, together again, basking in the October sunshine.

ACKNOWLEDGMENTS

While I have many, many people to thank for this book—many more than I'll be able to thank here—I wanted to tip my cap to a handful of people whose contributions stood out.

I'm thankful for everyone who spoke to me and provided input for this book. Two interview subjects in particular, Dave Moretti and Roger Samuels, went above and beyond, opening their homes to me when I visited San Jose for a reporting visit in 2015 and opening their hearts in the years since. Dave, you promised not to hold back if we spoke in person, and you weren't kidding— your honesty stands out to me, along with your friendship. Roger, I've adored talking to you about San Jose baseball and your playing days, and life, and it's so special to finally be able to play catch with my son using the glove you sent him when he was born.

I'd also like to mention Richie Lewis, whose candor and character made him such a joy to speak to. Richie was larger than life despite his five-foot-six-inch height. I was crushed to learn of his death in late 2020 and hold him and his family in my thoughts.

Special thanks to journalists Jane Mitchell and Jules Roberson-Bailey for their insights from their momentous interviews with Ken.

Book writing is *hard*. Writing a book like this one can be a difficult, lonely process, and some of the connections I've made in the book industry have helped to make this process a lot less lonely. My literary agent, Joe Perry, believed in this project the moment I sent him my proposal, and his insight and guidance have been a dream. To the team at Abrams Press, especially Jamison Stoltz and Garrett McGrath, I'm forever thankful for the class and professionalism you've brought to every step in the publishing process—the look and feel and shape of this project, beginning with the cover, are better than I could have ever dreamed.

I'm so thankful for the friendships I've made as I developed as a book writer and ghostwriter. Shelley Moench-Kelly helped me believe in myself and trust my gut, while Julie Broad, Jaqueline Kyle, and the Book Launchers team have reinforced the values of goodness and integrity, and it's been such a joy to work together.

Dave Jordan and Michael Stahl both welcomed me into the baseball book fraternity with open arms—I owe you big-time. Other writers who inspired or influenced me include John Branch, Jane Leavy, Peter Golenbock, Peter Kerasotis, Jeff Pearlman, Brad Balukjian, and Steve Kettmann.

My years in New York media have shaped me as a storyteller and person in so many ways—it's inspiring to work with the best of the best each day and try to match up. To Zach Haberman, it seems to keep coming down to you and me. Trust is hard to find, and so is someone so committed to getting the story right (or with such a great recall for movie quotes). My friendship with Clemente Lisi has outlasted the Steak 'n Shake in Midtown (we waited in the cold when it opened) and has stretched across what feels like a million different newsrooms and assignments. What a great mentor, and a hilarious person, and a card collector, too. Erle Norton took a chance on me twice when he didn't need to, and I'm forever thankful for that. Others who influenced me or whose friendship stands out include Laura Thompson, Chelsea Stahl, Meera Jagannathan, Jason Silverstein, Ginnie Teo, and Terence Cullen.

Marie Hardin has encouraged me ever since she was my journalism professor at Penn State . . . and she's still encouraging me as the dean of the Donald P. Bellisario College of Communications. She and her husband, Jerry Kammer, have offered me endless support and two crucial lessons: One, get the story right. Two, keep writing.

My friends kept me going whenever I hit a rough patch. Casey Coyle is a damn good lawyer, and an even better friend—he stayed on me and motivated me, talking through the book's narrative and keeping me on track. Justin Van Wyen provided a constant sounding board, even if it was a busy day at Olive Garden and they were trying to shove us along to seat someone else. We had a lot to talk about! We always have a lot to talk about. Leslie McRobbie is the coolest person I know, and such a caring friend—I'm so proud of who she is and the impact she's had as a teacher and educator. Margaret DeAngelis has believed in me since the beginning of my career, and here we are all these years later, and her support has only strengthened; more later, as always. Pat McShane is a true connoisseur of 1990s baseball, and even if we don't always see eye to eye on everything, there's no questioning the dominance of the Reds' Nasty Boys bullpen. Trudi Gilfillian is always quick with a pick-me-up or a postcard or a listening ear at the perfect time.

My parents have shaped and influenced me, and this project, in so many ways. They encouraged my reading and writing, and nurtured my love of baseball, and helped me find balance and stability when I'd find myself drift-ing. I don't know of many moms who would show up to Phillies games hours early—or stay hours after the final pitch—so her kids could try to get autographs of Greg Vaughn or Bobby Abreu, but my mom did that. To my brother, Zach, thanks for the walk down memory lane and talking about 1990s baseball. My grandparents have shown me what it means to be successful and live a rich life, and their love has been a continuous resource. Thanks to my in-laws, too, for the childcare help at the drop of a hat, warm meals, and support whenever I've needed anything.

To Suzy—you've been so helpful and patient during the decade this project was coming together, adjusting plans so I could talk to some random player, or listening to countless stories about Casey Candaele, or Hal Lanier, or the 2001 Texas Rangers, or the 1998 World Series (even for a Yankees fan, that pitch against Tino was strike three). You're my best friend and the best editor I've ever had, and this book couldn't have happened without your warmth and patience and support. I love you so much.

And last but not least to Dean, who has kept me grounded and centered during this journey—and whom I look forward to telling more about Ken Caminiti when he's a little bit older.

NOTE ON SOURCES

This book relies on ten years of research, hundreds of documents and media reports, and interviews with four hundred different sources, stretching across Ken's life and its themes. I've noted those that provided significant input below.

CHAPTER 1: BATMAN

Jane Mitchell, the longtime TV journalist who profiled different sports figures for Channel 4 San Diego with her *One on One* series, was a favorite of Ken's, and her feature on Ken that aired in early 1997 was among Ken's most important interviews. It also included home movies of Ken at a young age and interviews with his parents, and the insight therein helped to shape this and other chapters. Another source worth noting was a masterful feature on Ken's life, "Fatal Errors" by Mark Zeigler, that was published October 31, 2004, in the *San Diego Union-Tribune*. Key interview subjects relied on in this chapter include Peggy Weeden, Chris Camilli, Roger Samuels, Nick Duerksen, Dave Moretti, Sharon Rossell, Kim Eicholtz-Novielli, and Claudia Henderson Druhan.

CHAPTER 2: THE VALLEY OF HEART'S DELIGHT

Lee and Yvonne's genealogical and family records are available on Ancestry.com, as well as through the Cook County (Illinois) Clerk's Office Vital Records, and relevant pages of their Tuley High School yearbook were provided by historian Dan Maxime. Basic records of Lee Caminiti's military service were verified through the National Archives' National Personnel Records Center. The family's places of residence and Lee's employment records were verified through searches of city directories and newspaper archives. The record of Ken's birth was published on April 22, 1963, in the *Hanford Sentinel*, accessed on Newspapers.com.

CHAPTER 3: (NOT SO) BIG MAN ON CAMPUS

Interviews with dozens of sources—including Hal Kolstad, Vito Cangemi, John Belmont, Mark Buesing, Michael Volzke, Hardy Watkins, Tammy Ivancovich Cabri, Dave Collishaw, Jeff Melrose, Jackie Vitale, Chris Camilli, Dave Moretti, Jim Evans, Mike Thorpe, Walter Wellsfry, Dino Sontag, Ron Deetz, Tim Cogil, Vic Druhan, Frank Blefari, Mike Sullivan, Harriet Armstead, Tim Halverson, Will Vince, Dean Yoder, and Mary McNiel Valle—helped to shape this chapter about Kenny's high school years. Records and stat sheets provided by Kolstad also helped to provide insight into Ken's and other players' statistics, while Leigh High School yearbooks for 1978–82 offered a window into Ken's athleticism and the Leigh campus culture. Interviews with John Oldham, Jerry McClain, and Sam Piraro also provided insight on the college process.

CHAPTER 4: COLLEGE TRY

Roger Samuels provided a lot of perspective on the culture surrounding John Oldham's program at San Jose City College, as did Mark Triplett, Joe Cucchiara, Max (Greg) Sosebee, and Billy Smith. Ken's quotes to his father about wanting to quit baseball—and Lee's urging him to stick with it—were documented in Lawrence Baldassaro's book *Beyond DiMaggio: Italian Americans in Baseball*, published in 2011 by University of Nebraska Press, a story Baldassaro recounted in an interview with the author. It was a joy to speak to Ken's college colleagues, such as Gene Menge, Chad Roseboom, Dana Corey, Mark Webb, Kevin Sullivan, Jeff Crace, John McLarnan, Rudy Escalante, and Dan Bajtos. SJSU figures like Lawrence Fan and Carolyn Lewis were insightful, and records provided by the San Jose State University media relations office were beneficial. Rick Schroeder and Bob Liebzeit had important stories to share. The author relied on archives of the *Spartan Daily*, accessed at the San Jose Public Library and online, for quotes from Ken and Menges about specific games and moments.

CHAPTER 5: RED, WHITE, AND BLUE

Newspaper accounts on Newspapers.com offered a window into the Team USA tour in 1984—as did interviews with players such as Don August, Oddibe

McDowell, Cory Snyder, Sid Akins, Bobby Witt, and Chris Gwynn. Ken's quotes on the Team USA tour came from Steve Carp's reporting in the *Mountain Democrat* and *El Dorado News* on July 11, 1984. Ken's frustrations about playing time, and ultimately getting cut from the team, were affirmed in interviews with numerous friends of Ken's, such as Dave Moretti and Mark Webb. Rick Schroeder, David Coffing, Dan O'Brien, and Gary Hughes offered meaningful perspectives on the scouting and draft process that led Ken to wind up getting selected by the Astros.

CHAPTER 6: BUS RIDES AND EMPTY BALLPARKS
Sitting in the Yankee Stadium dugout with Gary Tuck and listening to his stories about the Columbus Astros' 1986 championship run was especially meaningful for the author, as was a meetup in Manhattan with Rob Mallicoat. The author reconstructed Ken's game-by-game minor league statistics and team records by digging through box scores and game recaps found in various newspapers on Newspapers.com. Interviews with Ken's minor league teammates include Anthony Kelley, Karl Allaire, Scott Houp, Jim O'Dell, Mark Reynolds, Larry Ray, Tim (Earl) Cash, Jeff Livin, Jeff Bettendorf, Nelson Rood, and Richard Johnson. Coaches and personnel such as Don Miers, Charley Taylor, Dave Cripe, and Larry Lasky, as well as opposing players—Rocky Coyle, Doug Scherer, Jimmy Jones, and Tom Dodd—offered lots of meaningful insight. Speaking to Roger and Betty Ann Jones, and their son Kirk, was such a joy, as was Melodee Lange Christensen. John Trautwein (founder of the Will to Live Foundation) and Adam Peterson both offered input on the Southern League all-star game and the watches that quickly stopped working. Hank Aaron's quotes to the Southern League all-stars can be found in "Aaron Warns Stars of Drugs' Effects," by Ernie Kastner, in the July 14, 1987, issue of the *Greenville News*.

CHAPTER 7: HOUSTON, WE HAVE LIFTOFF
Insight on Ken's first major league game pulls from various sources, including Major League Baseball video posted on YouTube and newspaper accounts such as Neil Hohlfeld's reporting in the *Houston Chronicle*, "Astros' Future Haunts Phillies," along with interviews with Hal Lanier, Alan Ashby, and Rocky Mitchell. Jules Roberson-Bailey, the CNN/SI producer who interviewed Ken in 2002 ahead of his *Sports Illustrated* cover story, confirmed that Ken spoke to her about his use of greenies early in his major league career. Information about the

development of the Astrodome comes from a 1965 film, *The Astrodome*, which has been digitized by the Houston Public Library and Houston Metropolitan Research Center. Other interview subjects whose reflections aided the chapter include Billy Doran, Terry Puhl, Kevin Bass, Matt Galante, Charley Kerfeld, Denis Menke, Bill Wood, and Kevin Gross. Ken discussed religion and his lack of self-confidence in his 1997 interview with Jane Mitchell, who provided a copy of the segment to the author. Video from the August 10, 1987, Giants-Astros game is available on YouTube. Joan Ryan's column on Ken, "The Homecoming," appeared in the August 11, 1987, issue of the *San Francisco Examiner*. Numerous San Jose friends of Ken's confirmed details of the party thrown after he returned as a major leaguer.

CHAPTER 8: DOWN

Details of Ken's traffic stop on March 20, 1988, are maintained by the Osceola County Clerk (his last name is misspelled in the online system as "Camimiti"). Interviews with Hal Lanier, Chuck Jackson, Kevin Bass, Billy Doran, Denis Menke, Bill Wood, and other Astros players and personnel provided context on the season. Ken's records with Triple-A Tucson were reconstructed through newspaper reports and box scores published by the *Arizona Daily Star*, while his quotes appeared in an article by Ron Somers, "Toros' Caminiti Cools His Cleats," published May 7, 1988. Players such as Nelson Rood offered insight into the budding friendship between Ken and Craig Biggio. Ron Karkovice detailed his run-in with Ken in an interview.

CHAPTER 9: WINTER BALL

Journalist Thomas Van Hyning provided much-needed context on Ken's time playing in Puerto Rico—his knowledge and insight were meaningful. Tom Gamboa, Ken's manager in winter ball, was especially helpful, as was his Mayaguez teammate Tom Pagnozzi. Game and season records from Ken's time in Puerto Rico were pulled from coverage in various newspapers and *Baseball Almanac*.

CHAPTER 10: JOB SECURITY

Lou Gorman's comments about the rumored Wade Boggs trade were reported by Steve Buckley of the *Hartford Courant* in "Gorman Taking Calls on Boggs, but

No Tempting Offers So Far," on February 2, 1989. The Associated Press wrote about Houston's plans at third base for Billy Hatcher, Ken, Craig Reynolds, and Chuck Jackson ahead of the 1989 season. Art Howe discussed his relationship with Ken in an interview, and it was also covered in news reports at the time, including "Astros Banking on Caminiti at Third Base" by Mike Forman of the *Victoria Advocate* on March 25, 1989. Ken's defensive highlights appeared in a 1990 team video celebrating the twenty-fifth anniversary of the Astrodome, as did the twenty-two-inning game between the Dodgers and Astros. Statistics from Ken's 1989 season were found on Basebal-reference.com. Adrián Beltré's quotes about Ken appeared in an article by Mike Berardino of the *Sun-Sentinel*, "Can't Dodge Destiny," published March 5, 1999. It was insightful speaking to Matt Williams about Ken; they were contemporaries and friends and carried a lot of respect for each other. Details of Biggio's (and Ken's) arrests were obtained in newspaper accounts.

CHAPTER 11: FEEL THE HEAT

Interviews with Michael Hart, Tom Koppa, and Rex Jones were insightful, while Sheigla Murphy's perspectives on addiction provided much-needed expertise. Stories of Ken's addictions were shared by many sources, some quoted within the chapter. Gerald Young's own struggles with addiction were confirmed by people close with Ken and supported by reports of Young's 1995 arrest, in which he "told police he was a pro ballplayer with a cocaine habit," according to the Associated Press.

CHAPTER 12: FRESH FACES

Art Howe and Luis Gonzalez were both candid in interviews about the third-base challenges Ken faced during 1991 spring training and the eventual decisions to place Gonzalez in left field and Jeff Bagwell at first base. Quotes from Ken and Bagwell come from reporting by Allen Wilson of the *Orlando Sentinel* for the article "Caminiti Lets Astros Know Who's at 3rd," published March 14, 1991. Every one of my interview subjects from Ken's early Astros days spoke fondly of Casey Candaele, and it was a joy to speak to Casey myself. Details from Kendall's first game, and Ken's quotes, came from "Caminiti Hits Big Blast for Little Lady," by Neil Hohlfeld, from the July 7, 1991, edition of the *Houston Chronicle*.

CHAPTER 13: LONG ROAD

The story of Hal Newhouser and Derek Jeter is recounted from Buster Olney's 1999 *New York Times* article "Derek Jeter: The Pride of Kalamazoo, Bound for Greatness." Interviews with the Astros' front office staff of the early 1990s include Dan O'Brien and Bill Wood. Comparisons of the Astros' infield to the Philadelphia Athletics infield of 1912 and 1913 follows David Schoenfield's "The Best Infield of All Time? The Answer May Surprise You," published January 13, 2016, on ESPN.com. Phil Nevin was a thoughtful and reflective interview subject, as was Eddie Taubensee. Tony DeMarco covered the Astros' "Astro-nomical mystery tour" for the *Fort Worth Star-Telegram* on August 18, 1992, while Kelly Candaele's reflections of Ken and his brother were detailed in "Postcards from the Edge: The Houston Nomads," published by the *New York Times* on August 16, 1992. Sid Bream shared his perspectives on Ken's collision with Greg Olson in an interview. Ken's quotes on Olson's injury were reported by Tom Saladino of the Associated Press in articles published September 19, 1992.

CHAPTER 14: EARTHQUAKE

This chapter, outside of the final one, was the most difficult to report and write. . . . The chapter is based on interviews with three people who attended rehab with Ken—Ryan Burda, Cindy Popp, and J. Hutton Pulitzer—along with Terry Yates, Ken's lawyer, and Astros personnel such as Art Howe, Bill Wood, and Fran Pirozzolo. Tom Pagnozzi was also insightful. Information and quotes pull from Jack Etkin's "Caminiti Turns Around Life, Career" for the *Rocky Mountain News* on May 3, 1995, and "Pain Killer," by Ross Newhan of the *Los Angeles Times*, published September 27, 1996.

CHAPTER 15: STRIKE, YOU'RE OUT

Andy Stankiewicz had a significant impact on Ken's life following his stint in rehab, and likewise played an important role in describing his perspectives to the author. Players for the 1994 Astros such as Doug Drabek, Chris Donnels, Mike Felder, and Sid Bream, along with owner Drayton McLane, participated in interviews. Video of Ken's game-winning double on Opening Day is available on YouTube. Quotes from Ken and Bob Watson about facial hair appeared in Jayne Custred's July 20, 1994, article for the *Houston Chronicle*, "Letting Their Hair Down." Neil Hohlfeld's writing in the *Houston Chronicle* was a source throughout this book, probably none more influential than "High and Dry," published July 10, 1994. Other reports about Ken's sobriety include Tom Krasovic's "Caminiti Let Booze Go, Took Hold of Career," published July 10, 1995, in the *San Diego Union-Tribune*. Insight into Ken's struggles maintaining his sobriety were shared by Dave Moretti and other sources. Blake Blackwell's meeting with Ken was detailed in the January 13, 1997, *San Diego Union-Tribune* article "Getting a Lift." Details on the blockbuster Astros-Padres trade were shared by Dick Freeman, Randy Smith, Tal Smith, and Drayton McLane.

CHAPTER 16: NEW BEGINNINGS
It was so special for the author to speak to Bruce Bochy—unless otherwise noted, all quotes by Bochy were based on a personal interview. Charles Steinberg was helpful in understanding the Padres' front office, while Merv Rettenmund and John Flores were also interviewed. Larry Dierker wrote about Ken's being honored by the Italian Sports Hall of Fame of Houston for the *Houston Chronicle* on July 11, 1995, in "Thanking Caminiti for the Memories."

CHAPTER 17: GETTING A BOOST
Dave Moretti was interviewed for the first time for this book in 2014, and he's participated in dozens of on-the-record conversations since then, filling in gaps and answering questions about his efforts to help Ken. This chapter relies on interviews from Brian Johnson, Bip Roberts, Phil Garner, Glenn Wilson, Greg Stejskal, Dean Armitage, and Larry Duensing. A radio broadcast of the Padres' September 19, 1995, game was obtained by the author, and Ken's quotes following his historic home runs come from Associated Press coverage. Bob Nightengale's July 15, 1995, article in the *Los Angeles Times*, "Steroids Become an Issue," remains an influential piece of writing read more than twenty-five years later. "Pud" Galvin's use of PEDs has been covered in numerous articles, including by Robert Smith in "A Different Kind of Performance Enhancer," NPR, March 31, 2006. Hank Aaron wrote about his use of a pep pill in *I Had a Hammer*, cowritten with Lonnie Wheeler, published in 1992 by HarperTorch. Dr. Daniel Hanley's quotes about IOC testing for steroids were published by the Associated Press in July 1976. Two books—*The Male Hormone* and *Steroid Nation*—were especially meaningful resources for the author in understanding performance-enhancing drugs. Videos of Jose Canseco being taunted during

the 1988 playoffs are available on YouTube. A copy of MLB's drug policy and prevention program memo, dated June 7, 1991, is available online at www .steroidsinbaseball.net/assets/memo.pdf. Video of Ken's landing on his shoulder, and subsequent issues, were included in Jane Mitchell's *One on One* profile of Ken that aired in early 1997.

CHAPTER 18: LEGEND

Video of Ken's throw from his butt was posted on YouTube by MLB, as was video of the August 16, 1996, Padres-Mets game. Video from Ken's "Snickers" game was obtained from Major League Baseball. Interviews were with Kevin Towers, Ted Leitner, Andy Strasberg, James Hayashi, Rob Deer, Bob and Griffin Tewksbury, Homer Bush, Merv Rettenmund, Shaun Rachau, Patty Cahill, Amy Schneider, Chris Gwynn, Glenn Erath, and Brian Jordan. Tom Krasovic's reporting on Ken with the *San Diego Union-Tribune* was some of the most insightful of Ken's career, such as the April 23, 1996, feature "Caminiti Corners the Market." Another key article was "The Bionic Man," which ran on November 13, 1996. Other quotes of Ken's used in this chapter, including those about his efforts to stay in the lineup or his style of play, came from reporting by John Schlegel of the *North County Times*, including the May 14, 1996, article "A Pitch, Then Some Punch from Cammy." His quotes about injuring his hip appeared in print on April 17, 1996, in the article "Ashby's 4-for-4 Par for Coors," while Ken's comments about getting named to the All-Star team came from a July 8, 1996, article by Shaun O'Neill of the *North County Times*, "Reluctant Caminiti Named an All-Star." Greg Vaughn was an important source, and it was meaningful to discuss the friendship that developed between him and Ken. And it was always a joy to talk to the late, great Tom Reich. The VHS *Keep the Faith* detailing the Padres' 1996 season was a helpful resource. Bill Russell's comments on Caminiti, the comments that were so hurtful to Mike Piazza, came from Lawrence Rocca's article in the September 20, 1996, *Orange County Register*, "Russell Votes for Caminiti." Video of the Padres-Cardinals playoff games is available on YouTube.

CHAPTER 19: PLANES, SPRAINS, AND AUTOMOBILES

Information about the extent of Ken's injury was reported by Tom Krasovic in the *San Diego Union-Tribune*; interviews with Catherine Ondrusek and Dave Moretti offered independent vantage points that both spoke to Ken's recovery process. OPS+ statistics come from Baseball-reference.com. Video of Ken's appearance at the 1997 ESPYs was provided to the author by Maggie Vision Productions. Krasovic wrote about Ken's truck breaking down in a February 19, 1997, article, "Contract for '99 Would Let Cammy Buy Reliable Truck." The author is humbled and thankful at the candor displayed by Dave Moretti and Richie Lewis—the topics they discussed aren't easy ones. Details about changes in Ken's personal life starting in 1997 were confirmed by multiple sources in and around the Padres. Krasovic wrote about the flight near-tragedy for the *Union-Tribune* on July 12, 1997, in "Moores' Pilot Makes Padres' Save of Year."

CHAPTER 20: TG

It's sad that Ken and Tony Gwynn aren't here anymore; the author wishes he had been able to speak to Gwynn before the Hall of Famer's death in 2014.

CHAPTER 21: CAPTURE THE FLAG

Interviews with Bruce Bochy, Peter Kerasotis, Dave Stewart, Greg Vaughn, Jim Leyritz, and George Arias helped to shape the chapter. Ken's quotes about his home run off Kerry Ligtenberg came from "Caminiti Strikes 1st Blow" by David O'Brien of the *South Florida Sun-Sentinel*, October 9, 1998, while his comments after winning the pennant came from Mark Sauer's "Bubbling Over," which was published in the *Union-Tribune* on October 15, 1998.

CHAPTER 22: FALLING DOWN

Videos of the 1998 World Series are readily available; of note is *A Season of Heroes*, a video account of the Padres' 1998 season, in which Ken's interview following Game 1 appeared.

CHAPTER 23: MOVING ON

I enjoyed talking to Steven Callan, whose softball team beat the team of base-ball stars, 26–7, at Roger Clemens's charity event. Randy Hendricks, too. Russ Johnson, Billy Wagner, and Jack Howell were great interview subjects. Comments by Dave Moretti about a steroids shipment being intercepted were matched with elements from "The Report to the Commissioner of Baseball of an Independent Investigation into the Illegal Use of Steroids and Other Performance Enhancing Substances by Players in Major League Baseball," also known as the Mitchell Report, which is available online at mlb.mlb.com/mlb/news/mitchell/index.jsp.

Interviews with David Indermill, Tim Purpura, and Sean Cassidy were difficult but insightful. The author spent years attempting to track down Cassidy following an anonymous post on a blog site about his encounter with Ken; elements of his story were later verified by text message records of another person who interacted with Ken during his rehab assignment in New Orleans. Kirk Radomski discussed his encounter with Ken in an interview and also wrote about the exchange in his book, *Bases Loaded: The Inside Story of the Steroid Era in Baseball by the Central Figure in the Mitchell Report*, published in 2009 by Hudson Street Press. Jose Lima's and Ken's quotes appeared in an article by Anthony McCarron of the New York *Daily News* on September 1, 1999, "Astro Vet and Bat Wake Up at the Right Time." Wagner, Brian Jordan, Mike Remlinger, Scott Elarton, Bobby Cox, Larry Dierker, and Walt Weiss all offered insight in interviews about the 1999 NLDS.

CHAPTER 24: WARNING SIGNS
Dave Matranga proved to be a meaningful source for this chapter, as did Larry Dierker, Matt Galante, and Gene Coleman. Ken's comments on his return to San Diego were included in Tom Krasovic's April 24, 2000, article in the *Union-Tribune*, "Caminiti Refuses to Forgive, Forget." Aaron J. Lopez wrote about Ken's injury for the Associated Press on June 15, 2000. Reflections on Ken's meeting with Maria were provided by her son, Robert Silva-Romero, over the course of multiple interviews. Evan Grant's February 2001 feature on Ken for the *Dallas Morning News*, "After Battling Alcoholism, Injuries, Ken Caminiti Relishes Chance to Restart Career with Rangers," really captured Ken's essence and Nancy's perspectives on his struggles.

CHAPTER 25: OLD DOG
Ken's and Johnny Oates's quotes were included in a March 17, 2001, article by T. R. Sullivan of the *Star-Telegram*, "Caminiti Working Out Kinks." Bobby Cox, the legendary Braves manager, was reached by phone in 2016—his insights were meaningful, as were perspectives shared by Brian Jordan, Wes Helms, Jesse Garcia, Merv Rettenmund, and Steve Karsay.

CHAPTER 26: LOST AND FOUND
Details of Ken's 2001 arrest were contained in Harris County law enforcement offense records obtained by the author. Other records outlined his conditions

of community supervision. J. Hutton Pulitzer, Cindy Popp, and Ryan Burda all participated in interviews discussing difficult but crucial topics. Linda and Mystic Martin also proved to be very helpful. Judge Hatten and Ken's reactions from court were included in Carol Christian's reporting in the *Houston Chronicle* on March 22, 2002, "Former Astros Player Caminiti Pleads Guilty to Drug Charge."

CHAPTER 27: THE TRUTH WILL SET YOU FREE
Jules Bailey and Tom Verducci both participated in interviews, offering their perspectives on the interviews they conducted with Ken in 2002. John Covington, who was with Ken in Las Vegas, was also helpful. Video of Bob Fiscella's CNN coverage that included Ken's on-camera statements was obtained by the Vanderbilt Television News Archive.

CHAPTER 28: RELAPSE
Aaron Crumpton proved to be a valuable source, as did Gus Gerard and Tracy Burns.

CHAPTER 29: GREATEST DAY
Rick Licht wrote about the final series at Qualcomm Stadium for Today's Knuckleball (https://web.archive.org/web/20160815181327/http://www.todaysknuckleball.com/nl/san-diego-padres/guest-column-remembering-ken-caminiti/) and also recounted stories from that weekend for Mark Zeigler's haunting "Fatal Errors" for the *Union-Tribune* on October 31, 2004. Interviews with John Moores, James Hayashi, and John D'Acquisto were meaningful for the author.

CHAPTER 30: THE END
Insight into Ken's final weekend was obtained through interviews with Robert Silva-Romero, along with reporting such as "The Final Hours of Ken Caminiti's Life" by William Weinbaum and Jeremy Schaap of ESPN (November 3, 2004) and "Superstar's Last Days in the Bx." by Murray Weiss of the *New York Post*.

EPILOGUE
Video of the March 17, 2005, hearings in Washington, D.C., is available on C-SPAN's website.

INDEX